*You are my witnesses*

# *You are my witnesses*

## The message of the **ACTS** of the Apostles

Gordon J. Keddie

EVANGELICAL PRESS

EVANGELICAL PRESS
12 Wooler Street, Darlington, Co. Durham, DL1 1RQ.


*First published 1993*

**British Library Cataloguing in Publication Data available**

ISBN 0 85234-307-8



Printed in Great Britain by the Bath Press, Avon.

# Contents

**Part IV: The first missionary journey**



**Part V: The second missionary journey**



**Part VI: The third missionary journey**



**Part VII: The road to Rome**

# Preface

Christians have always found the book of Acts to be enjoyable, exciting and encouraging reading. Here, most personally and immediately, are our own 'roots' as the followers of Jesus. It is the history of the Christian's beloved country, the body of Christ, and the description of what it means to be a citizen of heaven while living upon the earth. Whereas the four Gospels expound the person and work of Jesus as the Saviour who came to save his people from their sins, the book of Acts recounts how the Holy Spirit came and savingly applied the message of the gospel to multitudes of people across the Roman world, through the ministry of the apostles and the newborn church of the New Testament era. If the Gospels focus on the accomplishment of redemption, Acts describes the application of redemption. If the Gospels tell us what the gospel *is*, Acts tells us what the gospel *does*.

Acts is unique in that it is pre-eminently the history of *the work of the Holy Spirit* in the church. The key to the meaning of Acts lies in two themes from Jesus' closing ministry among his disciples. The first, prior to his death on the cross, is his promise of 'another Counsellor', who would lead the disciples into 'all truth' (John 14:16; 16:13). The second, from after his resurrection, is the promise of the 'Great Commission', in terms of which they were called to preach the gospel to the whole world in the assurance that he would be with them always, 'to the very end of the age' (Matt. 28:18-20). These two great promises come together in Acts, as Luke tells the story of the first thirty years of the Christian church. These are the 'acts' of the Holy Spirit, the second Counsellor, who is as surely and objectively present with the people of God as was Jesus, their first Counsellor, in his ministry upon earth. Jesus goes; the Holy Spirit comes. And the result is that God's people are enabled to do 'even greater things' than he had done while with us in the flesh (John 14:12). The birth, growth and development of the New Testament church, including her ministry at the end of the second millennium since Christ, is unintelligible apart from these foundational truths. Acts, rightly understood, establishes that the normative condition of true churches is that of enjoying the poured-out presence of the Holy Spirit in her ministry and in the heart of every believer.

That this appears to be contradicted by the evident powerlessness and lifelessness of much of what is called the church is an argument, not for his non-existence or powerlessness, but for the need of reformation and revival by the Holy Spirit, and the vigorous proclamation of the gospel of Jesus Christ. This does not depend on how we handle the question of the extraordinary gifts of the Holy Spirit. It is not a 'charismatic' issue. Even if, as is argued in these pages, the special gifts of the apostolic period have ceased, the church remains 'apostolic' in everything that is of the essence of being the church of Jesus Christ. We are not less apostolic on account of the closure of the canon of Scripture and the cessation of revelation-word gifts. The living presence of the Holy Spirit is the very heart of the apostolic age, and that will mark the progress of the gospel church until the day the Lord returns.

Acts is also unique in that it sets out the New Testament's *doctrine of the church* in the practical context of the dynamics of a generation of church growth. Beginning, as it were, from a standing start, the church spreads as an organism, instituted and organized by the revealed Word of God. The ministry and government did not evolve, as men put their minds to the best practical way to run things. Rather, the Lord set apart men to serve him in the 'body of Christ'. The fact that we have multiplied so many conflicting forms of church government over the centuries is a testimony to how our itch for visibly grander organization so easily overpowers the simple structure with which God endowed the church at the beginning. The church of the apostles rebukes the ecclesiastical bureaucracies and hierarchies on both sides of the Reformation and calls for a return to the unadorned elegance of the New Testament way. Of this, more later. Suffice it to say that it is the conviction of this commentator that if the church of Acts is in any sense a model for us today — and there can be no doubt that it is — then it at least argues that the prelate- and committee-ridden churches of our day represent church government 'gone to seed'. They are, for the most part, unrecognizable in the pages of the New Testament.

Last, but not least, it is striking how the *evangelistic impulse* bursts from every page of Acts. The church marched across the ancient world on a powerful wave of enthusiasm for Jesus Christ. The recapture of this open-faced, unashamed and self-sacrificial love for Jesus and for lost men and women is surely the most pressing need for everyone who professes to be a Christian. Luke conveys a dynamic sense of the spiritual warfare in which the church was engaged. Acts is the record of costly campaigning against a fiercely resistant enemy, over the eternal destiny of lost men and women. The sounds of battle echo from almost every scene. But so also does the scent of victory, as lives are changed and the light of Christ spreads from nation to nation! The message for our day could not be clearer. We too have a world to win for Christ! We too must reap, or our world will perish!

The following exposition is intended to be accurate, readable and practical. I have kept discussion of technical exegetical points to a minimum and indicate in the notes where help may be found on some of the more vexed questions. My hope and prayer is that something of the liveliness of the exultant spirit of the apostles and their church may shine afresh in our hearts and lift up our hearts to Jesus, our Saviour and our King!

Gordon J. Keddie
State College, Pennsylvania

# Part I

## The Day of Pentecost

Acts 1-3

# 1.
# Prelude to Pentecost

**Please read Acts 1**

*'Do not leave Jerusalem, but wait for the gift my Father promised'* (Acts 1:4).

Had Jesus Christ never risen from the dead, it is most unlikely that we would ever have heard of him or his disciples. All would have melted into the oblivion of falsified prophecy and unfulfilled promise. How, then, did the shattered followers of Jesus become the vanguard of a faith which within three centuries would dominate the Roman world? The answer is that Jesus Christ really did rise from the dead! As the *risen* Saviour, he appeared to the eleven disciples and, over a period of forty days, gently ministered to them in their confusion and discouragement, rekindling their spiritual lives and welding them into an effective team for the preaching of the gospel message of salvation. During this time the watchword was 'Wait!' They were to **'wait for the gift [the] Father promised'** (1:4). In four specific matters they had to be prepared for the work they were to do: there was a message to proclaim (1:1-2), a promise to receive (1:3-5), a vision to grasp (1:6-11) and a leadership to be revived (1:12-26).

## A message to proclaim (1:1-2)

The economy of Luke's introduction is breathtaking. In one sentence he outlines three basic characteristics of the apostolic church.

### *The continuity of the message* (1:1)

The 'former book' is Luke's Gospel. Luke presents Acts as the sequel and, not least, the divinely inspired account of the birth and progress of Christ's body, the church. This is no mere collage of myths and legends, compiled and concocted by men who wished to provide a rationale for their preconceived faith. This is sober history, as is also the history of Jesus of Nazareth.

*A Christ-centred message* (1:1-2)

Luke, in his Gospel, **'wrote about all that Jesus began to do and teach, until the day he was taken up into heaven'**. Christ both *did* and *taught*, the point being that Jesus' message was confirmed by his pattern of life and, not least, the miracles which he performed. He proved himself to be 'a teacher who has come from God' (John 3:2). Furthermore, the implication is that what Jesus *began* to do and teach will *continue* to be taught and done through the ministry of the apostles. It is one continuous work of revealing the fulness of gospel salvation in Jesus Christ (Heb. 2:3).

*Chosen and equipped* (1:2)

Those who truly speak for Jesus do not appoint themselves. The apostles were *chosen* by the Lord and *instructed through the Holy Spirit.* 'We should be convinced of the divine calling of the apostles,' says John Calvin, 'so that we should learn to have regard, not to men, but to the Son of God from whom the call comes ... that no one may claim the honour for himself.'[1] We may also be confident of the message, because it is the work of the Holy Spirit as he leads Jesus' disciples to minister the gospel.

## **A promise to receive** (1:3-5)

Jesus never leaves his followers to fend for themselves, without the necessary resources with which to serve him effectively. Thus it was, says Luke, that **'after his suffering'**, Jesus showed himself to the apostles and **'gave many convincing proofs that he was alive'** (1:3). Over the period of **'forty days'** prior to his ascension, the risen Jesus — living proof of the resurrection and his victory over sin and the grave — gave the Eleven a refresher course in all he had earlier taught them.[2] Luke sums up this teaching under two general headings: the kingdom of God and the baptism of the Holy Spirit.

*The kingdom of God* (1:3)

The kingdom of God is simply the rule of God. At its heart it is the acknowledgement of God as King. In the Old Testament period it had been manifested in and through Israel. The Davidic monarchy in particular, promised in Deuteronomy 17, afforded a picture of the better kingdom to come — that of the Messiah, who would be revealed in the fulness of time (Dan. 2:44; 7:13-14). Finally, with the advent of Christ, that kingdom was said to be 'near' (Mark 1:15). His life, death, resurrection and, as yet, future bodily return at the end of the age seal the coming of the kingdom (Acts 17:31; Phil. 2:10-11).

This kingdom has come into a world which largely resists its claims. It overlaps with the present age in which evil remains unvanquished. At Jesus' first coming, writes F. F. Bruce, 'the age to come invaded this present life; at his second coming the age to come will have altogether superseded this present age'[3] (Fig.1).

**Figure 1** — The overlap of God's kingdom and the present age

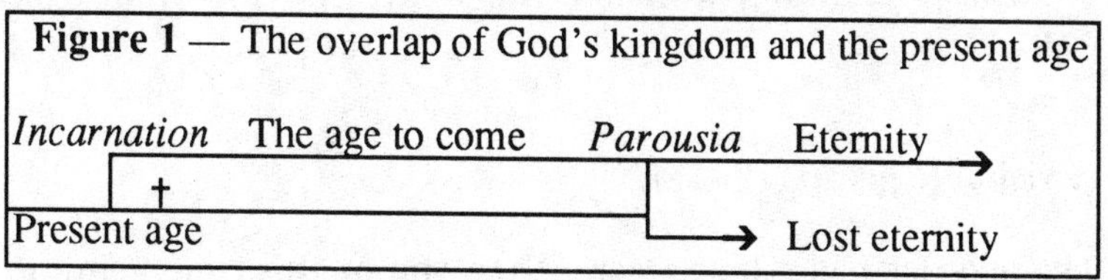


Christians belong to both kingdoms (Eph. 2:6; Col. 3:1-3) — having become citizens of God's kingdom by faith in Christ. 'The beginning of this kingdom,' says Calvin, 'is regeneration; the end and fulfilment of it is blessed immortality.'[4] God's kingdom is not *of* this world, but is very definitely *in* this world and Christians are called to live here and now in terms of their higher allegiance to their true King, the Lord Jesus Christ, who is sovereignly in control of both — 'head over everything for the church' (Eph. 1:22).

*The baptism of the Holy Spirit* (1:4-5)

The release of the power of God's kingdom upon the apostles and the church was to come with the decisive endowment of a gift from God: **'in Jerusalem'** and **'in a few days'** they would be **'baptized with the Holy Spirit'**. This had already been foreshadowed by the water-baptism of John (1:5; Luke 3:16). Jesus had spoken of the coming of the Holy Spirit (John 7:37-39; 14:16,26; 16:13) and had given a pledge of the as yet future Pentecost on the day of his resurrection (John 20:22). The significance of this event can hardly be overestimated. George Smeaton rightly called it 'the greatest event in all history, next to the incarnation and atonement',[5] for it would be the official inauguration of the new order of history in Jesus Christ. For the apostles themselves, and for all believers ever after, it would mean experiencing the power of the Holy Spirit in terms of an explicit personal manifestation of his presence in our innermost being and in a way never before known in the life of the people of God. The Holy Spirit, as the promised Comforter, took the place of Christ's bodily presence.[6] An unparalleled, irreversible transformation would take place in the way in which men and women would come to know God.

The fulness of God's light, shining in the face of Jesus Christ, would now be grasped by everyone who believes in the Saviour through the renewing and illuminating work of the Holy Spirit in the heart.

### A vision to grasp (1:6-11)

The apostles had a lot to learn. **'Are you at this time going to restore the kingdom to Israel?'** they asked (1:6). They seemed to think that 'the kingdom' would be a restored theocracy — a revived Jewish state — like David's monarchy, only with greater glory under Jesus' kingship. But this betrayed a deficient grasp of the scope of the gospel.

#### *A lack of vision* (1:6)

They had no vision for the future *worldwide* extension of the kingdom. 'Israel' was as wide as they could see. Their eyes did not yet reach beyond the horizon to a world of many tongues and nations, which would be gathered in by the preaching of the gospel. This arose, of course, from a failure to understand the *spiritual* nature of the kingdom, which, in the coming age (the New Testament era), would be characterized by the rule of Christ in the hearts of believers, bringing every aspect of life and thought captive to Christ. To **'restore the kingdom to Israel'** looked backwards to a national, temporal and discretely local manifestation of divine lordship. True restoration, however, was to be much more than turning back the clock, even to the best of the past. It was to mean nothing less than the universal manifestation of the age to come in the present age. It was to be heaven on earth in the hearts, lives, labours and societies of men, as these became transformed by the power of the gospel.

*Jesus' programme for the church* (1:7-8)

Jesus answered the apostles' question directly. There was to be *no date-setting* about the Day of the Lord. It would not be an 'at this time' kind of thing. The full establishment of the kingdom would take time — time in which they and others must serve the Lord in the world. Knowing the date would not have helped them anyway, especially if they had known it was thousands of years in the future. They must meanwhile focus on their commission. Scripture teaches clearly that the date of the consummation of the kingdom is hidden in the secret will of the absolutely sovereign God who foreordains all that comes to pass (1:7; Mark 13:32-33).[7]

Meanwhile, Christ's followers would be *equipped* for the task, for they would **'receive power'** when the Holy Spirit came upon them (1:8). The implication, later to be confirmed in the experience of the church, is that, once come, the Holy Spirit would always remain to empower the true church while the world lasts. The church would never be left to act in her own strength, but would be enabled to follow the clear leading and working of the Spirit.

They were to be *witnesses* to Jesus to the ends of the earth (1:8). Spirit-filled power is not political, but evangelical. It is designed to 'bring salvation to the ends of the earth' (Isa. 49:6; Acts 13:47). They had work to do — as Calvin puts it, 'They must fight before they can hope to triumph.'[8] The word 'witness' is the Greek *martur* — the origin of the English 'martyr'. Witnessing for Christ is costly and self-sacrificial. The geographic references anticipate the outline of Acts, from Jerusalem (Acts 1-7), to Judea and Samaria (Acts 8:1 - 11:18) and the ends of the earth (Acts 11:19 - 28:31).

*The ascension — confirmation and commission* (1:9-11)

Jesus' resurrection appearances were all distinct visitations from his place of exaltation in glory at the right hand of God. He did not hide away somewhere on earth in between these appearances. The ascension is the final 'disappearance' of Christ and marks the end of his forty days with the disciples. Pentecost would follow ten days later. Jesus therefore departed in a style designed to convey finality. Even then it was not 'Farewell', but 'Au revoir', for as the apostles stood gazing at the heavens, two angelic messengers appeared to tell them that Jesus would return from heaven in a similar manner to that in which he had just departed! What is most striking is the initial question of the angels. It sounds as if they are chiding the apostles for being amazed at what has happened: **'Men of Galilee, why do you stand here looking into the sky?'** This seems hardly fair. After all, if the pastor ascended through the church ceiling at the end of a service, we would all be inclined to look upward in amazement!

What, then, is the import of these words? It seems to me that this is the 'application' of which the ascension itself is the 'sermon'. The apostles have been confirmed in their calling to be Christ's witnesses in the world. Jesus' appearing to them cements the absolute truth of the gospel message. The ascension then signals their imminent entrance upon their great commission to preach Christ throughout the world. The angels' question says, 'Now you must be up and doing. You must prepare your hearts for the great work the Lord is giving you to do! Looking up into heaven is therefore inappropriate. He will indeed come back in the same way. But, being assured of that fact, you must not spend any time looking up into the sky in anticipation of the event. Rather, you must set your eyes upon the work he is giving you to do!'

This challenge ought to be ringing in our ears today as freshly as in that moment when it was first uttered. Yet it often finds modern Christians indulging in our versions of 'sky-watching'! The date-setters and prophecy-mongers are sky-watching for the Second Coming, their enthusiasm apparently undiminished by the fact that Jesus has expressly forbidden such speculations, and the embarrassing reality that an expanding list of exploded false prophecies litters the past and brings a reproach on the gospel! The sermon-tasters and the seminar-hounds likewise gaze skywards for ever fresher 'insights', while the world perishes for lack of real Christian witness! In point of fact, we need neither wait nor look into the sky, because that for which the apostles waited — the Holy Spirit's outpouring — is a reality now! (1 Cor. 12:13). We *are* witnesses for Jesus! Let us stop dreaming and get on with the job!

**A leadership to be revived** (1:12-26)

The disciples remained in Jerusalem and **'joined together constantly in prayer'** (1:12-14).[9] 'Before they were first sent forth,' writes Matthew Henry, 'Christ spent time in prayer for them, and now they spent time in prayer for themselves.'[10] There were, of course, only eleven apostles, when there should have been twelve. The defection of Judas Iscariot still cast a shadow over the infant church and represented a breach in the completeness of the apostolate! This posed a question: how could the church enter upon her ministry in the world without some definitive restoration from the damage done by Judas?

Surely it was to address this problem — the need for the visible renewal of the leadership — that Peter convened the meeting recorded in 1:15-26. Peter's opening greeting, **'Brothers'** (literally, 'brothers men' — *adelphoi andres*), indicates an all-male gathering, perhaps an *ad hoc* assembly of the leading disciples of Jesus, proto-elders meeting in what looks very like a pre-run of the later mature 'Council of Jerusalem' (Acts 15).[11] Clearly the church had begun to function as an organism, with a body-life and a spiritual government and leadership, even before Pentecost.

*The failure of Judas Iscariot* (1:16-20)

Judas Iscariot is the archetypal traitor. What is often overlooked is that the tragedy of Judas is also the failure of *leadership*. As such it has the utmost relevance for the plague of moral failure among the leadership of churches in our own day. Judas was a disciple and one of the Twelve. For three years he had **'shared in this ministry'**, says Peter (1:17). He was *not* the kind of person one expects to go over to the opposition. Nevertheless, he apostatized from his calling and ministry and rejected the Lord Jesus Christ. 'What will it avail us', asks Matthew Henry, 'to be added to the number of Christians, if we partake not of the spirit and nature of Christians?'

Luke records the details of Judas' tragic death (1:18-19). According to Matthew's account, Judas 'hanged himself' (Matt. 27:5). Luke adds the gruesome detail that as he fell, **'His body burst open and all his intestines spilled out.'**[12] Later on, Judas' blood-money for betraying Jesus — the thirty pieces of silver — was put to the purchase of a field (the Potter's Field) to be a cemetery (see Matt. 27:6-7). In this sense, **'Judas bought a field.'** Appropriately enough, the local people were soon to call that field **'Akeldama, that is, Field of Blood'** — thereby fulfilling Zechariah's prophecy of the final rejection of the Messiah (Zech. 11:12-13; Jer. 32:6-9; Matt. 27:9).[13]

Judas' death itself, says Peter, was the fulfilment of Scripture prophecy: **'Brothers, the Scripture had to be fulfilled which the Holy Spirit spoke long ago through the mouth of David concerning Judas...'** (1:16). Peter goes on to quote from two of the psalms to prove the point (1:20). Psalm 69:25 is applied to the *removal* of Judas from this earthly scene: **'May his place be deserted; let there be no one to dwell in it.'** The immediate context in Psalm 69:22-29 is directed at the reprobate enemies of the Lord and calls for divine justice to be meted out. Psalm 109:8, on the other hand, is applied to the *replacement* of Judas by another in his office as one of the apostolate: **'May another take his place of leadership.'** This reaches beyond the judgement upon Judas and provides the scriptural basis for the choice of a successor. We are reminded of the more general principle that God's purposes can never be frustrated — as Matthew Henry puts it, 'Christ's cause shall never be lost for want of witnesses.'[14]

*A new apostle (1:21-26)*

The number of apostles had been 'fixed by Jesus to correspond to the twelve tribes of Israel (cf. Luke 22:30; Matt. 19:28)'.[15] Filling the vacancy was therefore not a matter of administrative efficiency, but a specific requirement of God's purpose for the church as revealed in Scripture. **'Therefore it is necessary,'** says Peter (1:21). The leadership of the apostolic church must be *complete*. Notice also that this reconstitution of the Twelve is a once-for-all action of the Holy Spirit in the church. This is not contradicted, but rather confirmed, by the later calling of Paul as the apostle to the Gentiles. This was also a once-for-all appointment and only serves to emphasize that all modern attempts to choose 'apostles' entirely ignore the unique conditions surrounding the true apostolate appointed by Christ.[16] Notice that Judas' replacement had to be **'a witness with [them] of his resurrection'** — a simple fact that both defines who may be an apostle and settles for ever the invalidity of any claim for a continuing office of apostle. We are very definitely in the post-apostolic period!

Matthias was chosen at the leading of the Holy Spirit. First, two men were selected as fulfilling the stated requirements for an apostle, possibly by common consent of the entire company present. Then, lots were cast to choose between them. The lot fell upon Matthias and was seen as conclusive as to the mind of God in the matter (Prov. 16:33). This is the last occasion in which this venerable Old Testament method of finding God's will was used, for hereafter the Holy Spirit would lead the church in the setting apart of her ordained leadership.[17]

*Lessons for leadership*

Allowing for the unique character of both the apostolic leadership and the choice of Matthias, we must still reckon with the fact that this affords us important lessons for the leadership of the New Testament church today. All Scripture is designed not merely to *inform* our intellect, but to *reform* our faith and practice. It would be a mistake to let the uniqueness of the event described here become a reason for failing to reflect on what does continue to apply to the church in succeeding generations. Consider the following points:

1. It is often assumed that nominal, lukewarm church members are the greatest hindrance to the progress of churches and the gospel. As great a problem as this is, Scripture suggests that the *failure of leadership* — 'the Judas factor' — is a greater enemy by far. Backsliding members can damage a church and eventually reduce it to impotence, but an apostate pastor, or ungodly elders and deacons, can destroy it in no time at all. Heresy, like Marxist revolution, is a movement of the élite, not the ordinary people. It is talented, but unbelieving, leaders who spearhead the decline of churches. Furthermore — and we saw this with the 'tele-evangelist' scandals in the USA in the 1980s — millions of people outside the church can be confirmed in their contempt for Christ and the gospel by the hypocrisy and immorality of his erstwhile servants. Beware of 'false teachers'!

2. True leadership is exercised in response to the *call of Christ* and in *obedience to God's Word.* Judas had the former outwardly, but denied the latter inwardly. Judas stands for ever as the proof that

a man may exercise leadership in the church and be a dissembler and an unbeliever. Pray that the Lord would send men after God's own heart to be your pastors and elders!

3. True leadership is a matter of *heart-commitment* to the Lord, allied to God's call and God's gifts. Today, leadership is too often defined in terms of techniques which will produce success that is quantifiable. In churches this means numbers — programmes, buildings and the like. In Scripture, however, it is imitation that is at the heart of effective leadership — the imitation of godly leaders, who themselves are imitators of the Lord Jesus Christ (1 Cor. 4:16). Leadership is from the heart and then from the front — by example as well as precept (Heb. 13:7).

4. Leadership in churches is to be *collegiate*. There is to be no 'one-man band' ministry and no demagogic pulpiteering. A plurality of elders is to lead each local church. Decisions are to be collective — most significantly, they are to emerge from the concert of unified prayer and devotion to the Lord (Acts 14:23; Titus 1:5-7).

5. Leadership is *service*, not prestige and power. There is, to be sure, authority in church leadership that is powerful even to the extent of touching on eternal things (Matt. 18:15-20; 1 Cor. 5:4-5). Christ was the suffering Servant who was obedient to death, even death on a cross. His servants must lead in terms of the fellowship of his sufferings and in the giving of themselves for those within their charge and for whom they must give account (Heb. 13:17).

The renewal of the apostolic leadership was the prelude to the coming of the Holy Spirit at Pentecost. It remains a continuing challenge to our own need for and practice of Spirit-filled leadership in the church.

# 2.
# The coming of the Holy Spirit

**Please read Acts 2:1-13 and John 20:19-23**

*'I will ask the Father and he will give you another Counsellor'* (John 14:16).

The Day of Pentecost is often called the 'birthday' of the church. This is somewhat of a misnomer, because it tends to obscure both the essential unity of the church throughout the Old and New Testament periods and the fact that the Holy Spirit was active among the true people of God even in the days of the older covenant. Even so, it is true that the fulness of the work of the Holy Spirit was definitively revealed and powerfully released upon God's people in a new way at Pentecost. What burst onto the world stage that day was the fruition of all that the prophets had foretold, all that John the Baptizer had heralded and all that Jesus had accomplished from his incarnation to his ascension. Neither the world nor the church, neither the apostles nor the believers, neither the living nor the unborn would be the same again! Never again would unbelief be as ascendant in the universe as it was on the day Christ was crucified, because henceforth, and until heaven comes, the church would grow and spread until the whole innumerable multitude of the elect would be brought to saving faith in Jesus Christ through the proclamation of the everlasting gospel!

The second chapter of Acts records this epoch-making event, from the coming of the Holy Spirit (2:1-13), to Peter's preaching of Christ as Saviour (2:14-41) and on to the resultant growth of the church (2:42-47). We shall confine our attention here to the first section of the chapter. This unfolds in four sections, dealing successively with the day itself (2:1), the signs of the Spirit's coming (2:2-3), the gifts associated with his coming (2:4-11) and the response of the public to what had happened (2:12-13).

**The Day of Pentecost** (2:1)

**'When the day of Pentecost came, they were all together in one place.'** Pentecost is so called because it is the fiftieth day (Gk *pentekostos*) after the presentation of the first fruits of the harvest, which took place on the first day of the week after Passover (Lev. 23:15-16). This 'day of Pentecost' is the Lord's Day (Sunday) fifty days (seven weeks) after that first Lord's Day on which Jesus rose from the dead. To the Jews it was known as the Feast of Weeks (Exod. 34:22) and was later understood to be the anniversary of the giving of the law at Sinai (Exod. 19:1).[1] The question immediately posed is, of course, 'Why was this God's chosen day for the outpouring of the Holy Spirit?' Three reasons suggest themselves.

*Maximum publicity*

Some might regard this as an unworthy motive. The Lord, however, has an infallible eye to what will best promote his cause and kingdom and he was well aware that Pentecost would see very large numbers of visitors in Jerusalem from all over the known world, Jews and proselytes, who were there for the Passover season. 'Thus the Jewish feasts served to toll the bell for gospel services.'[2] We do not have special speakers in our churches when most folk are away on holiday. The Holy Spirit therefore baptizes the church in the presence of the maximum possible audience!

*Heightened expectations*

Many of those who were in Jerusalem at that time, especially from distant places, were the most zealous and enthusiastic of the Old Testament believers. Some may well have had a heightened expectation of the imminence of the coming of the Messiah. Some may have believed that the 'seventy "sevens" (i.e. weeks)' of Daniel 9:24 had expired and that the 'kingdom of God was going to appear at once (cf. Luke 19:11)'.[3] Is it not a certainty that the Lord prepared many people for this mighty revelation of the power of the Holy Spirit and the preaching of Jesus Christ? Even today, the Lord prepares the hearts of men and women to listen to the gospel and to receive Christ as their Saviour.

### *Theological significance*

The symmetry of divine revelation always implies a profound theological significance for the mighty acts of God. Most obvious is the parallel with the Passover (Fig. 2).

**Figure 2** — the Passover parallels

| Old Testament | | |
|---|---|---|
| Passover (Egypt) → | 50 days → | Pentecost (Sinai) |
| *redemption/lamb slain* | | *first fruits/giving of law* |
| **New Testament** | | |
| The cross → | apostles waiting → | Holy Spirit given |
| *redemption/blood of Christ* | | *the gospel preached* |

Christ is the true Passover of which the annual sacrificial lamb, from the Exodus on, was only a shadow (1 Cor. 5:7). The first-fruit of his atoning death was to be the outpouring of the Holy Spirit at Pentecost (cf. James 1:18; Rom. 8:23). Both the death of Christ on the cross and the Holy Spirit's coming at Pentecost constitute the once-for-all fulfilment of the meaning of the centuries of annual Passover and Pentecost celebration in the Old Testament church. The sacrifice, in the person of the Lamb of God, is complete and actually secures salvation for sinners. He saves 'his people from their sins' (Matt. 1:21).

In this light, we can understand why the outpouring of the Holy Spirit has a literally epoch-making significance for the *spiritual experience* of the apostles and the whole church for ever after. The Spirit applies the benefits of the cross. Before his crucifixion, Jesus told the disciples — then confused about much of what Jesus was doing and saying — that after he was gone, they would be taught 'all things' and be reminded of everything he had said to them (John 14:26). Jesus' death and resurrection had to precede the coming of the 'Counsellor', the 'Spirit of truth' who would guide them into all truth (John 16:7,13). Only when Jesus was glorified was the Holy Spirit to be given to, and received by, believers; only then would believers experience the Spirit as 'streams of living water' flowing within them (John 7:38-39).

To say, then, that the cross is the pivotal event of human history is no high-flown abstract or academic assessment. It touches the very heart of human experience and therefore the very life and destiny of the world. Why? Because the self-revelation of God in the person and work of Jesus Christ and the consequential reality of the work of the Holy Spirit in the changing of people's lives confronts the world with a new reality. The old is swept away and the new is unveiled. The Holy Spirit comes specifically at Pentecost for 'the promulgation of the evangelical law, not as that to one nation, but to every creature'.[4] The gospel now goes to all nations. And for all who turn to Christ in saving faith, the Holy Spirit's indwelling is a reality. Christ, by the Holy Spirit, lives in our hearts through faith! That is why, since Pentecost, things have never been the same again in the world — nor will they ever be while the world lasts.

## **Signs of the Spirit's coming** (2:2-3)

The apostles were 'together in one place' (2:1) when the Holy Spirit came upon them in power. Two signs heralded his coming.

### *1. A sound 'like the blowing of a violent wind'*

The imagery of wind in Scripture points to both the revelation of God and the work of the Holy Spirit. In Ezekiel 37:9 the wind ('breath' in NIV) comes forth from God to revive the dry bones. The Holy Spirit, as that wind which 'blows wherever it pleases', brings men and women to the new birth and conversion to Christ (John 3:8). It was sound without wind which **'filled the whole house'** and was instantly recognized as a miracle **'from heaven'**.

### *2. Tongues of fire*

The **'tongues of fire'** added a visual sign to the invisible sound of the wind. Fire speaks of the presence of God, as in the burning bush (Exod. 3:2-4); but also of the power and demonstration of the Holy Spirit (Isa. 6:6-7; Ezek. 1:13). Jesus came 'to bring fire on the earth' (Luke 12:49) and to baptize 'with the Holy Spirit and with fire' (Matt. 3:11). We have no reason to explain these 'tongues of fire' away in naturalistic terms, as one writer has done, as 'Christians seeing a deeper meaning in the sun's rays streaming through ... the arches of the Temple'.[5] By analogy with the sound of the wind, these were miraculous appearances of an unconsuming fire — a visible but heatless fire. And so God set his sign unmistakably upon the apostolic company, indicating the 'constant residence' of the Holy Spirit with them.[6]

These signs point up the connection between miraculous signs, new word-revelation from God and the public attestation of those whom God sends to bring his inerrant Word to the world (Christ, the prophets, the apostles and other authors of Scripture). Periods of divine revelation are invariably accompanied by 'signs and wonders'. This was true in Sinai at the giving of the law, and in Moses' ministry. It was true at Pentecost and in the ministry of the apostles (see 2 Cor. 12:12; Gal. 3:5; Heb. 2:1-4). The other side of this coin is the cessation of such extraordinary signs and wonders during periods when there is no new revelation — as today in the aftermath of the closing of the canon of Scripture.

### **Gifts of the Spirit** (2:4-11)

Inwardly, the apostles and the 120 were **'filled with the Holy Spirit'**. He entered their hearts in a profound and powerful way, took hold of their faculties and transformed them. This translates into a quantum leap in personal holiness. 'The transforming power of the Spirit so filled them that the timid became bold, the selfish self-denied, the arrogant humble, the ambitious aspirants after distinction ceased to seek great things for themselves.'[7] They were 'more weaned from this world, and better acquainted with the other'.[8]

Outwardly, the apostles **'began to speak in other tongues as the Spirit enabled them'**. This extraordinary gift had been promised to them by the Lord (Mark 16:17). It would attract notice on later occasions during the apostolic period (Acts 10:46; 19:6; 1 Cor. 12:10) and eventually draw a warning from the apostle Paul against the kind of tongue-mania that arose in Corinth (1 Cor. 14:2-40). Paul did not forbid speaking in tongues (1 Cor. 14:39), but was able to say that 'Tongues ... will be stilled' (1 Cor. 13:8) — a remark strongly suggestive of their imminent cessation.

The nature of these tongues may be gleaned from the testimony of the people who had gathered around the apostles, drawn first by the sound and then by the tongues themselves. These people came from all over the Roman world — **'both Jews and converts to Judaism'** (2:9-11). Three basic points emerge.

1. The tongues were *languages native to the hearers but unknown to the speakers*. Smeaton notes that the view that these were ecstatic gibberish is 'a modern [nineteenth-century] German speculation devised to escape the full admission of the extra-ordinary miracle'.[9] Modern tongues are invariably of the open-syllable gibberish variety and, charismatic claims to the contrary, defy all characterization as genuine languages — i.e., translatable tongues in which sound and meaning are demonstrably connected. The apostles spoke genuine languages of particular peoples and this was a miracle wrought by the extraordinary power of the Holy Spirit.

2. These tongues were *a sign to unbelievers* attesting to the power of God. Paul establishes this basic truth in his rebuke of the disorder in the Corinthian church over tongues (1 Cor. 14:22). The purpose of tongues was *not* to edify the church, but to attest the power of God before those who opposed him — in particular, unbelieving Israel. In this connection, Paul quotes Isaiah 28:11-12 to show that apostolic tongues were a covenantal sign rebuking covenant-breaking Jews: '"Through men of strange tongues and through the lips of foreigners I will speak to this people, but even then they will not listen to me," says the Lord.' This sombre view of their significance therefore relates as much, if not more, to the rejection of reprobate Israel in the destruction of Jerusalem in A. D. 70 as to the conversion of the 3,000 on the Day of Pentecost and the subsequent growth of the church (which was largely among the Gentiles).

3. The sign of tongues is inseparably bound up with *the revelatory activity of God.* This activity continued in the New Testament church, accompanied by prophecy and tongues, until the completion of the New Testament Scriptures. The closure of the canon of Scripture, in itself, implies the cessation of these extraordinary signs. Conversely, the insistence on the continuance of tongues and prophecy today implies new and direct revelation from God through this means. This sets up practical tensions between the authority of these utterances and that of the Scriptures. These are not resolved by assertions that what comes up in tongues will not contradict the Word of God. A man who believes that God has said

something to him that is a new and direct revelational insight is not likely to retreat from it, even in the face of a clash with the Scriptures. It is no accident that all cults and many heterodox strands of teaching have their genesis in so-called 'revelations' and become established by the practical subordination of Scripture to their 'new light'. Wherever religious experience escapes the exclusive control of the Holy Spirit through the Word, the result has been the entrance of intense subjectivism, doctrinal individualism and, sooner or later, outright heresy.

The uniqueness of Pentecost offers a helpful corrective to any desire to speak in tongues today. This first instance of the gift of tongues occurs in connection with the once-for-all outpouring of the Holy Spirit upon the New Testament church. The 'larger lesson', as Richard Gaffin has put it, 'is that while individual experience is precious and indispensable to being a Christian, it is not to be our primary concern. That concern is the coming of the kingdom of God, the eschatological lordship of Christ over all creation established in "the fulness of the time" (Gal. 4:4), particularly by his death, resurrection, ascension and Pentecost. Here too we may rest content that the words of Jesus in Matthew 6:33 apply: Seek first the kingdom of God and his righteousness and all these things, experience included, will be given to you as well.'[10]

**Amazement or amusement?** (2:12-13)

One man's miracle is another man's madness. The miracle of speaking in various languages struck the people who heard it in entirely different ways. Some were positive in a perplexed kind of way; others negative, even abusive. However great the evidence of the reality of God's power may be, it is easy enough to reject it when your mind is already made up. The attitudes we bring to any encounter with challenging and mind-boggling events — call them predispositions, pre-commitments or presuppositions — are never easily overthrown. We tend to interpret our experience in terms of these basic underlying commitments. And there is, of course, the fact that extraordinary events do boggle the mind! They take us into new areas beyond our experience and challenge both our ignorance and our inexperience before we can assess their credibility and their implications.

So it was with the crowd's response to the apostles that day. Some responded with amazement. They recognized that they were hearing **'the wonders of God in [their] own tongues'** (2:11). They did not write the experience off. On the other hand, they did not know what it was all about. This is quite understandable, since this was the introit rather than the homily. Peter's preaching, in plain old Aramaic, would attack the question of the meaning of it all and issue in the conversion to Christ of **'about three thousand'** (2:14-41). They asked the correct question, because they did have the right to be astonished as well as a duty to desire an understanding of these phenomena (2:12).

Others, however, merely scoffed and **'made fun of them'**, charging, **'They have had too much wine'** (1:13). John Calvin thought that anyone with 'any drop of sound understanding in him' should have been 'shaken even to hear of the tongues' (i.e., by a second-hand report). 'How beast-like then must men be who see with their eyes and yet mock and essay by their jests to scoff at the power of God.'[11] Blind eyes cannot see the brightest sun. These mockers were the future mission-field for the infant church. Their opposition here was only the barometer of their spiritual state and a reflection of the common need of humanity for a Saviour who would shed his light abroad in the darkness of the human condition.

Pentecost continues to challenge men and women today. The Holy Spirit — the Paraclete (i.e. the Counsellor or Comforter) promised by Jesus — has come. In his coming, Christ is proclaimed as the risen Saviour who triumphed in his death and resurrection to redeem men and women from their enslavement to the myriad bondages, corruptions and consequences of sin, both in time and eternity. The Holy Spirit ministers as the Spirit of Christ. He declares Christ as he accompanies the message of the gospel to the hearts of men and women. The coming of the Holy Spirit proves that the invisible, absent Jesus is still in business, that he rules from heavenly exaltation as King of Kings and sends out his servants, filled with the Holy Spirit, to spread the message of his free grace and life-giving love. The question is: are you listening?

# 3.
# Christ is preached

**Please read Acts 2:14-41**

*'God has made this Jesus, whom you crucified, both Lord and Christ'* (Acts 2:36).

The great declaration of the first sermon of the infant church is that Jesus is both Lord and Christ. It is no overstatement to say that this is the irreducible core of all true preaching of God's Word. Where Christ is not preached, the real meaning and thrust of Scripture are not being opened up. Sermons may proclaim the best morals, tease out the finest points of doctrine or display the tidiest exegesis. If, however, they fail to hold up Christ as the only Saviour of sinners and do not press the claims of his love on the consciences of the hearers, they have missed the point of whatever text was chosen, for all Scripture, rightly understood and explained, points us to Christ. It may seem difficult to preach Christ from all of the Scriptures, but that is surely more a function of our lack of understanding than of any difficulties or deficiencies in the Word of God itself. Peter's sermon provides the church with a model for *all* of her preaching and exposition, much as the Lord's Prayer affords a template for the prayers of believers. The whole point of Christian preaching *is* Christ and the apostolic preaching strains every sinew to press this home to the heart.

The basic elements of apostolic preaching are all in Peter's great sermon. These are four in number: first, the announcement that the age of fulfilment is now; second, an exposition of the person and work of Jesus Christ; third, an appeal to the Scriptures to prove that Jesus truly is the Christ (Messiah); and, fourth, a call for people to repent and turn to Christ for salvation.[1]

**The age of fulfilment has come!** (2:14-21)

Peter, like all fishermen, was a down-to-earth fellow. He shows a bit of the street-preacher's art when he takes his cue from the scoffers' charge that their speaking in tongues was a result of their being drunk. F. F. Bruce sees this exchange in terms of good-natured jesting on both sides.[2] Peter does not, however, appear to be using the language of banter. He rises to speak with all the authority of one who is filled with the Holy Spirit. And if there is a wryness to his riposte, he certainly does not make light of the spiritual blindness of the scoffers: **'Listen carefully to what I say. These men are not drunk, as you suppose. It's only nine in the morning!'** (2:14-15). He simply reminds them of the absurdity of their charge — the barb, of course, being that they must face the fact that there is a far more serious meaning to this phenomenon and it has implications for their own lives and relationship to God! With no beating around the bush, Peter makes his real point, which was not to defend the apostles but to emphasize that what was happening was the fulfilment of what had been prophesied centuries before. This, says the apostle, **'is what was spoken by the prophet Joel'** (2:16). He then goes on to quote Joel 2:28-32. R. C. H. Lenski notes that the construction in the original Greek text — the passive 'what *was spoken*' together with '*by* (or "through") the prophet ...' — wherever [it] occurs in Scripture, state[s] in brief the entire doctrine of verbal inspiration, to wit, that in all Scripture the real speaker is God, and that the holy writers are only his media, instruments, mouthpieces.'[3]

The quotation from Joel's prophecy is remarkable, not only because of the fact that Pentecost is its specific fulfilment, but also because it is an example of the divinely inspired interpretation of prophecy. We are not left to wonder if 'this' is a prophecy of 'that'. We are told very simply and with all the authority of revealed truth that 'this' is indeed 'that'! Hence Peter's modification of Joel's text, with the replacement of 'After this ...' with **'In the last days ...'** and the addition of **'God says'** (2:17; cf. Joel 2:28) and **'and they will prophesy'** (2:18; cf. Joel 2:29). The thrust of all this is sevenfold:

1. Joel foretold the *coming of the Holy Spirit* in connection with the promised revival of the covenant people of God (2:17).

2. That outpouring of the Spirit is fulfilled *from Pentecost on*. The expression 'in the last days' refers to a period of time. From that

Day of Pentecost until the completion of the 'last days', the Holy Spirit would be with the true people of God (2:17).

3. The Holy Spirit would touch men and women of *all nations* and not just the covenant people, the Jews. At Pentecost the universality of the gospel became an irrevocable fact for the whole human race (2:17).

4. The coming of the Holy Spirit would be evident among God's people, in terms of certain *gifts* of the Spirit. Old and young, male and female — **'my servants'** — will variously **'prophesy ... see visions ... dream dreams'** (2:17-18). Joel was referring to the fact that God revealed himself in these ways in his (Old Testament) day and only by a very few prophets. Peter is saying that henceforth (the New Testament era), all believers will be prophets, in that they will have a full understanding of the revelation of God in Jesus Christ (Jeremiah 31:34).[4]

5. The 'last days' will be marked by certain *signs and wonders* (2:19-20). The entire period is telescoped within these verses. The signs of Pentecost and the signs of the last day of all appear to merge in this verse.[5] Again, 'signs' are associated with periods of new revelation — namely, at the first coming of Christ, culminating in Pentecost, and at the second coming of Christ, which will be the culmination of human history.

6. The **'great and glorious day of the Lord'** (2:20) is most naturally associated with the Day of Judgement and the Second Coming of Christ. Many commentators, including John Calvin, Matthew Henry and Keil & Delitzsch, see this as a reference to the kingdom and rule of Christ as his judgements go forth in parallel with the ministry of the Holy Spirit. All of his judgements, from the destruction of Jerusalem to the last great day would be included. The text just does not tell us enough to resolve this question — it is certain, however, that history will answer it for us in due course.[6]

7. During this period of the 'last days', the Lord will *save people from their sins* — for **'Everyone who calls upon the name of the Lord will be saved'** (2:21). Lenski calls this 'the really important statement in Joel's prophecy'.[7] The 'last days' are pre-eminently the era of the gospel of Jesus Christ. Salvation, not judgement, is the leading motif. This is pre-eminently the age of salvation, the era of the outpouring of the love of God in Jesus Christ!

**The man Jesus is both Lord and Christ!** (2:22-24)

J. A. Alexander has brilliantly summarized Peter's train of thought as he led his hearers to Christ: 'This is not drunkenness but inspiration — it was predicted centuries ago — on the fulfilment of that promise is suspended your personal salvation — and the promised Saviour is the man you crucified.'[8] Peter has come to the heart of the matter. Who is this Lord, who will save everyone who calls upon him? Who is the Lord who is behind all that was happening that day as the Holy Spirit came upon the church? Is he simply 'God' — Jehovah, Elohim, Adonai — as he revealed himself in the Old Testament? No! He is none other than **'Jesus of Nazareth'**, whom they killed, but whom **'God raised from the dead'**!

What looks to us like a simple, run-of-the-mill declaration of the gospel truth about Jesus was at that moment the most shocking thing Peter could have preached to a crowd of pious Jews! He was saying that Jesus was the Messiah and the only Saviour of sinners! He set out four facts that were beyond all disputing.

1. Jesus was **'a man'**. They knew who he was and knew a lot about him.

2. Jesus was a man **'accredited by God to [them] by miracles, wonders and signs'**. This was accepted fact (Luke 7:16; 11:20; Heb. 6:5).

3. It was also why they, **'with the help of wicked men, put him to death by nailing him to the cross'**. There was no disputing these facts either.

4. But Jesus had not remained dead, for **'God raised him from the dead, freeing him from the agony of death.'** There were plenty of witnesses.

What did all this mean? Peter makes two basic points. First of all, it happened **'by God's set purpose and foreknowledge'**. Jesus did not die by chance. Human wickedness did not overthrow the plan of God. God planned it all — this was predestined from all eternity! Secondly, Jesus' death was not for ever, because **'It was impossible for death to keep its hold on him.'** Why? Because his resurrection was just as much planned as his sufferings! The risen Jesus is the promised Redeemer! Peter nails his colours to the gospel mast!

**The Scriptures foretold the exaltation of the risen Christ** (2:25-36)

To agree that the man Jesus was accredited by God is one thing. Plenty of prophets had been accredited by 'miracles, wonders and signs'. To accept the assertion that he is the divine Messiah requires more proof. Peter turned once again to the Scriptures, to show that the resurrection of the Messiah was indeed foretold in God's Word and to argue that the resurrection of Jesus is the only fulfilment of these promises.

*The resurrection of Christ* (2:25-32)

Peter first quoted David's words in Psalm 16:8-11 (2:25-28). David speaks in lyrical terms of his gladness, rejoicing and hope, **'because you will not abandon me to the grave, nor will you let your Holy One see decay'**. Peter pointed out that since David did die and never rose bodily from the dead, he could not be the 'Holy One' of whom he spoke. He therefore spoke prophetically, not autobiographically! Believing God's promise[9] that **'He** [God] **would place one of his descendants on his throne,'** he saw what was ahead and, in the spirit of prophecy, **'spoke of the resurrection of the Christ, that he was not abandoned to the grave, nor did his body see decay'**.

The extent to which David understood his own divinely inspired utterance is beside the point. It is axiomatic that the prophecies of the Old Testament were veiled in mystery, even to the prophets themselves. Christ is their unveiling and the New Testament is their authoritative interpretation. If people had ever wondered how David could say such amazing things about himself, they now had the answer. He was really speaking about Jesus Christ! Peter makes this perfectly clear: **'God has raised this Jesus to life, and we are all witnesses of the fact.'** So Peter links the risen 'Holy One' of Psalm 16:10 with the 'Lord' of Joel 2:28 and the coming of the Holy Spirit that very day (Acts 2) and pulls them all together in Jesus as the promised Saviour of their own Scriptures!

*The heavenly exaltation of Christ* (2:33-36)

The next obvious question would be: where is this risen Jesus today? Why can he not be here to tell all this, if indeed the grave could not hold him? Anticipating such questions, Peter gives the reason and supports it from the Scriptures. Jesus is **'exalted to the right hand of God'**, has received the **'promised Holy Spirit'** from God the Father and, says Peter, **'has poured out what you now see and hear'**. That this was foretold in Scripture is clear from Psalm 110:1 (2:34-35). Peter's point, once again, is that David was writing about something far, far greater than himself. This psalm is thoroughly Messianic (see Heb. 5:6; 7:17,21).

The sense of the first verse is well expressed in a singing version of the psalm:

> Jehovah to my Lord has said,
> 'Sit thou at my right hand
> until I make thy foes a stool
> whereon thy feet may stand.'[10]

The first 'Lord' is God the Father; the second, God the Son. David's 'my Lord' is Christ. Christ is exalted in triumph to the right hand of the Father. Peter can therefore say, **'Let all Israel be assured of this: God has made this Jesus, whom you crucified, both Lord and Christ'** (2:36). Here is a startling model of what it means to preach Christ. R. C. H. Lenski notes: 'Peter minced no words. He preached plenty of gospel but drove straight home with the law. And he was content with that. There was no sentimental pleading of the kind that so often defeats itself. No sinner does God a favour by accepting Christ. Peter preached the divine truth in all its power; the effect took care of itself.'[11]

## The gospel call to salvation (2:37-41)

The balance of law and gospel has often been a hard one to strike. Suffice it to say that where there is no declaration of God's law and the consequences of breaking it, the gospel is reduced to little more than a programme of psychological enrichment — a cure, perhaps, for bad feelings and social ineptitude, but certainly no salvation from the just judgement of God and a lost eternity. Where the law is over-preached, the gospel recedes to distant impotence, overwhelmed in the experience of the hearers (if any can bear to sit under such dismal preaching) by a depressed sense of helplessness, without the rising hope of redemption and victory. Where the issues of sin, death and hell are squarely faced and the good news about Jesus Christ as Saviour is proclaimed, the Holy Spirit changes lives. In this respect, the Day of Pentecost was indeed a model for the church for ever after: preach Christ and people will be saved!

*Convicted of sin* (2:37)

The first response to the Holy Spirit had been amazement and questions. The second response of many present was conviction of their sin. They were **'cut to the heart'** and asked the apostles, **'Brothers, what shall we do?'** They felt their naked guilt before God and knew the utter helplessness of being unable to save themselves. Their hearts were filled with honest and humble contrition and their spirits truly broken of pride and self-reliance before the Lord (Ps. 51:17). This is what the 'law-work' (as the old preachers called it) is all about, as it relates to the preaching of the gospel: real sorrow for sin, self-judgement that says from the heart a sincere and anguished *'mea culpa'* — 'I have sinned!' — and then immediately looks upward to the Lord for deliverance. 'Those that are convinced of sin would gladly know the way to peace and pardon (cf. Acts 9:6; 16:30).'[12]

*Called to repentance* (2:38-39)

'Brothers, what shall we do?,' is the desperate heart-cry of people who cannot see a way out. Peter's call to **'repent'** is, as Matthew Henry neatly observes, 'a plank after shipwreck'.[13] Repentance (Gk *metanoia*) is the turning round of the whole man — the decisive forsaking of sin and self-sufficiency and the embracing of personal faith in and discipleship to the Lord Jesus Christ.[14] At its heart, repentance involves what the *Shorter Catechism* calls 'a true sense of sin' and a 'grief and hatred of sin'.[15] This is more than 'feeling sorry', even if that is as intense as a despairing and suicidal remorse (2 Cor. 7:10).[16] Why? Because it is inextricably bound up with an 'apprehension of the mercy of God in Christ'. Jesus is *always* looked to and embraced by faith in the experience of evangelical repentance. Sorrow, without turning to Christ, is no more than the carnal disappointment and self-pity that goes with not getting away with what one wants to do!

Peter answers his deeply concerned hearers by pointing out five things that must happen (2:38). He tells them both what they are to do, and what God will freely give, that they might enter into new life in Christ.

1. They are to **'repent'** — not merely of the one sin of complicity in the death of Christ, but of their sinful condition of heart before God, together with the comprehensive range of their actual sins — that which constitutes the basis of their actual estrangement from God. **'Every one of you'** indicates that none can excuse themselves of the need of repentance, on whatever grounds they might imagine themselves to be right with God at the present.

2. They are to be **'baptized'** — i.e., they are to receive the external sign and seal of entrance into new life in Christ. This is the public mark of belonging to the Lord — the sign and seal of the covenant of grace. It is, of course, water-baptism, symbolizing the washing of regeneration — the inward renewal wrought by the Holy Spirit.

3. This must be **'in the name of Jesus Christ'**. This is not the formula used for baptism (Matt. 28:19), but the distinguishing mark of *this* baptism from other baptisms known among the Jews, notably proselyte baptism and John's baptism. The baptism is the seal of what Christ has done.

4. It is **'for the forgiveness of your sins'**. Assurance that their sins were forgiven was bound up with the reality of their repentance and faith. Baptism outwardly sealed the promise of forgiveness to inward repentance. An unbaptized Christian is therefore a contradiction in terms. Hence the close connection of repentance, baptism and forgiveness here.[17]

5. As a result they will **'receive the gift of the Holy Spirit'** — the gift, not the gift*s*, for 'The *gift* of the Spirit is the Spirit himself, bestowed by the Father through the Messiah; the gifts of the Spirit are those spiritual faculties which the Spirit imparts, "dividing to each one severally as he will" (1 Cor. 12:11).'[18] All believers receive the Holy Spirit when they believe. No later so-called 'second blessing' experience is required in order for Christians to receive him.

The promise of the saving work of the Holy Spirit is not for them only, but for their **'children'** and for **'all who are far off'** (2:39).[19] In other words, God promises to save all who repent and call upon the name of the Lord, both in the line of generations ('you and your children') and from all the nations of the world (those who are 'far off' are the Gentiles and their children, Isa. 57:19).[20] This promise extends to **'all whom the Lord our God will call'**. The call is the effectual call of the gospel. It is as if Peter says, 'Yes! You who hear us today! The promise of the Father is for people in all nations, whether Jew or Gentile; it is for your children and succeeding generations; it is all of grace; it is full salvation through Christ alone. The Lord is going to call people to himself, to the reality of forgiveness of sins. He will give them the gift of the Holy Spirit. This is what is happening on this Day of Pentecost! This is what will happen throughout the world in the hearts of all who believe in Christ!'

*Converted to Christ* (2:40-41)

Much more was said that day. The air was one of electric expectancy and exercised earnestness. There was nothing of the dull decorum of many modern churches, where passionless sermons echo from empty pews and unresponsive people watch the clock and think about Sunday dinner. Peter preached and taught and always pleaded, **'Save yourselves from this corrupt generation.'** Even the outpouring of the Spirit only saved a portion of that 'unbelieving and perverse generation', as Jesus had called it (Luke 9:41). The true measure of Pentecost was the conquest of the nations, not the response of the Jews. That generation, except for Christians, was to perish in A. D. 70 with the temple and the superseded shadows of the Mosaic ceremonies.

But that Pentecost was memorable enough, for **'Three thousand were added to their number that day,'** having accepted Peter's message and received Christian baptism. Jesus had said that the apostles would do greater works than he (John 14:12). 'The conversion of these three thousand with these words', observes Matthew Henry, 'was a *greater work* than the feeding of four or five thousand with a few loaves.'[21] In one day, the church grew more than in the entire ministry of Jesus! Could there be a clearer demonstration of the power of the Spirit and the sure promises of the Lord? Where Christ is proclaimed — which means, where the Word concerning Christ is opened faithfully — there the Holy Spirit is powerfully active to convert men and women to Christ. This promise remains in force today and calls the church to faithfully proclaim the gospel of Jesus Christ and reap the harvest of lives transformed by the work of the Holy Spirit.

# 4.
# The growing church

**Please read Acts 2:42-47**

*'And the Lord added to their number daily ...'* (Acts 2:47).

'Church growth' is all the rage these days. Never has there been such an emphasis on growth as in these last decades of the twentieth century. A very extensive literature describes and dissects both growth and decline and offers a myriad of suggestions about how to grow new churches and revitalize old ones. No doubt this has arisen largely in response to the catastrophic collapse of what may only loosely be termed 'Christianity' in the Western countries where once it was the dominant influence. Seeing the writing on the wall, many Christians have given themselves to the project of turning the situation around.

To the extent that this has called the churches to re-examine the scriptural teaching on the nature of a lively and growing church body-life and embrace a fresh and full-orbed obedience to the Lord together with the faithful proclamation of the gospel, this has been a timely stimulus to forsake the too-often defensive, inward-looking attitudes which have turned too many fellowships into spiritual ghettos.

On the debit side, however, 'church growth' is more often than not an exercise in method and technique, the effectiveness of which is measured by statistics. In practice it is, as J. I. Packer has put it, 'in the grip of a secular passion for successful expansion'.[1] When David counted his fighting men, it was sin (2 Sam. 24), but in the baptized sociology of the 'church growth' approach to effective ministry, counting is good — because numbers are always what makes the difference, for without them there is neither analysis nor prediction and no means of establishing programmes that have a 'proven' track record.

The Bible is very interested in the growth of the church and, without encouraging any great attention to statistics, records some figures which are apparently designed to show something of the extent of the power of God to change lives and events. We know, for instance, that 'more than five hundred of the brothers' were witnesses of Christ's resurrection, that 'about a hundred and twenty' gathered in Jerusalem at Pentecost, that 'about three thousand' were converted that day and that the church numbered 'about five thousand' men a short time later (1 Cor. 15:6; Acts 1:15; 2:41; 4:4). Thereafter, there is complete indifference to numbers.[2] Even in the account of Pentecost and its aftermath, the numbers are merely illustrative of the effect of the Spirit's outpouring. The weight of the inspired record is on the qualitative aspects of the apostles' preaching and the responsiveness of the converts.

The essential characteristics of a living church are wonderfully exemplified in the few sentences which record the activities of the believers immediately after Pentecost and their conversion (2:42-47). The weight, as we shall see, is overwhelmingly upon a full-orbed personal discipleship that is fully integrated with the lives of our brothers and sisters in the church.

## **Personal commitment** (2:42)

The fact that all who repented were to be baptized (2:38) indicates the vital role of the church as a Christ-instituted *organization* in the pastoral oversight and mobilization of those who, by that baptism, are publicly marked as *members* of Christ's body. From the beginning, the leadership, as appointed by Christ, exercised discipline in connection with their ministry of the Word and the sacraments. No one could be a Christian, apart from the church as an institution, for only in the context of the gospel ordinances and the apostolic ministry could there be genuine validation of any individual's confession of Christ. Individualistic, free-lance, unconnected and 'secret' Christians were and remain a contradiction in terms, for both Spirit-led desire and scriptural duty impel believers into the fellowship and discipline of a true gospel church. Many professing Christians today operate in practice as their own 'church', and speak in disparaging tones of 'the institutional church' as if it were congenitally aberrant. This view has no support in the New Testament, as is plain from the inception of the church on the Day of Pentecost. The organic wholeness of that body shines through in the way the believers committed themselves to the people of God. The pictures in Acts of the emerging pattern of church life confirm that this was no merely voluntary association of otherwise individualistic believers, but a body made up of people called by the Lord and welded together in loving and submissive discipleship under his sovereign lordship and the pastoral oversight of the ministry of his church.

The growth and development of the early church is unintelligible apart from this perspective. Here is a body, organic in personal commitments and mobilized under leadership for kingdom work and witness — and we see this in every aspect of her body-life from that very first day. Four aspects of the personal commitment of the new believers are highlighted in 2:42.

1. **'The apostles' teaching'** refers to the ongoing instruction given by the apostles, as opposed to the doctrine, or system of truth, held by the apostles. Clearly, the latter was the goal of the former. But the text focuses on the enthusiasm of the people for sound preaching and teaching.

2. **'Fellowship'** (Gk *koinonia)* is Christ-centred mutual affection and action and includes everything from joining in worship to conversations, meals and working together in all the activities of the Christian community as it grows internally and reaches out externally. 'It denotes the unanimity and unity brought about by the Spirit. The individual was completely upheld by the community.'[3] As Matthew Henry says with his usual pithiness, 'Wherever you saw one disciple, you would see more, like *birds of a feather*.'[4] J. A. Alexander defines this fellowship as 'mutual communion, both by joint repasts [fellowship meals] and sacramental feasts [frequent communions] and charitable distribution [mercy ministry]'.[5] Sharing and spreading their mutual love for Jesus and for one another was their grand obsession.

3. **'The breaking of bread'** refers to the frequent celebration of the Lord's Supper, which appears to have been observed at the close of a main meal — something that was to cause problems in Corinth (1 Cor. 11:17-34). Because of its distinctly Christian and congregational nature, they observed this in homes, rather than in the temple.

4. **'Prayer'** was a priority. The context suggests frequent prayer *meetings*, while certainly including private and family prayer.

Corporate prayer is one of the universal essentials of healthy church life as well as a vital component of the individual Christian's prayer life.

These add up to an experiential frame of reference for every Christian's involvement in church life: the Christian wants solid teaching and more of it, wants to share whole life and whole-hearted fellowship with brothers and sisters in the church, wants to sit at the Lord's Table in celebration of his salvation in Christ, wants to pray in secret, in the family and with the church. These are every Christian's basic personal spiritual goals. If they are not your goals, you need a change of outlook!

## **Sharing a common life** (2:44-46)

The description of how these goals were effected in the days after Pentecost poses the question, to what extent this early apostolic pattern ought to be a model for us to imitate. The reason for this is simply that the initial intensity with which the new converts committed themselves to their faith was expressed in ways which could only be sustained for a short period and would eventually have to give way, as indeed they did, to what we might call a more 'regular' pattern of personal and church life. Notice the two points in which their devotion was most extraordinary.

### *Everything in common* (2:44-45)

They **'were together and had everything in common. Selling their possessions and goods, they gave to anyone as he had need.'** This remarkable expression of generosity echoed the outpouring of the Holy Spirit they had just experienced. At the same time, it arose from the peculiar circumstances of the infant church. It was a feast time in Jerusalem. Many of the new converts had come from a distance. They were rejoicing in their new faith and fellowship. It was hardly the time to head for home. They needed more time to be taught the things of the Lord, to be discipled by the apostles and to forge the kind of personal relationships with other believers which would strengthen and equip them to be faithful witnesses for Christ wherever he sent them. But staying in Jerusalem meant having certain unanticipated needs. Many in the 'family of believers' needed practical help (Gal. 6:10). The 'community of goods' was a spontaneous and loving response to the particular situation facing the church.

Without mandating some required renunciation of private property and a kind of 'Christian communism', this does, nevertheless, afford an example of what Christians can and will do when love for the Lord is applied to real need. Love does not seek its own good, but rather the good of others (1 Cor. 13:5) and gives even more than it is able (2 Cor. 8:3-4). The Lord's command to the rich young man to sell all that he had and give it to the poor was not an absolute command to every Christian to do likewise. Nevertheless, it did emphasize the underlying principle of all Christian liberality: namely, that all that we have belongs to the Lord and ought to be directed to serving him.

*Everyday worship* (2:46)

The believers also met together in the temple courts **'every day'**. A young Christian once asked his pastor why he thought people should attend two services on the Lord's Day. 'After all,' he protested, 'the Bible doesn't say we have to have two services.' 'Well,' said the pastor, 'I'll agree that you don't need to come twice on Sunday, provided you agree to do what the Bible says.' 'O.K.! Fair enough,' said the lad. 'Right,' said the pastor, 'I'll see you on Monday morning ... and Tuesday ... and Wednesday ... and we'll follow the apostolic pattern in Acts 2:46!' His point, of course, was not to make a law out of the Acts 2:46 pattern, but just to emphasize that when you love the Lord and thirst after true worship, sound teaching and living fellowship, you don't stay at home and waste your opportunities, whatever they may be! The new believers simply longed for more spiritual food. That is the principle. That is the motive which took them to the fellowship every day! It should take you to church whenever the door opens!

The same is true of their desire to meet together in their homes and is the reason for their **'glad and sincere hearts'**. That tells us a great deal about our coldness and insularity, our lack of hospitality, our complaints about 'having to go to church'! It is certainly true that normal lives need to be ordered. We just cannot go from house to house day in and day out. There are six days for work — only one, the first of the week, is reserved for rest and worship by God's command. Every day cannot be another Day of Pentecost. It is not surprising, then, to find that the apostolic church eventually settled down into a pattern of life that integrated with the proper demands and responsibilities of work and business (1 Thess. 4:11-12). Even so, the abiding theme of the Christian life is a thirsting for communion with God (Ps. 63:1-5; 84:1-4). This is why we always see the joyous sharing of lives where there are lively Christians and growing churches.

## **Attractive public witness** (2:43,47)

That first post-Pentecost period was unique in that it was attended by many miraculous signs performed by the apostles. This created a widespread sense of awe (2:43). As the days passed and more people became Christians — and their lives overflowed with grace — this made a deeper impression still on the population in general. They enjoyed **'the favour of all the people'** (2:47). It is often forgotten that persecution is usually initiated by the small circle of power-brokers in any society and that the greater mass of ordinary people, were they left to themselves, would just as well 'live and let live'. It remains a basic principle of evangelism that righteous living is a positive influence upon the unconverted in general: we are to let our 'light shine before men, that they may see [our] good deeds and praise [our] Father in heaven' (Matt. 5:16). It is your duty, Christian friend, to be winsome and attractive in your witness for Christ. The Hollywood image of the Christian as a hard-nosed, censorious kill-joy is not always off the mark. Many Christians are better at protesting against the evils of the day in the strident tones of implacable righteousness, than at reaching out with quiet and loving concern and compassion to those who desperately need to be won for Christ. Christians are to be clothed with the *beauty* of holiness.

## **The Lord added to their number** (2:47)

The numbers were increased **'daily'** by **'those who were being saved'**. The inspired historian observes pointedly that it was **'the Lord'** who added to their number. As on a later occasion, it would be a Paul that might plant, and an Apollos that might water, but it is always God who gives the growth — who actually works the supernatural transformation of regeneration and conversion. God is sovereign in salvation: the church is his embassy to this lost world. And so, divine sovereignty and human agency intertwine in faithfulness to bring men and women to Christ and cause the church to grow across the world.

The experience of many churches today, certainly in this country, seems a world away from the excitement and expectancy of Pentecost. A little reflection, however, will show that this need not be the case, for the same gospel and the same Holy Spirit are speaking to the same sinners albeit in widely differing cultures and times. Let me suggest some relevant points.

First of all, we are like the apostolic church in that we are *a minority in a hostile environment*. The difference is that we seem to be on the way down, while they were definitely on the way up. The fact is that we can turn this insight to advantage — by understanding that God calls us, in our generation, to attack the problem of human rejection of the Lord with a vigorous obedience that has no regard to cost and no attention to 'success' as a measure of 'effectiveness', or an excuse for resting on supposed laurels (if 'successful') or retreating into defeatist inactivity (if 'failing').

Secondly, the *Holy Spirit* is as much with faithful disciples of the Lord Jesus Christ today as he was in the first century A.D. Allowing for the unique once-for-all aspects of the apostolic period, we have every reason to pray and witness expectantly for conversions today.

Thirdly, our consuming passion must be for *personal holiness* — not 'success'. Leave the increase with the Lord; your task and mine is to fix our eyes upon Jesus and walk in his ways before God and the world. Attractive loving holiness *is* evangelism every bit as much (and sometimes a good deal more) than a polished presentation of the gospel.

Finally, *God will give growth according to his purpose*. What a promise and what a comfort — a promise that he will fill heaven and not lose one soul he means to save; a comfort, in that we have every encouragement to persevere, however slow or faltering we think our witness may be, knowing that he is faithful to ensure that his Word will not return to him empty or fruitless!

# 5.
# When God heals

**Please read Acts 3:1-10**

*'In the name of Jesus Christ of Nazareth, walk'* (3:6).

Miracles are God's headlines. They grab our attention and lead us to listen to the message of his Word. This was certainly one of the principal functions of the miracles performed by the apostles during and after Pentecost. Even if the 'classic' New Testament miracles of the apostles have ceased, this is still true, for when we read about these miracles in the Scriptures or when we see the extraordinary acts of God in history and in people's lives — many of which may well defy all human explanation — we are given pause to think about what the Lord is saying to us.

After Pentecost, 'Many wonders and miraculous signs were done by the apostles' (2:43). In our present passage, we are told about just one of these — the healing of a lame beggar at the temple gate called 'Beautiful'. This event poses two principal questions for modern Christians. The first is simply: what did this miracle mean for the apostles, their ministry and the church — and, not least, for the beggar himself? The second is the theological, and very practical, question as to how we are to view miracles today. Should we expect miracles? And what are we praying for when we pray for healing from some illness? We shall seek to address these two questions as we study this remarkable healing miracle.

## **The beggar's need** (3:1-5)

Peter and John encountered the beggar as they went up to the temple **'at the time of prayer — at three in the afternoon'** (3:1). The beggar had been lame from birth. Luke adds later that he was over forty years of age, perhaps to emphasize that this was a problem of long standing (4:22). The beggar asked them for money (3:3). Peter spoke to him and the man turned to him expectantly, only to be told that Peter had no money but would give him what he could. He then commanded the man: 'In the name of Jesus Christ of Nazareth, walk!' (3:6). Peter took him by the hand; he got up, found he could walk and went with the apostles into the temple court 'walking and jumping, and praising God' (3:8). The people, who knew him well, were 'filled with wonder and amazement at what had happened to him' (3:10).

*Neglected!*

We are naturally inclined to think that the beggar was in need because he had a chronic disability. He was no 'drop-out' from society. He was not lazy. He just happened to be crippled and all he could do was beg. But he was in need, surely, not just because he was a cripple, but because he was *neglected* by those who should have helped him! Why can we say this? Because the law of God declared that there were to be 'no poor' among God's people (Deut. 15:4-11). How was this to come about? God said that the Lord's people — the covenant community — were to take care of them! There were to be no poor among them (Deut. 15:4). Yet there would always be poor people in the land (Deut. 15:11). Therefore, says God, 'I command you to be open-handed.' God's people, from the elders (government) to the people (individual mercy-giving) were to provide for the poor.

What, then, does this tell us about the state of the Old Testament church? Putting it another way, suppose one of the members of your church was discovered begging at the church door every Sunday — what would it say about your church? The *fact* of the beggar being at the temple gate tells us that, while he was sustained after a fashion by the charity of individuals, the church as an organization (instituted by God, mark you) was apparently not bothered about his plight. This ties in with Jesus' rebuke of the Pharisees: 'You give a tenth of your spices — mint, dill and cummin. But you have neglected the more important matters of the law — justice, mercy and faithfulness. You should have practised the latter, without neglecting the former' (Matt. 23:23). The man had begged all his days. Where then was the organized obedience, compassion, sharing, giving, mercy and love of the Old Testament church? It had neglected the need at its own door. It had closed its eyes to its God-given responsibility to care for its own poor and needy brothers and sisters.

*The real need*

The beggar was used to being neglected and a beggar. If the church had no vision for his need, he had also probably lost sight of his real need and had no vision for his own life. How do we know this?

For one thing, he asked for *money*! (3:3). He was just trying to survive, no more, no less. He asked for money, of course, because that was what passers-by could give him and it could purchase what he needed in order to subsist — that is, to be a live beggar as distinct from a starved-to-death beggar! He was forced by circumstances to exist from day to day on the hand-outs of the worshippers.

Furthermore, his life was entirely circumscribed by his destitution and he was therefore a man with *no hope* of accomplishing whatever aspirations to usefulness he might otherwise have had. He had no future but to beg and to make it through another day.

His real need was therefore for something far greater than money. He needed a place within the fellowship of the covenant community that recognized his dignity as a child of God and that integrated him into the work and witness of the people of God. It seems almost silly to say this in view of the hopelessly decayed spiritual state of the Jewish church, but this in fact was the goal of the Mosaic law in requiring open-handedness to the Lord's poor. He needed a truly caring community, with encouragement, help, a place of usefulness, a sphere of work, a place to serve God with a thankful heart. Perhaps you are asking, 'Doesn't this just boil down to the fact that the man really needs more money (a social security cheque to stop him needing to beg), a job (work specially created for people with his disability) and a new pair of legs (not likely, but maybe the National Health Service could do something)?' Yes, these things are true enough — as far as they go. But there is a vastly deeper dimension to his need which alone can give meaning and substance to these temporal helps. That is the spiritual and covenantal dimension. And it is this which comes to the fore in what happens through the ministry of Peter and the Lord's provision for the lame man.

If we need reinforcement of this truth from the negative side, we need only look at the emptiness and despair left by two generations of cradle-to-the-grave welfarism in a country like Britain. Good intentions and lavish redistribution of other people's wealth did not produce a better or a more prosperous country. One does not need to be a prophet to predict that the other extreme of a soulless capitalism will fare no better, even if it does give some incentive to work hard and be a 'success' in worldly terms. When the full-orbed blessing of life in covenant with the Lord is missing, the best of human effort will fall short of the mark or even overleap itself and fall on its head. The fundamental condition for a joyous and meaningful life is still Jesus' words in the Sermon on the Mount: 'But seek first his [God's] kingdom and his righteousness, and all these things will be given to you as well' (Matt. 6:33).

## **The Lord's provision** (3:6-10)

When we talk about 'answers to prayer', we far too often assume that 'Yes' is the only real answer. True prayer, however, ought to be as ready to take 'No' for the Lord's answer, as a 'Yes'. We tend to trust our feelings and our sense of persuasion so much that we almost always assume for all practical purposes that what we are asking for is already the Lord's will. Consequently we can find it very difficult to accept it when the Lord closes a door. We are not told how pious the beggar was, but we can be sure that he expected something tangible from the apostles. What a surprise was in store for him!

### *'What I have I give you'* (3:6-8)

There was no money for the beggar. **'Silver or gold I do not have...'** says Peter. Peter was broke! There is no reason to believe he would not have given the man something, had he the means to do so. This is not to be used as an excuse for a tight-fisted attitude to the needy, even if it does prove that there are other ways to help meet real needs. The Lord made sure Peter had no cash on him just so that he could demonstrate his life-giving compassion in the most dramatic way. And the universal application for the church in every age is that we are called to the ministry of mercy and a constant attitude of readiness to help those in need.

Peter did not tease the lame man: **'...what I have I give to you. In the name of Jesus Christ of Nazareth, walk.'** The heart of gospel compassion, of the love of Jesus Christ, is to give what you have — that is to say, that which God has given you, in his grace. Peter had no money, but he had the love of Christ. He cared. He was moved by the man's plight. And the Holy Spirit moved Peter to do something for him that would completely overshadow the combined hand-outs of his long and sad career as a beggar.

That 'something' was to be a miracle of healing! The disciples had earlier been commissioned and specifically gifted by the Lord to 'heal the sick' (Matt. 10:8). Significantly, the invocation of the name of the Lord preceded the healing command. The miracle then served to attest the truth that the man Jesus of Nazareth was indeed the Christ, the promised Messiah. Peter's formula is chosen for maximum public relations impact: 'Jesus Christ of Nazareth' combines his office as the Messiah promised in the Scriptures ('Christ' = Messiah = Anointed One) with his incarnation as the eternal Son of God who took our flesh ('of Nazareth' = 'the carpenter's son' Matt. 13:53-56). It is the power of the risen Christ which heals and saves! And so believers confess: 'He reached down from on high and took hold of me' (Ps. 18:16).

If God is sovereign in all his redeeming works, it is also the case that the recipients of his blessings are usually called to respond with an act of will. The raising of both Jairus' daughter and the dead and decomposing Lazarus would be notable exceptions. Here, the man is commanded to *walk*. He is to answer the healing word from God with an *effort* that is an earnest of credible responsiveness. Peter even helps and encourages him by **'taking him by the right hand'** (cf. Ps. 73:23-24). As the Lord touches his crippled feet, Peter touches his outstretched hand. The hand that was cupped in expectation of a gift of money received the loving grasp of the Lord's power to heal! That physical contact says, 'I care; I am with you; believe what I say; the Lord is with you; rise up on your crippled feet; *act* on the call; don't say, "It's impossible"; **Walk!'**

Then 'the impossible' happened, for **'Instantly the man's feet and ankles became strong. He jumped to his feet and began to walk'** (3:7-8). He was healed after all these years! And he could not leave the apostles, for he **'went with them into the temple courts, walking and jumping and praising God'** (3:8). Well might he have sung the words of the psalmist:

> 'Praise the Lord, O my soul,
>     and forget not all his benefits—

who forgives all [my] sins
  and heals all [my] diseases;
who redeems [my] life from the pit
  and crowns [me] with love and compassion'
(Ps. 103:2-4).

We see just how powerfully transforming the work of God is in a human life. Notice four aspects to this in the case of the crippled beggar:

1. He *confessed* the goodness of God from his heart.
2. He went joyously to *worship* the Lord.
3. He *witnessed* to the mercy of the Lord in public.
4. He had a *new life* to live — his life would never be the same again.

Of course, we would readily concede that a man who experienced such a miracle could be expected to be dramatically affected by the experience. We would be enthusiastic too, were we to see a miracle or two in our lives! But let me ask this: if you have been given good health all through your life and with it the gifts and capacities to live, work and provide for yourself and your family, is that really less of a work of God's infinite love and sovereign grace than the Lord's restoration of the beggar? Why do you take for granted all the blessings you have enjoyed all along? Did the Lord owe you these good things? Are you more entitled to them than the beggar, who was deprived of them? For all that he had been healed miraculously, the beggar would never get back 'the years that the locusts had eaten' — the prime years of young manhood. You have had the freedom to use these years. You therefore have *more* cause to be praising God, since he has never allowed you who have had good health to be afflicted with the disabilities which the beggar and many like him today have had to cope with. The 'normality' of your experience of life ought to be the very reason you rise up to praise the Lord with exultation and joy!

*They were filled with wonder and amazement* (3:9-10)

If everything from Olympic victories to scientific achievements can excite the wonder of the masses, then it should be no surprise that the healing of the crippled beggar set all Jerusalem in a buzz. Bogus 'healings' and even rumours of 'miracles' will do as much, but this was the real thing! As one of God's 'wonders and miraculous signs', this meant at least three things.[1]

First, the miracle was a mighty evidence of the *lordship* of Jesus Christ as the risen Saviour. Such 'signs and miraculous wonders' pointed to the Lord and attested the message of his Word and the ministry of his servants. This was the reason why the apostles were given these wonders to perform (John 14:12). The Lord's enemies certainly understood this, albeit in a perverted hostile fashion (cf. 4:14-18).

Second, the miracle was also evidence of the *compassion* of the Lord Jesus Christ for lost and suffering humanity. The healing of diseases is a parable of the permanent and eternal healing of salvation through faith in Jesus Christ. The diseases that threaten us most are those of the soul — the unregenerated human nature, with its unhallowed, self-destructive affections and lusts that make war on our own being (1 Peter 2:11). Jesus came to save, because of his love for the people, the lives of those who would perish in darkness and rebellion had he not purposed to die in their place.

Last but not least, the miracle was a call to *come to Jesus Christ* as the only Saviour of lost men and women. It said that healing, in terms of the comprehensive spiritual claims of gospel redemption, is a possibility for you, *now!* It calls those who are not Christians to come to Christ, to receive him as the Saviour, to bring their souls in repentance and tears to ask for 'peace in believing'. And it speaks continuously to all who are already Christians to 'receive not the grace of God in vain' (1 Cor. 15:2, AV).

Charles Simeon, that great Anglican evangelical of the nineteenth century, reserves the last word of application for those who think themselves right with God: 'We expect you no longer to continue the poor, low, grovelling creatures ye have been; but to show to all around you, that you are endued with power from on high, and enabled to "walk even as Christ himself walked". We expect you to shine as lights in the world; yea, the world itself expects this of you. If you profess to have experienced the converting grace of God, the world will ask you, and with reason too, "What do ye more than others?" And they should be made to see that there is in divine grace an energy and a power to which they are utter strangers; and an efficacy for which they know not how to account.

Dear brethren, ye must live above the world: ye must delight yourselves in God. Ye must not be afraid of man: nor, if man ridicule and revile your devotion to God, must ye regard it as of the smallest moment. Gratitude to the Saviour must fill your souls. To him you must consecrate all the powers he has renewed; and the whole of your life must henceforth be devoted to the praise of his grace, and to the glory of his name.'[2]

# 6.
# The true healer

**Please read Acts 3:11-26**

*'The Christ, who has been appointed for you — even Jesus'* (3:20).

All miracles of healing — past, present and future — are, in themselves, temporary in their effects. Unless the Lord returns in our lifetime, each of us will die and our body return to the dust. This fact alone ought to put any thirst for 'healings' in perspective. It ought at least to tell us that, however desirable it is to be healthy and live a long life, this will all be to no avail for the eternity to follow if our hearts are not right with God. The most basic fact of life remains that we are 'destined to die once and after that to face judgement' (Heb. 9:27). The real issue with which we are confronted by the healing of the lame man is not so much the *healing* as the *healer*. The physical healing was, to be sure, an outpouring of God's loving compassion upon the lame man. It changed his life completely. But, as Peter was at pains to make clear in the address that followed the healing, Jesus Christ is the true healer — both of the lame man's legs and also of his old lost and undone nature. For he gave him a new heart with which to worship and praise his Redeemer.

## Christ rejected (3:11-15)

Peter did not want anybody to think that it was the apostles' **'own power or godliness'** that had made the lame beggar walk. Lloyd Ogilvie observes that the apostle here 'picked out the two qualities among the Jews which were the greatest source of pride — moral impeccability and religious diligence'.[1] So, when people crowded around in their amazement and curiosity over the miracle, he took care to let them know both that this was the work of God in glorifying **'his servant Jesus'** and 'not the work of men', and that their greatest need was for the very same Jesus Christ, through whom the man was healed, but whom they had rejected and nailed to the cross.

Peter set forth his argument with the most elegant simplicity. He contrasted God's treatment of Jesus with the way men had treated him. Every clause serves to intensify the enormity of the crime and magnify God's reversal of the intended effects of human sin. The structure can be set out as follows:

***God* ... 'glorified his servant Jesus'** (3:13).
***You* ... 'handed him over to be killed'** (3:13).
***You* ... 'disowned him before Pilate'** (3:13).
***You* ... 'disowned the Holy and Righteous One'** (3:14).
***You* ... 'killed the author of life'** (3:15).
*But* ***God* ... 'raised him from the dead'** (3:15).

In this way, Peter rapidly shifted the focus from the healing event to the gospel itself! For the true meaning of the healing was actually to be found in the sufferings, death and resurrection of the Lord Jesus Christ! In the process, Peter sets a double example which preachers of the gospel everywhere ought to be imitating in their own ministries. The first is his willingness to confront sin head-on; the second is his determination to move swiftly to the heart of the gospel and commend Christ to sinners as their only hope for what ails them!

The first part — confronting their sin — is achieved by means of five points of contrast.

*The power of God* (3:12)

This healing did not come from man's power, but from the power of God. John Calvin, in his lively way, reminds us that because we have a tendency in matters miraculous 'to slip away from God to his creatures, it is very important to prevent this error in good time'.[2] Hero-worship in the church is a cloud that comes between the believer and the Lord, and blights the purity and single-mindedness of his worship of God. *All* the glory belongs to God!

*The revelation of the God of our fathers* (3:13)

This was no new religion, but the revelation of **'the God of our fathers'**. Identification of the source of the miracle as **'the God of Abraham, Isaac and Jacob'** was as good as saying to them, 'Remember *who* your God is! Remember what he has *done* in the history of our covenant people! Remember what he has *said* to us in his Word through the prophets about his purposes of redemption! The Scriptures expressly forbid even listening to what false teachers have to say!' (Deut. 13:3). Peter had to assure them from the start that this was the work of the God of their fathers. Only then could he go on to speak of Christ. As Calvin neatly puts it, 'He says that he is bringing in no new religion such as would draw the people away from the law and the prophets.'[3]

*The glory of Jesus* (3:13)

This was more than merely a miracle, for God was glorifying his servant Jesus. Again, note the language of continuity connecting the 'God of our fathers' with Jesus. Jesus is **'his servant'** — an evocation of Isaiah's prophecy of the Messiah as the suffering servant (Isa. 52:13, cf. 53:1-12). This was no isolated act of compassion in which some man happened to be healed. It was the coming of Messiah as a result of the eternal love of God for his world, so that 'By his wounds we are healed'! (Isa. 53:5).

*The Jesus you killed* (3:13-15)

This sensational event ought certainly to amaze us, but it is about our sins that we ought to be most concerned! Peter did not mince words. While 'careful to give no needless offence', he laid on his hearers 'the guilt they had contracted in crucifying their Messiah'.[4] They handed him over to be killed; insisted upon it when Pilate wanted to let him go; rejected him in favour of releasing a murderer; in sum, they killed the author of life. Again, the language is chosen both for meticulous accuracy and maximum effect. Jesus is **'the Holy One'** of Isaiah 31:1; 41:14 and 43:14; he is the **'Righteous One'** (Gk *dikaion,* Acts 7:52; 22:14; James 5:6, cf. Isa. 32:1; Zech. 9:9); and the **'author of life'** or 'prince of life' (Gk *archegos*). He was the incarnate Son of God, but they killed him.

*The Jesus who has risen from the dead* (3:15)

The Jesus they killed, says Peter, is the risen Christ to whom they must answer. Conviction of sin is the intended response. We killed the author of life, but God raised him from the dead. Charles Simeon rightly says that, while we of succeeding generations did not personally kill Jesus, we have nevertheless shown the same hostility as the Jews 'against him, *as revealed in the gospel*', for 'we have refused to acknowledge him in his proper character' and 'have rejected him, with a scornful preference for our most deadly lusts'.[5] Peter's words for his Jewish hearers do not let any of us Gentiles off the hook. Nevertheless, even in this comprehensive rebuke there is a marvellous ray of light — the words **'but God'**. God raised Jesus to life. And there could only be one reason for that to be relevant to the human race. And it is that God meant to give life, in Christ, to a people he intended to save and make his disciples.

**Christ proclaimed** (3:16-23)

From a little implicit 'law', Peter passes to some very explicit gospel! If they are guilty of the death of Jesus, they surely need the life that Jesus has won for all who trust in him. The keynote is struck in Peter's explanation of the healing of the lame man: it is **'Jesus' *name* and the *faith* that comes through him that has given this complete healing to him, as you can all see'** (3:16). F. F. Bruce has pointed out that 'In the faith and thought of every nation the name is inextricably bound up with the person.'[6] He goes on to show how 'the whole content of the saving truth revealed in Jesus is comprised in his name (Acts 4:12; 1 Cor. 6:11).'[7] The lame beggar had been healed when Peter declared, 'In the *name* of Jesus Christ of Nazareth, walk' (3:6). Now Peter explains that he was healed through his **'faith in the *name* of Jesus'**.

There is, of course, nothing magical about the *sound* of Jesus' name. The name is indicative of the person. The invocation of the name is the invocation of the power and authority of that person. Faith in that name which is 'above every name' (Phil. 2:9) is faith in the person and work of Jesus Christ as Saviour and Lord.

Ogilvie notes that 'There is no record of Peter using the word "faith" before that day, not even in his message on Pentecost morning.' Now, in his proclamation of Jesus Christ, he 'stresses the essential, crucial role of faith'.[8] He also describes who Jesus is and what he has done. There are three main points.

*The giver of life* (3:16-20)

As Jesus renewed the life of the beggar — healing for the body and new faith in his heart — so he would be the giver of life to all sorts of people. The message is three-fold.

Firstly, there is *hope* for lost people. Peter 'encourages them to hope that, though they had been guilty of putting Christ to death, yet they might find mercy'.[9] Without minimizing their guilt, Peter does put it in perspective by acknowledging two things: one, that they **'acted in ignorance'** and, two, that this was the means by which God fulfilled the prediction of the prophets **'that his Christ would suffer'** (3:17-18). Neither their ignorance, nor the plan of God, removed their responsibility or excused the sin. The Jews freely chose to kill Jesus.

But these two facts shed a wonderful light on their predicament, just because Jesus' death was for sinners. The awful realization that our sin consisted in a blind and ignorant rejection of the only one who could save us and that God purposed to use this to effect the very salvation we were ignorantly refusing, is calculated to melt hard hearts. What love can compare with the love that lets our sins be the instrument of delivering up the perfect sacrifice for sin — a sacrifice which so soon returns in the call of God to believe in Jesus for our own salvation by his free grace?

Secondly, *turn* to the Lord, now: **'Repent, then, and turn to God...'** (3:19). Repentance and faith are the two sides of the door to salvation (20:21). Truly turning *from* sin is inseparable from truly turning *to* the Lord. They are essentially of a piece and boil down to giving up the former negative attitude to Christ in favour of the viewpoint of the God of Abraham, Isaac and Jacob — namely that Jesus *is* the divine Messiah. This is no mere intellectual change of opinion, but nothing less than the receiving of Jesus Christ as a personal Saviour and making a commitment of loving discipleship to him.

Thirdly, you will receive *new life!* Peter earnestly encourages this faith-commitment by showing that it will issue in the Lord's blessing of our lives from the past to the present and then on into the future. Our past slate is washed clean: our **'sins [will] be wiped out'** when we turn to the Lord (3:19). Forgiveness of sins is absolute, in Jesus Christ. The blood of Christ removes all barriers to reconciliation with God. Our present will be transformed. We shall enjoy **'times of refreshing ... from the Lord'** (3:19). For, 'if our sins be forgiven us, we have now reason to be of good cheer'.[10] Like the healed beggar, we shall have every reason to be walking and jumping and praising God! And our future is heaven itself: a day is coming when **'he [will] send the Christ'** (3:20). The following verse (3:21) clearly implies that the coming of Christ promised in 3:20 must be at the consummation or *parousia,* when he has subjected everything under his feet (cf. Heb. 2:8). Until that great day, he must remain in heaven. In the meantime, every Christian's future is shaped by his expectant anticipation of the return of the Lord. We have *forgiveness* for the past, *joy* for the present and *hope* for the future!

*The heavenly Advocate* (3:21)

Any impatience that the risen Jesus had not immediately appeared to lead his new believers to the rapid establishment of his kingdom was now dispelled by Peter when he declared that Jesus **'must remain in heaven'** until the time for fulfilment of the prophesied restoration of all things. This is the doctrine of the 'session' of Christ — he *sits* at the right hand of God (Ps. 8:5-6; Heb. 2:6-10; cf. Ps. 110:1; Col. 3:1) — a teaching that became increasingly prominent in the apostolic ministry (Acts 5:30-31; Rom. 8:34; Eph. 1:19-23; cf. 1 Cor. 15:25-28; Phil. 2:9-11). Peter does not elaborate on the details of the heavenly ministry of Christ at this point. We know, however, that he is our constant *advocate* with the Father (1 John 1:5 - 2:1), and that he continues, by the gift of the Holy Spirit, to nurture lively faith in his followers, such that we are spiritually raised up with Christ and seated with him in the heavenly realms (Eph. 2:4-6). And he exercises 'all authority' as the Mediator-King, who is 'head over everything for the church, which is his body' (Matt. 28:18; Eph. 1:20-21).

*The incarnate Prophet* (3:22-23)

If there were any lingering questions as to how the man Jesus could really be the divine Messiah and this be in accord with the Word of

God as it stood at that point (the Old Testament), Peter moved to reassure his hearers by quoting from Deuteronomy 18:15-19. Moses, he said, had prophesied of Jesus Christ! Jesus was the great **'prophet like me from among your own people'**. This explained why the carpenter's son could be the resurrected Jesus Messiah. The last Moses was the Son of God incarnate! Even the Samaritans knew that the Messiah would come (John 4:25). Jesus had taught that the era of the prophets had ended with the fulfilment of Malachi 4:4-6 in the ministry of the last Elijah, John the Baptizer (Matt. 11:13). John had paved the way for Jesus, who is the final prophet. As *the* Prophet, Jesus must be heard. At the transfiguration, the Father declared: 'This is my Son, whom I love; with him I am well pleased. Listen to him!' (Matt. 17:5). Refusal incurs being **'completely cut off'** from the covenant community. There is a heart-felt plea in these words, for it is as if Peter says, 'If you won't take my word for it, hear Moses — for he speaks of the same Jesus, whose salvation I proclaim in your hearing today!'

## **Christ received** (3:24-26)

The apostle's argument rises to its climax. It really is very simple and straightforward. The prophets *all* foretold Messiah's coming (3:24). '[You are] **heirs of the prophets and of the covenant'** (3:25; Gen. 22:18; 26:4). Therefore, 'the blessing is for you, in his **servant**', Jesus Christ (3:26), which further implies the need to 'repent and turn to God'.

### *An earnest invitation*

In spite of all the earlier emphasis on guilt, this is a thoroughly positive appeal to the hearts of the audience. Peter appealed to the Jews as 'heirs of the prophets and the covenant'. He was saying they were privileged to belong to God's people. In this way, says Calvin, 'He encourages them again to receive the grace of God offered them in Christ.'[11] Even though they had killed Jesus and even though the actual spiritual state and practical devotion of the Old Testament church was in such a decayed state, God had not summarily rejected them. They were still God's people. God was not ready to write them off. Peter thus appeals to 'the highest motives'.[12] Let them return to the Lord, who has been blessing them all along.

But how does this apply to the non-Jews of the world? What about us, who are 'foreigners to the covenants of the promise'? (Eph. 2:12). Not surprisingly, there is a shift of focus in the way the apostles later appeal to the Gentiles, who have no Old Testament background. On Mars Hill, Paul appeals to the Greeks on the basis of their awareness that there is a God — symbolized by their altar inscribed 'To an unknown god' (Acts 17:23). The point of contact had to be their basic humanity, as created by God. So Paul noted that we are all 'God's offspring' (17:28-29) and proclaimed Christ from that starting-point, without any reference to the Hebrew experience. God loves his world and plans to save people, whom he has made in his image, to be his body, the church. We are appealed to as human beings who can think, who have a relationship to our Creator already, who have consciences and a sense of destiny beyond the grave, who know there is a difference between right and wrong and, however low we may have sunk, are aware that there is a reckoning some day, if not in this life then in the world to come.

The *covenant* emphasis, however, speaks of God's sovereign grace (3:25). God reached out to us. His grace is unconditional and given with absolute sovereignty from his side. This says something as special as it is humbling: God simply and sovereignly means to save sinners in spite of themselves! Even when we were going our own way — when we were still spiritually dead in our sinful ways — Jesus Christ died, the just for the unjust. The sinless Son of God *became* sin before his Father-God to bear the penalty of sin and win eternal life for a people whom he would bring to saving faith in their generations as he worked out his purpose in history.

*The gospel message is Jesus Christ*

God's promise to Abraham was that **'through your offspring** (Gk *to spermati* — the dative singular of 'seed') **all peoples on earth will be blessed'** (3:25; Gen. 22:18). Paul later will point out that this 'seed' is singular, not plural, and refers to the one person, the Lord Jesus Christ! He is the *seed* of the promise to Abraham (Gal. 3:16)! The fulfilment comes in Christ. The reality is experienced in Christ, through personal faith. 'The healed beggar is a sample of that blessing; Peter's sermon is the offering of all the spiritual riches of that blessing' — first to the Jews, but ultimately to all nations.[13]

### *Personal discipleship to Jesus*

The real evidence of salvation is personal holiness and practical discipleship. 'If saved at all, it must be from their sins, not in them.'[14] We must turn, but it is Christ who turns us. Christ blesses **'by turning each of you from your wicked ways'** (3:26). 'Christ turns us, but so that we ourselves turn (Jer. 31:18).'[15] To turn from our sins means to turn to Christ in new life. This is the true healing, for he is the true Healer. 'If the healing of a man's body was such a source of joy,' wrote Charles Simeon, 'what must the healing of the soul be? The truth is that sin is the one source of all the misery that is upon earth; and the restoration to a measure of their pristine holiness in Paradise will restore them also, in the same proportion, to their pristine happiness. Holiness, insofar as it is wrought in the soul, is the commencement of heaven upon earth.'[16]

Come, Lord, when grace hath made me meet
Thy blessed face to see;
For if thy work on earth be sweet,
What will thy glory be?
My knowledge of that life is small,
The eye of faith is dim;
But 'tis enough that Christ knows all,
And I shall be with him.

(Richard Baxter, 1615-91).

# Part II

# Jerusalem and the Jews

Acts 4 - 8

# 7.
# Holy boldness

**Please read Acts 4:1-31**

*'Lord ... enable your servants to speak your word with great boldness'* (4:29).

Wherever Jesus Christ is faithfully proclaimed, opposition is never long in coming. It is no accident that the most virulent attempts to suppress the Christian movement recorded in Acts came, not from pagans, but from the Jewish leadership, the Sanhedrin — the ruling body of the residual Old Testament church. The first instance of this was our Lord's examination and trial prior to his crucifixion (Matt. 26:57-67; Mark 14:53-65; 15:1; Luke 22:66-71). Others soon followed, a vivid reminder of Jesus' own teaching that no servant is above his master and that Christians therefore can expect hatred from those who hated him first (John 13:16; 15:18). The apostles as a group (Acts 4:5-21; 5:21-40); then Stephen, whom they martyred (Acts 6:12 - 7:60); and finally Paul, once the persecutor of Stephen (Acts 22:30; 23:15; 24:20) all faced the murderous ire of the ecclesiastical establishment.

The pattern was set for all of history to come. The New Testament church has proclaimed Christ as the risen Saviour against a grumbling groundswell of opposition, which from time to time has erupted into a volcanic torrent of persecution for the Lord's people. Paradoxically, this has not issued in defeat, but has occasioned the most notable victories for the Lord's cause and kingdom, wrought in that 'unconquerable fortitude' with which the Lord endows his people.[1]

## Arrest and trial (4:1-7)

Peter and John were arrested (4:1-4). This was evidently prompted by the Sadducees, who were the majority, 'liberal' party in the

Jewish church and who, over against the traditionalist-ritualist Pharisee minority, rejected the doctrines of the resurrection, future retributive judgement and the existence of angels (Matt. 22:23-28; Acts 23:8). They were greatly disturbed by the apostles' **'proclaiming in Jesus the resurrection of the dead'** and by the increasing following the Christian faith was gathering — now **'about five thousand'** men (4:2,4). And they determined to suppress their preaching.

In the trial itself (4:5-7) the Sadducees sidestepped the embarrassing problem that a cripple really had been healed by a miracle by confining their attentions to the question of the **'power'** or **'name'** by which the apostles had done what they had done. The bureaucratic mind-set always seeks to protect its power by jealously guarding pretended exclusive claims to authority. They wanted to hear the apostles admit to an authority other than their own — specifically, the authority of the Jesus they had condemned to death seven weeks earlier. Then they could 'legally' neutralize what they had already decided was a threat to the established order.

Jesus had warned the disciples to expect this kind of thing: 'They will treat you this way because of my name, for they do not know the One who sent me' (John 15:21). Christians need not be surprised when they find the church establishment and the law of the land applied to their disadvantage. We also need not be discouraged by this. Why? Because the courts of human injustice are the best arenas for powerful testimonies to the grace of God in the gospel of Jesus Christ. And persecution for righteousness' sake has always had the attendant promise of the happy possession of the kingdom of heaven (Matt. 5:10).

### **Giving an answer** (4:8-20)

If Peter felt any fear, it is not discernible in anything he said. His reply might indeed have come from the very portal of heaven. With a majestic simplicity and courageous forthrightness — what John Owen, referring to the gift of holy boldness, calls a 'free, enlarged spirit, attended with an ability of speech suited unto the matter in hand'[2] — the apostle confesses Christ before the men who murdered his Master. This is what it means for a Christian to be a martyr — to 'witness' (Gk *martur*) in the teeth of threatened danger and the fear that silences the tongue to save the skin. Martyrdom is always associated in our minds with last words on the scaffold and heroic death, but the Scripture does not lock it up with murdered saints. The witnessing Christian is a true martyr on every occasion in life in which he stands up and is counted for Christ against the world's opposition and, in so doing, gains the victory over the pressures that would shut his mouth and let the moment pass in silence.

Small wonder, then, that when we analyse Peter's reply, it is thoroughly God-centred. Indeed, it is thoroughly trinitarian, for, filled with the Holy Spirit, he testifies in the name of the Son of God and in obedience to God the Father. There is nothing of the power of man in this, otherwise Peter would have failed as surely as he did when he denied Christ in the high priest's yard (Matt. 26:69-75). This time, the Lord gave him victory.

*They were filled with the Holy Spirit* (4:8)

Jesus had promised: 'Now when they bring you to the synagogues and magistrates and authorities, do not worry about how or what you should answer, or what you should say. For the Holy Spirit will teach you in that very hour what you ought to say' (Luke 12:11-12, NKJV). That time had come, and Peter's special need was answered by a special moment of the Spirit's infilling.[3] The work of the Spirit should not, however, diminish the force of what is emphasized elsewhere in Scripture, that we are *commanded* to be filled with the Holy Spirit (Eph. 5:18). Obedient co-operation with the Spirit is indispensable to living a good and godly life (see Eph. 5:22 - 6:9; Col. 3:16 - 4:1). The filling of the Spirit, therefore, is 'not a matter of unusual or spectacular experience (although something of that may at times be involved), but Spirit-worked obedience to Christ as that comes to expression in the basic, everyday relationships and responsibilities of life'.[4] The normal experience of Christians is to see God working in us 'to will and to act according to his good purpose', even as we 'continue to work out [our] salvation with fear and trembling' (Phil. 2:12-13). The third person of the triune God is the inward agent of the work of God in the soul of man. Because of the filling of the Holy Spirit, every believer can know the freedom of which Paul speaks to Timothy: 'For God did not give us a spirit of timidity, but a spirit of power, of love and of self-discipline' (2 Tim. 1:7). We are neither alone nor left to our own resources. The Spirit is within us (Ezek. 36:26-27).

*They spoke in the name of the Son of God* (4:8-12)

When Peter addressed the Sanhedrin, he turned to the Second Person of the triune God, the Lord Jesus Christ, and preached the very heart of the gospel. He asserted three basic truths about Jesus.

First, *Jesus is alive!* Why was the cripple healed? Peter's answer scythed through the scepticism and hypocrisy of his interrogators. He threw down the gauntlet of the gospel with the most uncompromising clarity: **'It is by the name of Jesus Christ of Nazareth, whom you crucified but whom God raised from the dead, that this man stands before you healed'** (4:10). He claimed no power for himself. He offered no secular-scientific explanation. He simply ascribed the healing to a miracle of the risen Christ. His authority was 'the name' of Jesus. By calling Jesus, **'Jesus Christ of Nazareth'**, he identified the man 'Jesus ... of Nazareth' as the divine 'Christ' (the Messiah) and confessed him as the Lord from heaven. This was to invoke the presence and power of God.[5] His was the authority; his was the healing! And the healed cripple before them was the objective, irrefutable proof! The challenge to the council could hardly have been more provocative to them, for this Jesus was the man they had put to death!

Secondly, their opposition to Jesus was *predicted in Scripture* (4:11). Why did the *church leaders* not welcome Jesus as the promised Messiah? Peter went straight to the point: Jesus is **'the stone you builders rejected, which has become the capstone'** (quoted from Ps. 118:22). They did not understand their own Scriptures or their father David! Therefore, instead of building the church of God, they were in fact tearing it down, or, rather, trying to build their own false church on a foundation other than that which God had given. The churches of our own day which no longer believe or preach the Word of God and deny the great doctrines of the faith are no different in principle from the Christ-denying Old Testament church of apostolic times — and their destiny will be no different in practice, if, like the Sanhedrin, they continue to reject the Jesus of Scripture.

Thirdly, the claims of Jesus Christ are *exclusive* — **'Salvation is found in no one else'** (4:12) — not in the bare, legalistic righteousness of the Pharisees, nor in the sceptical anti-supernaturalism of the Sadducees, and certainly not in any Christ-rejecting form of religion. There is **'no other name under heaven given to men by which we must be saved'**! The decree of God is that Jesus Christ is the only Saviour. He is the 'one mediator between God and men' (1 Tim. 2:5). Peter told the Jews what they most needed to hear, but least wanted to heed. This is the task of the church in every generation. Without such clear witness-bearing, the world will perish. By means of it, martyrs may suffer, but sinners are saved.

*They obeyed God the Father* (4:13-20)

Peter must have wondered how the Sanhedrin would react to his ringing affirmation of the risen Jesus as the promised Messiah. Humanly speaking, he could well expect imprisonment and death. After all, no servant is above his master — as Jesus had said — and Jesus had been nailed to a cross by this very body of men!

The *witness* of the apostles astonished the members of the Sanhedrin (4:13-14). Four facts left them utterly speechless:

1. The **'courage'** (Gk *parresia* — boldness) of Peter and John impressed them greatly (4:13).
2. The fact that the apostles were **'unschooled'** (Gk *agrammatoi*) and **'ordinary'** (Gk *idiotai*) amazed these Jewish leaders (4:13).
3. They recognized that the apostles **'had been with Jesus'** (4:13).
4. The **'man who had been healed'** was standing before them, a living evidence of the apostles' claims (4:14).

All the basic components of testimony-bearing are present in this remarkable moment of self-awareness on the part of the Sanhedrin. The Jewish leaders saw, firstly, *renewed lives*, filled with a confidence not their own; secondly, *transformed minds*, clothed with a wisdom not their own; thirdly, clear evidence of the *lordship of Jesus Christ* in their lives; and, fourthly, clear evidence of the *historical reality* of the redeeming power of the Lord. The voice of God speaks to the world through these basic realities. Indeed, the very fact that people can be so virulent in their opposition to the gospel is itself a witness to the effectiveness of the message's thrust. This tells us also that the cutting edge of Christian witness does not depend on *our* notion as to 'how we are doing', but the unbelievers' perception of what we *are*, even as the truth pierces consciences. Our part, as ambassadors for Christ, is to think and act in a Christian manner and let the Holy Spirit do his work.

They still tried to *silence the preaching of the gospel* (4:15-18).

Thwarted by a combination of their evil consciences, irrefutable facts and fear of public opinion, the Sanhedrin could only engage in some low-key damage-control. They placed a gag-order on the apostles, in the vain hope that it would somehow hinder the church.

How little some things change! The modern equivalents of the Sadducees populate the corridors of power in the large, established churches of our time and continue to preside over the decaying shells of denominations which for decades have been more adept at declaring what they do not believe, than in promoting anything approximating to the teaching of Scripture and their own historic but now disregarded doctrinal standards. The 'Sanhedrins' of Lambeth and Rome, and elsewhere, continue to darken counsel with words without biblically informed knowledge (cf. Job 38:2). Conspicuously silent on the actual content of the infallible Word of God, the claims of the Lord Jesus Christ and the holiness required of us by our Father-God, they defend without shame their unbelief in such clear scriptural truths as the deity, substitutionary atonement and resurrection of Jesus Christ and the eternal condemnation by a holy God of all who refuse to come to Christ in faith and repentance!

Peter and John *refused to be silenced* (4:19-20). They courageously threw down the gauntlet of spiritual liberty: **'Judge for yourselves whether it is right in God's sight to obey you rather than God'**, and went on to affirm the impossibility of not preaching the gospel of Jesus Christ: **'For we cannot help speaking about what we have seen and heard.'** The Holy Spirit will not be muzzled! God will not permit his truth to be suppressed! However great the danger that threatens, there will be Christians who obey God rather than men (cf. 5:29). Why? Because they love their Saviour more than they fear what men can do (1 Cor. 9:16). Indeed, it is opposition and persecution which not only test the mettle of Christian people, but are frequently the arena in which lives, churches, communities and nations experience spiritual revival.

### Free to proclaim the gospel (4:21-31)

The Sanhedrin had no alternative but to release Peter and John. Even they had to bow to public opinion. Governments should be a restraint to the wickedness of people, but sometimes, in the good providence of God, the people are a restraint to wicked rulers (e.g.

1 Sam. 14:45). In this case, the miracle of the cripple's healing could not be denied and this simple fact shut them up to grumbling impotence, so **'After further threats, they let them go'** (4:21-22). The underlying lesson is that we have a profound freedom to proclaim the good news of Jesus Christ which can never quite be taken away! In the strength of our Lord and with the words given by our Comforter, the Holy Spirit, we are freed from the limitations that men would impose by their bogus authority and lethally tyrannical power.

When the martyr Donald Cargill (1619-1680) was delivering his final words on the scaffold, he was interrupted by the rolling of his executioners' drums. He paused, and with a smile declared to the crowd, 'Ye see we have no liberty to speak what we would, but God knoweth our hearts.' He then went on to prove that he possessed the true freedom, which not even an executioner can take from a child of God: 'And now this is the sweetest and most glorious day that ever mine eyes did see... The Lord knows that I go on this ladder with less fear and perturbation of mind, than ever I entered the pulpit to preach... Now, I am near the getting of the crown which shall be sure, for which I bless the Lord, and desire all of you to bless him that he hath brought me here, and made me triumph over devils, men, and sin.'[6]

Even the worst opposition to Christ will in the end serve the purpose of God. This is the iron that will sharpen our iron (Prov. 27:17). This remains true even for those who are silenced by martyrdom! Christ will not be denied! The hostility of so many to Christian testimony-bearing is proof positive that he cannot be ignored — it is also the harbinger of Christ's victory and kingdom!

How appropriate that the Lord's people, reunited with the apostles, should **'raise their voices together in prayer to God'**! (4:23-31).[7] When many might have convened a planning meeting to discuss their response to the new political situation and the authorities' ban on preaching and proselytizing, the apostles held a prayer meeting! There are two lessons for Christians in the apostolic example. On the one hand, they took their enemies' threats very seriously. They neither laughed off the danger carelessly, nor shrank back in paralysed fear. On the other hand, they turned to the Lord with confidence and godly petitions, that he would sustain them and protect them as they openly ministered for Jesus Christ.[8]

The prayer itself addresses God as the Creator (4:24) who has revealed himself through the Holy Spirit in the Scripture (4:25), and goes on to quote Psalm 2:1-2 as the explanation of the opposition being faced by the church (4:25-28). The **'kings of the earth'** are rising up against God's **'holy servant Jesus'**. This, however, is entirely within the sphere of the absolute sovereignty of God: they only did what God's **'power and will had decided beforehand should happen'**. Consequently, they pray for boldness to continue to speak the Word of God and for the Lord to continue to do great things through them (4:29-30).

The Lord's answer was immediate: **'They were all filled with the Holy Spirit and spoke the word of God boldly.'** And this remains the Lord's promise for Christians today. He calls us to holy boldness. He equips us for holy boldness. He will make us fruitful through holy boldness. This is what it means to be truly free — in Jesus Christ. Like the apostles we are free to serve the Lord. We are free from the fear of men and all that they can do, because we know that God is in control of all things and, above all, we know *whom* we have believed, and are persuaded that he is able to keep that which we have committed to him, against that great day, when Jesus comes to judge the living and the dead (2 Tim. 1:12).

# 8.
# All things in common

**Please read Acts 4:32 - 5:11**
*'They had all things in common'* (4:32, NKJV).

'Brotherly love', wrote Thomas Manton, 'is such an affection as knits the hearts of Christians to one another, as if they had but one heart and one soul in common amongst them.'[1] Such was the spiritual unity of the newly Spirit-filled church. Little wonder, then, that it immediately bore fruit in what remains the most remarkable example of community life that the world has ever seen.

We cannot but be amazed and challenged by their practical generosity — the so-called 'community of goods' which involved not only the sharing of possessions, but of property as well. We first saw this in the aftermath of the outpouring of the Holy Spirit and Peter's inaugural sermon at Pentecost. Many believers sold their possessions and 'gave to anyone as he had need' and opened their homes and tables to their Christian brothers and sisters (Acts 2:42-47).

'As in the teachers there was an immediate increase of holy zeal,' remarks Charles Simeon, 'so was there in the hearers a visible augmentation of heavenly love.'[2] This is the vital connection: real love for the Lord produces real love for the Lord's people. That love of their Saviour drew them together in a remarkable unity of heart and mind and led them to give freely of themselves and their substance for the collective good of the body as a whole. Thus they bequeathed to human history both a luminous picture of the lively spiritual condition of the emerging Christian church and, for the rest of time, the practical standard for loving, self-giving and Christ-centred church-community life.

## **Sharing what they had** (4:32-37)

The sheer scope of the economic sharing in the Jerusalem church is a standing indictment of too many churches in our own day. Such generosity is today only too conspicuous by its absence. The lack of it cannot be covered up by the distribution of canned goods at annual harvest thanksgivings, or limpid protestations that government social welfare programmes have eliminated need and the needy in our communities. The contemporary church needs to learn afresh the lessons of the first Jerusalem congregation.

What are these lessons? Just that where there is true spiritual unity in Christ and the powerful preaching of the true gospel, there will be such transformation in people's lives that everything — economics included — will be devoted to the service of the lordship of Christ and the good of all his people.

### *True unity in the faith*

These Christians were **'one in heart and mind'** (4:32). In churches riven by differences and even outright animosities and rivalries, it is convenient to ignore the biblical fact that the most basic evidence of saving faith — a true heart-love for Jesus Christ as Saviour — is spiritual oneness with other believers. The conjunction of *believing* (Gk verb, *pisteuo*), the *heart* (Gk *kardia,* the centre of the personality) and the *soul* (Gk *psuche,* the 'life' of the body[3]) is profoundly deliberate, for it indicates the comprehensive captivity to Christ of the whole man and, since the 5,000 or so church members were **'one'** in these matters, also the bonds which had drawn the people of God together in harmony.

The evidence and only proof that this unity was real was to be seen in the way the Christians actually behaved towards one another. Without the slightest compulsion, they began to see their possessions as a stewardship from the Lord, resources to be shared with those in need. Negatively, they ceased to view them as for their exclusive use; positively, they regarded them as for the blessing of all God's people. This is the force of the expression **'all things in common'** (NKJV). They stood ready to expend their own wealth for the benefit of the neediness of others.[4]

Here then is a test of the seriousness with which you practise Christian unity. Do you say you believe in the essential spiritual unity of believers in Christ? Fine! Do you take every opportunity to join together in worship and praise? Good! Do you rejoice in fellowship around God's Word and in meeting together for prayer? Do you share in the support of the Lord's work by faithful giving of money and time? All this is a blessing! But are you ready, voluntarily and joyfully, to give of your capital resources ('lands or houses', 4:34)?

*Practical generosity*

The engine of liveliness in the church was the powerful proclamation of the **'resurrection of the Lord Jesus'**. This is a synecdoche: one part (resurrection) standing for the whole (the gospel of Jesus Christ). Without the Spirit-accompanied preaching of the gospel in all its aspects, nothing good will happen in the church. The resurrection is the crowning proof of the efficacy of the cross (1 Cor. 15:16-20). Resurrection faith is living faith. The **'great power'** of the apostolic preaching issued in the **'much grace'** which **'came upon them all'** (4:33).

'Grace' is the unmerited favour of God. Here it is represented in its effect upon the believers. Grace received from the Lord becomes grace poured out on others. As required **('from time to time')** and in proportion to the problem **('as [anyone] had need'),** believers sold property and gave the proceeds to the apostles for the church's ministry of mercy. The plenty of some filled the need of others. Thus, by a happy, grace-grown willingness, the gospel fulfilled in the New Testament church what the law had failed to achieve in Israel — there **'were no needy persons among them'** (4:34-35; cf. Deut. 15:4; 2 Cor. 8:13-15; 9:7; Gal. 2:10; 1 John 3:17). Can this be said of your church today?

*Son of encouragement*

As an example of the believers who sold some property to help the poorer Christians, Luke singles out one man — best remembered by his second name, **'Barnabas'** (4:36-37). He was a Levite from Cyprus, who was later to become a prominent figure in the missionary expansion of the church (Acts 9:27; 11:19-26; 13:2,42-52; 15:2,12,36-41). This is no doubt why he is mentioned here. Here was a man who spans the ministry of both the Old and New Testaments — the Levitical priest become gospel preacher and presbyter. But he was a leader in more than sound words. He devoted capital assets to the relief of fellow-believers' hunger and privation. He led from the front with an example for us to follow. In recognition of his selfless, giving, godly character, Luke appropriately describes him as the **'son of encouragement'**.[5] He remains as an encouragement to our own practice of Christian kindness.

## Ananias and Sapphira (5:1-11)

In contrast to Barnabas, Ananias and his wife Sapphira paint a sorry and discouraging picture. Hypocrisy is ever an evil mask. Even their names leave an acidulous after-taste, for his name means 'God is gracious' and hers 'beautiful'. They had 'name[s] that [they were] alive' (Rev. 3:1, NASB), but carried a lie in their right hands (Isa. 44:20). The story is as dramatic as it is familiar. Like many of the more prosperous Christians, Ananias and Sapphira sold a property in aid of the apostles' mercy fund. They kept back some of the money, but evidently gave the apostles to understand that all of the proceeds had been given to the Lord. In this way they affected a show of commitment and generosity, which was in fact no more than a 'swindled pretence of loyalty to the Lord and the Body'.[6]

They might well have gone undetected, had not Peter discerned their deceit and exposed their hypocrisy. How did Peter know what they had done? Was it by a direct 'revelation of the Spirit'?[7] Or was it the special gift of discerning the spirits, referred to by Paul in 1 Corinthians 12:10?[8] The former is probably closer to the mark, since Peter not only exposed their sin but was also given the task of pronouncing God's judgement on the couple. This amounts to a 'package' of direct revelation from God — far more than even the most profound capacity for spiritual discernment.[9]

The unmasking of the hypocrisy remains one of the most disconcerting of divine judgements ever recorded and an endless source of questions and debate. Peter pointed out to Ananias that the property, and the money it yielded, was his to do with as he chose. He could have kept it. He could have given any portion of it to God or men. But he chose to cast the shadow of a lie across his gift by saying one thing and doing another. We can hear the incredulity of the apostle as he challenges this misguided course of action: **'What made you think of doing such a thing? You have not lied to men**

**but to God.'** If Peter could hardly fathom it, Ananias was completely devastated, for he **'fell down and died'** (5:4-5). Three hours later Sapphira was to join her husband in the grave, when she was similarly confronted with their provocation of the Spirit of the Lord (5:9-10).

*Why such a severe judgement?*

Ananias and Sapphira claimed to be Christians. They had joined themselves to the infant church, committed a portion of their resources to the relief of the needy and must have done so in the knowledge that they might face great personal cost in future as part of such a vulnerable minority group. What went wrong? What we need to grasp is *the character of their sin.* They were not required to give anything to the apostles (this was over and above any regular support for the church's ministry). Neither was the amount of money important in itself. The problem was that they honoured 'the feet of the apostles more than the eyes of God'.[10] One cannot but think of days not so long gone when churches would publish an annual list of members' givings, over which the self-satisfied could pore at their leisure and indulge their sense of usefulness to the church! Today we are hardly more subtle and no less carnal. Donor plaques adorn the halls of many Christian institutions, parading in public the giving which our Lord expressly declared should be done in secret (Matt. 6:1-4).[11] Jesus knew how seductive and deceptive a *show* of godliness could be. He knew that the removal of public recognition would go a long way to sort out those who were out to please other people from those who were devoted to serving the Lord.

Ananias and Sapphira chose the wrong side of this divide. Just look at the anatomy of their sin.

First, they showed *contempt* for God. Knowing that he had to know about their crookedness, they went right ahead without apparent fear of divine justice. Behind their outward generosity they had in fact embraced the satanic lie that God could be deceived with impunity (Gen. 3:4). In their spiritual blindness they did not see that to lie to men as they did was actually to lie to God and seek to rob God of his glory. This is the heart of all sin: it puts man's will on the throne of God and challenges God to do something about it!

Secondly, they acted in *a spirit of unbelief.* In contrast, the exercise of living faith in Jesus Christ does not hatch plans to deceive people.

Thirdly, they *despised the church of Jesus Christ.* They were concerned to impress God's people; yet prepared to secretly deceive them and to abuse a God-honouring plan that had been designed to benefit needy people.

This sin has no doubt been replicated on innumerable occasions in the last two thousand years and people have not been dropping dead in the act of their deception. Why then did Ananias and Sapphira receive such unique and instantly draconian punishment? The answer is to be found in the parallel with the very similar case of Achan, recorded in Joshua 7.[12] Achan and Ananias each illicitly appropriated portions of that which had been devoted to the Lord and did so at the beginning of a new phase in the life of the people of God — the former at the entrance into the land of promise, the latter at the inauguration of the New Testament church. The church was the fulfilment and embodiment of that of which the promised land was the foreshadowing.

This remarkable parallel renders intelligible the Lord's very rare suspension of his longsuffering handling of human sin. Almost everywhere else — even with respect to the destruction of the Canaanite nations, in which he waited more than four centuries until their sin 'reached its full measure' (Gen. 15:16) — God has shown himself very 'slow to anger, abounding in love' (Ps. 103:8). 'The sin of Ananias and Sapphira', writes Francis Schaeffer, 'was followed by judgement, because sin would have stopped the church's advance... If this sin of acting from bad motivation in order to be superficially accepted by the church had been allowed to grow in the church's heart, the whole advance would have been endangered. But after the judgement, the early church went on in power.'[13] God decisively demonstrated his righteous might and gave notice of his determination to preserve his church.

*What was God teaching the church?*

This dark episode was recorded at the beginning of the New Testament church to remind us that 'The Lord detests the sacrifice of the wicked, but the prayer of the upright pleases him' (Prov. 15:8). As such, it was altogether appropriate that **'Great fear seized the whole church and all who heard about these events'** (5:11).

God was teaching his people to fear him with the fear that is the beginning of wisdom. If anyone objects that his summary execution of Ananias and Sapphira was out of proportion to their sin, he should remember that everyone who dies in his sins without a personal, saving knowledge of Christ, dies the same death as the hypocrite couple. The drama of sudden judgement ought not to obscure the fearful reality of death without Christ. Every day millions pass into eternity. The sanitized sedation of much modern dying is only a screen behind which immortal souls, torn from expiring bodies, face the judgement seat of God. The lost will always be surprised by hell, however long and apparently unpunished their lives of sin (Isa. 33:14).

For Christians there is in this a message of bright promise. If Ananias and Sapphira warn us, Barnabas is the model for our lives. The future belonged to the sons of encouragement and the very crushing of the hypocrites proved that 'The Lord who had battled the forces of evil and won was not about to give up the infant church to Satan's ploy of spiritual pretence. The Lord's movement was pressing on!'[14] Let your own heart be right with the Lord! His Holy Spirit is with all believers, leading them to have 'all things in common' and to go forward in the happy fellowship of those who love the Lord Jesus Christ and keep his commandments.

# 9.
# Reactions to the gospel

**Please read Acts 5:12-42**

*'More and more men and women believed in the Lord'* (5:14).

Spectacular events always attract attention. If even 'magic' shows, which are just clever entertainment, can draw excited audiences of all ages, it is little wonder that the **'miraculous signs and wonders'** performed by the apostles — real healings verified by the highest people in the land — commanded the attention of the Jews and set all of Jerusalem in a ferment of wonderment and anticipation. This universal and intense interest in the miracles, first of Jesus and then of the apostles, was by no means indicative of a uniform *inward* reaction. In their hearts people were responding in various ways to the import and significance of these events for their own lives.

It is clear from the flow of the narrative that the judgement of God against Ananias and Sapphira — itself a miraculous sign — concentrated the minds of not a few and led many to think very seriously about the claims of the gospel. The sudden deaths of Ananias and Sapphira were a witness to the church for all time to come that God is altogether holy and righteous and perfectly just in his judgements. He is not to be lied to, or to be approached with our lips when our hearts are far from him. It is no accident that the first use of the word 'church' (Gk *ekklesia*) in Acts is in connection with the concept of awestruck reverence for God: 'Great fear seized the whole *church* and all who heard about these events' (5:11). In coming to know God, it is first 'fear' and then 'Father!' Believing fear is in fact freedom from the fear that men fear — the doubting terror of which Franklin D. Roosevelt once said, 'We have nothing to fear but fear itself.' The fear of the Lord is just one component of the perfect love that casts out that other fear.

There are four recorded classes of reaction to the ministry of the apostles in our passage: those of the believers (5:12); the uncommitted onlookers (5:13); the liberal churchmen (5:17-32); and the pragmatic moderates, led by the Pharisee Gamaliel (5:33-40). The fruit of this ferment was the continuance, unabated, of the proclamation of the gospel of Jesus Christ (5:41-42).

**The believers** (5:12)

Luke records that **'All the believers used to meet together in Solomon's Colonnade.'** This vast structure enclosed the temple court and provided ample room for thousands of Christians to come together to hear the apostles' preaching. These public meetings of the whole church were at once the principal vehicle for the corporate worship and preaching ministry of the infant church and the cutting edge of her evangelization of the Jewish people. They met as one united body in the temple courts 'every day' (2:46). This is not to minimize the significance of the house-to-house fellowship meetings and the individual witness of believers throughout the city in the life of the church, but it serves to remind us that the primary, regular, irreducible, life-changing, evangelistic, worship assemblies of the church are her public gatherings. Small-group ministry, as it is called today, is a necessary and vital part of the body-life of the church, but it is ancillary to and supportive of that public ministry to the whole fellowship.[1]

Luke, then, gives us a picture of the aggressive liveliness of the church's witness in these days of her infancy. Two characteristics are particularly in evidence.

The *power of the Holy Spirit* was powerfully manifested amongst them (5:12). **'Miraculous signs and wonders'** were being done among them.[2] Calvin notes the contrast with the judgement-miracles which took the lives of Ananias and Sapphira: 'He [Luke] returns to miracles of a different kind which are more in line with the gospel, viz. those by which Christ bears not only witness to his power, but also to his goodness, so that he may attract men to himself by the delightfulness of his grace. For he came to save, and not to condemn, the world (John 3:17).'[3] The Reformer goes on to emphasize that miracles are handmaids to faith. They are inseparable from the ministry of God's Word. Furthermore, bodily healing speaks of the spiritual grace of Christ and his purpose of healing on a far more profound plane.

Secondly, the believers *met together* (5:12). The church is a gathered people, joining together to worship the Lord (Heb. 10:25). Their love for the Lord issued in an open-faced enthusiasm for the fellowship of corporate worship and the body-life of the assembly of Christians. The apostles' preaching of God's Word would have been at the heart of these gatherings, for they thirsted to know more about Christ. They rejoiced to worship God: Father, Son and Holy Spirit. They exulted together in the wonder of their salvation, in the assurance that their Saviour, as John Owen so exaltingly expresses it, 'sees more beauty and glory in the weakest assemblies of his saints, coming together in his name, and acted and guided in his worship and ways by his Spirit, than ever was in all the worship of Solomon's temple when it was in its glory'.[4] The very fact that they met together in the temple could only have elevated their sense of God's grace towards them as a people. The temple had become, as Jesus had thundered, 'a den of robbers' (Mark 11:17). Jesus' followers were now the true temple of the Holy Spirit and they were living out that truth in the courts of the very building which had preached for centuries the promise of the Messiah and the life everlasting.

## **The uncommitted** (5:13-16)

The bulk of the people remained uncommitted. They saw the miracles, they heard the Word of God opened up in faithful preaching. They **'highly regarded'** the apostles and their followers. They could see they were the real thing. There was something that rang true about them. They practised what they preached. Transformed lives and newborn winsomeness touched the hearts of many onlookers and kindled an interest in this new message about Jesus the Messiah. 'There is', says Calvin, 'a certain secret majesty in holy discipline and in sincere godliness.'[5] Yet they held aloof. **'No one else dared join them'** (5:13). They were afraid. The cost was too great. They were not yet persuaded to follow the Way.

But God was at work. 'Satan's deadly chains,' in Calvin's phrase, were being broken by the Holy Spirit and **'More and more believed in the Lord and were added to their [the church's]**

**number'** (5:14). The Lord takes his time to save us, because we need time to be persuaded and to be broken from our past enslavement to sin. This burgeoning of living faith was accompanied by healing on a massive scale, such that even the shadow of Peter was thought by many to be efficacious (5:15-16).[6]

## **The 'liberals'** (5:17-33)

In his seminal work on theological liberalism, *Christianity and Liberalism*, J. Gresham Machen defined that movement as 'rooted in naturalism — that is, in the denial of any entrance of the creative power of God (as distinguished from the ordinary course of nature) in connection with the origin of Christianity'.[7] By this measure the Sadducees were the 'liberals' of their day, for they were 'anti-supernaturalists' who, among other things, 'denied the existence of angels and spirits and repudiated any idea of a resurrection (Acts 23:8)'.[8] They, not the more conservative Pharisees, were the first to oppose the church (4:2). They were an elite minority who favoured the *status quo* and 'were opposed to the preaching of the resurrection, not merely because it was contrary to scepticism, but because it was connected with a Messianic movement'.[9] The religious establishment nailed its true colours to the mast — as it has continued to do in our own day — and trained its guns on those who had unfurled their banners on account of the truth (Ps. 60:4, AV).

The attitude of these establishment clerics, says Luke, was one of **'jealousy'** (5:17). Since the Greek word used *(zelou)* is from the root *zeo*, 'to boil', the picture given is of men who were simply 'steaming' over the apostles' preaching! The vaunted tolerance with which 'liberals' treat all shades of scepticism and false teaching rarely extends to those who promote the truth of God's Word! These were, of course, the men who had voted to put Jesus to death. Later they accused the apostles of being **'determined to make us guilty of this man's blood'** (5:28). If they did not have bad consciences over Jesus' death, they were certainly aware of the political consequences for them should large numbers of people believe that the man they had killed had risen from the dead and was the promised Messiah and the Son of God. Small wonder, then, that the apostles promptly found themselves in jail. They were not there too long. Just as promptly they were released by the miraculous intervention of an angel of the Lord and told to preach the gospel — **'the full message of this new life'** (5:20) — in the temple courts.

The account of the discovery of the escape underscores the unique significance of the event as a 'sign and wonder' analogous to all that the apostles had themselves been performing (5:12). The doors were still locked and the guards were still in place, but the prisoners were preaching in the temple. This was God's way of saying for all time that no one under heaven will silence the gospel of Jesus Christ. This one miracle stands as a sign and symbol of the myriad of normal non-miraculous ways in which the Lord preserves his church in a hostile world. All of history confirms the fact that the fiercest persecution has utterly failed to stop the Christian faith from spreading — in our day most notably in places like China and the countries of Eastern Europe.

The apostles' attitude to the Sadducean jailing and the attempt to silence them is equally significant for Christians throughout history. We too **'must obey God rather than men'** (5:29). Peter's defence before the Sanhedrin actually sets out the basic programme for the church's preaching. Notice the parallelism in the way Peter expresses his thought in verses 29-32:

A. *Obedience to God:* 'We must obey God rather than men!'

B. *The resurrection of Jesus:* 'God ... raised Jesus from the dead.'

C. *The Saviour who lives:* 'God exalted him ... as Prince and Saviour.'

C. *The salvation Christ gives:* 'that he might give ... forgiveness'.

B. *The truth of the resurrection:* 'We are witnesses of these things...'

A. *Obedience in the Spirit:* 'the Holy Spirit ... given to those who obey'.

Peter spoke right to the point of the Sadducees' opposition and did not mince his words: 'You try to silence the church by naked authority — we must obey God and let the chips fall where they may. You reject the resurrection of the Jesus you killed — we preach the risen Jesus as the truth of which we are witnesses. You refuse to repent and believe in Christ as Saviour and Lord ("Prince") — we proclaim the exalted Christ as the giver of the only salvation!' Yet this is a manifesto for Christians in every generation, whether they are under persecution or not. We must, as Charles Simeon has said, 'imitate ... the holy Apostles in their zeal and love; and whilst you look to Christ for salvation yourselves, endeavour to make him known to the whole world, as their Prince, and as "the Author of eternal salvation to all them that obey him"'.[10]

**The moderates** (5:24-40)

The fury of the 'liberals' was to founder on the pragmatism of the 'moderates'. The world that opposes Christ is not monolithic. Human nature is very effective at dividing and conquering itself! In the Sanhedrin the more conservative Pharisees were not eager to support the Sadducean reasoning for suppressing the apostles and their followers. They were opposed to the Sadducees' sceptical anti-supernaturalist rejection of the doctrine of resurrection and were not enamoured of their political supremacy. They had no love for the apostles' doctrine about Jesus. But, after all, Messianic movements had come and gone many times before, so why get in a big stew about this one? More to the point, why appear to support and therefore strengthen the Sadducees on an issue like this, when there was an opportunity to clip their wings a little, without much risk? Doctrine and politics conspired, in God's providence, to spare the church some persecution at a vital point in her young existence.

The counsellor of moderation was Gamaliel, a grandson of Hillel, the founder of a dynasty of teachers and a school of rabbinic scholarship that was to endure for centuries. The apostle Paul was one of his students (22:3). Gamaliel was a model of many modern 'churchmen'. He was carefully 'balanced' in his views. He avoided all extremes. He was cautious, not wanting to make any rash decisions. And he had a wide political base, for he was a Pharisee, a revered teacher and was **'honoured by all the people'** (5:34).

Gamaliel likened Jesus and his movement to two minor characters of their recent past, Theudas and Judas the Galilean. Both men had been killed and their followers had subsequently melted away. So, he reasoned, why not wait and see? The leader was dead, so why add more blood to the affair? After all, he added with a pious clincher, **'If their purpose or activity is of human origin, it will fail. But if it is from God, you will not be able to stop these men; you will only find yourselves fighting against God'** (5:38-39).

At least one commentator thinks this was 'very wise counsel' and believes that Gamaliel 'in his wisdom and training ... saw and felt the authenticity of these men'.[11] What is certainly true is that it won the day and was instrumental in plucking the apostles from the tender mercies of the Sadducees. The question as to whether the counsel was wise is not resolved by an appeal to the results, but is to be measured against the standards of *truth*. For example, is it true that endeavours of human origin always fail, say, within a human life-span? Gamaliel, after all, implied that if he and the others waited long enough, they would see a decisive result. How long, then, should we give Hinduism or Islam to fail, before we decide they are not of God? Conversely, how long do these and other philosophies such as evolutionism have to last for us to decide they are of God? Has truth never been overthrown? Does evil always speedily fail?

Gamaliel's counsel was not an appeal to *truth*, but one of *indecision* based on a kind of studied agnosticism about the truth or falsehood of the gospel of Christ. He just could not make up his mind. Moreover, he could not see how anyone else could make up his mind. He 'belonged to that class of men', as R. C. H. Lenski puts it, 'whom the most convincing evidence does not convince'.[12] They still look for more, for another sign (Matt. 12:39). The evidence of Christ's ministry, of his resurrection, and of the apostolic preaching was not enough for Gamaliel. Like his modern descendants in the religious establishments of Western Europe and the main-line denominations of America, he preferred doing theology by committee consensus and political expediency, than by any serious appeal to Scripture and the evidence.

Besides, he did not have a heart for the Lord — and in this respect he did know his own mind. Here he was *decisive* even in his indecision! He had decided *not* to believe that Jesus was the promised Messiah! He was quite prepared to sit in judgement over Christ and had no difficulty putting him in the same class as those two deluded pseudo-messianic visionaries, Theudas and Judas. Indeed, he had already been party to crucifying Christ and showed no remorse over his death. We may thank the Lord for using him to overthrow the excess of the Sadducees, thereby sparing the church worse persecution, but we should also recognize that he was still a despiser of the Christian faith, albeit a cultured one.

The positive principle that we must learn and apply for ourselves from all of this is well stated by John Calvin: 'What is "of God" is bound to stand, even if the whole world is against him. Therefore faith, which is sustained by the eternal truth of God, ought to remain unshaken against any assaults whatever of Satan and men. Even if heaven falls, our salvation is secure, for God is its Author and Protector... Because the teaching of the gospel has its foundation in God, no matter how many men fight against it or shake it, yet it will remain secure.'[13]

It may be argued that Gamaliel's pragmatism prolonged the apostles' earthly life, but it is beyond all debate that the same pragmatism could never bring him to eternal life. The apostles lived. They were flogged, admonished to cease preaching **'in the name of Jesus'** and released (5:40). They had cause to be thankful for Gamaliel's moderation, but they had not the slightest intention of either following his example or obeying his orders. Preaching Christ was their life. As Paul would later put it, to live was Christ and to die could only be gain (Phil. 1:21).

### **Christ is proclaimed** (5:41-42)

How did the apostles respond to the Sanhedrin's judgement? Their backs had been ploughed into gore by painful flogging. They knew that next time they might not escape execution. Yet they were not cowed by their experience or afraid of future suffering.

They *rejoiced in their sufferings for Christ.* In a wonderful oxymoron (a figure of speech which brings contradictory terms together to reinforce the point being made) Luke sums up their exalted spirits: they rejoiced because they were **'counted worthy of suffering disgrace'** (5:41). The 'disgrace' was specifically the humiliation of the flogging. Their wounds, or stripes, were a badge of honour, an echo of the suffering of their Saviour. His stripes had healed them (Isa. 53:5, AV); theirs were the seal of their faith in him. Peter later reflected on this connection when he wrote, 'He himself bore our sins in his body on the tree, so that we might die to sins and live for righteousness; by his wounds you have been healed' (1 Peter 2:24).

They went right on *preaching the gospel.* The authorities had no right to muzzle the gospel. The apostles were prepared to continue to obey God rather than men and preach the very truths that were so obnoxious to the Jewish council. **'Day after day',** they proclaimed **'the good news that Jesus is the Christ.'** This was 'the opposite of indecision'.[14] They loved the risen Jesus, they loved to do his will, they were ready to face the consequences without fear or complaint and they did all this happily, because they knew whom they had believed and were convinced that he was able to guard what they had entrusted to him against that day, in which he will appear to judge the living and the dead (2 Tim. 1:12). This remains the commission of the true church of Jesus Christ and the response of Jesus' followers in every generation to the life-changing message of the gospel of the risen Christ.

O happy day, that fixed my choice
On Thee, my Saviour and my God!
Well may this glowing heart rejoice,
And tell its raptures all abroad.

High heaven, that heard the solemn vow,
That vow renewed shall daily hear
Till in life's latest hour I bow,
And bless in death a bond so dear.

(Philip Doddridge, 1702-51).

# 10.
# A man full of faith

**Please read Acts 6**

*'They saw that his face was like the face of an angel'* (6:15).

The church *is* people — people brought to faith by the preaching of the gospel and the renewing work of the Holy Spirit. The best-known people in the book of Acts are no doubt the apostles Peter and Paul. Nevertheless, we encounter many other characters in the New Testament, and some of them are, as it were, stepping-stones to the next phase in the story of the growth of the church. Luke, like any good historian, illumines his times by carefully interweaving personalities and issues with the chronology of the major events.

Barnabas, for example, is introduced as a generous contributor to the apostles' benevolent fund. Why is he singled out? After all, were others not as generous as he? The answer is that Luke uses the historian's craft to kill several birds with one stone! He first of all wanted to show how the church cared for the poor, and so establish the standard which was ever after to motivate Christians and guide the church's response to the needy. Then again, he set Barnabas in contrast with Ananias and Sapphira and used this to illustrate something of the nature of both faith and hypocrisy and, not least, the holiness and justice of God. Finally, he simply took the opportunity to introduce us to the same Barnabas who would later become a prominent and effective missionary church-planter.

With the mention of Stephen, we are taken a step further. As with Barnabas, the starting-point is the problem of caring for the needy. We meet Stephen as one of the first deacons and go on to become witnesses of his martyrdom. But the story does not end there, for as Stephen passes into eternity, we get a glimpse, almost in passing, of a man named Saul of Tarsus, and yet another link is added to the chain! In this context the biography of Stephen is arguably the first great milestone, after Pentecost, in Luke's account of the advance of the gospel, for it brings us to the threshold of the evangelization of the non-Jewish world and prepares us for the conversion of Saul, who, as the apostle Paul, becomes the towering figure of the rest of the book of Acts.

## **Appointed** (6:1-7)

Christian work is always labour-intensive. Virtually every pastoral duty is conducted at conversational speed and, with the exception of preaching and teaching, with one or a few people at a time. The simple arithmetic of the Christian ministry is that a pastor without a team of workers to support him will be strained to the limit in even a small congregation of no more than 200 members. One-man ministry is very limited indeed. From the beginning the apostolic church operated on teamwork. The Twelve ministered as a team. But as the church grew rapidly and settled into a life of its own, needs arose which they just could not handle effectively. Like many a minister after them, they found themselves drawn into tasks which consumed the time they needed to be spending on what was their central calling of preaching the gospel.

### *The problem: neglect of the Hellenist Jewish widows* (6:1)

Ministry to the needy had grown as the church expanded, and the strain soon began to show. The **'Grecian Jews'** alleged that their widows were being neglected in **'the daily distribution of food'**. The 'Grecian', or Hellenist, Jews came from the western dispersion of the Jews and were native Greek-speakers. The 'Hebraic Jews' were from Palestine and the eastern dispersion and spoke Aramaic. Clearly, some folk were falling through the apostles' welfare net and it was beginning to look as if the Hellenist believers were being overlooked, if not discriminated against. The cultural diversity of the church, then as now, posed a threat to her unity and challenged the Christians to sink long-standing sinful prejudices in the interest of sharing the love of Christ without a shred of partiality.

*The proposal: a special ministry of mercy* (6:2-4)

In response, the apostles instituted an organized ministry of mercy, to be conducted by men set apart to what we now know to be the biblical office of deacon (1 Tim. 3:8-13). The 'remote foundation' of this office, says John Owen, lies in Christ's words, 'The poor always ye have with you,' (John 12:8)[1] and the charge to promote the 'preaching of the gospel among the poor'.[2] The church would always have need of a diaconal ministry to the poor. Peter vividly describes this as the ministry of tables (*diakonein trapezais* — literally, 'to serve tables', NIV, **'wait on tables'**) and distinguishes it from the **'ministry of the Word of God'**(6:2). He thus established a fundamental division of labour within the church: namely, that while the *elders* were to devote themselves to **'prayer and the ministry of the Word'** (6:4), the *deacons* would give themselves to the ministry of mercy.[3]

The fact that many modern 'deacons' are little more than committee men administering church finances and property only serves to highlight how far the diaconate has fallen from the New Testament pattern. The apostles envisaged a powerful, personal mercy ministry. Their proposal that the church elect seven of their own number, who were to be **'men ... known to be full of the Spirit and wisdom'**, indicates that this was to be a roll-up-your-sleeves, hands-on ministry requiring a reputation for spiritual maturity and an enthusiasm for helping people.

*The provision: the election of deacons* (6:5-7)

Seven men were duly elected and presented to the apostles for solemn ordination to their task with prayer and the laying on of hands. **'Stephen'** is described as **'a man full of faith and of the Holy Spirit'** — the stuff of which martyrs are made. **'Philip'** is the evangelist (8:4-7,26-40). **'Nicholas'** has been associated, though on rather slender evidence, with the group called the Nicolaitans (Rev. 2:6,15).[4] Of the other four men, little or nothing is known.

The diaconal care of the widows by these men did not merely solve an internal problem in the church — it resulted in the spread of the Word of God and the growth of the church, not least through the conversion of a large number of priests (6:7). A church that cares for its own members is the only kind of church that is capable of caring for new people. To live the gospel is to love the lost. The mercy ministry of the deacons, as a necessary adjunct to the preaching and pastoral ministries of the elders, is vital to the evangelistic witness of the church, and reflects the fact that our Lord himself 'went around doing good' and teaches us to do the same (10:38; Matt. 5:16).

## **Accused** (6:8-14)

The world is an unfair place. Bad things do happen to good people. Oppression has violently invaded the lives of even the gentlest of God's people and rarely has this been more dramatic than in the case of Stephen, the first martyr of the Christian era.

### *A faithful witness* (6:8)

Stephen's name is the Greek for 'crown' *(stephanos)* and he was indeed crowned with the gifts and graces of the Holy Spirit in remarkable measure. First set apart as a deacon, he soon began to exhibit the gifts associated with the apostles themselves, doing **'great wonders and signs among the people'**. From the 'ministry of tables' he had gone on to exercise a teaching ministry, for, as Calvin observes, he was 'unremitting and undaunted in spreading the teaching of the gospel'.[5]

### *A false accusation* (6:9-14)

Stephen's ministry, says R. B. Rackham, triggered 'a revolution in the attitude of the Jews to the church', in which the death of Stephen was to be 'the signal for the first persecution'.[6] The key may well be the fact that Stephen was a Hellenistic (Greek-speaking) Jew. Stephen's ministry must have been making inroads into his native section of the Jewish community, for vigorous opposition soon arose from among those Jews of Roman (the Freedmen), North African and Asian origin (6:9).[7] Prophets are notoriously without honour among their own kith and kin! The controversy followed the usual, predictable lines, so familiar to all who have faithfully proclaimed the Christian message.

Firstly, *unreasoning passion* transforms the discussion from a reasoned exchange on the merits of the case into a one-sided exercise in hatred and vituperation. The more impressive Stephen's **'wisdom'** and **'the Spirit by whom he spoke'** (6:10), the more made up were the minds of those who were determined to reject manifest truth. The gospel always divides its hearers, for the 'aroma of Christ', as Paul says, is 'the smell of death' to those who are perishing and the 'fragrance of life' among those who are being saved (2 Cor. 2:15-16).

Secondly, efforts are made to outflank the message by *discrediting the messenger.* As in football, playing the man can be easier than playing the ball, especially when you have neither skill nor principles! And so, a trumped-up charge of blasphemy is levelled at godly Stephen (6:11).

Thirdly, to the end of silencing the man, *authority* is invoked (6:12). The Lord's enemies seek to *suppress* the truth 'by their wickedness' (Rom. 1:18). Stephen's trial echoes that of Jesus, right down to the charge of blasphemy, the false witnesses and the reference to the destruction of the temple (Mark 14:56-58). Even though the Jews twisted and politicized what Stephen had preached, so as wrongly to make him out to be a subversive and a revolutionary bent on destroying the existing order by violence (6:13-14), the truth is that the preaching of the gospel of Jesus Christ *did* herald the beginning of a new order and sounded the death-knell of the old. Stephen's preaching aimed to change lives and the weapons of his warfare were spiritual. It was the Lord, however, who had prophesied the destruction of the temple and the sacrifices and it would be the Romans who, in A. D. 70, would obliterate the old order for ever.

## **At bay** (6:15)

Most men might blanch under such threatening accusation, but Stephen had **'the face of an angel'**. He was perfectly composed. Not the fear of men, but the fire of God, was in his soul. He was beyond intimidation, beyond the temptation to recant, beyond the grasp of persecuting power in all but his body.

How was he able to respond to false accusation and impending death with such single-minded strength? Let me suggest four reasons.

1. He *expected opposition*, because he knew the gospel was out of line with the world's way of thinking. He knew 'that the teaching of the gospel can never be handled in such a cautious and moderate way that it is not subject to misrepresentations. For Satan, who is the father of lies, always devotes himself to his business.'[8] This happened to Jesus (John 2:19-22); it would happen to Paul (Rom. 3:8; cf. 6:1) and it is the norm for all Christian witness (1 Cor. 2:14). Stephen was not surprised. Forewarned by truth, he was forearmed for evil.

2. He had a *clear understanding* of God's Word. He knew what he believed and had no reason to retreat from his doctrine. Too many Christians can be dogmatic in their shallowness and later have real cause for doubt and shame when their errors are exposed. Stephen, like the psalmist, could declare God's statutes before kings and not be put to shame, because he truly delighted in the Lord's commands and could say, 'I love them,' with a whole heart and a holy intelligence (Ps. 119:46-47). He did not embarrass either himself or the Lord and his Word by careless and imprecise statements of biblical teaching or extravagant and vitriolic attacks upon his hearers. Sarcasm and sloppiness have no place in our witness for Christ. We must walk a straight line with both love for truth and love for lost people.

3. He had borne *faithful testimony* to the Lord Jesus Christ. Stephen's 'wisdom and the Spirit by which he spoke' had been tested and found powerful for Christ (6:10). He had been graciously and precisely faithful to God's truth. His later defence proves how well he understood the Scriptures and the significance of God's covenant dealings with Abraham, Moses and David and the people of Israel (7:1-53). Stephen did not water down the message in anticipation of objections he knew would inevitably arise. He did not hide hard truths in soft evasiveness. Today, for example, we are encouraged not to use words like 'sin' in personal evangelism, because we will put people off. The same goes for much bigger theological terms like 'justification' and 'sanctification'.[9]

There is certainly something to be said for not bamboozling people with big words, or difficult theological phrases. Rolfe Barnard, the American evangelist, used to preach sound Calvinistic doctrine round the backwoods of the Bible Belt in the U.S.A., among people who had often been taught by staunch Arminian preachers to hate the slightest mention of election and predestination or total depravity and the bondage of the will. When he preached on 'total depravity' he would initially not use that term, but just showed from the Bible that we were all 'plumb lost'! Barnard knew his audience. He stuck to biblical language — including the word 'sin'! — and he did not shrink from teaching the plain unvarnished truth of the Word of God. This is the unvarying calling of the church of Jesus Christ. We are to preach the Word — and leave the results in God's hands.

4. Stephen had *lived a holy life* before God and the world. Nothing will enable a Christian to stand before persecutors with 'the face of an angel' other than 'a conscience clear before God and men' (Acts 24:16). The Holy Spirit, who so filled him in his ministry in the synagogue, now filled him, according to promise, in the moment of his great trial (Matt. 10:19-20; 13:11-13; Luke 12:11; 21:14-15). What confronted the fury of his unbelieving persecutors was the transparent holiness of a life made new by Jesus Christ. All his sins were thrown on Christ and sunk in saving grace through the Redeemer's sacrifice for sin. All their sins were still upon them and bade fair to sink them into a lost eternity.

The Sanhedrin looked intently at Stephen and what they saw, says R. C. H. Lenski, caused 'a hush' to fall upon them: 'They were gripped by that light on Stephen's face'; they were 'struck but not moved'.[10] It was they, not Stephen, who stood before the bar of judgement! From the human viewpoint, Stephen was at bay and cornered by the world's power; from the eternal perspective, a saint was judging the world and calling upon men to repent towards God and believe in the Lord Jesus Christ and flee the true wrath which was to come!

# 11.
# The first martyr

**Please read Acts 7:1 - 8:1**

*'But Stephen, full of the Holy Spirit, looked up to heaven'* (7:55).

All the panoply of perverted power was arrayed against Stephen. He faced his accusers alone. The charges were for capital crimes and the murderous intent of the court was perfectly clear. Stephen was the designated example for any who might give credence to the Messianic claims of Jesus of Nazareth.

As usual in such cases, the façade of a fair proceeding was at least initially maintained: **'Then the high priest asked him, "Are these charges true?"'** (7:1). It did not matter that the sentence had already been determined. Without an abject recantation, Stephen was a dead man. Still, he would, as we say today, 'have his day in court'. He was to be permitted his 'apology' (Gk *apologia*) — that same defence which is every Christian's calling and of which the apostle Peter says, 'Always be prepared to give an answer *(apologia)* to everyone who asks you to give the reason (*logos* ='word') for the hope that you have' (1 Peter 3:15).

There is, of course, nothing here of the being sorry or the regret which we today associate with 'apologizing' or offering an 'apology'. The sense is rather that of legal or formal defence — for example, like that of Martin Luther fifteen centuries later, when he declared to the Emperor Charles V: 'I can do nothing else; here I stand, so help me God! Amen.'[1] For Stephen, the moment had come for him to declare his testimony to the assembled leadership of the Jews, and give to them and to the world the reason for the hope that was in him.

**Apologia** (7:1-53)

'Stephen's reply', observes John Calvin, 'could appear at first glance absurd and unsuitable.'[2] Stephen does not *directly* answer the charges of blasphemy and sedition, but embarks on a voyage through the Old Testament which he never completes and in which he barely alludes to the cross and never so much as mentions the name of Jesus! You certainly will not find this approach in today's evangelistic manuals! On the face of it, Stephen would seem to have buried the gospel message about Jesus under a mountain of extraneous Old Testament details!

A look beneath the surface, however, reveals a different picture. Both the method and content of Stephen's argument actually evidence a masterly grasp of the Scriptures, as well as a consummate skill in confronting his judges with the claims of Jesus Christ. In this light we shall see that his defence is a powerful example of the fulfilment of Jesus' promise that the Holy Spirit would give his followers the words to speak whenever they were hauled before their persecutors (Mark 13:9-11).

Stephen appealed to the Word of God. The very structure of his speech reveals his unreserved acceptance of the authority of Scripture. It also reflects a clear view of the progressive unfolding of God's covenant as the Lord revealed himself to his people over the centuries and the canon of Scripture was brought to fulness and completion. Stephen's method was to compare Scripture with Scripture in terms of this redemptive-historical development.[3] From Abraham (7:2-8) and Joseph (7:9-16), through Moses (7:17-43) and the history and meaning of the tabernacle (7:44-50), to a devastating application to his accusers (7:51-53), Stephen showed that the fundamental issue in all of Scripture concerned the goal and fulfilment of all these covenant promises — promises which centred in the person of the coming Messiah. He — the 'Righteous One' of Stephen's speech (7:52) — is the key to this covenant, the meaning of the Jews' history as the people of God, and is none other than the Jesus whom they had crucified, but who had risen from the dead!

*Abraham — an everlasting covenant* (7:2-8)

Stephen's first words are both the keynote of his defence and the first shot in his rejection of the blasphemy charge: it was **'the God of**

**glory'** (7:2, quoting Septuagint of Ps. 29:3) who had called Abraham from his native land in Mesopotamia and promised the possession of Canaan to him and his descendants, when he had neither land nor children. This was sealed with a **'covenant of circumcision'**, in terms of which he became the progenitor of the patriarchs and the tribes of Israel (7:8). They were indeed a privileged people, bound in covenant with the living God! There was no disagreement here! Stephen had established his orthodoxy and had laid out the true and universally accepted basis for the interpretation of Jewish history and doctrine.

*Joseph — free grace versus jealousy* (7:9-16)

Now Stephen introduces his first disquieting note. The **'patriarchs'** proved something of a disappointment. They were jealous of their teenage brother Joseph and sold him as a slave into Egypt. But **'God was with him'** and raised him to great power in Egypt. Irony of ironies, when famine struck the whole area, it was the heathen, thanks to Joseph, who had food and to spare, while — Stephen drives a barb into Jewish consciences — **'our fathers could not find food'** (7:11). But God was gracious and provided relief and a home in Egypt, through the very son they had so despised and abused many years before! God showed up the brothers' bad attitude by turning their victim into the vehicle of undeserved blessings!

*Moses — deliverance versus unbelief* (7:17-43)

Generations went by and the time came, says Stephen, for God to **'fulfil his promise to Abraham'** (Gen .15:16). By this time Israel had grown from the original seventy-five who came to Egypt in Joseph's day, to a sizeable nation. They had, however, been reduced to slavery and forced to **'throw out their newborn babies so that they would die'** (7:19). God then raised up Moses to be their deliverer and, over the space of eighty years, first prepared him and then employed him to bring Israel out of Egypt and to the threshold of the promised land.

Again Stephen contrasts God's goodness through his servant with the repeated resistance of the **'fathers'** (7:25,35,39-41). He quotes Exodus 32:1 to show that they turned from God to idolatry during their Sinai wanderings. Then he very deftly reminds them that this was no isolated occurrence in their long history. He quotes from Amos 5:25-27 to show that what started in Sinai culminated in the Babylonian exile some eight centuries later! Who had really spoken **'words of blasphemy against Moses and against God'**? (6:11). Stephen implies the obvious answer. They and their fathers, not Stephen and his Saviour, were the guilty ones!

It is at this point that Stephen begins, in the language of prophecy with which they were well acquainted, to preach Christ to the Sanhedrin. Moses was indeed the deliverer from God (7:25,35), but he saw himself only as a forerunner of **'a prophet like me from your own people'** (7:38, quoting Deut. 18:15), namely the promised Messiah. Stephen again invites the Jews to draw their own conclusion: if they rejected the prophet whom Moses foretold and who was now proclaimed by Peter (Acts 3:22-23) and Stephen, who were the ones really guilty of blasphemy against Moses?

*The tabernacle — spirituality versus formalism* (7:44-50)

Having dealt with the first charge, no less effectively for his rather indirect approach, Stephen goes on to the second, namely, that of rejecting the temple and the law of Moses (6:13-14). He warmly acknowledges the divine institution of the tabernacle and its successor, the temple built by Solomon (7:44-47). Far from being against the temple, he is very much aware of its true meaning and significance. God, he said, does **'not live in houses made by men'** (7:48), because, as he said through the prophet Isaiah, **'Heaven is my throne and the earth is my footstool'** (7:49; Isa. 66:1-2).

Stephen had already shown from Scripture that the promise to God's people, the covenant with them and their redemption had been in place *before* the temple was ever built. In highlighting the essential spirituality of the temple, he was quietly suggesting that it was a transient phenomenon in God's plan and that the same promise, covenant and redemption were done no disservice by the passing of earthly tabernacles!

And, of course, this all ties in with the advent of the true Prophet foretold by Moses, the free grace seen in Joseph's life and ministry and the everlasting covenant given to Abraham. Stephen could have mentioned Jeremiah 31:31-34 and tied that revelation of the 'new covenant' explicitly to Jesus, but he had already made the point in a quietly effective way.

*The only possible conclusion* (7:51-53)

If the council was incapable of drawing its own conclusion, Stephen set it out for them in no uncertain terms. This was no mere legal defence, but a ringing proclamation of the truth of God! Stephen, in effect, passed sentence upon the court — a vivid demonstration of the fact that 'The saints shall judge the world' (1 Cor. 6:2). In doing so, he succinctly defined the empty, formal religion of his accusers and laid on their seared consciences, with a clarity they could deny but not escape, the fact that they, and not he, were guilty of blasphemy against the Bible's God, the Bible's Moses and the Bible's worship and laws! And in this Stephen has left us a searching outline of the most basic characteristics of the lifeless, nominal Christianity so common today, and an example of what it means to confront a lost world with its real condition and its real needs. We might call these characteristics the 'five points of formalism'.

1. *Stubborn unwillingness to admit, and repent of, sin.* They are **'stiffnecked'** people, just as God has been saying for centuries. They hang on like grim death to their error, prejudice and self-righteousness and will not change their ways.

2. *An exclusively outward form of religion.* They are **'uncircumcised'** in their hearts and ears. They are outward, not inward, followers of God (Rom. 2:28-29). They need to be 'born again' (John 3:7) and 'believe in the Lord Jesus' with their whole hearts (Acts 16:31).

3. *A natural aversion to the work of the Holy Spirit.* Instinctively and wilfully, they **'resist the Holy Spirit'** who accompanies the message of the written Word to their consciences (1 Cor. 2:14).

4. *A decisive rejection of the person and work of Jesus Christ.* They reject **'the Righteous One'** — the very one to whom all of the Scriptures always pointed. They will not come to him for salvation and they do not want him to be their Lord (John 1:11).

5. *A rebellious and disobedient attitude to the will of God.* They do not **'obey'** the **'law that was put into effect through angels'**. They simply ignore the bits of the Bible they do not like and recast the teaching of the rest to suit their own sense of what is right, thereby asserting their autonomy from God (Rom.1:21-32).

Stephen presented the apostate church leaders with a most vital decision: they could turn to Christ and live ... or perish in their sins.

**Apotheosis** (7:54 - 8:1)

The reaction was violent: **'They were furious and gnashed their teeth at him'** (7:54). There was no civility, far less receptivity or repentance! 'We are warned by these examples,' says Calvin, 'that we must not entertain the hope that the Word of God will call everybody back to soundness of mind; and this teaching is very necessary to maintain our perseverance. Those who carry the burden of teaching cannot perform it and carry it through faithfully, without bringing themselves into a sharp clash with those who despise God.'[4] If the gospel cuts right across every natural inclination of unconverted people, it is particularly infuriating to unbelieving clerics and church members.

*A living faith* (7:55-60)

There is a *uniqueness* about Stephen's death. He was the protomartyr of the New Testament era. He is the first to die explicitly in the name of Jesus. Therefore, as R. B. Rackham observes, 'The occasion is worthily marked.'[5] He was given a vision of heaven in which the triune God revealed himself as being with his servant and already welcoming him into glory. As at the baptism of Jesus, 'Heaven was opened' (Luke 3:21) and Stephen was **'full of the Holy Spirit ... and saw the glory of God, and Jesus standing at the right hand of God'** (7:55-56). Just as Isaiah saw the glory of the pre-incarnate Christ 'and spoke about him' (John 12:41), so Stephen was given a direct revelation of the glorified and risen Saviour—an experience shared only by Paul (9:3-9) and John (Rev. 1:9-20). 'Thus,' says R. C. H. Lenski, 'The Holy Spirit himself completed Stephen's address for him, completed it in a most miraculous way and with the most effective gospel word.'[6]

Jesus had told that same Sanhedrin that a day would come when they would see 'the Son of Man sitting at the right hand of the Mighty One and coming on the clouds of heaven' (Matt. 26:64). That day was yet future, but the Lord had republished his decree through Stephen's testimony and had done so in such a way as to serve notice not merely on them but on the entire world and for all time. That the council made the connection is clear from the fury with which they responded (7:57-58).

There are also aspects of Stephen's martyrdom that are *common* to all who are called upon to witness to Christ before a hostile and persecuting world. Two characteristics stand out in the sixtieth verse.

The first is an *unreserved trust in the Lord Jesus Christ.* As he died, Stephen, in words recalling those of the dying Jesus (Luke 23:46), threw himself on the love of Jesus his Saviour: **'Lord Jesus, receive my spirit.'** A confiding trust in the Lord and a rising assurance of his salvation turn away the sting of death and the grave. Many a martyr has testified in his dying agonies to this self-same sense of serene composure and holy confidence. Thomas Bilney, for example, though enveloped in the flames of his martyr pyre, was heard to utter repeatedly the name of Jesus and the word, 'Credo' ('I believe').[7]

Secondly, there is a heart-felt *love for the enemies of Christ.* **'Lord, do not hold this sin against them,'** cries Stephen, clearly reflecting the first of Jesus' words from the cross (Luke 23:34). This is perhaps the ultimate application of the fifth petition of the Lord's Prayer (Matt. 6:12), for as Stephen enters into the eternal experience of forgiveness of sin and salvation in Christ, he evidences the forgiving spirit of a man who knows the meaning of God's free grace. He desires the salvation of the lost, even including those who are putting him to death. And then he **'fell asleep'** and passed into the presence of his Saviour and his Father-God.

*A planted seed?* (8:1)

Present that day, and **'giving approval to [Stephen's] death'**, was a young Pharisee named Saul of Tarsus. The Greek word used means more than a bare approval — it connotes enthusiasm and means 'to consent with delight'. Saul was still an inveterate enemy of the gospel. He had yet to meet with Christ. But was a seed planted in Saul's mind that day by Stephen — a seed that would germinate on the Damascus road, as the Lord convicted him of his sin and brought him to the same faith for which the martyr had perished? Saul had heard Stephen's defence, he had seen Stephen looking up to heaven, and he had witnessed Stephen's apotheosis. He, indeed, was very probably the eyewitness source of Stephen's defence before the Sanhedrin from whom Luke derived the details of his account.[8] Matthew Henry has suggested that Paul, as the apostle to the Gentiles, guided Luke's choice of the word *suneudokein* ('to consent with *delight*'), so that there would be no question of toning down his guilt for Stephen's death.[9] This may or may not have been the case, but it reminds us that God purposes to save people when they are still at war with him. Saul would see just how gracious and merciful God could be to sin-blinded murderous people, when he was later converted by the very Jesus whom Stephen had proclaimed. Stephen's ministry had already become part of Saul's spiritual pilgrimage on the day he looked with pleasure on the martyr's shattered corpse. He did not know it then, but he had passed a milestone on his own pilgrimage to the foot of the cross.

# 12. Reaching out

**Please read Acts 8:1-40**

*'Then Philip ... told him the good news about Jesus'* (8:35).

Stephen's death unleashed a **'great persecution'** upon the church in Jerusalem. Even as godly men buried him and mourned his loss, Saul of Tarsus set about destroying the church (8:2-3). From one point of view, the young church had been handed a crushing defeat. And yet, as is so often the case in human experience, repression produced the very opposite effect from what was intended. As the pruning of a bush stimulates new growth, so the making of martyrs was to multiply disciples and intensify commitment. It was not because suffering and death were inviting prospects. What caught people's attention was the transparent testimony of these early Christians to the saving love of Jesus Christ and the obvious contrast between this and the usual response of real criminals when they were hauled before the authorities.

Tertullian, the second/third-century apologist, noted that whereas 'evil-doers ... deny when accused ... do not easily or always confess' and 'lament' when condemned, Christians tell 'quite another story... Not a man of them is ashamed ... not a man regrets — unless, indeed, that he was not a Christian earlier. If he is denounced [as a Christian], he glories in it; if he is accused, he does not defend himself; when he is questioned, he confesses without any pressure; when he is condemned, he renders thanks.' Tertullian asks, 'What sort of evil is that which has none of the native marks of evil — fear, shame, shuffling, regret, lament? What? Is that evil where the criminal is glad, where accusation is the thing he prays for, and punishment is his felicity?'[1]

True Christian witness, however imperfect, shines with sufficient heavenly light that even a lost world cannot deny its essential character. And since this witness draws attention to Christ, it brings people under the influence of the gospel in a living, powerful way. This is why persecution invariably issues in growth for the church. When Christ, crucified for sinners, is proclaimed to lost people, he draws many of them to himself. He said this would happen (John 12:32). And so it was in and through the martyrdom of Stephen and the persecution of the apostles' fledgling church.

## **Overthrowing prejudice** (8:1-4)

The immediate result of Saul of Tarsus' persecuting ministrations in Jerusalem was to scatter **'all except the apostles'** throughout **'Judea and Samaria'** (8:1). This is hyperbole, for we are immediately informed that many remained in Jerusalem — some of them because they were in prison! (8:3). The exodus was none the less very considerable and amounted to a forced dispersion of evangelistic zeal throughout the territories of the Jews and Samaritans. They **'preached the word wherever they went'** (8:4). The word 'preached' is the Greek *euangelizomenoi,* meaning literally 'evangelized'. These Christians evangelized. They were not all professional 'preachers' or, to use that ugly modern expression, 'full-time Christian workers'. They were simply full-time Christians. All that they said and did preached Christ. Some, like Philip, preached in the sense of giving sermons. But most preached with their daily lives, in whatever they did, and God blessed that witness with abundant fruitfulness.

The dispersion also achieved something of world-changing significance. It took the good news of salvation by grace beyond the historic confines of the Old Testament people of God, and ushered in the fulfilment of God's promise of redemption for *all* the nations of the world. This cut right across the entrenched religious and racial prejudices of the decayed Judaism of the first century A.D. It was bound to be hugely offensive to the Jewish establishment and later was to occasion further persecution from that quarter.

Two case studies signal this transition. These represent the nations hitherto beyond the pale of the Old Covenant. They also exhibit two radically different responses to the gospel message. They are Simon the sorcerer (8:5-25) and the Ethiopian eunuch (8:26-40). At the centre of the account of Philip's ministry to these men lies the event of the so-called Samaritan Pentecost, which declared once and for all, in the most emphatic way, that the fruit of the Jerusalem Pentecost was meant not only for the Jews, but for the nations beyond — the Samaritans and the Gentiles.

### To Samaria — Simon the sorcerer (8:5-25)

Philip **'proclaimed the Christ'** in Samaria (8:5). That is to say, he preached Jesus as the promised Messiah. Here is the heart of the gospel in a few words. The good news *is* Jesus Christ. The divine Son came and took a human nature, died a human death as the atonement for human sin and the substitute for human sinners, and rose again from the dead for the salvation of every human being who would believe in him, confessing him as their Saviour and Lord (John 3:16; Rom. 10:9). God's good news is *not* 'what Jesus can do for you' or 'how you can find new meaning through Jesus' — that is, the modern pseudo-gospel of self-fulfilment.[2] The good news is *who* Jesus is — 'the Christ' — and *what* he has accomplished by his death and resurrection. He died for the ungodly. He died to save his people from their sins. The good news is the *accomplished fact* of his once-for-all, finished, victorious, substitutionary atonement as he pays the penalty of sin and reconciles lost people to his Father.

#### *The conversion of the Samaritans* (8:5-13)

When Christ is proclaimed in terms of who he really is and what he has really done — **'the good news of the kingdom of God and the name of Jesus Christ'** — people's lives are changed (8:5,12). The apostolic sequence is: Christ is proclaimed; miraculous healing attests the message; people take careful notice; conversions to Christ result and joy erupts spontaneously among the new believers (8:6-8). Aside from the miracles, which were not the invariable attendants even of apostolic preaching, the experience of the work of God in the church today follows the same basic pattern as it did in Samaria. If there is little power and joy in many modern churches, it suggests there is a pressing need for the earnest preaching of the cross and the effectual outpouring of the Holy Spirit. Joy is the normal fruit and evidence of the Lord's working among us.

Furthermore, inroads were made into the more obvious manifestations of the kingdom of darkness. A sorcerer named Simon, who had sufficiently impressed the credulous Samaritans to be styled by them **'the power of God, the one called Great'** (8:10),[3] made a profession of faith, received baptism and, astonished by Philip's miraculous signs, followed the evangelist everywhere (8:13). The later evidence that Simon was not truly converted to Christ only serves to show, as John Calvin puts it, how 'difficult it is to pick out hypocrites'.[4] (It also explodes the false doctrine of 'baptismal regeneration' as taught by Rome and, among Protestants, the so-called Churches of Christ, the Campbellites.)[5] For all that — which remained to be revealed — the transformation of the Samaritans was as real as it was amazing. For, as John Dick so beautifully observes, 'Notwithstanding, however, the veneration in which Simon was held by the Samaritans, no sooner did the Evangelist appear, than the mimic wonders of magic shrunk before the genuine works of omnipotence.'[6]

*The Samaritan Pentecost* (8:14-17)

News of Philip's missionary success soon reached Jerusalem. The apostles sent Peter and John to Samaria. Why an *apostolic* delegation? Because, says Luke, **'The Holy Spirit had not yet come upon any of them; they had simply been baptized into the name of the Lord Jesus'** (8:16).

The obvious question is, of course, 'Why was there a time-lapse between the Samaritan's *believing in Christ* and their *receiving the Holy Spirit*?' Comparison with the Day of Pentecost points us to the answer. Firstly, the Samaritan ministry included none of the supernatural phenomena associated with Acts 2:1-11. Secondly, it did not conform to the pattern for receiving the Holy Spirit set out in Acts 2:38-41. Thirdly, it involved no reception of the Holy Spirit until Peter and John came and ministered among them, with prayer and the laying on of hands.[7]

This indicates a special circumstance calling for a special action. This was the first New Testament ministry outside Judea and must be set in the context of the long-standing hostility of Jews towards Samaritans. The presence of the apostles and their instrumentality in the outpouring of the Holy Spirit upon the Samaritans (which, in conformity to the great event of Pentecost among the Jews, would have been visible), constitutes a once-for-all official reception of the Holy Spirit sealing the unity of their church. The Samaritans truly believed, and in truth had the Holy Spirit, but had not 'been distinguished by the sign of the Spirit's presence'.[8]

Acts 8:14-17 has been used, improperly, to promote the view that baptism with the Holy Spirit is a normative post-conversion experience, a so-called 'second blessing'. The once-for-all significance of this Samaritan 'Pentecost' and the later Gentile 'Pentecost' (Acts 10:44 - 11:17) for each ethnic group republishes and confirms the meaning of the original, definitive coming of the Spirit at Pentecost among the Jews, namely that the promised Paraclete of John 14:26 is now openly and clearly with the people of God throughout the world to the end of the age and that all who come to Christ in faith do so in terms of the baptism of the Holy Spirit.

*When faith is less than real* (8:18-24)

Simon had made a credible profession of faith, had received baptism and enthusiastically attended on Philip's ministry. When he saw how **'The Spirit was given at the laying on of the apostles' hands'**, that credibility crumbled and the deeper layers of his undiscerning heart were exposed. He promptly offered to pay money that he might have the apostles' gift for himself. The old sorcerer had burst out of the new believer! The apostle's judgement is devastating: **'May your money perish with you ... your heart is not right before God'** (8:20-21).

Peter had got to the root of the matter, and Simon gave his name to the practice of 'simony' — the buying of influence and office in the church, especially in the pre-Reformation era. But Simon's real sin was nothing so restricted as a mere department of official corruption. It was rather the sin of unbelief. The offer of money only proved that Simon did not grasp the nature of the gospel itself, or of the work of the Holy Spirit. He had a kind of 'faith' — what in theology is called 'temporary faith'.[9] This was characterized by an apparently sincere conviction that the gospel is true and by an observable conformity to the norms of Christian behaviour, and yet it was in one whose heart was not regenerate, who was actually unconverted, who had not denied self, who had not repented towards God and had not truly believed in the Lord Jesus Christ. This is the rocky soil of Jesus' parable of the sower: 'Those on the rock are the ones who receive the word with joy when they hear it, but they have no root. They believe for a while, but in the time of testing they fall away' (Luke 8:13).

Not surprisingly, real repentance is no more intelligible to Simon than real faith. Peter's call for repentance (in 8:22-23) is answered by thinly disguised evasion. Simon piously asks for prayer, instead of confessing his sins and mending his ways (8:24). He just will not see Peter's point, however much he fears the power he was so ready to buy with his money. He will not repent, for he is **'captive to sin'** and loves it more than life.

*The work goes on* (8:25)

The failure of Simon is not the last word. The apostles return to Jerusalem, preaching throughout Samaria. The time foretold by Jesus to the woman at the well had dawned: 'neither on this mountain [Gerizim] nor in Jerusalem' would true worship be offered to God, for 'the true worshippers' had come, by grace through faith in Jesus Christ, to 'worship the Father in spirit and in truth' (John 4:21,24).

## **To Africa — the Ethiopian eunuch** (8:26-40)

From an example of preaching to masses of people in a city, the spotlight now switches to focus on ministry to a single individual on a journey. Allowing for the twin facts that it was direct revelation from God which first sent Philip down the Gaza road and a miracle which took him away to Azotus at the end, the actual substance of his encounter with the Ethiopian stands as a wonderful model for one-to-one personal evangelism.

Three steps are discernible in Philip's *proclamation of the gospel of Christ.*

*The Lord's leading* (8:26-29)

God sent **'an angel'** to tell Philip to head south on the road to Gaza. One the way he met an Ethiopian eunuch,[10] the Chancellor of the Exchequer of his country and evidently a proselyte of the Old Testament faith. The **'Spirit'** then directed him to stick close to the man's chariot. Philip obeyed his instructions and waited for whatever the Lord would bring next — surely a lesson of universal application for all Christians. God wants every Christian to be consciously 'on call' throughout the course of daily life, for whatever opportunities he may bring for bearing witness for the Saviour.

*Love for the lost* (8:30)

It was a case of instant opportunity. Philip ran up, heard the man reading aloud from Isaiah and, in a natural and, no doubt, genial manner asked *the* great question, which may be asked of anyone reading the Scriptures: **'Do you understand what you are reading?'** Here is the essence of evangelism: having such a love for the lost as to *want* to touch their lives for Christ. It is so much more common for us to hesitate, to fear causing offence, to feel we are intruding — in other words, to be *self*-conscious to the degree that we hold back and lose the moment for potentially fruitful contact. Philip acted on the practical principle that the road to Gaza could be the road to hell for that Ethiopian, if he shirked his evangelistic responsibility. He was determined that by God's grace and his outreach, it would be his road to eternal life.

*Pointing to Christ* (8:31-35)

It is admittedly rare to find as teachable a spirit as Philip found that day in the Ethiopian. The man humbly acknowledged his ignorance and invited Philip to sit with him in the chariot. He had just been reading Isaiah 53:7-8 and wondered who was the **'sheep'** for **'the slaughter'** spoken of by the prophet. Philip's response was to **'begin with that very passage'** and tell him the **'good news about Jesus'**.

Philip scratched where it itched. He started at the very point at which the man had a question. For this he had to know the Scriptures — and, not least, the power of God in his own heart. He knew that Isaiah's 'sheep' for 'the slaughter' was Jesus. So it was easy for him to proclaim his Saviour. But it would not have mattered which passage the man had been reading. Philip knew the Christ-centred meaning of the Old Testament.

Here then is a pointer for every Christian. How can you be a better evangelist? First, *know the Bible thoroughly*. Love it, as the psalmist did, and 'meditate on it all day long'! (Ps. 119:97).

Secondly, *love people* enough to risk taking each opportunity as it arises. Be there, ready to speak, and it is certain to happen. Pray for these moments to occur. Thirdly, *begin with people, where they are*; you apply the gospel to their particular needs or interests.

Philip always had his eyes on Jesus. He did not get side-tracked into discussions of obscure points — an easy thing to do with prophetic Scriptures. And he did not talk 'church' — denominations, numbers, programmes. He kept to the point — the good news about Jesus. He pointed to Jesus as directly as he could. So should modern Christians, for (eternal) lives are at stake!

*Receiving Jesus Christ* (8:36-40)

The Ethiopian was clearly a man with a sincere and profound interest in God's Word. He was not embarrassed to be seen in public with a Bible in his hand. He redeemed the time on his travels with serious reading. He had all the characteristics of someone who was being awakened to the issues of life by the Holy Spirit. He sought answers; he acknowledged his ignorance; he was ready to learn and, although a high official, humble enough to invite a bold young man to be his teacher. 'How much progress he made in a short time,' says John Calvin,[11] noting his conviction that there was nothing to hinder his receiving baptism. Philip knew this man truly had a saving trust in Jesus Christ, and duly baptized him in a roadside stream, which some speculate to have been the Wadi el-Hesi, north-east of Gaza.

Philip was then, by a miracle, taken away to preach the gospel elsewhere, leaving the Ethiopian to go **'on his way rejoicing'** (8:39). 'For can one imagine a more genuine ground for joy,' asks Calvin, 'than when the Lord not only opens the treasures of his mercy for us, but pours out his heart on us (if I may put it like that), in giving us himself in his Son?... Then does the sky begin to look serene, and the earth tranquil; then is conscience set free from the saddening and fearful sense of the wrath of God, is liberated from the tyranny of Satan, emerges from the darkness of death and beholds the light of life... Let us learn to despise the world and all its allurements, so that Christ may make us truly glad.'[12]

That joy was now on its way to Africa. It had swept through Samaria. It was soon to come to the Greeks and the Romans and wing its way across the world, from sea to sea and to the uttermost ends of the earth.

On hilltops sown a little grain,
Like Lebanon with fruit shall bend;
New life the city shall attain;
She shall like grass grow and extend.

Long as the sun his name shall last.
It shall endure through ages all;
And men shall still in him be blessed;
Blessed all the nations shall him call.[13]

# Part III

# Damascus and the Gentiles

Acts 9 - 12

# 13.
# A chosen instrument

**Please read Acts 9:1-31**

*'This man is my chosen instrument ...'* (Acts 9:15).

Having described the first major result of Stephen's martyrdom — the ministry of Philip the evangelist — Luke now takes up a second consequence of the martyr's death, in the person of a 'young man named Saul' (7:58). Saul was an up-and-coming defender of his faith. He approved of killing heretics like Stephen and was eager to see the Christian church in Jerusalem destroyed. As he tells us himself, he was motivated in all of this by an extreme zeal for the traditions of his fathers (Gal. 1:14), for, according to the 'strictest sect' of the Jews' religion, he 'lived as a Pharisee' (Acts 26:5).

The Pharisees as a class were the rigorous legalists, renowned in their day for their meticulous knowledge of Scripture and their precision in elaborating rules and regulations for faith and life. James Renwick Willson pinpointed the problem when he noted that they 'departed from the simplicity of the Word of God, despised the righteousness of God which is by faith, and went about to establish their own righteousness... Instead of looking through their sacrificial rites, to the Lamb slain before the foundation of the world, for the sins of his elect people, and by whom an everlasting righteousness was to be brought in, and to whom these rites directed the worshipper, they endeavoured to weave for themselves a robe of righteousness, by an external performance of ceremonial duties and an adherence to the laws of Moses. Their doctrines took away entirely the foundation of the true religion, a fundamental and prominent principle of which has ever been, justification by the righteousness of Christ Jesus alone. Saul embraced fully this system, and was in every respect a bigoted Pharisee, and zealously attached to the righteousness of the law.'[1]

Saul the Pharisee bore all the marks of a man who correctly discerned the threat which this new **'Way'** posed to his chosen belief-system. He was desperate to crush it — he breathed out **'murderous threats'** against the church. He was obsessed about this. He scoured the synagogues to seek out Christians and get them to 'blaspheme' (i.e., confess Jesus as God). He put 'many of the saints in prison and when they were put to death ... cast [his] vote against them' (26:10-11). Saul hated the followers of Jesus and dedicated himself to suppressing them and their new-found faith. Jesus, however, had other plans for this fire-breathing Pharisee.

**Saved** (9:1-9)

The transformation of Saul of Tarsus into Paul the apostle has long been regarded as *the* great example of what it means for someone to be converted to Christ. The 'Damascus road experience' has often been thought of as a standard for true conversion to Christ, as if anyone who did not have a dramatic conversion was possibly not truly converted. This flies in the face of the fact that there is the widest range of 'conversion experiences' in Scripture from the quiet conversions of a Nathaniel, an Ethiopian official or a Lydia, to the dramatic transformations of the woman of Samaria and the Philippian jailer (John 1:46-49; Acts 8:36; 16:14; John 4:29; Acts 16:27-33). There is even a case of someone apparently regenerate from the womb! (Luke 1:41,44,80). Indeed, of all the conversions in the New Testament, Saul's is so unique as to be unrepeatable in any other person. Why? Because it was effected by a personal post-resurrection appearance of the risen Christ which had the express purpose of setting him apart as an apostle! (22:14-15; 26:16-18; 1 Cor. 9:1; 15:7). No one need expect to repeat Saul's conversion experience in this, its most dramatic, aspect.

On the other hand, the various basic elements in what it means to be truly converted to Christ are discernible in the way the Lord dealt with him, and emphasize for us the absolute necessity of closing with Christ in personal faith. Jesus' words on another occasion apply to every human being: 'Unless you repent, you too will all perish' (Luke 13:5). How does this become an experiential reality? First, there is a divine initiative; secondly, a word bringing conviction of sin; thirdly, a call to faith in Jesus Christ and, fourthly, a charge to committed discipleship.

*The divine initiative* (9:3)

As he neared Damascus, Saul had war in his heart. His quarry would soon be cornered. This heresy called 'the Way' would be delivered a blow which would drive another nail into its coffin. The Christians in Damascus, for their part, knew what was coming and did not look forward to their approaching encounter with the young Pharisee (9:13-15). Their prospects looked grim. And yet, in one astonishing moment, all that was to change.

The arm of the Lord is not too short that it cannot save (Isa. 59:1). Confronted by inveterate despisers of Jesus Christ like Saul of Tarsus, we find it difficult to grasp with confidence the hope that is latent in this promise. But against all obvious indications, Saul was arrested by the invincible grace of God[2] and was to meet his intended victims, not as their persecutor, but as their brother in Jesus Christ, his Saviour and theirs! A **'light from heaven'** — a powerful manifestation of heavenly glory, brighter than that Syrian noonday sun — stopped him in his tracks (26:13). God had sovereignly laid hold upon his life! He did not grasp it yet, but he had in fact found the Saviour he had not sought! (Isa. 65:1).

The first step in anyone's salvation, and Saul's is no exception, is the sovereign initiative of God. For Saul, that was a unique self-revelation of the risen Christ in the blinding light of his glory. For all who will ever come to Christ, it is the invisible, effectual calling of the Word and Spirit of God, together with the Spirit's regeneration of the heart and the subsequent conscious turning of the sinner to the Lord in the repentance and faith of gospel conversion to Christ.

*Conviction of sin — the voice of Jesus* (9:4)

The whole company was felled in awestruck fear by this appearance of the light of the glory of God. Then Saul, though not the soldiers, heard the voice of Jesus saying, **'Saul, Saul, why do you persecute me?'** There could have been no gentler way of convicting anyone of his sins. Jesus had in one moment proved that he had risen from the dead, that he was the promised Messiah, that he was the divine Son of God, that he was the reigning King over all things for his church (Eph. 1:22) and that he was the judge of sinners and also the author of the way of salvation. His words to Saul were an overture of grace in the form of a rebuke. They assumed the truth of Jesus' own Messianic claims and of his innocence, and that of his followers, from the charge of being blasphemers against God; and they protest against the injustice of the persecution of the church.

These words of Jesus show us that the first entrance of conviction of sin into a sinner's heart has to be more than a simple awareness that he has done bad things — there must also be a sense of shame that he has rebelled against the God who is 'the light' and who is full of grace. Years later, Paul recalled in his address to King Agrippa that the Lord had also said, 'It is hard for you to kick against the goads' (26:14). Like every other unconverted person, Saul had wilfully suppressed the truth in his rejection of God, the true message of his Word and his only begotten Son, Jesus Christ (Rom. 1:18). He had fought the stirrings of his conscience and kicked against 'unsettling thoughts, questions and misgivings'.[3] Saul had, however fleetingly, entertained at least the notion that there might be some truth in the Christians' claims. Now he had been brought lower than his knees with the dawning and terrifying realization that these Christians were right about Jesus after all.

*Conversion to Christ — the call to faith* (9:5)

Saul was now, in Calvin's words, 'somewhat tamed, but ... not yet Christ's disciple'. Disarmed and disorientated, suspended between past and future, between heaven and hell, groping for some understanding of what was happening, he cried out, **'Who are you, Lord?'** The answer, **'I am Jesus, whom you are persecuting,'** identified both the sinner and the Saviour, and rebuked the old Saul, while calling him to his new life as a believer in Christ. Notwithstanding the miraculous appearance of Jesus in light and voice, 'It was the truth itself, the simple truth as it is in Jesus, which effected the conversion of Paul, and herein it resembles the case of every other sinner.'[4] Paul now knew that Jesus was alive and that the claims of the apostles were true. And he knew this with the effectual conviction which the Holy Spirit and the Word had applied to his innermost being. Paul responded as a new believer, 'What shall I do, Lord?' (Acts 22:10). His old pride was broken, his old goals in life shattered. He acknowledged Christ as Saviour and Lord. He had been saved by the free grace of God through faith in the Jesus he had so recently despised!

*A charge to committed discipleship* (9:6-9)

The Lord told Saul to get up and go into Damascus, where he would be told what to do. Evidently the Lord also told him that he was to be his 'servant' and 'witness' to bring the nations 'from darkness to light, and from the power of Satan to God' (Acts 26:17-18). Nevertheless, Saul had a long way to go. There were many practical changes which needed to be made in his life and he had a lot to do in order to win the confidence of the Christians he had been so bent on persecuting. This would take time. In fact it was to be some thirteen years before he was set apart for his ministry as the apostle to the Gentiles (13:1-2). The Lord has a plan for everyone who trusts in him, but the path of discipleship is one of growing knowledge of Christ and widening obedience to his revealed will. The first steps in Saul's journey were taken in helplessness and vulnerability, as in his blindness he reflected on the meaning of his past and the prospect of his future.

**Sealed** (9:10-19)

The Lord had already prepared a reception for Saul in Damascus. He had spoken to a disciple named Ananias in a vision and told him to go to the house of Judas on Straight Street, where he would find the blinded convert at prayer (9:10-11). When Ananias expressed his fears about Saul, whose reputation and commission had preceded him, the Lord assured him that the fearsome Pharisee was now his **'chosen instrument'** to preach the gospel to **'the Gentiles and their kings'** and **'the people of Israel'** (9:15).

Saul was *chosen*. This word[5] carries the concept of much more than an immediate choice made at that moment of time. It denotes a sovereign and eternal choice — that of divine election (Eph. 1:4-5,11; Rom. 9:11; 11:5; 1 Thess. 1:4; 2 Peter 1:10). God chose Saul in eternity, on the basis of 'the purpose of his will, without any foreseen faith or merit of Saul's own, and this choice had burst into history in his conversion.

Saul is declared a chosen *instrument*. The idea is that of a 'vessel'[6] — a utensil designed for a vital and helpful purpose, something which can receive, hold and dispense those things that are given to it. As applied to a new Christian like Saul, it emphasizes three aspects of discipleship. The primary focus is upon the *gift* of God's grace. 'We have this treasure [the knowledge of God in the face of Christ] in earthen vessels [our mortal body] (2 Cor. 4:6,7,11, AV). Secondly, we are reminded that our service is a *calling* to God's service. Christians, in other words, exercise a calling which is not only given, but sustained by God. Calvin notes that, 'The word *instrument* shows that men can do nothing, except in so far as God uses their labour according to his will. For if we are instruments, he is strictly speaking the only doer: the power and capability of acting are in his hands.'[7]

Finally, Christian service is *costly* service. Saul would be shown **'how much he must suffer'** for Christ's name (9:16). Instruments, say in surgery, are never unscathed by use. Scalpels become blunt and need to be kept sharp. Eventually the day comes when their work is done. Jesus' followers have work to do and time to redeem ... and only for a season, for soon they fly to glory.

Saul was also *sealed* as God's chosen instrument. Through the ministry of another chosen instrument of God, Ananias, Saul's sight was restored, he was formally given the filling of the Holy Spirit by the laying on of hands, and was baptized there and then (9:17-18). This was a unique and definitive event of preparation for his apostolic ministry (thirteen years later). We are reminded of Samuel's anointing of David, years before his actual assumption of the throne of Israel. God's seal was set on Saul of Tarsus. The triad of physical healing (eyes), reception of the Holy Spirit (heart) and baptism (public sign and seal of belonging to Christ), all came together as the formal beginning of his witness as a Christian.

### **Sent** (9:19-30)

The church is the essential context in which new Christians are both recognized and nurtured. The Bible has no place for Christians who chart their own individualist courses and ministries, out of fellowship with the regularly organized visible church. The expression 'institutional church' is, in our day, virtually a term of abuse. The church of the apostles was, however, the church instituted and institutionalized by her head, the Lord Jesus Christ. No one had any right to ordain himself to the ministry or the eldership (Heb. 5:4).

And so, when Saul was converted, two things had to happen. He had to be received into the church and had to accept the pastoral guidance of the church.

*Received into the church* (9:19-22)

Saul was immediately received into the fellowship of the visible church. Luke says he **'spent several days with the disciples in Damascus'** (9:19). The very ease of this statement masks something of the uniqueness and glory of the church as the one society in the world in which the reconciling love of God is to be found healing hurt lives. Where else would a fierce enemy of just three days before be embraced with heart and soul as one of the brethren? Only among those who had first been so loved by Jesus Christ, when still his enemies, and saved by grace to be his beloved friends!

Luke then says that **'at once'** Saul **'began to preach in the synagogues'** (9:20). This has led some to conclude that he went from persecuting Pharisee to Christian preacher in the space of little more than a week. As a result, many young Christians have been encouraged to seek a leadership role, including preaching and teaching, soon after they are converted, often with sadly harmful results to themselves and the church. It is often argued that if the youth are not involved in the leadership of the church and given such responsibilities at the earliest opportunity, their present enthusiasm and future commitment will be dampened and enfeebled.

It should be noted, first of all, that Saul himself testifies that after his time with Ananias, he 'did not consult any man', but went 'immediately into Arabia and later returned to Damascus', where he stayed for three years (Gal. 1:17-18). His first priority was to be taught by God, not to be propelled immediately into a position of leadership.

On the other hand, it was certainly not long before Saul was back from 'Arabia' (not modern Saudi Arabia, but the desert to the east of Palestine), and vigorously preaching Christ in the synagogues. Luke omits mention of the hiatus, because it was, no doubt, a rather short period. As a Pharisee and a graduate of the school of Gamaliel, Paul would have been expected to speak in the synagogues. He was no novice in the Scriptures. He was an accomplished theologian before his conversion. His conversion meant that his already well-furnished intellect was now illumined with the light of the Holy

Spirit. More than one penny must have dropped in his mind, as he began to grasp the Christ-centred themes of the prophets he otherwise knew so well. Saul unconverted had the credentials of a theologian; Saul converted was endowed with the spiritual unction of a true divine.

Notwithstanding his fine academic accomplishments, his thorough knowledge of the Scriptures and his status as a converted celebrity, his introduction to his apostolic calling was restrained and gradual. The message of Saul's early ministry stands in sharp contrast to the thirst for 'involvement in leadership' too often encouraged in new Christians today. And that message is: seek to be taught of God; sit under a solid ministry of God's Word; learn patiently the things of God and work quietly within the fellowship of God's people, under the guidance of the elders God has raised up to be your shepherds.

After his return from 'Arabia', Saul preached the gospel — **'that Jesus is the Son of God'** — to such effect that opposition began to arise, fuelled by the frustration resulting from their chagrin that he had not only abandoned the Pharisaic cause, but was able repeatedly to **'baffle the Jews ... by proving that Jesus is the Christ'** (9:21-22). It is worth noting that Saul's success as a Christian apologist translated not into the mass conversion of the Jews, but into their hardening in opposition to the gospel. Sound doctrine is no guarantee of its own instant acceptance. Minds that are made up do not wish to be confused by God's facts. Saul was a thorn in the flesh of unbelieving Judaism, and like all truly prophetic preachers of the Word before and after him, he learned that the word of truth is as much a 'smell of death' to the reprobate lost as it is 'the fragrance of life' to those who believe (2 Cor. 2:16).

*Pastoral guidance from the church* (9:23-30)

For the best part of three years, Paul ministered in Damascus, with the result that he had to flee for his life. Luke's **'after many days'** is not to be seen as not allowing for Saul's three-year ministry — he means, 'as many days were drawing to an end' (9:23-25).[8]

Saul then went to Jerusalem, where the remnant of the persecuted church, now largely scattered throughout Judea, was at first suspicious and aloof. This, however, was the occasion for Barnabas, the 'Son of Encouragement' (4:36), to exercise genuine pastoral courage and introduce Saul to the apostles. Saul stayed with Peter for a fortnight (Gal. 1:18:24), preached **'boldly in the name of the Lord'**, and once again had to be helped by his brothers in the church to escape a plot against his life (9:26-30). They sent him to his home town of Tarsus (near Adana, in modern Turkey) and there he was to stay, out of the mainstream of church life as recorded in Acts, for almost a decade. We know nothing of his activities during this period of silence between Acts 9:30 and 11:25, except that this was very probably the time in which, even while in relative obscurity, Saul suffered the loss of 'all things' referred to in Philippians 3:8, and suffered some of the privations recorded in 2 Corinthians 11:23-29.[9]

**The blessing of God** (9:31)

Saul's departure from Judea appears to have removed the sting of offence which so inflamed the Jews to violent persecution — an irony, perhaps, in view of the fact that his presence figured prominently on *both* sides of the ferment over the emergence of 'the Way'. Whatever the reason for the lull in persecution, the church had weathered the first great threat to her existence and began to enjoy the fruits of steadfast testimony to her risen Saviour. **'It was strengthened; and encouraged by the Holy Spirit, it grew in numbers, living in the fear of the Lord.'** 'Sometimes,' writes Matthew Henry, 'the church multiplies the more for its being afflicted, as Israel in Egypt; yet if it were always so, the saints of the Most High would be worn out. At other times, its rest contributes to its growth, as it enlarges the opportunity of ministers, and invites those in who at first are afraid of suffering.'[10] Times of peace for the church are times to be redeemed, for it is the *whole church* which is the chosen instrument of God to reach the world, whether in season or out of season. While Saul awaited his recall to the public arena, the apostolic church continued to reach out in good times, as they had in bad. This too is our calling today.

# 14.
# A new direction

**Please read Acts 9:32 - 11:18**

*'I now realize ... that God ... accepts men from every nation'*
(10:34)

The persecutions abated. With Saul's conversion and his removal from the public eye, the steam seems to have gone out of the Jewish efforts to destroy the followers of Jesus. The church was growing in grace, and many people were being converted to Christ. The gospel was on the move. Luke records that 'The church throughout all Judea, Galilee and Samaria enjoyed peace, being built up; and, going on in the fear of the Lord and in the comfort of the Holy Spirit, it continued to increase' (9:31, NASB).[1] The spiritual condition of the growing church comes out clearly in the order and flow of Luke's thought, expressed in two parallels, as follows:

A. 'being built up' (spiritual growth of church).
B. 'going on ... in the fear of the Lord' (means of growth).
B. 'and ... in the comfort of the Holy Spirit' (means of growth).
A. 'it continued to increase' (numerical growth of church).

Luke first says that they were 'being built up' (Greek: *oikodomeo*, literally, 'building a house'). The idea here is of edification or *spiritual* growth. Believers were continuing in the 'fear', or reverential awe, of 'the Lord' (Jesus). Their consuming commitment was to the kind of discipleship in which their Saviour would rejoice. They also continued in 'the comfort' of 'the Holy Spirit', who was living in their hearts, illumining their minds, and lifting their souls as they witnessed a good confession for Christ day by day. Luke's whole point is that spiritual growth consists in 'going on' with an obedience that looks upward in reverent fear to the Lord's will, and a steadfastness that is sustained inwardly by the indwelling Holy Spirit. As a consequence, the church 'continued to increase'. People were converted to Jesus Christ. Numbers increased. The fruit of holiness was the growth and extension of the church. The gospel went out in the demonstration of the Spirit's power (1 Cor. 2:4).

It is at this point that Luke turns our attention to Peter and introduces us to the events which established for ever the global implications of the gospel. On the Day of Pentecost, the fulness of the power of the Holy Spirit burst forth upon the world. In order for this fact to be etched for ever in the annals of the history of redemption, the Holy Spirit was also poured out, first, upon the Samaritans and now upon the Gentiles. Jews, Samaritans and Gentiles were all thereby made aware, for all time, that the gospel of Jesus Christ was for the whole world and was no longer bound up with the Israel of the older covenant.

**Preparation** (9:32-43)

We last saw Peter returning to Jerusalem after the Samaritan Pentecost (8:25). He subsequently engaged in itinerant ministry to the scattered Christian groups north of Jerusalem. This eventually took him to the coastal regions of western Palestine, where his ministry was to be attended with miraculous signs and many conversions to Jesus Christ. A man named Aeneas was healed of paralysis in Lydda, while a woman named Tabitha was raised from the dead in Joppa, the latter following almost to the letter the actions and words of Jesus when he raised Jairus' daughter (Mark 5:40-42).[2] The purpose of these miracles was, as always in the Acts of the Apostles, to attest the authority and validity of the apostolic message, and be a means of drawing many to Christ. **'Many people believed in the Lord,'** and Peter was afforded more opportunities for continuing ministry in the area, for some time (9:42-43).

But there was more to it than even these remarkable blessings from God. The very names of the two who were healed give us a clue to the deeper significance of these events. 'Aeneas' is a Greek name, while 'Tabitha' is of Syrian origin.[3] While this does not prove that they were Gentiles, it does indicate some non-Jewish connections, and it points to the fact that the gospel was beginning to touch the Gentile world, as it had the Samaritans. Peter did not yet know it, but the church had a future among all the nations. In fact, God was preparing Peter for a new direction for the church's ministry. Four things in particular underscore this reality.

Firstly, Peter's very *effectiveness* in the ministry — by the gift and in the power of the Spirit — could only prepare him for the further leading of the Holy Spirit. Lloyd Ogilvie notes that 'The church was being conditioned by immense success in preparation for a new direction.'[4] When we experience the blessing of God, we are being equipped and encouraged by the Lord to forge ahead in faithful discipleship.

Secondly, the *healings* in Joppa prepared Peter to face a healing that he needed in his own thinking about the gospel. We know, from what follows in Acts 10, that on the question of the relationship of the church and of Jesus Christ to non-Jews, Peter carried in his heart a great deal of the baggage of traditional Jewish prejudice against the Gentiles. God was preparing to confront his unholy prejudice, and open his heart to all the lost peoples of the world.

Thirdly, the ministry in Joppa placed Peter *within reach* of the man whom God had chosen to be the catalyst for the great change in which the church would resolve for ever the crisis concerning her ministry to the Gentiles, namely, the Roman centurion Cornelius. Peter stood at a door, the existence of which was entirely hidden to him. Such are the mysteries of God's providence. Matthew Henry observes that 'Though Peter might seem to be buried in obscurity here in the house of a poor tanner by the seaside, yet hence God fetched him to a noble piece of service ... for those that humble themselves shall be exalted [Matt. 23:12].'[5]

Fourthly, the process of change in Peter's attitude to whole-world ministry for Christ *had already begun* and was witnessed by the fact that he stayed for some time in the house of Simon the tanner. Under the Old Testament ceremonial law, contact with a human corpse was regarded as a defilement, to be cleansed by a prescribed ritual purification (Num. 19:11-13). It appears that in Peter's time, orthodox Jews attached the same odium to occupations which involved dead animals. Producers of leather and skins, like tanners, were required to live a certain distance away from Jewish villages and pious Jews would have nothing to do with such people. It is therefore arguably a mark of Peter's liberation from the ceremonial law of the Old Testament and the Pharisaic accretions upon that law that he was prepared to lodge with Simon. For Peter, the gospel had already as much transcended, as it had fulfilled, the weak and beggarly elements of the former publication of the law under Moses.

## **Prospectus** (10:1-23)

The prospectus for the new order of gospel ministry in the world was revealed in two remarkable visions — one to the Roman soldier Cornelius, and the other to Peter the apostle. They were, as Ogilvie points out, 'part of one central vision the Lord had for his church'.[6]

### *Cornelius' vision of the angel* (10:1-8)

Cornelius was an officer in the garrison at Cæsarea. He was '**God-fearing**' — a Gentile follower of the Old Testament faith, who had not become a 'proselyte' by submitting to circumcision. Evidently a godly man, he was noted for his '**devout**' family, his giving '**generously**' to the needy and the fact that he '**prayed to God regularly**' (10:1-2).

During his regular prayer-time one day — '**at about three in the afternoon**' is the 'ninth hour', the time of the evening sacrifice in the temple at Jerusalem and a favoured hour for private devotion for pious Jews away from the city — Cornelius had a vision in which an angel appeared to him and told him to send someone to Joppa, to bring Peter up to Cæsarea (10:3-8). This was God's answer to his prayers and devotion, which had '**come up as a memorial offering before God**'. Cornelius had clearly prayed for a greater knowledge of the Lord and of his will. He had prayed in living faith. And the Lord's answer was to bring him the apostle Peter with the good news of the risen Messiah.

### *Peter's vision of the animals* (10:9-16)

As Cornelius' messengers covered the forty kilometres to Joppa, the Lord was preparing Peter for his encounter with Cornelius. He had been up on the roof of Simon's house praying. Afterwards, while waiting for lunch, he '**fell into a trance**' and saw a vision of '**heaven opened and something like a large sheet being let down to earth**

**by its four corners'**. This sheet **'contained all kinds of four-footed animals'**, and included **'reptiles'** and **'birds'**, which Peter was told by a voice to **'kill and eat'** (10:9-13).

Peter was hungry enough, but was not tempted. He responded in terms of the Old Testament dietary laws, which had declared some of these animals unclean (Lev. 11). Birds and reptiles were out, as were certain quadruped mammals. Cud-chewing, cloven-footed mammals were clean, but even then, they had to be prepared with 'ritual propriety'.[7] Peter was emphatic in his refusal: **'Surely not ... I have never eaten anything impure or unclean.'** The voice, however, responded with an equally emphatic contradiction of the apostle's Levitical orthodoxy: **'Do not call anything impure that God has made clean.'** And for good measure, the whole vision was repeated a second and a third time (10:14-16).

This was nothing less than an abrogation of the Levitical dietary laws and may be seen as a follow-up to Jesus' teaching in Mark 7:1-19, in which he told his disciples that 'Nothing that enters a man from the outside can make him "unclean".' By the time Mark penned the Gospel, this was clearly understood, for Mark comments, 'In saying this, Jesus declared all foods clean.' The Lord had set aside the dietary distinctions for ever, and had done so, although Peter was some way from grasping this, to make an even greater point, namely, that there was no partiality with God towards the Jews and against the Gentiles, as under the older covenant. The barrier between the two was gone (Eph. 2:14). The new covenant in Jesus' blood would encompass all nations. The theocratic separation of the Israelite commonwealth had fulfilled its purpose. Now the whole earth would rejoice in the coming of the Son of Man!

*The meaning of the visions* (10:17-23)

The vision was unmistakably clear — about the dietary question. When Peter **'was wondering about the meaning of the vision'**, it was its relationship to events present and future that gave him pause. What was it to do with anything? It was surely more than a menu! How did it apply? What did the Lord have in store for him? Answers began to unfold almost immediately. Cornelius' servants arrived, asking for Peter, and simultaneously, the Lord followed the vision with his Word for the apostle. 'Right then,' Peter later records, 'the Spirit told me to have no hesitation about going with them' (11:11).

And so the plans were laid to set out next day for Cæsarea and a meeting with Cornelius.

Peter knew the meaning of his vision. He must associate with Gentiles. He was, as Calvin so beautifully puts it, 'conquered by the authority of God'. And so, he adds, 'We must quietly submit ourselves to God, and when his will is known, all that there is left for us to do is to run quickly to where he calls.'[8]

**Persuasion** (10:24 - 48)

The meeting of Peter and Cornelius was inevitably charged with high anticipation and excitement. Even without the drama of visions of angels and audible voices from heaven, Christians today can easily identify with the tremendous sense of the presence of God and of the leading of his hand in the circumstances and coincidences of his providence. Cornelius was the more overwhelmed. God had sent him Peter. So when Peter appeared, Cornelius fell at his feet, not in worship as if he were divine, but in a **'reverence'** that was nevertheless excessive for any man, even if he were an apostle. Peter returned humility for humility: **'Stand up ... I am only a man myself'** (10:24-26). A word, surely, for the preening preachers and prattling prelates of our day!

What followed filled out the meaning of the two visions and marked the sea-change in the ministry of the church which would pave the way for the emergence of Paul as the apostle to the Gentiles and the launching of the missionary journeys which would take the gospel to the ends of the earth. Notice also how the triunity of God — Father, Son and Holy Spirit — is unfolded in the preaching of Peter and the outpouring of the Holy Spirit.

*The Father — for Gentiles also* (10:27-33)

Peter had accepted what God had taught him in the vision and he shared this with the company in Cornelius' house, in what was a model of unaffected humility and a wonderful instance of how grace can melt away the barriers of a powerful tradition. He had seen the real point of the vision, which was not so much that he should cease to regard some animals as 'unclean' for food, but that he should not **'call any *man* impure or unclean'** (10:28, emphasis mine).

Nevertheless, he still did not grasp *why* he was sent to Cornelius (10:29).

Cornelius duly explained his vision and, with it, the purpose of Peter's visit: **'We are all here in the presence of God to listen to everything the Lord has commanded you to tell us'** (10:30-33). God had drawn these non-Jews to seek him. They were Old Testament believers waiting expectantly for the promised Messiah. God was their Father-God, as much as he was to Israel of old! And what a congregation! What wonderful enthusiasm for the Word of God! Well might we cry to God today that people everywhere would give such a reception to those who come to them with the gospel! Well might we pray that ministers everywhere would preach only what the Lord has commanded them to preach! And well might we rejoice to receive *everything* that God is teaching us in his Word! The implication was inescapable. The gospel was for the whole world!

*The Son — the Gentiles' Saviour* (10:34-43)

Peter was overwhelmingly gripped by the truth that **'God does not show favouritism,'** and immediately proclaimed the gospel of Jesus Christ to his first Gentile audience. His message, of which Luke records only a summary, was perfectly adapted to the specific needs of his non-Jewish audience. He made five main points.

First, there is no favouritism with God (10:34-35). He is perfectly just in his judgements and his invariable criteria are *holy fear* and *doing righteousness*. And he always was just. He had made this abundantly clear long before Peter discovered it (Gen. 4:7; Deut. 10:17; see also Rom. 2:10).

Furthermore, Jesus' claim to *lordship over men and nations* was already known to the Caesarean Gentiles: they knew that Israel had heard the **'good news of peace through Jesus Christ'**, and that he was proclaimed **'Lord of all'** (10:36). Peter emphasized the universality of the gospel, not as an afterthought or an accommodation to Gentile realities, but as essential to the person and work of Christ from the beginning.

Thirdly, Jesus' *teaching and his healing ministry* were well-attested and were common knowledge among the Gentiles in Palestine, and these were clear objective evidence that **'God was with him'** (10:37-38).

Fourthly, the apostles were eyewitnesses of Jesus' *death, burial and resurrection* (10:39-40; 1 Cor. 15:4-8). This is the heart of the gospel: the atonement which Jesus effected by his substitutionary sacrificial death in the place of sinners. They also were given the task of proclaiming him as *judge of the living and the dead;* a reference to the Day of Judgement and the Second Coming of Christ (10:42).

Lastly, he noted that *all who believe in Christ* will receive forgiveness of sins (10:43). The Old Testament prophets proclaimed the gospel, albeit in the shadows of incomplete revelation. Now, in Jesus, God's way of salvation is made plain! 'But that amounts to nothing else,' rejoices John Calvin, 'but to embrace him, as he is set before us in the gospel, with a sincere attitude of mind. So faith depends on the promises.'[9]

*The Holy Spirit — the Gentile Pentecost* (10:44-48)

As Peter was preaching, Pentecost came to the Gentiles.[10] The Holy Spirit **'came on all who heard the message'** and they spoke in tongues and praised God. This sealed, as much for the Jews as for the Gentiles, the fact earlier revealed to Peter that the gospel of Jesus Christ was for 'all the families of the nations' (Ps. 22:27). These Gentile believers were therefore not to be denied baptism and, with it, the recognition of their inclusion in the membership of the church of Jesus Christ. They were no longer to be what they were under the Jewish church — a second-class fringe of 'proselytes' or 'God-fearers', recognized as believers yet denied full acceptance into the life of the people of God. The 'dividing wall of hostility' had been demolished: 'For through him [Jesus Christ] ... both [Jew and Gentile] have access to the Father by one Spirit' (Eph. 2:14-18).

**Praise** (11:1-18)

It was not long before Peter had to face the as yet unenlightened prejudices of his believing Jewish brothers. On returning to Jerusalem, he was called to account for his ministry among the Gentiles and duly recounted the story of these momentous events and pressed on them the only reasonable conclusion: **'If God gave them the same gift as he gave us, who believed in the Lord Jesus Christ, who was I to think that I could oppose God?'** (11:17).

When we set this marvellous submission to the Lord's will over against the breaches of fellowship which exist between Christians today, we can only be convicted that we have hardly begun to learn the lesson the Lord taught Peter. Doctrinal disagreements are one thing. There are bound to be cases where good men differ. Sometimes this has issued in denominational organizations devoted to maintain these distinctive principles, because they were sincerely deemed to require ecclesiastical separation as a testimony to their truth. Sad to say, divisions of principle are too often attended, and then completely overshadowed, by prejudicial and self-righteous attitudes, even when the differing groups are actually united in their commitment to the Bible as the inspired Word of God. Many denominations preach the same gospel and believe in the same Jesus as their Saviour and Lord. They share most of the body of their doctrine. But because of a particular teaching or perhaps some event in their history, they become, in practice, enemies to each other, while professing the same Prince of Peace! Our cities, villages and rural areas are littered with the sad fruit of such attitudes: two or three churches in close proximity, geographically and even doctrinally, but practically at war with each other as far as fellowship and personal relations are concerned! Is it perhaps possible, that, to use Peter's expression, some of these divisions might just be manifestations of a determination to 'oppose God'?

Even admitting sincerely-held doctrinal disagreements, ought there not to be a mutual love between those who are truly the children of God, purchased by the blood of Jesus Christ his Son, and baptized by the Holy Spirit? Peter's anti-Gentilism was subdued by the overwhelming conviction that these were people for whom Christ had died. He repented of the sin of 'favouritism' and embraced them simply and exclusively because they were fellow-believers, in whose hearts the Lord had effected a saving change and biblical faith. This too will be the first mark of genuine spiritual revival among us — when those of 'like precious faith' really rejoice in one another and love one another, even when they differ on church government or baptism or a myriad of less substantial doctrinal punctilios.

In contrast to today's dried-up divisiveness, the spiritual liveliness of the Jerusalem church shines brightly with gospel grace. Having heard Peter, they dropped their objections and **'praised God'**, rejoicing in the conviction that God had **'granted even the**

**Gentiles repentance unto life'** (11:18). Praise is always the first response to a new experience of God's goodness. Only fresh water can come from such a pure spring! In that one afternoon they embraced, with glad hearts, the greatest change in the make-up of the church that the world has ever seen! And yet, two thousand years later on, there are still churches riven by ethnic exclusivity, cultural favouritism and historical animosities, which hold revival at bay by resisting the example of the apostolic church in its readiness to put to death the prejudices of past and present, in the interest of a future blessed by the transforming grace of God.

## Echoes in our daily lives

The new direction taken by the early church is history. It has happened and it is irrevocable. The challenge remains, however, for every Christian and every church fellowship. God expects us to apply his principles with a whole heart and a generous spirit. There are bridges to build with new believers from diverse cultural backgrounds. There are wounds to heal with others from a similar background. There are plenty of opportunities to share the love of Christ. But it is costly work. It costs us our entrenched prejudices, our little self-righteous feelings of superiority, our false enjoyment of imagined purity and our coldness to many for whom the Lord has the warmest affection. The Bible is plain enough on these matters. The Holy Spirit still leads the church into the truth of the Word of God. But are we ready to listen to his voice and go where he commands? Peter listened — and obeyed. And if you love Jesus, so will you.

# 15.
# First called 'Christians'

**Please read Acts 11:19-30**

*'The disciples were called Christians first at Antioch'* (11:26).

One of the great fallacies of human history is the notion that problems can be solved by sheer power. Florida oystermen dredged up the starfish infesting their oysterbeds, chopped them up and threw the 'bits' back into the sea, only to discover that they had unwittingly increased the population of starfish, because the 'bits' regenerated their missing parts![1] In human experience, we have invariably seen the violent suppression of political and religious movements result in the multiplication of followers for the cause so persecuted. The *proscription* of many a group has become the *prescription* for its growth and ultimate success!

There is no more powerful example of this theme than the expansion of the Christian church down the centuries and across the world, while under persecution. We are, in the West, perhaps more acquainted with the converse. When the churches became fashionable and prestigious, they began to depart from the doctrine and devotion of the Scriptures, became cold and loveless and soon rotten from the core in their complacent unbelief (Amos 6:1-7; Rev. 3:14-18). Faithful ministry today in the West takes place largely amidst the ashes of such spiritual neglect and apostasy. In happy, glorious contrast, witness the churches of countries like Korea, Romania and a myriad of other places, where Christians have passed through the fires of controversy, hardship and outright persecution. Disciples have multiplied and devotion has increased! The truth is that the church's mettle is tested, her testimony powerfully refined and focused, in the arena of confrontation with a hostile world that is offended by the straight message of Christ's truth.

It is not an accident that the followers of Jesus were first called

'Christians' in the context of scattering through persecution and witnessing against a background of opposition. Under pressure, the fundamental spiritual character of Jesus' followers shone with a brilliant lustre. Here were the practical marks of the true people of God exhibited for the world to see.[2] In the account of the church in Antioch, we can discern no fewer than five basic characteristics of the church of Jesus Christ. True churches are evangelizing (11:19-21); believing (11:22-24); doctrinal (11:25-26); Christ-centred (11:2b) and giving and caring (11:27-30).

**Evangelism** (11:19-21)

Persecution in Palestine dispersed Jesus' followers far and wide. They were to be found by this time on the Mediterranean coast in what is now Lebanon, over on the island of Cyprus and also in northern Syria, in the ancient city of Antioch. Wherever they went, they were found **'telling the message'** of the gospel of Jesus Christ, but **'only to Jews'** (11:19). They were enthusiastic for Christ, but as yet remained wedded to the exclusivity of their Jewishness. The scales which fell from Peter's eyes in Cæsarea remained in place, for the most part, among the Jewish believers of the Christian diaspora.

There were, however, some converted Jews of Hellenist origin who hailed from Cyprus and Cyrene, in North Africa. These ethnic Jews from Greek-speaking societies were not so inhibited by the wall of partition which was a much more powerful reality to the Jews of Palestine. They were thoroughly integrated with Greeks in daily life, language and culture, and it was natural for them to **'speak to Greeks also'** as they shared their new faith with people of similar culture. As a result, **'The Lord's hand was with them, and a great number of people believed and turned to the Lord'** (11:20-21). Heathen Greeks were converted to Jesus Christ! And so, the actual work of the Holy Spirit in people's lives interpreted infallibly the Lord's words in the 'Great Commission' about making disciples of *all nations* (Matt. 28:19-20).

The fact that the Palestinian Jews could not bring themselves to accept the practical requirements of the plain meaning of Jesus' words tells us a great deal about the strength of our personal prejudices and our unsanctified assumptions. Today, every existing racial, ethnic, social and economic division in the human race is represented in the very institution which should, by God's grace, transcend such distinctions. Modern evangelistic methods even make the perpetuation of such divisions a principle for effective church growth, by telling churches to 'target' specific groupings, even narrowing this down to a particular age-range or marital status.[3] It will always be a struggle to overcome unholy worldly prejudices in the church, but it is a battle never to be shirked. Diversity in unity — with the unity in Jesus Christ — is to be fostered and cherished among God's people. It is itself a powerful evidence of the healing power of the gospel, to a world that is enslaved to its divisions and hatreds.

A living church is an evangelizing church, for those who know what it is to be saved by God's grace through faith in Jesus Christ want to see others come to him. This is a litmus test of our commitment to our calling, in Christ, to spread the gospel message to friends, neighbours, communities and nations. Our light must shine!

## Personal faith (11:22-24)

The conversion of Gentiles in significant numbers could only excite tremendous interest through a predominantly Jewish church. As in our day, the Christian 'grape-vine' was fully operational. In no time at all the news came to **'the ears of the church at Jerusalem'**, and they promptly sent Barnabas to see what was going on (11:22). This, in itself, suggests an important point of application: never to be satisfied with gossip-type reports. These invariably engender more suspect notoriety than good report and accurate assessment. Gossip is non-accountable information and it is a fact of life that the absence of accountability is the sure prescription for misleading notions and ill-informed conclusions. Christians and churches ought to be exemplary in this regard and check their sources before entertaining stories about churches, ministers, or individuals which might prove to be prejudicial to the integrity of other folk and the progress of the gospel.

Barnabas's deputation proved to be a wonderful blessing to the church — and remains so for us today. In two ways, he was to be the means of catalysing the transformation of the church's outreach from that of a mission to the Jews to a mission to the whole world.

Barnabas was to be the midwife for the emergence of Paul's ministry to the Gentiles, and Antioch was to be the laboratory in which the church was prepared for her dramatic emergence upon the world scene.

*Encouragement* (11:23)

Too many fact-finding missions turn out to be more interested in *fault*-finding, but Barnabas was never a man to look for problems where there were none. What he found in Antioch gladdened his heart. There was abundant evidence of the grace of God and, true to his designation as the 'Son of Encouragement' (4:36), he **'encouraged them all to remain true to the Lord with all their hearts'**. This was the spirit of revival, where every heart and every relationship within the fellowship feels the breath of the Holy Spirit and the grace of God bathes every hurting soul. How many of our congregations could bear the scrutiny of a Barnabas and leave him rejoicing in our love for the Lord and our happy harmony with one another? Antioch stands for ever as both a rebuke and an encouragement, to the end that we might enjoy the fullest blessing of the Holy Spirit's power.

*Fruitfulness* (11:24)

Barnabas found an open door for a solid ministry of preaching and teaching. In our day, when so much emphasis is placed on the techniques of ministry, as opposed to the personal character of the minister, it is a healthy corrective to see what God thinks is really important. Luke mentions three things about Barnabas, all of them personal characteristics born of the work of God in his life. He was, first of all, **'a good man'**. '"Good" is a rather pale translation of *agathos*,' says R. C. H. Lenski.[4] This is no mere external niceness or morality, but is the 'goodness' of a heart renewed by the Spirit and informed by a living faith in Christ; the 'goodness' of spiritual discernment and wisdom. It is the highest and most humbling praise that can be accorded to any human being. He was a good man, because he was God's man. Secondly and thirdly, he was full of **'the Holy Spirit'** and **'faith'**, as was Stephen (6:5). This was the engine of his goodness. He knew the Lord and loved him with his whole heart. He had experienced a saving change. The Holy Spirit had regenerated his heart (John 3:3,5-8). He had turned in faith to Christ as Saviour and Lord (John 3:16). And therefore he preached a gospel that lived in his heart.

The result was that **'A great number of people were brought to the Lord.'** There was fruit from the faithful ministry of Barnabas. His deputation trip turned into a church-planting mission. He saw the need and threw himself into the work. What began so quietly with the personal witnessing of a few enthusiastic believers soon burgeoned into a growing church. Here is another test of the life of any Christian fellowship: is it characterized by an enthusiastic, encouraged faith, which looks to the Lord in the joy of new-found salvation?

**Truth** (11:25-26)

A third mark of a living church is a thirst for the knowledge of the truth of God's Word. The sad reality is that in pulpit and pew across the land, this seriousness about Bible exposition is, as the Americans say, 'as rare as hen's teeth'. The legacy of a century of theological liberalism and its abandonment of the Bible is a dying socialist-unitarian churchianity. Furthermore, this anti-doctrinal movement almost conquered even the professedly Bible-believing churches in the last quarter of the twentieth century, in the process substituting ecstatic experiences, entertainment, pop-psychology and self-improvement for the solid and biblically experiential exposition of the Word. Among the more 'traditional' churches, unenthusiastic, unenergetic preaching and a flowery, literary pulpit style that masked the absence of real applicatory exposition, together with lay non-involvement in church life, round out a picture of declension.[5]

Antioch represents the cure for this ill. The demand for spiritual food sent Barnabas in search of help and led him to Saul of Tarsus. Saul had been out of the public eye for some eight years. Today, this would have been deemed a waste of talent, and Saul would have immediately been propelled onto the evangelical 'famous speaker' circuit and provided with writers to 'ghost' a series of best sellers, dispensing the wisdom of his handlers in the clothes of his sensational about-turn in life. God was not in a hurry, however, and only when the need arose among Gentile converts was Saul called from the obscurity of Tarsus to begin the ministry that would eventually take him across the Roman world. **'So for a whole year Barnabas and Saul met with the church and taught great numbers of people.'**

### **Christ-centred** (11:26)

The love of the church at Antioch for the Lord Jesus Christ was so obvious to the community around them that it was in Antioch that they **'were called Christians first'**. Luke has already recorded the reasons: they loved the message of Christ and spread it abroad, naturally and winsomely; they loved the Lord with a shared, harmonious spirit of faith; and they loved the truth and thirsted to be taught everything that God had revealed. One has the impression of a fragrant devotion and of an unassuming holiness. There is no hint of the self-righteousness, the strife or the stridency which mark the public perception of Christians and churches in our time. The modern church in the West has expended much of its 'goodwill' by being obviously less than consistently Christian. In Antioch, the world saw the freshness and graciousness of a new-found faith at work and it made a powerful impact.

And here is how we know when our witness is really on God's track: it is when the *world* can easily and accurately pin-point the essence of our faith. Too often, Christians or churches are known for some peculiar doctrine, which, because it is their 'distinctive position', they defend out of all proportion to the real weight given it in Scripture. Another becomes known for attitudes to other Christians, because it is perceived as being most concerned to tell the world how wrong 'they' are. Still others are known for their coldness to visitors. The list could go on. In Antioch, they were known as 'Christians' — people who followed Christ. Even if this was a nickname and used as a jibe, it tells a story. And that story is that the believers at Antioch were identified by the 'man in the street' as belonging to Jesus Christ in deed as well as word. Their witness clearly pointed to Christ and this was not lost on the community.

### **Giving and caring** (11:27-30)

There was a terrible famine in the east during the reign of Claudius (c. A. D. 44-46). Luke records that this famine was the subject of a predictive prophecy by a man named Agabus, a Christian, while on a visit to Antioch at the time of Barnabas' and Saul's ministry there. He was one of a number of New Testament prophets — people with the gift of prophecy which, in tandem with the gift of speaking in foreign tongues, formed the revelatory word-gifts of the apostolic era. Agabus' prediction **'through the Spirit'** galvanized the young congregation into a major effort to help the Christians in Judea, which they must have been given to understand would be a hard-hit area. They organized a congregational *mercy ministry*, specifically for the relief and the relief-work of the church in Judea, on the principle that their plenty should be shared to help the need of others (2 Cor. 8:13-15), and that while they should do good to all men, they should especially care for the household of faith (Gal. 6:10). Secondly, they collected *special offerings* for this mercy mission, separate from the regular support of the church and given by **'each according to his ability'** (11:29). Finally, they administered the fund *through the regular church leadership*, as the accountable, and responsible agents of the collective financial ministry of the church: sending it **'to the elders [in Jerusalem] by Barnabas and Saul** (11:30).[6]

What this represents is a fifth practical mark of a true church. It is one which lovingly, generously and eagerly does all that it can to alleviate the sufferings and privations of others. The Lord promises his blessing on this ministry (Ps. 37:19-21; 41:1-2; Matt. 5:7; 6:1-4) and it is plain from all of Scripture that mercy ministry is inseparable from lively faith and fruitful church-life. There has been a tendency in recent years for evangelical Christians to leave 'welfare' in the hands of the state and, perhaps in reaction to the 'social gospel' type of teaching, to regard it as somehow not the work of the church and therefore in some sense 'unspiritual'. This was never the case in the past and is insupportable from Scripture. Christian love can only be shown to whole people, soul and body. It is simply a matter of faith and works — and faith without works is dead (James 2:14-16).

'In Antioch,' observes Lloyd Ogilvie, 'the new age of the church had begun. No wonder they were called Christians. Perhaps for the first time, their inclusive faith deserved the title.'[7] This is the challenge for Christians today — to live up to our name and to do so by making our goals thoroughly apostolic in word, thought and deed — evangelizing, believing, sound in doctrine, centred in Christ and giving and caring, because he first loved us.

# 16.
# Persecution and progress

**Please read Acts 12**

*'But the word of God continued to increase and spread'* (12:24).

The account of the growth of the church in Antioch ends with a reference to the mission in which Barnabas and Saul took the collected mercy funds to the elders in Jerusalem for relief from the famine predicted by the prophet Agabus (11:30). The actual accomplishment of that mission is recorded in Acts 12:25. Sandwiched in between is an account of the career of Herod Agrippa I, including his persecution of the church in Jerusalem and his sudden death at the age of thirty-four (12:1-24).

It might seem from this that Barnabas and Saul went to Jerusalem before Herod's persecution, somehow managed to escape capture during it and returned to Antioch after his death. The actual sequence of events is, however, a little more complicated. Barnabas and Saul were in Antioch around A. D. 43-44, when Agabus prophesied of the famine to come (11:28). That famine did not occur until A. D. 45 or 46. Herod Agrippa I died some time after the Passover in A. D. 44, before the famine. His persecution of the church in Jerusalem (12:1-24) took place *at the same time* as Barnabas and Saul were in Antioch, gathering funds for the as yet future famine. So, although the visit of Barnabas and Saul to Jerusalem is mentioned in 11:30, no doubt for the sake of completing the account of the church at Antioch, it did not take place until *after* Herod's death, probably late in A. D. 44 or early in 45. Luke preferred to tell the complete story of the mission by Barnabas and Saul before speaking about Herod and the persecution, leaving only the record of their return to Antioch to round out this section of Acts (12:25).

**Persecution, prayer and preservation** (12:1-17)

Through his friendships with the Roman emperors Caligula and Claudius, Herod Agrippa had, from small beginnings, acquired Galilee and Peræa (A. D. 39), and Judea and Samaria (A. D. 41), and come to rule over what is now Israel and Jordan. He thus largely restored the kingdom of his grandfather, the misnamed Herod 'the Great'. Since the persecution in which Stephen had been martyred, the church had enjoyed peace and prosperity, but with the new king, things soon took a turn for the worse.

*Herod strikes* (12:1-4)

This latest Herod unleashed a second persecution upon the church. Christians were arrested and the apostle **'James, the brother of John,'** was martyred, becoming the first apostle to follow the Lord in his death, just as Jesus had prophesied (Mark 10:39). When Herod saw how this raised his standing in public opinion, he turned the screws a little tighter and **'proceeded to seize Peter also'**, planning to put him on **'public trial after the Passover'**.

Why had this happened after a decade of peace? Most commentators think it was related to the addition of Gentile converts to the church. Only then did the practical challenge of the new faith to the old Jewish practices become clear. The early Jewish Christians went on living as devout Old Testament believers. They continued to observe the law, including the dietary regulations. They looked like Jews, because they were Jews. There had been Messianic cults before, and so, after the first persecution died down, people got used to the Christians and learned to live with them. When Gentiles came into the picture in larger numbers, however, attitudes born of ancient prejudice, and also of unbelief, reared their heads. The spirit of Saul of Tarsus, before his conversion to Christ, revived and turned once more upon the church. 'During the restraint which Providence sometimes imposes upon the wicked,' writes John Dick, 'they may seem to be favourably disposed toward religion, and may treat good men with apparent respect and kindness: but the enmity of their hearts to truth and holiness is not diminished and waits only for a favourable opportunity to discover itself. For a short time, the sun may shine, and the sky may wear the aspect of serenity, but the clouds will return, and the storm will again beat upon the heads of the righteous.'[1] Christians today, take note!

*God's people pray* (12:5)

The imprisoned Peter was guarded twenty-four hours a day and chained between two soldiers — Herod, one presumes, had been told how easily Peter and John had once escaped from the high priest's jail (5:19). The apostle was helpless and faced certain death after the Passover. **'But,'** says Luke with majestic understatement, **'the church was earnestly praying to God for him.'**

It is striking how many Christians regard prayer as a *last* resort, after all else has failed. It is certainly true that the church had no physical means of securing Peter's release. Herod was in complete control of the situation and the majority of the populace supported him. Even so, it must be stated that prayer was still the church's *first* resort in their trouble. Prayer properly *precedes* whatever other actions, if any, may be decided upon. Prayer also *prevails* while the need exists. As Aaron and Hur had to hold up Moses' arms for Israel to prevail over the Amalekites at Rephidim, so Christians must 'pray without ceasing' while there is any question about the outcome of the battle. This is a vital test of the reality of a person's faith. Those who are really trusting the Lord pray first, and then act while continuing to look to the Lord. Those who trust themselves act first, and then pray only in desperation, and to whoever will hear.

It is also worth noting that fervent perseverance in prayer, although it has the promise of power and effectiveness (James 5:16), does not in itself guarantee the outcome. There is no reason to doubt that the church prayed just as faithfully for the apostle James, who perished, as they did for Peter, who was spared. The difference is not that the one diet of concerted prayer 'worked' and the other did not. The point is that God answers in terms of a will that is hidden from our view, while at the same time calling us to pray for what seems to us at the time to be good and desirable. In prayer, Christians do not, in any case, merely seek to get their own way: their requests are set in the context of seeking God's way, and trusting that he will bless us with whatever he deems best for us.

*Peter is delivered* (12:6-17)

On what might have been his last night in this world, and while the Lord's people were very much awake, in prayer for him (12:12), **'Peter was sleeping'** (12:6). To sleep in the face of death testifies to a remarkable composure before the Lord! One wonders, however, if Peter would have slept at all if he had known that **'an angel of the Lord'** was about to deliver him, miraculously, from his captors!

The angel woke him; the chains fell off; the guards remained asleep; Peter and the angel passed through three gates; they walked the length of a street — and the angel disappeared! (12:7-10). It all must have seemed like a dream to Peter (don't we all regularly experience the fantastic in our dreams?) — until, that is, he **'came to himself'** in the street and realized that he really had been delivered and was going to get away scot-free from Herod's clutches (12:11).

When Peter arrived at the home of John Mark's mother, where a prayer meeting had been interceding for the apostle throughout that night, there was disbelief among the believers when Rhoda the servant girl reported that Peter was knocking at the door (12:12-17). When she **'kept insisting'** it really was Peter, some thought, **'It must be his angel'** (12:15). Lenski aptly assessed the atmosphere at that moment: 'These disciples could not shake off their mortal fears for Peter and leapt to the conclusion that he was already dead, and that his guardian angel had come to tell the sad news. It was a wild idea, but fears inspire weird notions...'[2]

This highlights something all Christians experience in their most personal and faithful prayers: there are times when we pray, truly believing that *God is able* to do what we ask for and even 'to do immeasurably more than all we ask or imagine', yet with a definite sense that what we pray for is *humanly impossible*. Then, when the Lord does the 'impossible', we can hardly credit it, until at last the facts overwhelm our doubts. It was, of course, by a mighty miracle that Peter was delivered. But are the inscrutable movements of God's hand in our everyday experience less replete with evidence of his immediate involvement in our lives? The *means* by which he interacts with us today may be less 'miraculous', but are they less amazing in their influence, coincidence or effects? Have we not prayed for the 'impossible' quite frequently? And have we not seen it happen from time to time, and all through the mediation of 'normal' but otherwise wholly unpredictable events? Let us, therefore, when we pray, 'approach the throne of grace with confidence'! (Heb. 4:16).

**Pride and punishment** (12:18-23)

Naturally enough, Herod did not see Peter's escape as an answer to prayer. His fury was to cost the guards their lives. Having failed to find his erstwhile victim, he went off to Cæsarea, where he had to resolve a dispute with Tyre and Sidon. Herod did not rule these cities, but controlled the hinterland, which provided their food supplies. He had evidently placed some pressure on them, perhaps through an embargo, and this had persuaded them to sue for peace (12:18-20).

*'God's voice and not man's'* (12:21-22)

Herod's moment of glory duly arrived. It was, says Josephus, the occasion of games to celebrate the return of the Emperor Claudius from Britain. All the dignitaries of the realm were present — it was an 'invitation only' gathering of the *demos*, the body politic.[3] It was a glittering occasion, a moment of triumph for the thirty-four-year-old king. Herod gave an oration, in the course of which he was suitably magnanimous to the Tyrians and Sidonians. It must have been quite a performance — enhanced no doubt by Herod's magnificent robe of silver cloth, which, according to Josephus, glittered in the sun — for the people shouted out, **'God's voice and not man's!'** (12:22, literal translation).[4] Herod had been offered his own divinity!

*'Eaten by worms'* (12:23)

Herod knew full well that such a suggestion was impossible for a Jew to entertain. But God was not on the throne in Herod's heart. He **'did not give praise to God'**. He did not instantly and inwardly reject the blasphemy for himself, and he did not rebuke his sycophantic subjects for their gross sin against the living God.

God therefore visited an immediate judgement upon him and, in so doing, laid low both the pride of Herod and the presumption of his subjects. Herod was **'eaten by worms'** — probably a case of long-standing affliction, brought to its dramatic conclusion by the angel's miraculous power. Josephus says he collapsed, but lingered in misery for five days. Herod is reputed to have admitted that his predicament was the result of accepting blasphemous praise. In any event, **'He ... died'** (literally, 'breathed out his soul'). The maggots of his own sin had eaten him up, as they will for all who will not come to Jesus Christ that they might have life (John 5:40).

**Power and progress** (12:24-25)

The Word of God **'continued to increase and spread'**. Barnabas and Saul carried out their mercy mission and returned to Antioch. The Lord provided peace for the church and relief from the coming famine. There is a symmetry to all of this. The Word feeds hungry souls as the mercy ministry feeds hungry mouths. The Lord makes Peter's defeat into a triumph, and Herod's triumph into a defeat. Peter could sleep before the day of his (anticipated, but not actual) execution, while Herod enjoyed thoughts of divine immortality on the day of his (actual but unanticipated) destruction.

In the twinkling of an eye, the Lord transformed a situation for the Lord's people that seemed to be one of unrelieved gloom. Herod's last fling could have stifled the movement, already in progress in Antioch, to spread the Christian gospel to the Gentile nations across the world. So it is throughout history. Looming defeat amazingly turns around and paves the way for victory. Christians in Korea have seen this. Christians in Eastern Europe are beginning to see it. One day, seemingly impregnable Islam will crumble before the Lord Jesus Christ. The kingdoms of this world will, by grace or by judgement, become the kingdom of our Lord and of his Christ (Rev. 11:15). Peter gloried in Christ, even on 'death row', because he knew whom he had believed, and that he was able to keep that which he had committed to him, against that day (2 Tim. 1:12). Where do you stand? Whom do you serve?

# Part IV

## The first missionary journey

Acts 13-15

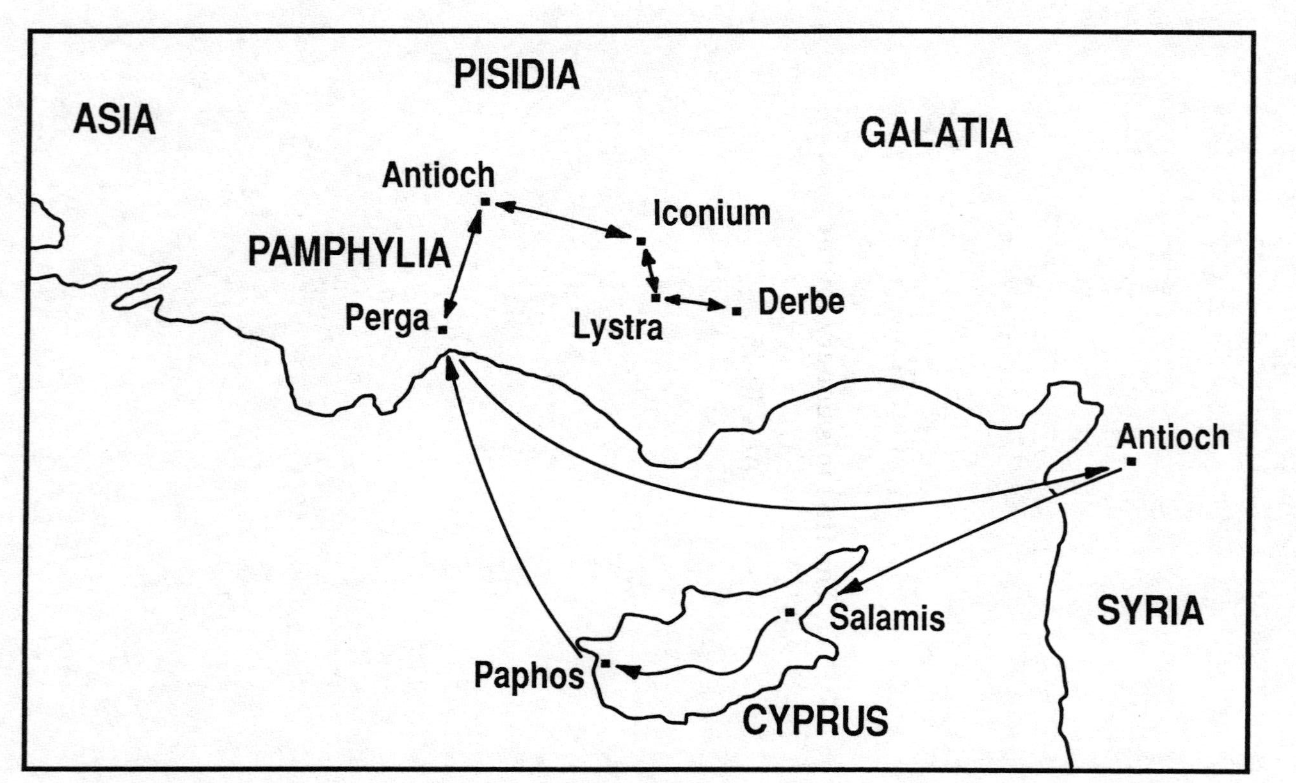

PISIDIA
ASIA
GALATIA
Antioch
Iconium
PAMPHYLIA
Perga
Lystra
Derbe
Antioch
Salamis
SYRIA
Paphos
CYPRUS

# 17.
# Free indeed!

**Please read Acts 13:1-48**

*'If the Son sets you free, you will be free indeed'* (John 8:36).

The spread of the Christian gospel to the nations of the world was to be the greatest advance for true freedom in the history of the human race. This is no overstatement, because, in the last analysis, Christian freedom is the only real freedom in the world. All else is a species of bondage, a variation on the theme of spiritual death. The political freedom with which the counsels of modern nations are obsessed reinforces the point. Along with earthly comforts, it falls under Jesus' timeless caveat: 'What good will it be for a man if he gains the whole world, yet forfeits his soul?' (Matt. 16:26). It is not that temporal freedoms — from oppression, persecution, unemployment, sickness, etc. — are unimportant. They are properly to be seen as blessings from God and evidence of the rolling back of the effects of the fall of man into sin, in Adam. But they are often as temporary as they are temporal, and do not constitute the fundamental spiritual liberty of heart and soul that alone can transcend the transience of the best the world can offer and, indeed, be the only basis for, and guarantee of, whatever freedom human societies may enjoy. God has put eternity in the human heart, which is why we thirst for a deeper and more abiding reality than the tinsel favours of this passing scene.

The watershed year for the Gentiles was to be A.D. 45. A lively church of Greek converts had grown up in Antioch in Syria, under the ministry of Barnabas and Saul of Tarsus. In Antioch, they were first called 'Christians'. The Jewish Christian leadership in Jerusalem accepted this development as from the Lord and it is clear that everybody realized that they stood on the threshold of a great new direction for the church's witness in the world. When Barnabas and

Saul returned to Antioch, having accomplished their famine relief mission to Judea, it was not the end of a story, but the beginning of an epoch. In fact, that epoch had already begun at Calvary, with the death and resurrection of Jesus. Christ died to be the Saviour of the world. Now the world was to hear the good news!

**Free to go to the Gentiles** (13:1-3)

There were five **'prophets and teachers'** sharing the leadership of the church in Antioch: Barnabas and Saul, Simeon Niger, Lucius and Manaen. Perhaps the last three were the 'men from Cyprus and Cyrene' who had begun the church's ministry to non-Jews and so made it into the multi-racial fellowship it had become.[1] Clearly, their ministry was developing and they were beginning to see ever-wider possibilities for a ministry not only to Gentiles in Antioch, but to the peoples of the entire Roman Empire and beyond. If Gentiles could be converted to Jesus Christ in Antioch, they could be converted anywhere. So, they must have reasoned, since they are not all going to come to Antioch, we must go to them and preach the gospel wherever they may live! Such was the genesis of what is now called the first missionary journey (see Map 1, p.150).

Barnabas and Saul surely felt a powerful *inward call* from God to be missionaries to the nations. And yet this was not enough. They knew that the ministry of the gospel itself was something that no one can just take to himself (Heb. 5:4). They were not free to be self-appointed, 'lone ranger' preachers. God had instituted a church, with an order, a leadership and a membership, and from whom and through whom his ministers would be recognized, confirmed and sent out to their ministries. Their inward call would be ratified by the *outward call* of the body of Christ. This was no formality, no mere procedure of checking credentials and issuing the right papers. The church was seriously concerned to be of one mind with the Lord in this venture.

The church gave herself to **'worshipping the Lord and fasting'** (13:1). They knew that this was the evangelistic Rubicon for the apostolic church. Hitherto a Jewish church with Gentile converts, they knew that this step would mean a multi-racial church with only a Jewish origin. So they prayed — earnestly and long enough to put aside eating. The result was that the **'Holy Spirit'** said, audibly, that they should **'set apart'** Barnabas and Saul to the work to which he had already called them (13:2). This miraculous word-revelation points to the vital role of the church as a body in relation to her own ministry. Today we do not expect audible guidance from the Holy Spirit, but guidance we do expect, through the prayers and the counsels of the church. When we also take into account that the apostolic leadership in Jerusalem had previously sanctioned the mission to the Gentiles (Gal. 2: 7-9) and that Saul already had the inward call to the work (9:15; 22:21), we have a clear mandate for the church to exercise careful, prayerful responsibility in setting apart men to the ministry. The Antioch church might have rubber-stamped either the apostles' decision or Saul's inner call, but they did neither. They sought the mind of the Lord themselves.

Thus persuaded, the 'prophets and teachers' commissioned Barnabas and Saul — **'They placed their hands on them and sent them off'** (13:3), this ceremony symbolizing the endowment of gifts and calling, which the Lord had *already given*. In being 'set apart' by the church they were publicly, and for all time, authorized by God himself to take the good news of Jesus Christ to the Gentiles. There would still be objections from the Judaizers, as we shall see, but, like the Berlin Wall in 1990, the 'dividing wall of hostility' between Jew and Gentile was about to come tumbling down for ever (Eph. 2:14).

### **Free to proclaim the Word of God** (13:4-12)

The two missionaries were the right men for the job. Both were thoroughly cosmopolitan in culture and experience. Barnabas hailed from Cyprus and Saul, here for the first time called by his Roman surname, **'Paul'** (13:9), has been aptly described as 'a man for all nations and all seasons'.[2] Their ministry in Cyprus may have been a kind of 'warm-up' for future trials in more remote places, but it had the basic challenges which have faced all ground-breaking ministries ever since.

*They made the most of their opportunities* (13:4-5).

They preached **'the word of God in the Jewish synagogues'** as soon as they arrived in Salamis. Why did they go to the Jews, when they had just been sent to the Gentiles? Calvin points out that the latter commission did not 'depose them from the office which they had heretofore exercised'.[3] They took whatever opportunities arose to carry out the Great Commission (Matt. 28:19-20). Gospel preaching ought to be the most classless activity on earth.

*They were prepared to confront the opposition* (13:6-11).

In Paphos, the Roman proconsul Sergius Paulus **'wanted to hear the word of God'**. A member of his entourage, a **'Jewish sorcerer and false prophet'** named Bar-Jesus (i.e., Son of Jesus) or Elymas, did his best to **'turn the proconsul from the faith'** (13:7-8). It was an open challenge, defying not only Paul's message, but the very sovereign power of God to bring a man to saving faith. 'In general, the duty of ministers', wrote Charles Simeon, 'is to "have compassion on them that are ignorant and out of the way," and to "instruct in meekness them that oppose themselves": but there are occasions whereon it is necessary for them to "rebuke men sharply", and with all authority (Heb. 5:2; 2 Tim. 2:25; Titus 1:13).'[4] Paul did not mince his words. He looked Elymas in the eye and, under the direct inspiration of the Holy Spirit, exposed the man's true character. He was **'a child of the devil'** — a striking irony for a man named 'Son of Jesus' (Bar-Jesus). He opposed **'everything that is right,'** was **'full of all kinds of deceit and trickery'** and gave himself to **'perverting the right ways of the Lord'** (13:10). His immediate punishment would be a temporary blindness — the same affliction Paul himself had experienced ten years before on the Damascus road!

God is not mocked and he will never permit his message to be suppressed. We are not given Paul's role as the voice of direct divinely inspired judgement on any person's soul, but we have warrant to confront sin with the Word of God, in meekness and humility, yet with firmness. We are free, by God's appointment, to proclaim the gospel of Jesus Christ and give a reason for the hope that is in us. Christians are not called to be so 'nice' (in the world's terms) that they drop the subject of Christ and his 'right ways' at the slightest objection. Sergius Paulus' eternal destiny was at stake: more than that, so was the very integrity of the gospel and the Saviour for Cyprus and beyond. God opened the door. Elymas tried to close it. Paul stood fast and the Lord blew away the opposition.

Today, even without the overtly miraculous, God does the same for those who witness faithfully for him. Jesus is Lord.

*They saw both success and failure* (13:11-12)

Sergius Paulus believed. Elymas groped about, his soul as darkened as his eyes. They represent the only two basic categories of humankind: the lost and the found. The gospel always divides its hearers (2 Cor. 2:15-16). Paul was prepared to win some and to lose some. He did not look back and wallow in doubts and recriminations, asking, 'What if...? What if ... I'd been gentler with Elymas? Or just backed off and prayed for these men?' Paul prayed 'without ceasing', planted the Word and let God give the increase (1 Cor. 3:6).

**Free from condemnation** (13:13-43)

From Paphos, the apostolic team sailed to Perga, near Antalya in modern Turkey, at which point John Mark **'left them'** for Jerusalem — a departure Paul later characterized as desertion (13:13; 15:38-39). We are not told why Mark left. We do not need to know all about other people's failings: we just need to work at overcoming our own. Mark went on to be a missionary and the writer of the Gospel that bears his name. He appears also to have been reconciled to Paul in later years (Col. 4:10; 2 Tim. 4:11; Philem. 24).

From Perga, Paul moved inland to Pisidian Antioch, where he was invited to speak in the local synagogue on the Sabbath day. Luke, who was present, has preserved for us the contours of Paul's masterly exposition of the gospel. The sermon was in three parts, each marked by direct address to the audience: **'Men of Israel ... Brothers ... Therefore, my brothers'** (13:16,26,38). These are: first, the *preparation* as Israel's history leads to Jesus (13:17-25); second, the *proclamation* of fulfilment in Jesus' person and work (13:26-37) and, lastly, the *provision* of salvation, through faith in Jesus (13:38-41; for a full outline see page 156).

*Preparation — history and Jesus* (13:16-25)

The argument parallels Stephen's defence (7:1-53). It is a review of God's dealings with Israel since her Egyptian period fifteen

**An apostolic sermon outline**
delivered by Paul in Pisidian Antioch (13:16-41)

**Israel's promised Saviour**

*Introduction:* the call for a hearing, identifying the audience as the covenant people of God (13:16)

I. *Promise:* the history of Israel leads to Jesus (13:17-25)
- A. Moses to David (13:17-22)
- B. David to Jesus (13:23)
- C. John the Baptizer and Jesus (13:24-25)

II. *Proclamation:* fulfilment in Jesus (13:26-37)
- A. He came to us (13:26)
- B. He died on a cross (13:27-29)
- C. He rose again (13:30-31)
- D. He is the Saviour promised to the fathers (12:32-37)
  - 1. Psalm 2:7 (13:33)
  - 2. Isaiah 55:3 (13:34)
  - 3. Psalm 16:10 (13:35-37)

III. *Provision:* saving faith in Jesus (13:38-41)
- A. A call to faith in Jesus Christ (13:38-39)
  - 1. Forgiveness of sins in him (13:38)
  - 2. Justification by grace, through faith in him (13:39)
- B. A warning against unbelief — Habakkuk 1:5 (13:40-41).

centuries before. Three interwoven themes appear: God's covenant faithfulness in making them prosperous and giving them their inheritance in Canaan (13:17-19), Israel's recurrent ingratitude and folly (13:18,21) and the provision, through David and his descendants, of the promised Messiah, the one heralded by John the Baptizer, **'the Saviour Jesus'** (13:22-25; see also Ps. 89:20; 1 Sam. 16:7,12; Isa. 44:28; Rom. 1:4). The key expression here is: **'God has brought to Israel the Saviour Jesus'** (13:23). Paul echoes Peter: 'God has made this Jesus ... both Lord and Christ' (2:36). Jesus' advent is no chance event, no fortuitous birth: it was the culmination of history, brought to maturity by the sovereign will of the living God!

*Proclamation — fulfilment in Jesus* (13:26-37)

This was no theoretical or abstract consideration: **'this message of salvation'** has been sent to *them* — in the history of Israel, now culminated in Jesus. But what had happened? Firstly, the people *rejected* the one they ought to have recognized and received! (13:27; John 1:11). Secondly, in so doing, they actually *fulfilled* the very prophecies read in their hearing every Sabbath day! (13:27). They killed Jesus on **'the tree'** (13:29; Deut. 21:23). God **'raised him from the dead'** and so transformed their very rejection of him into the occasion of Jesus' accomplishment of salvation for his people. This is the **'good news'** which God had promised the fathers of Israel and has now fulfilled **'for us'** — namely, **'raising up Jesus,'** not only from the dead, but as the Son who is exalted a Prince and a Saviour (13:32-33; 5:31).

It is important to note that the gospel is clearly defined here. It is not, 'What Jesus can do for you.' Still less is it to be psychologized and subjectivized into 'feeling like a new person'. The gospel is not to be confused with its application. It is what Jesus *did* in his death, burial and resurrection. Our faith, our sanctification and the blessings of God in our lives are the *fruit* of the gospel, not the gospel itself. Jesus is the divine Son of God (Ps. 2:7); Jesus fulfilled the covenant promise of God not only for the Jews but for all nations (Isa. 55:3; see the whole chapter); and the risen Jesus alone saw no decay and so fulfilled the prophetic word (Ps. 116:10).

*Provision—faith in Jesus* (13:38-41)

The point of the gospel is, of course, that people believe it. The salvation won by Christ must be appropriated personally by faith in him. Through Jesus, **'Forgiveness of sins is proclaimed'** (13:38). In other words, Jesus' death satisfied the justice of God and brought reconciliation between God and lost and guilty people (Col. 3:13). The gospel does what the law of Moses could never do: justifies **'everyone who believes'** (13:39). Calvin is still correct when he says that these are 'principles' which are not learned in the 'schools of the philosophers' — or the psychologists, educationalists and scientists — namely, 'That mankind is condemned and drowned in sin, and that there is in us no righteousness which is able to reconcile us to God; that the only hope of salvation rests in his mercy ... and that those remain under the guilt, which fly not unto Christ.'[5]

The juxtaposition of justification through faith in Jesus Christ and the inadequacy of the ceremonies, rituals and works of the law underscores the futility of seeking to be right with God through the very best of self-generated human effort. 'All our righteous acts are like filthy rags' (Isa. 64:6). 'Therefore no one will be declared righteous in his sight by observing the law; rather, through the law we become conscious of sin' (Rom. 3:20; cf. Gal. 2:16; 3:10-11; 5:4-5).

The necessity of personal, experiential faith in Jesus as Saviour is emphasized by Paul's warning, also drawn from Israel's long record as a nation of backsliders. He quotes Habakkuk 1:5, which had warned the Jews of a coming invasion by Nebuchadnezzar that would demonstrate God's sovereignty in history and his judgement of Israel's sins. The principle applies to all who reject God. 'Repent or perish' is written over the portals of every life that is ever lived.

The modern pseudo-gospels, that proclaim a 'salvation' of health, prosperity and self-fulfilment and avoid the subject of 'guilt in regard to sin and righteousness and judgement', are exposed as dangerous frauds. Jesus sent the Holy Spirit to 'convict the world' of these things (John 16:8), but much modern preaching merely massages the ego and entertains the senses instead of challenging the mind and heart. The recovery of the Bible's theology of God's wrath is essential to any revival in the modern church. People who are taught not to face their sinful nature, and the sins they practise, cannot learn to fear God. And whatever else they may seek in the way of physical and psychological creature-comforts, they will not come to Jesus Christ for what the Bible defines as salvation, until and unless they begin to take seriously what the Lord actually says in his Word about the human predicament and its only solution — the gospel of Christ. None of those who heard Paul that day in Pisidian Antioch could ever say later, to men or to God, that no one had told them the real truth both about their deepest need and the way of salvation.

Speaking of the kind of pastors and teachers who explain away or water down these most essential and vital elements of gospel truth and preach 'a different gospel — which is really no gospel at all' (Gal. 1:6-7), Brownlow North would later write with awesome solemnity, 'I do not believe there exists a more miserable being, even amongst the lost themselves, than a lost minister shut up in hell with his congregation.'[6] Those who have been made free from condemnation through the blood of Christ are free to spread the message of the cross, in which all who believe in him will themselves be 'free indeed' (John 8:36).

*A positive response* (13:42-43)

Success in evangelism is not automatic, but it is the subject of God's promise. There will be rejection, but some will come to Christ (1 Cor. 2:14-17). Gospel seed will find soil in which to germinate (Matt. 13:8). Paul's preaching immediately won him an invitation to preach again the following Sabbath. Interest had been kindled among the people in general and many **'Jews and devout converts to Judaism'** appear to have been converted to Christ, for they followed Paul and Barnabas and the latter **'urged them to continue in the grace of God'** (13:43). They were free to be Jesus' men and women, to enjoy the 'glorious freedom of the children of God' (Rom. 8:21).

## **Free to be lights in the world** (13:44-48)

Opposition soon arose to Paul's ministry. The next Sabbath, when **'the whole city'** (i.e., Gentiles) came to hear him, **'the Jews'** were overcome with **'jealousy'** and became abusive towards the apostle's message (13:44-45).

The mere threat of this kind of thing is enough to silence many modern Christians ahead of time. We are so inhibited by the thought of people being upset by anything we say, especially in matters of religion. We can talk, in the church, about the 'offence of the gospel' as a necessary and unavoidable fact of Christian witness in a lost world, but we freeze when we touch the shadow of a real unbeliever. Bold Christians embarrass us. We hold back. We avoid confronting the unconverted. We hope that our lives, without words, will lead people painlessly (for us, especially, but also for them) to Christ.

This is a crucial area of failure among Christians in the West today. Yet there is another way. It is found in the apostles, but it is also abundantly evident in some parts of the world at the present time. I have been privileged to enjoy fellowship with the pastor and members of the Korean church in State College, Pennsylvania. What is most striking about these Korean believers is the freshness of their faith, the seriousness with which they search the Scriptures and the uninhibited freedom with which they speak of their Saviour. We Western Christians often seem tired and inhibited by comparison, weighed down by our long history and the experience of living in a spiritually declining society. We think first of objections to confronting the world and causing what we call 'unnecessary offence', and then devise our 'strategies' for evangelizing the lost. We are experientially boxed in. We possess little of the experiential freedom and abandonment to Christ characteristic of the apostles and, I believe, oriental Christians of today. My Korean friends live, spiritually, in an apostolic environment. They know what it means for life to come to a spiritually dead culture and bring overwhelming renewal through millions of conversions to Christ. Mostly within living memory, they have tasted the kind of victory for Christ that is long in the past for Christians in the West. Western Christians — converted people, not nominal church people (for the latter need to become real believers) — must recapture the apostolic freedom to be lights in the world for their Lord.

The apostolic missionaries show us the way: in the face of opposition, they were *confident* in the Lord. They exercised their freedom, in Christ, to answer their detractors **'boldly'** (13:46). They simply declared their faithfulness to their *commission* from God.

This had involved, first, bringing the gospel message to God's old covenant people: **'We had to speak the Word of God to you** [i.e., the Jews] **first'** (13:46). They had gone straight to the Jewish community, and they had not fudged the message: they had proclaimed Jesus as the Messiah, the only Redeemer of lost mankind. But this had been largely rejected. The statement that the Jews did not **'consider [them]selves worthy of eternal life'**, is a way of saying they had proved themselves unworthy of the salvation they had rejected, precisely because they believed the gospel of Jesus Christ to be beneath them. The thought that the faith of their promised Messiah could encompass Gentiles equally with Jews was too much for them. Why? Because they loved the notion that their type of observance of the law and their generations of privilege as *the* people of God entitled them to something which others could never have. The gospel message of justification by God's grace through saving faith in Jesus Christ cut through that pride of exclusivity and assurance of merit through religious observance — justification earned by man's best efforts — and exposed the loveless self-centredness of the shrivelled pseudo-faith of the

Judaism of the time. This is what legalism and ritualism do to the soul. They make people into twice-born children of hell, who trust their dead works, their illusions of self-produced merit before God, their blind reliance on the fantasy that God is pleased enough with sinners 'just the way they are' (cf. Matt. 23).

The apostolic commission, however, was to be **'a light for the Gentiles'** (13:47; Isa. 49:6). This, of course, was not something just thought up for the Christian church. It was in fact the mission and destiny of the true Israel of God. The Jews of Pisidian Antioch should have seen this in the Scriptures. They should have seen that God's covenant had *always* been one of grace; that keeping the law was impossible in a sinner and could *never* save them; that the blood sacrifices of the temple spoke of the final Lamb, who alone could atone for sin and whose free grace could alone reconcile lost people to a holy God. The godly Simeon had seen this when Jesus was still a baby (Luke 2:31-32). So had the thousands at Pentecost and many of their own number. But they had not.

The Lord does not flog dead horses. There comes a time in his dealings with the unbelieving when he leaves them to reap the consequences of their rejection of his overtures of grace. The blessing passes to those who will listen. The Gentiles, in ever larger numbers, were coming to Christ. They **'honoured the Word of the Lord; and all who were appointed for eternal life believed'** (13:48). People respond as they will, but the sovereign will of God is served none the less. Here is a key to the boldness of Christ's servants. Whatever the decisions of men, however uncertain our prospects of success, God is sovereign. He does his will among the armies of heaven and the inhabitants of the earth. And it is the privilege of the Christian church to minister that gospel by which the elect ('all who were appointed for eternal life') are found and come to believe in Jesus Christ.

# 18.
# Coping with rejection

**Please read Acts 13:49 - 14:28**

*'And the disciples were filled with joy and with the Holy Spirit'* (13:52).

Discouragements in the Christian life and in the work of the gospel are, says Lloyd Ogilvie, like 'splinters in our pride'.[1] Even one little discouragement seems to outweigh any number of substantial encouragements. Setbacks, failures, rejections, discouragements — call them what you will — tend to get under our skin. They are blemishes on what we want to be a perfect record of progress. They tell us that more is needed than our best efforts in order to avoid setbacks. They remind us of our frailty. They tempt us to think that the Lord may not be completely in control of his own work. In the end, discouragements can become occasions of the sin of not believing that God 'in all things ... works for the good of those who love him' (Rom. 8:28), and of not trusting in him as the one who always 'does as he pleases with the powers of heaven and the peoples of the earth' (Dan. 4:35).

Few of God's people ever faced as much rejection and discouragement as the apostles and preachers of the early church. Paul, for example, testifies about his frequent imprisonments, floggings and close encounters with death, how he went without sleep, was shipwrecked, in danger from bandits, rivers, Jews, Gentiles, in city, country and at sea (2 Cor. 11:23-33). How did he, and suffering Christians down the centuries, cope with discouragement? Only by learning from the Lord who said, 'My grace is sufficient for you, for my power is made perfect in weakness' (2 Cor. 12:9). How this was realized in the cauldron of personal Christian experience can be seen in the events which overtook the apostolic team in the remainder of their first missionary journey. They were expelled from Pisidian Antioch (13:49-52); they fled from Iconium (14:1-7); they were stoned in Lystra (14:8-19); but they fought the good fight of faith from Derbe and all the way back through Lystra, Iconium and Antioch (14:20-28).

**Expelled from Pisidian Antioch** (13:49-52)

The preaching of the gospel was blessed with great success in Antioch. In fact, it **'spread through the whole region'**. This was the last thing the enemies of Christ wanted to see, so they stirred up trouble for Paul among the ruling classes of the city, no doubt exploiting their traditional fears of anything that might appear to threaten the status quo and, with it, their privileges and authority. The authorities promptly expelled Paul and his companions (13:49-50).

With all the 'open doors' for the gospel among the people, this governmental fiat could have been all the more discouraging for the apostolic team. But they show no signs of despondency in their threefold response.

First, they **'shook the dust from their feet in protest'** (13:51). 'Thus,' remarks Matthew Henry, 'they left a testimony behind them that they had a fair offer made them of the grace of the gospel, which shall be proved against them in the day of judgement... Thus Christ had ordered them to do, and for this reason (Matt. 10:14; Luke 9:5).'[2] There is no twentieth-century 'self-doubt' here! No 'post-mortem' to see if evangelistic 'strategies' should be modified. They had been faithful. The door had closed. They saved no pity for themselves, for they knew it was all needed by lost people who had rejected Jesus so boldly. Oh, for such holy confidence today!

Secondly, they **'went to Iconium'** (13:51). They had the world to reach. They simply took the road to the next city on their itinerary. There is no shortage of work for Christ's church in this spiritually starving world.

Thirdly, far from being discouraged, they were **'filled with joy and with the Holy Spirit'** (13:52; Matt. 5:11-12). They rightly saw their expulsion as evidence that they were doing something right! Our perennial craving for everybody's approval is always a snare. We need to die to it, for, as Jesus tells us, 'Woe to you when all men speak well of you, for that is how their fathers treated the false prophets' (Luke 6:26). Our joy must be found in the opposite direction — the praise of God rather than that of men (John 12:43; Romans 2:29).

## Flight from Iconium (14:1-7)

Iconium, the modern Konya, lay fifty-six kilometres to the west of Antioch. Paul preached in the synagogue **'so effectively'** that **'a great number of Jews and Gentiles believed'** (14:1). Subsequent events followed much as they had in Antioch. The unbelieving Jews stirred up opposition. The missionaries, however, persevered for **'some considerable time'**. They preached boldly and the Lord **'confirmed the message of his grace'** by enabling them to perform various miracles (14:3).[3]

Some Christians assume that if only we had miracles like these today, performed in the public eye and witnessed by masses of people, we would see people turning to Christ in greater numbers.[4] The Scriptures show, however, that 'evidence' is not a converting ordinance. 'Facts' and 'education' do not change minds that are steeped in contrary precommitments and presuppositions. The miracles attested the message, but it was the message and the accompanying power of the Holy Spirit that converted people to Christ. Against all the evidence of the truth and power of the gospel, the same coalition of malcontented religious and civic leaders plotted to **'ill-treat and stone'** Paul and company (14:5).

He who fights and runs away, lives to fight another day. 'When you are persecuted in one place,' says Jesus, 'flee to another' (Matt. 10:23). The Lord never encourages the so-called 'martyr complex'. The missionaries' response was to flee. They had more important things to do than die in Iconium. So they trudged south-west into Lycaonia and there **'continued to preach the good news'** (14:6-7). 'In times of persecution ministers may see cause to quit the spot, when yet they do not quit the work.'[5]

## **Stoned in Lystra** (14:8-20)

Paul and Barnabas did not yet know it, but they had jumped 'from the frying pan into the fire! A stoning escaped in Iconium is overtaken by an actual stoning in Lystra! Yet at first, as so often happens in evangelism and new ministries, the missionaries were greeted with enthusiasm.

A congenitally crippled man was miraculously healed by Paul (14:8-10). The crowd was amazed, as they should have been, but immediately jumped to the wrong conclusion. Their presuppositions overwhelmed the evidence and led them to an erroneous interpretation of the miraculous event. They ascribed divinity to Paul and Barnabas! Paul, as the **'chief speaker'**, they identified as Hermes, messenger of the gods, and Barnabas, they concluded, must be Zeus, the supreme god of Olympus. To cap it all, the local **'priest of Zeus'** appeared, ready to offer sacrifices to the two of them! (14:11-13).

It was, of course, a case of rejection in the form of acceptance. The Lycaonians had the wrong end of the stick entirely. They saw only the miracle; they were unconcerned with the content of Paul's message. This should be a corrective to the temptation to overestimate the effectiveness of 'signs and wonders' as persuaders of men's minds. It takes the living and active Word of God — 'sharper than any double-edged sword' — to penetrate 'even to dividing soul and spirit, joints and marrow' and to judge 'the thoughts and attitudes of the heart' (Heb. 4:12). The Lycaonians' hearts were still committed to their pagan religion. The apostles therefore moved swiftly to ensure they understood the point of their ministry and the claims of Jesus Christ.

They first refused all glory that is properly due to God alone. They **'tore their clothes'** and went into the crowd to persuade them that they were **'only men'** (14:14-15).

Secondly, they proclaimed the truth — that they had come with the **'good news'**, to tell them to **'turn from these worthless things to the living God, who made heaven and earth and sea and everything in them'** (14:15-17). Paul, you will notice, chooses his subject very carefully. He does not immediately launch into a full statement of the gospel and the person and work of Christ. He starts from the point where he discerns that they are. He begins with the doctrine of God: the living God who created all things versus the false gods they have been worshipping. He then anticipates the question as to why they hadn't heard of this doctrine before. Paul's answer is that they had! God had indeed **'let all nations go their own way'** in the past, but he **'had not left himself without testimony'** — the universal testimony of the 'everlasting covenant between God and all living creatures' made with Noah, in terms of which 'seed-time and harvest' would 'never cease' as long as the earth endures (Gen. 8:22). God does reveal himself in his creation, which includes his provision for our daily lives and our own sense of being creatures belonging to a Creator (Rom. 1:20-23).

This was an invitation to them to stop, reflect and go on to further explanation of the apostles' message. But so great was the blind religious frenzy of these pagans that **'Even with these words, they had difficulty keeping the crowd from sacrificing to them'** (14:18). It took intervention by Jews from Iconium and Antioch, who hated the gospel enough to follow the apostles to Lystra, to turn the crowd against the apostles. They caught Paul, stoned him and left him for dead. The apostle did, however, survive and after a night's rest in the city was able to leave the next day for Derbe (14:19-20).

## **Success in Derbe and return to Lystra, Iconium and Antioch** (14:21-28)

The sheer resilience of Christian evangelists is one of the wonders of the New Testament period and remains so to this day.[6] No sooner had they arrived in Derbe than they again put themselves in harm's way by preaching the gospel! Then, having seen the conversion of a large number of people, they determined to go back to Lystra, Iconium and Antioch! How did they do it? Were they not afraid? Were they, as the saying goes, just 'gluttons for punishment'? The narrative of the apostles' completion of their first missionary journey suggests some answers which apply just as surely to us today.

### *They persisted in preaching Christ* (14:21)

The apostles' primary commitment was to their calling to preach the gospel, not to their personal welfare. *Not* to have proclaimed Christ would have been to abandon what was more than life itself. Pain in childbirth will not stop a woman who is committed to having a family! Pain in the ministry goes with the territory, but the ministry is life-giving labour. 'Woe to me,' said Paul, 'if I do not preach the gospel!' (1 Cor. 9:16).

*They were realistic in facing problems* (14:22)

Paul had no illusions about the cost of following Jesus. He knew that this world is hard and unfair and that it is starry-eyed fantasy to be thinking that we shall sail through it without a hitch. He also knew how discouraged Christians can become through bad experiences. Many years later, he reflected on this very time in his ministry to Timothy: 'You ... know ... what kinds of things happened to me in Antioch, Iconium and Lystra, the persecutions I endured. Yet the Lord rescued me from all of them.' Then he honestly and realistically sketched out for all time what real Christians can look forward to in the world: 'In fact, everyone who wants to live a godly life in Christ Jesus will be persecuted' (2 Tim. 3:10,12). Antioch, Iconium and Lystra were just the tip of an iceberg of personal suffering for Paul as a follower of Jesus (2 Cor. 11:23-29). 'Be not surprised at anything you suffer, nor be grieved at it,' concluded Charles Simeon. 'The inspired writers speak of your trials as a just occasion of joy (James 1:2,3,12). Only endeavour to improve them aright (1 Cor. 4:9-13); and you will never complain of the difficulties of the way, when you have reached your journeys end.'[7]

In practice, this means that when we realistically assess the way of the world — the way people are — we will not be shattered by disappointment over the way some will respond. Lloyd Ogilvie is surely correct when he says that '*Freedom from people* and their responses is essential to our effectiveness with them.'[8] In fact, we shall then be better placed to help them face the realities in *their* lives which need to be the subject of reflection, repentance and reformation. Related to this is our need for a clear understanding of the *causes of rejection.* If we are rejected because it is *Christ* who is being rejected, we not only cope with rejection, we shall draw extra power from it. We shall be confirmed in the right path and potential discouragement will become a cause for persevering.

Not the least of the encouragements to persevere is the goal of our faith. To know that **'We must go through many hardships to enter the kingdom of God'** provides a powerful incentive for faithfulness. We are, after all, on our way to heaven's glory.

*They passed on the work to new leadership* (14:23-25)

The apostles, in spite of their very special position in the church, never acted as though they were indispensable. They were ready to entrust the work to others. To that end, they set apart **'elders'**, probably after election by the people and examination by themselves, and left the churches they founded with a definite organization and leadership. This contrasts rather starkly with the practice of many, if not most, churches in the world today. These range from the elaborately hierarchical, with their multiple levels of clergy, from popes and archbishops to lowly curates, to the opposite extreme of the Protestant popery of the one-man ministry, in which the collegiate leadership of the church by a plurality of elders is subservient to a single will and personality. Such models have not the slightest whiff of a basis in the New Testament doctrine of the church, which clearly envisages pastoral leadership by elders, some of whom are set apart to labour in the word and doctrine full time (1 Tim. 5:17-18), to be assisted in the ministry of mercy and in temporal concerns by deacons (1 Tim. 3). Paul was ready to entrust these new churches to men who, themselves new Christians, were already mature in the faith. The work of the church is God's work and Paul rested in the assurance that he who begins a good work will certainly continue it to completion according to his eternal purpose.

*They rejoiced in God's work* (14:26-28)

Upon their return to Antioch in Syria, the apostles reported to the church **'all that God had done through them'**. This was pure encouragement. The things that could discourage — the railing of hostile people, the threats to life and limb, the pain of stoning, the fatigue of long miles on dusty roads — were all swallowed up by glorious victories for the gospel. Along their line of march, men and women, both Jews and Gentiles, had been converted to Christ. Churches led by their own elders continued to spread the good news abroad. The **'door of faith'**[9] opened to the Gentiles was the crowning advance in the Lord's work in the world. The promise of Cornelius' conversion (10:30-48) and the multi-racial church in Antioch (11:19-30) was being fulfilled in the multiplication of Gentile believers and churches along the trade routes of the Roman Empire. The air was full of excitement and expectation. The church had definitively 'broken out' of Jewry into the mainstream culture of the day and would never look back. The Gentile Rubicon had been crossed for ever!

Paul and his companions remained in Antioch **'a long time with the disciples'** (14:28). No doubt there was work to be done preaching, teaching and pastoring in church and community. But this time is perhaps mentioned more for the rest and recuperation it represents than for the labour it might also encompass. Rest, and that in the fellowship of other Christians, is as necessary in its own way to effective ministry as the spiritual cultivation of heart and mind.

In the communion of the saints
Is wisdom, safety and delight:
And when my heart declines and faints,
It's raised by their heat and light!

(Richard Baxter, 1615-91).

# 19.
# By grace alone

**Please read Acts 15:1-35**

*'It is through the grace of our Lord Jesus that we are saved'* (15:11).

The apostolic church was one church under the unitary leadership of the apostles and an expanding eldership — variously, but interchangeably, called presbyters, bishops or overseers.[1] From earliest days, the church had a simple but well-defined order. Elders and deacons were set apart to their particular tasks. Members were received upon profession of faith and the sacraments of baptism and the Lord's Supper were administered. Discipline was exercised, in which members who had fallen into sin and remained unrepentant were excluded from the church. The church was never individualistic: that is to say, people did not decide on their own charges whether to 'join' or 'leave' the church, as is too often the case in modern churches. The church was a corporate entity, in which pastoral oversight and spiritual authority were exercised by the leadership raised up by the Lord and set apart according to a church polity mediated by the divinely inspired guidance of the apostles.

This did not mean that there was neither controversy nor the threat of disunity. From the beginning, problems arose which needed to be resolved with pastoral, spiritual and judicial authority. The New Testament records such 'cases' as Ananias and Sapphira, the Hellenist widows, the acceptance of Saul (Paul); complaints against Peter's ministry to Gentiles in Cæsarea; the ordination of Barnabas and Saul and the ordination of elders in Lystra, Iconium and Pisidian Antioch (5:1-11; 6:1-7; 9:26-30; 11:1-18; 13:1-3;14:23).

It also seems clear from the record of those who engage in the ministry of the Word and sacraments that no one appointed himself to these tasks, the implication being that the church, through her God-appointed leadership, recognized and authorized those who were called to the ministry. The principles which are stated explicitly in later New Testament Scriptures were in operation from the start, although their practical development was related to need as it emerged progressively from the circumstances of the growing church.

It is therefore no surprise to find, early on, a question arising about the nature of membership in the church and to see the matter being dealt with through the collective leadership of the church, the apostles and elders, who met together in a deliberative assembly (15:6).

## **Disturbance** (15:1-3)

The problem arose because some men from Judea came to Antioch and promoted the view that circumcision, according to the law of Moses, was necessary for salvation.[2] They were opposed by Paul and Barnabas. The church must have been seriously riven by the dispute. There was no final resolution and so help was sought from the church in Jerusalem, still at this point the heartland of the Christian church, from which the problem had come in the first place. Paul, Barnabas and some other believers were deputed to take the case to the apostles and elders in Jerusalem.

It is impressive to see the orderliness and seemingly good spirit in which they sought to deal with the dispute. This is reflected in the way the news of the conversion of Gentiles was received along their path. **'This news made all the brothers very glad'** (15:3). The church was still one church, united in a glorious obsession with the gospel and the conviction that there is one truth by which the people of God are to be guided and ordered in one, undivided body. Every theological and practical controversy potentially threatens the unity of the church. In this case, the issue was fundamental to the meaning and application of the gospel itself. The intense conservatism of some of the Christian Jews was expressed in an insistence that certain regulations of the Old Testament law be required of non-Jewish converts as prerequisites for their recognition as members of the church of Jesus Christ. This is, of course, the so-called Judaizing controversy, which, notwithstanding the action of the Jerusalem Council, continued to dog the progress of the apostolic church and was to be the target of Paul's epistle to the Galatians.[3]

The heart of the matter is the tendency to *add to the Word of God* in defining who is, or is not, a Christian and thus expand the scope of what makes for a credible profession of faith to take in all sorts of unbiblical rules and requirements. The 'Judaizing' Christians in Antioch did not want to add some new *man-made* tradition of innovation, but desired to keep certain elements which had been God's will for the Old Testament church. The difficulty of dealing with this is obvious. How could what was good and holy until Jesus came become an improper imposition afterwards? The answer had already been given explicitly with respect to the dietary laws (10:10-16) and implicitly in the pouring out of the Holy Spirit upon the Samaritan and Gentile believers (8:7; 10:45-48). The maintenance of an Old Testament regulation (in this case, circumcision), when it had been replaced by a distinctively New Testament ordinance (baptism), was equivalent to imposing a man-made tradition even though God had originally given it to his people. Why? Because God had made it clear, through the teaching of Jesus and the apostles, that the latter was to be the ordinance of incorporation with his people for the whole New Testament era, until its culmination in the Second Coming of Christ (Matt. 28:19; Acts 2:38). The transitional nature of the first-generation church of the apostles, however, made this a sensitive and difficult matter with which to deal. Jewish Christians still attended services in the synagogues and observed the ceremonies at the temple (see Acts 21:26 for an instance of the latter involving the apostle Paul). Only with the destruction of the temple in A.D. 70 would the ceremonial aspects of the Old Testament pattern for godliness decisively recede from the practice of the church.[4]

### **Discussion** (15:4-18)

On arriving at Jerusalem, the delegates from Antioch were welcomed by **'the church and the apostles and elders, to whom they reported everything God had done through them'**. This gathering evidently consisted of the leadership (apostles and elders) and many of the membership, including those converted Pharisees who were putting forward the requirement that Gentiles **'must be circumcised and required to obey the law of Moses'** (15:5-6). This was the context for discussion of the issue.

The Jerusalem Council, as it has been named, was *a convocation of ordained elders* together with the apostles. The significance of this council, beyond the immediate decision which was made, lies in the fact that the apostles did not make the decision for the church, as could well have been expected of men of their unique position and gifts, but participated, for the purposes of this decision, as elders with the other elders, albeit as the 'first among equals'. It is for this reason that the Jerusalem Council is the great prototype of 'synods and councils', whether congregational or presbyterian, ever since. That prince of theologians John Owen observed that the churches 'did of old, and ought still, to meet ... for advice, consultation and consent' and that this 'is so fully expressed and exemplified in the two great churches of Jerusalem and Antioch (Acts 15) that it cannot be gainsaid'.[5]

Having convened for the purpose, **'the apostles and elders'** engaged in *a deliberative discussion* of the issue referred to them by the church in Antioch, namely, whether the Judaistic proposition that circumcision and a commitment to keeping Mosaic law were to be required of Gentiles (15:7). There was free debate and no papering over differences. The apostles let the elders speak before they joined in, thus showing the way for the future, when their uniquely revelatory gifts would be gone. Furthermore, it is clear, from what is said later, that their goal was to know the mind of the Holy Spirit in the matter (15:28).

This suggests a very practical point for church meetings today. So often they are about power, or money, or procedure. The 'committee men' manoeuvre to pass motions on reports and programmes, prepared long before behind closed doors by 'task forces' and 'think-tanks' drawn from a well-vetted ecclesiastical oligarchy. When the elders come together — if they ever do — they are invited to approve the work of others. For those who disapprove, a short time for ineffectual carping is allowed. Of deliberative debate, there is nothing. Even in Presbyterian assemblies, where, one might think, this principle would be most carefully preserved, the elders are either not expected to contribute much of any use to theological debate, or are prevented from doing so by the rules of order. The other 'E's — experts, executives, ecclesiastics and elitists — have hijacked the church's counsels! The Jerusalem Council calls the church of Jesus Christ back to God's way of seeking the mind of the Spirit on the issues confronting the doctrinal purity and the practical peace of the body of Christ — namely, by God-appointed elders in deliberative assemblies. The way the discussion unfolded in Jerusalem is the most vivid recommendation for God's way to solve the church's challenges.

*Saved by God's grace alone — Peter's argument* (15:7-11)

Peter rose, **'after much discussion,'** and proceeded to demolish the Judaistic viewpoint with arguments drawn from his own experience of ministry to Gentiles. He first described the conversion of the Gentiles as the *work of God* (15:7-9). It had been God, not himself, who had determined that, through his lips, Gentiles **'might hear ...the message of the gospel and believe'**. It was certain that God had *accepted* them, because he had given the Holy Spirit to them, just as he had to Jewish believers; and this was proved by the Gentile Christians' *faith*, which was no different from theirs (15:9). He then rebuked those Jewish Christians who would insist on *human works* — in this instance, circumcision and the law — as necessary for salvation (15:10). They should have known better! Their fathers could not bear the **'yoke'** of the law. It could not save them. They could not keep it. To suggest that this same yoke is necessary to being recognized as a true believer in Christ was, in effect, to deny their own profession of Christ as their Saviour! Worse! It was to **'try to test God'** — that is, to challenge his ability to save lost people by grace through faith in Christ *alone*! To make any action, however righteous in itself, an instrument of the justification of a sinner before God, when God has made it plain by precept and actual experience that it is by grace alone through saving faith in Jesus Christ, is to contradict the very essence of the gospel! Faith is in a category all of its own. Faith is not a 'work'. It is, to be sure, the act of the human heart casting itself upon the Lord, but it is pre-eminently the gift of God — as Paul later says 'so that no one can boast' (Eph. 2:9).

Rising to a glorious crescendo, Peter declared emphatically the very heart of the gospel (15:11). Salvation is by grace alone, both for Jews and Gentiles. Jesus' yoke is easy and his burden is light (Matt. 11:30). There is no place for the yoke of a law, which could only condemn us!

*Sealed with 'signs and wonders' — Barnabas and Paul testify* (15:12)

The two missionaries, whose labours had largely occasioned the controversy, supported Peter with testimony to the miracles attending the ministry to the Gentiles. These showed that God was working among them, as he had among the Jews.

*Prophesied in Scripture — James' speech* (15:13-18)

James, the brother of Jesus and writer of the epistle of James, was not an apostle. He delivered the *coup-de-grâce* to the Judaist argument with a direct appeal to the Word of God. God had already spoken on the matter! Quoting Amos 9:11-12, James reminded them that the prophet had declared that **'David's fallen tent'** was be restored and that this would involve the ingathering of **'all the Gentiles who bear [the Lord's] name'** (15:16-18). This is fulfilled, James says, in all that Peter had described (15:14). The church of Jesus Christ was all along intended to encompass both Jew and Gentile and, one by one without discrimination, they are brought to the same faith by the same grace of the same Lord. The gospel is for all nations. This, James showed, was 'the mind of God... in the Scripture'.[6]

**Deliverance proposed** (15:19-21)

The Lord's brother then proposed the motion that was to become the finding of the Jerusalem Council. This consisted of two main parts. The first was the definitive *doctrinal* answer to the Judaizers, which stands for all time: **'We should not make it difficult for the Gentiles who are turning to God'** (15:19). This verse is often passed over as a mere introit to the verses that follow, but it ought to be seen as standing on its own. It told the Judaizing party in the gentlest possible way — if they thought through all they had heard — that what they were asking for was not the Lord's will for the church, but was, indeed, even contrary to the gospel of God's free grace in Christ and the concomitant doctrine of justification by faith alone.

If ever there was a soft answer that would turn away potential anger, this was it. 'We should not make it difficult,' is an example of affirming a basic doctrine in a very practical way. The doctrine had been clearly stated by the previous speakers. There was no need for a bare restatement. There was need, however, to persuade people of its practical significance. And, at the same time, those whose views were being rejected needed to know that they were not being personally rejected, but were still warmly embraced within the fellowship of the Lord's people. They were believers and they had laid their views before the whole church in an orderly manner. Having received the considered judgement of the church, they could be expected to receive it with due submission in the Lord. They were certainly not to be made to feel that they had been foolish or were no longer welcome.

This is surely a model for resolving doctrinal and practical controversy today. Too often, church debates degenerate into fights and lead to unnecessary and ungodly division. The maintenance of truth never requires discourtesy or unpleasantness on the part of its advocates, even if those who oppose it are strident and contentious (2 Tim. 2:25). James deftly set the denial of any requirement of legal observances for salvation (the other side of which was the affirmation of the doctrine of salvation by grace alone through faith in Christ) in terms of not putting difficulties (i.e., unbiblical ones) in the way of Gentile converts being received into the membership of the church.

The second part is a *practical* four-point proposal (15:20) designed to foster unity in the church, by asking Gentile Christians to take particular care to distance themselves from their former manner of life. This was also, no doubt, designed to allay the fears of Jewish Christians, whose sense of what constituted a God-honouring lifestyle was formed by the regulations of the law of Moses. They needed to know that Gentile Christians were not adrift from practical godliness as properly defined by God's Word. James therefore addressed specific practical issues, where the teaching of the Scriptures — still confined to the Old Testament — challenged the accepted norms of Gentile behaviour and called for a conscientious application of biblical principles.

First, they should **'abstain from food polluted by idols'** (Dan. 1:8; Mal. 1:7-12). This had been offered at pagan temples as sacrifices to the gods and the surplus sold in the market. The question here was not primarily one of diet — that is dealt with in the third and fourth points — but concerned association with the pagan milieu from which the food had come. Questions of conscience later arose in Corinth on this very point. These were addressed by Paul, who made it clear that while there was no essential problem with eating this meat, there ought to be sensitivity to the tender consciences of those who, having come out of paganism, regarded consuming it as a sinful complicity with paganism (1 Cor. 8:1-13; 10:14-33).

Second, they should abstain from **'sexual immorality'** (Lev. 18; Matt. 5:27-30). The Gentile world, like that of television dramas and sitcoms today, treated promiscuous sexual relations as acceptable and part of normal behaviour. This was sin then and remains sin to this day.

Third, they should not partake of **'the meat of strangled animals'**. This is a reference to meat from which the blood had not been completely strained (Lev. 7: 22-27).[7]

Lastly, they should eat no **'blood'** (Gen. 9:4; Lev. 17:10-12; 19:26). This was the basis for the preceding point. Blood was symbolic of life and was to be reserved for sacrifice to the Lord, thus underscoring his role as the giver of life.

None of these, as John Owen points out, was a new imposition on the practice of the churches.[8] All were clearly taught in Scripture, even if all but the second were elements of old covenant piety that would eventually pass away when the full revelation of the New Testament was completed. The purpose of reiterating them here was to encourage a discerning sensitivity to practical godliness in a Gentile social-cultural milieu and a Jewish Christian ecclesiastical context. Gentiles were to examine critically their old habits and give no cause to anyone to accuse them of their old sins. They were also encouraged to be graciously accommodating to Jewish dietary sensitivities. For their part, Jewish believers needed to understand that Gentiles were not to be required to observe the Mosaic ceremonial law, now that the Messiah had come and published the gospel of sovereign grace in all its fulness.

**Decision** (15:22-35)

The decision was made to adopt James' proposal and send a letter with a deputation to all the churches in **'Antioch, Syria and Cilicia'** (15:22-29). This very winsomely conveyed the verdict of the council. Today it still vibrates with lively applicability.

First of all, the men who insisted on circumcision and the law were declared to be **'without** [the church's] **... authorization'** for their disturbing teaching. This almost unobtrusive dismissal underscores the solidity with which the church knew its doctrine. From the beginning, the apostles clearly taught that salvation was by the free and sovereign grace of God through faith in Christ and not through man's best efforts to keep the law and impress God with self-generated good works. Jerusalem held that line and closed the door to works-righteousness. Good works have a vital place in the Christian life, to be sure. They are, however, not the root, but the fruit of salvation, prepared by God in advance for us to do (Eph. 2:10).

Secondly, they emphasized that the decision 'see**med good to the Holy Spirit and to [the church]'** (15:28). Here is the purpose and the role of the church in the guidance and discipline of God's people. Jesus had promised that the Holy Spirit would lead them into all truth (John 14:26; 16:13). All decisions in churches, as well as in the individual Christian's life, ought to fulfil this condition. Not only does it tell us what God does with his church, but it defines the goal and prayer of the church. If what we do only seems good to *us*, without the evident leading of the Spirit, then we are simply not doing the Lord's work.

Thirdly, the council's four **'requirements'** — one permanent (sexual immorality), the others transitional and temporary — underscore the necessity and the blessing of the separated life for Christians: **'You will do well to avoid these things'** (15:29). Christians must bear a decisive testimony to the society in which they are placed — one which lives the righteousness of God before the world.

The result in the mission churches was encouragement and continued blessing through the ministries of Judas, Silas, Paul and Barnabas (15:30-35). The burden of Judaistic legalism was lifted. The gospel of Jesus Christ was lifted up before the Gentiles and the Holy Spirit continued to accompany the preaching of the Word with power, so that more and more people were being saved by grace alone. *Sola gratia! Soli Deo gloria!*

# Part V

## The second missionary journey

Acts 15:36 - 18:23

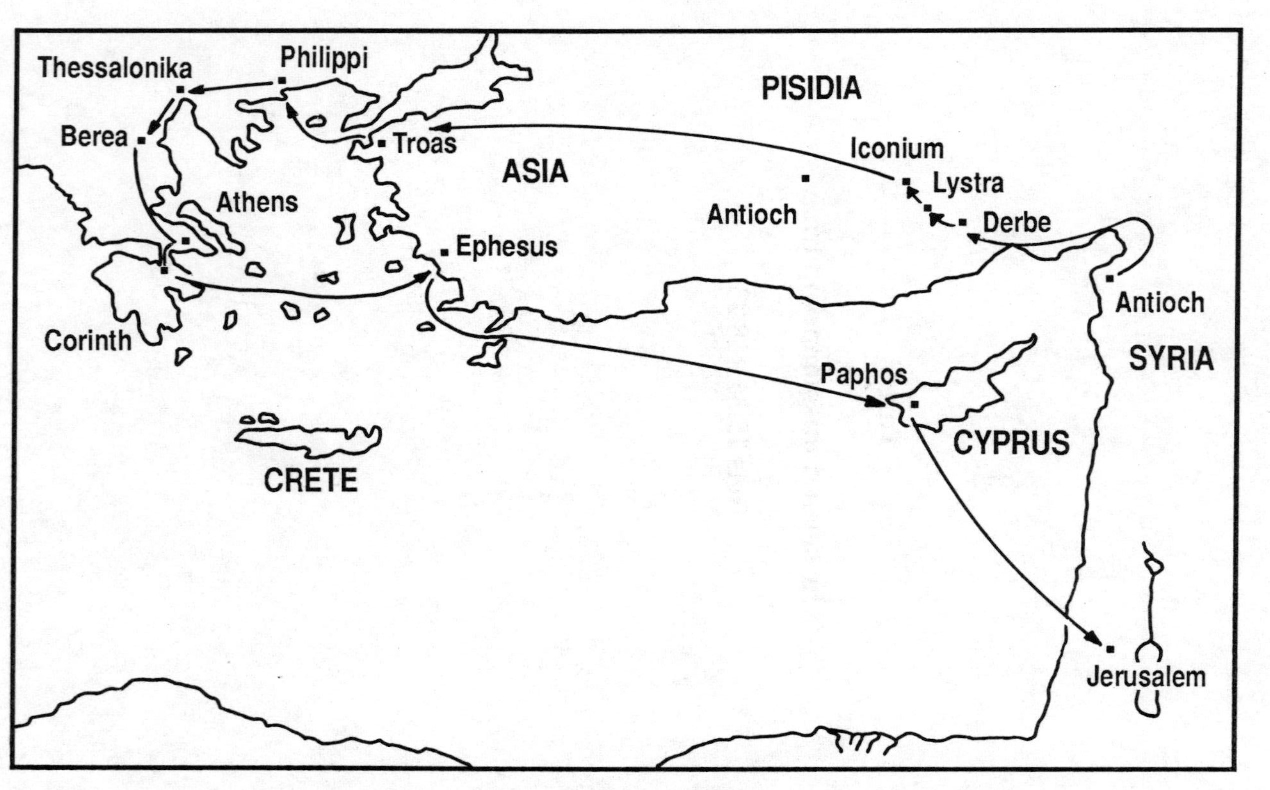
Thessalonika
Philippi
PISIDIA
Berea
Troas
Iconium
ASIA
Lystra
Athens
Antioch
Derbe
Ephesus
Antioch
Corinth
SYRIA
Paphos
CYPRUS
CRETE
Jerusalem

# 20.
# 'Come over and help us!'

**Please read Acts 15:36 - 16:15**
*'Come over to Macedonia and help us'* (16:9).

'It is the nature of divine grace,' says Charles Simeon, 'to be always operative, and never to remit its exertions, whilst there is any good to be done.'[1] The church cannot but be on the move. The gospel must reach out. The Christian wants to share his Saviour with a desperately needy world. From Antioch, to Cyprus and to the cities of Phrygia, Paul's first 'missionary journey' had brought new life in Christ to increasing numbers of Gentiles and Jews and planted many new vibrant churches. This was only the beginning. The gospel was still confined to a small corner of Asia. The heartland of the Roman Empire, with its Greek and Latin peoples, remained entirely to be evangelized. They beckoned, as do all unreached mission-fields, for the attention of the missionaries of Jesus Christ.

Our passage describes the beginning of the second missionary journey, the one in which the gospel first came to Europe. Europeans understandably see this as a momentous event. And so it is from the perspective of history. It is very doubtful, however, if Paul viewed the westward crossing of the Aegean Sea as intrinsically more significant than sailing from Syria to Cyprus, or walking from Iconium to Lystra! The hallowing of particular geographical boundaries would not have registered with the apostle Paul and the early Christians. What *was* vital to them was the leading of the Holy Spirit, whether he kept them from preaching in Bithynia or called them over to Macedonia. In any event, *the* great watershed in the church's mission had already been crossed — that between Jew and Gentile. It was in the course of continuing to reach the latter that Paul was called by God to minister in Macedonia and in Greece.

How this came about is unfolded in three stages, in which Luke shows us, successively, the underlying motive (15:36-16:5), the enabling power (16:6-10) and the resulting fruit (16:11-15) of the work of the Holy Spirit behind, in and through the apostle's ministry for Jesus Christ.

## **The underlying motive: the good of the church** (15:36 - 16:5)

Luke records two incidents which were significant in the life of the apostolic church. The first of these is the disagreement between Paul and Barnabas over John Mark (15:36-41) and the second concerns the addition of Timothy to the apostolic team (16:1-5).

### *A parting of ways* (15:36-41)

Paul, as we have seen, had suggested to Barnabas that they revisit the people and places where they had preached on their first journey. Barnabas wanted his cousin John Mark to accompany them, but Paul thought it ill-advised, on the grounds that Mark had deserted them on their earlier trip (13:13). Barnabas apparently could not accept Paul's position and went off with Mark to his native Cyprus. Paul chose Silas as his companion and, **'commended by the brothers to the grace of the Lord,'** set off through Syria and Cilicia, **'strengthening the churches'** (15:40-41). Luke does not specifically apportion blame, but there is no real reason to doubt that Paul correctly discerned Mark's lack of readiness for this particular mission. Later Mark did become an esteemed helper to the apostle (Col. 4:10; 2 Tim. 4:11; 1 Peter 5:13), but of Barnabas we hear no more.

There are perhaps two lessons in this, both relating to the good of the church. The first is that spiritual maturity is absolutely essential in those who are to be called to preach the gospel and lead God's people in service as elders and deacons (1 Tim. 3:1-10; Titus 1:5-9). The second is that disputes among Christians, not least those who lead the people of God, need to be resolved quickly. In this case a dispute, which John Calvin calls 'a light matter ... which might easily have been ended', quickly escalated into a tragic breach between two good men whose partnership had been forged by the Holy Spirit (13:2). We are admonished by this example 'that unless the servants of Christ are intent on keeping a sharp look-out, many chinks are open to Satan, by which he may steal in to disturb the harmony among them'.[2]

*A new team (16:1-5)*

Paul and Silas proceeded through south Galatia to Lystra (see Map 2, p. 180). There, a young disciple named Timothy was added to their company. Paul, we are told, **'circumcised him because of the Jews who lived in that area, for they all knew that his father was a Greek'** (16:3).

The question immediately arises why Timothy was circumcised at all, when the Jerusalem Council had just decisively rejected circumcision as a requirement for salvation. Clearly, Timothy was not circumcised *as a condition of church membership.* His recognition as a believer was not in question and Paul was not about to become a Judaizer! The reason given — 'for they all knew his father was a Greek' — shows us the true motive for his submission to this rite. The circumcision of Timothy was, like the dietary requirements of Acts 15:28-29, an accommodation to the Jewishness of the church for the sake of the peace and unity of the body. It was an exercise of unforced Christian liberty on the part of Timothy. Both Paul and Timothy would have realized that an uncircumcised missionary (as much as an idol-meat-eating Gentile Christian) would be a scandal to Jewish Christians schooled in the Old Testament law. As yet the New Testament revelation had not been completed and the church was in the transitional phase between the removal in principle of the Old Testament ceremonies and their practical disappearance. During this transition, New Testament Christians could continue to observe certain of these ceremonies just as long as they were regarded as 'things indifferent' *(adiaphora)* in relation to salvation, and therefore as matters of conscience for individual piety. On this basis and for the same reason that he circumcised Timothy, Paul was willing to participate in certain rites at the temple in Jerusalem (21:20-26). On another occasion, however, he firmly refused to have Titus circumcised because the pressure for this came from Judaizing legalists, who saw it as a term of membership to be forced on all Christians (Gal. 2:3; cf. Col. 2:11-12).

Timothy did not have to be circumcised. He did submit to it, however, freely and without compulsion and, very probably, on the recommendation of the apostle Paul, in order to accommodate the deeply seated convictions of the Jewish Christians. He exercised his Christian liberty out of regard to the weakness of his brothers in the faith (see Rom. 14 and 1 Cor. 8-9). 'The synagogue is to be buried with honour,' said a proverb, already old when quoted by Calvin.[3] Paul and Timothy honoured the piety of a passing era, for the sake of unity, peace and the building up of the church of Jesus Christ.

The time came, especially after the destruction of the temple in A.D. 70, when Judaistic practices passed from the church altogether. Sadly, questions of legalism and the infringement of the individual conscience still arise to challenge and disturb the church. Churches have often imposed unbiblical requirements on their members. These can be doctrinal peculiarities, but more often involve specific practices, like abstinence from alcohol and tobacco, observing specific dress codes and things like going to films or dances. Legalism always presses for new and higher hedges of man-made laws to be built around the actual provisions of God's revealed Word. Legalism removes from free individual consciences the responsibility God has given in his Word to exercise the judgement whether or not to engage in a particular activity and teaches for doctrines the commandments of men. Paul's teaching and practice — for example, his circumcision of Timothy in one situation and refusal to circumcise Titus in another — show us that there is a boundary between the church's power and the individual's right of private judgement. The church may require only what God requires. Individual believers may freely impose upon themselves, for the sake of others, restrictions of rights God has given them — for example, eating meat or drinking wine (1 Cor. 8:13).

### **The enabling power: the leading of the Spirit** (16:6-10)

Because of the attention paid to the entrance of the gospel into Europe, it is often entirely overlooked that Paul was **'kept by the Holy Spirit from preaching the word'** in several provinces of Asia Minor. They visited the churches formerly established in **'Phrygia and Galatia'** and no doubt preached throughout these regions, but they apparently were not permitted by the Lord to plant any churches in the provinces of **'Asia ..., Mysia ...'** and **'Bithynia'** (16:6-8). How the Holy Spirit prevented them from evangelizing in these areas we are not told, and it is idle to speculate. Whether by direct revelation, an inward conviction, outward circumstances or a word from a prophet (there were such in the New Testament church), or a combination of any of these, Paul was persuaded that wherever the Lord wanted him to preach the gospel, it was elsewhere. Why this happened becomes clear only when Paul had arrived in Troas, just across the Hellespont from Europe. There God gave him the vision of **'a man of Macedonia standing and begging him, "Come over to Macedonia and help us."'** This was conclusive for Paul. They were **'to preach the gospel to them'** (16:9-10).

This teaches us, first of all, that it is God who *sovereignly determined* where and to whom the gospel should be preached. God did not reveal his reasons for having Paul go to Macedonia, before Asia, Bithynia and Mysia. He certainly did not choose Macedonia because Macedonians were more worthy or because he foresaw they would believe! John Calvin comments that God reveals here 'that he has appeared openly to those by whom he was not sought, and that he has spoken to those who were not asking questions about him. For where do docility and a submissive mind come from except from his Spirit? Therefore it is certain that some are not preferred to others by their own merit, since all are quite equally hostile to faith by nature.'[4] Salvation is by grace alone. No one deserves to be saved. No one gives himself the new birth (John 3:3-8). No one even generates his own saving faith in Jesus Christ, notwithstanding the fact that it is the response and commitment of his uncoerced will (Eph. 2:1-10). Mercy is optional with God. 'I will have mercy on whom I have mercy, and I will have compassion on whom I have compassion' (Rom. 9:15).[5]

Secondly, and more obviously on the face of the text, God revealed the *need for the preaching of the gospel* in Macedonia. This is not to say that the provinces Paul had been prevented from entering were less in need of gospel grace. The whole world was lost and it would simply have been impossible to go anywhere that had no need of Christian ministry. Indeed, Paul's method had hitherto been very simple — he just moved on to the next town. What was new for him was being diverted from the next, most obvious target area and kept waiting for clear guidance as to his next sphere of ministry. When the Lord told him this was to be Macedonia, he also showed him that this was no arbitrary decision, but one moved by love for the lost. He therefore appealed to Paul's, and every Christian's, two deepest motives — his love for the Lord and his love for the lost. *The Lord called* him to Macedonia, but he did so in terms of the *Macedonians' need* of Jesus Christ. Are we not ourselves to be powerfully moved by the lost condition of unconverted people in our families, communities and nations?

Finally, we should note that God's call carried with it a certain *promise of effectiveness*. Without expecting visions like that of Paul, we may still take the promise of his vision as a working principle of Christian witness. God had a purpose for Macedonia. He had a purpose for Paul. He has a purpose for you. He has a purpose for the people among whom he has placed you. This is not a promise of invariable and uniform success. 'We may, like the Apostles,' says Charles Simeon, 'spread our net wide, and "toil all the night, and catch nothing"; but, if our Lord instruct us where to cast the net, we may hope to enclose a multitude of fishes.'[6] The Holy Spirit who calls men to preach Christ also prepares the hearts of people to receive him. When we plant and others water, God is at work to give the harvest.

## The fruit: the opening of a closed heart (16:11-15)

Responding to the vision of the man of Macedonia, Paul sailed from Troas and made his way to the Roman colony of Philippi (16:11-12). After the Lord's calling of Paul in a vision, one might be forgiven for anticipating spectacular success for his mission. We discover, however, that, there apparently being no synagogue in Philippi,[7] his first contacts were made with a women's prayer group in a quiet corner by a riverside and, as it turns out, the first convert in Europe was not even a European, but a woman from Asia — a very quiet beginning to the conquest of a continent! Calvin points up the reason so beautifully: 'The Lord carries through his works under a humble and weak appearance like that, so that his power may in the end shine out more clearly.'

### *Lydia's need of a Saviour* (16:13-14)

That first convert in Europe was **'a woman named Lydia'**. She was **'a dealer in purple cloth'** from Thyatira in Asia Minor — a successful businesswoman who owned a comfortable and well-staffed house (16:14-15). She was a Jewish proselyte — **'a worshipper of God'** — sincere, given to prayer and a follower of God. She was, nevertheless, still a stranger to the gospel. Her heart was closed to the Son of God and needed to be opened to receive him. Lydia was a most attractive character. She was a productive member of the community. She was a morally upright churchgoer. But she had a closed heart. She was unconverted.

Sinners' hearts can be closed to the Lord for many reasons and these must not be underestimated. James Buchanan surveys the many possible bars across the door of the unconverted heart: 'There is the bar of *ignorance*: many "hear the word" but understand it not; and the wicked one takes away that which was sown; there is the bar of *unbelief*, which rejects the testimony of God; there is the bar of *enmity*, for "The carnal mind is enmity against God; it is not subject to the law of God, neither indeed can be"; there is the bar of *presumption or pride:* "The wicked, through the pride of his countenance, will not seek after God; God is not in all his thoughts"; there is the bar of *discouragement and despair:* "Thou saidst there is no hope, for I have loved strangers and after them I will go"; there is the bar of *unwillingness:* "Ye will not come to me that ye might have life"; there is the bar of *worldly-mindedness*: "The cares of the world and the deceitfulness of riches, choke the word and it becometh unfruitful"; there is the bar of *sloth*: "A little more sleep, a little more slumber, a little folding of the hands to sleep"; there is the bar of *vicious passion and depraved habits,* any one bosom sin being enough to exclude the saving power of the truth: "For this is the condemnation, that light hath come into the world, and that men loved the darkness rather than the light, because their deeds are evil."'[8]

*Lydia's conversion to Christ* (16:14)

What bar, or bars, closed Lydia's heart, we are not told. What we do know is that **'The Lord opened her heart to respond to Paul's message.'** As Charles Simeon puts it, 'The Lord "knocked, as it were, at the door" of her heart, and constrained her to open to him; he fixed her attention to the subject Paul insisted upon, gave her an insight into it, inclined her cordially to embrace the truth, and thus subdued her to the obedience of faith.'[9]

You will notice the *twofold* work of the Holy Spirit in Lydia's conversion. On the one hand, he sovereignly **'opened her heart'**, convincing her of her sin, enlightening her mind, renewing her will and persuading and enabling her to embrace Jesus Christ as her Saviour. On the other hand, the Lord *opened the Word* through **'Paul's message'**. 'The Spirit's agency,' writes James Buchanan, 'does not supersede the use of the Word: on the contrary, truth read or heard is still the wisdom of God, and the power of God unto salvation.'[10] Word and Spirit come at the human heart from different directions but completely in concert: the two are inseparable in the conversion of lost people to Jesus Christ. The psalmist notes this: '*Open my eyes* that I may see wonderful things *in your law*' (Ps. 119:18). Paul reminds the Thessalonians that 'From the beginning God chose you to be saved through *the sanctifying work of the Spirit* and through *belief in the truth*' (2 Thess. 2:13).

*Lydia's new faith* (16:15)

Coming to faith in Christ has two immediate results in the new believer's life. Without the slightest fanfare, Luke records these evidences of Lydia's conversion.

She first made a *public profession of her faith,* exemplified in her receiving baptism for herself and her household (i.e., her dependants and servants). Baptism, as the sign and seal of the covenant of grace, ought to be recognized as *the* visible dividing line between the kingdom of darkness and the kingdom of light. While it is certainly true that we do not belong to the Lord because we are baptized, but are baptized because we belong to the Lord already, it remains a fact that baptism is the point at which the church, in the name of the Lord, recognizes what God has done and will yet do for the person receiving baptism. Baptism is not what we do to 'join the church': it is what the church does to seal what God has done in his everlasting mercy in Jesus Christ.[11] Had Lydia professed faith in Christ and not submitted to baptism, she would have been in effect denying her own profession of faith. That is surely why Luke mentions her baptism, but never records her words in professing Christ as her Saviour. Why? Because, without baptism, her words would have been empty. It was baptism which sealed the credibility of her confession of Christ!

The second fruit and evidence of the reality of Lydia's conversion was her transparent *enthusiasm for Christ's cause,* expressed in her warm hospitality to the apostolic mission team. With a fetching sweetness, Lydia links her invitation to the apostles' view of the sincerity of her faith: **'If ye have judged me to be faithful to the Lord, come into my house, and abide there'** (16:15, AV). She is saying, 'Now that I am one of you, let me give of my home and my life to help you in your ministry for Jesus.' She simply threw herself and her resources into the work of the gospel, without reserve and without delay! Her home became both a haven and a centre of witness for the apostles in their time in Philippi (16:40). These are the 'things that accompany salvation', which the Scripture says that God will 'not forget' — that is, the 'work and love you have shown him as you have helped his people and continue to help them' (Heb. 6:9-10). Lydia did not consider it a burden, but a happy privilege, to put herself out for the Lord and his people. Contrast the coldness of churches where, if the minister did not offer hospitality to newcomers, there would be none at all. Many professing Christians make no effort even to speak to visitors to their churches, far less offer hospitality. 'We should long and pant after opportunities of honouring our God ... we should account ourselves, and all we possess, as the Lord's property; and we should make it the one labour of our lives to "glorify him with our bodies and our spirits, which are his".'[12]

This was how the gospel first made an impact on Europe, in the conversion of Lydia. And this is your calling, if you are a Christian at all, wherever you are in the world of today!

# 21.
# 'What must I do to be saved?'

**Please read Acts 16:16-40**

*'Believe in the Lord Jesus Christ, and you will be saved'* (16:31).

People become Christians in all sorts of ways. Some, like Lydia, come to Christ very quietly. They are drawn, says Charles Simeon, 'by the attractive influences of his Spirit; causing his word to distil as dew upon their souls ... imperceptibly ... opening their understandings ... and inclining their hearts to embrace his truth'.[1] This is the experience of many who grow up in a Christian family and are exposed to the ministry of the Word and the Spirit in both home and church. Others may have a more or less dramatic conversion to Christ, as did the apostle Paul himself. Whenever a person's life is being lived in conscious and deliberate opposition to the gospel, the transforming power of God's grace involves the overthrow of deeply entrenched commitments. Such folk often experience the terror of God's law before they come to saving faith in Christ. They cry to the Lord out of a profound sense of lostness and the need of a Saviour.

So it was with the jailer in Philippi. His story offers a pointed contrast with the conversion of Lydia and highlights the truth that the Lord is never limited by circumstances or predispositions, when he reaches out in his sovereign love to bring men and women to faith.

## **Preparation: the healing of the slave girl** (16:16-24)

Paul might never have ministered to the Philippian jailer had he not first been the subject of some very embarrassing attention from a fortune-telling slave girl. This girl had followed Paul and his company around, loudly declaring that **'These men are servants of the Most High God, who are telling you the way to be saved.'**

*The spirit of divination* (16:16-17)

The girl had **'a spirit by which she predicted the future'**. The Greek text has 'a spirit of a python' *(pneuma puthona).* The 'python' was a large dragon in Greek mythology, which, until killed by Apollo, had guarded the oracle at Delphi, in the region of Pytho — hence the name. The word was applied to those who predicted the future or were held to be possessed by a spirit. We are more familiar with its (no doubt deliberate) use in the modern English satirical 'oracle' — the *Monty Python* television series of the 1970s and 1980s.

We should notice three things about the girl. First of all, she was indeed *possessed* of an evil spirit, as a result of which she was able to earn a great deal of money for her exploitative masters. Secondly, she was given to declare the *truth* about Paul, Silas and the gospel message — they were, she said, **'servants of the Most High God, who are telling you the way to be saved'**. And thirdly, she was thereby doing the devil's work by bringing the gospel into *disrepute.* The girl's activities are not to be attibuted to some mental or physical illness. Satan was seeking to overthrow the Lord's work and what she did was demonic — not genuine miracles from God, but 'lying wonders' designed to deceive people into thinking they are from God (2 Thess. 2:9, AV). The most dangerous errors are not the most obvious, but those with just enough of the truth to fool the undiscerning into swallowing them. Terrorists hide their bombs in radios and food containers. Poison is never more potent than when buried in some sweetmeat.

But why was the girl's *true* statement about Paul and his message bringing disrepute on the gospel? The answer is simply that, in the popular mind, it associated the gospel with the magic of the day. Satan was trying to wrest the initiative from God's messengers by hijacking their message and presenting it in a foreign context, which made it just another weird and wonderful phenomenon of the day. This was the very same method, by the way, which Satan employed in his temptation of Jesus in the wilderness (Luke 4:34,35,41).

Furthermore, the girl's condition reminds us that it is possible to know the bare bones of the truth of the gospel, without experiencing anything of its saving power. The word 'doctrine' begins with 'do' — truth loved is truth *done.* Living faith is faith lived. In themselves, the finest words do not prove a thing. Words only *promise;* it is deeds that *prove* the promise of the words. The girl's true words masked the lost state of her soul.

*The healing of the girl* (16:18)

**'She kept this up for many days.'** Imagine how you would feel if someone followed you around all day, saying, 'This fellow's a Christian! He can tell you how to be saved!' Would this help your Christian witness? Of course not! It would reduce the Christian message to a laughing-stock! Calvin is quite right when he argues that 'If Paul had acceded to that testimony, there would have been no longer any difference between the saving doctrine of Christ and the mockeries of Satan. The splendour of the gospel would have been enveloped in the darkness of falsehood and so would have been extinguished.'[2] Paul therefore could not let her attach herself in this way to his mission. He could not say, as many might today, 'Yes, she has problems in her theology and in her life, but she is telling people the truth in this instance, and we can use the extra publicity for the gospel.' Paul was **'troubled'** and knew that something had to be done if the gospel message was not to be entirely discredited in the eyes of the public.

It is worth noting that on another occasion, Paul rejoiced when Christ was being proclaimed, even if it was by men who opposed themselves to him (Phil. 1:18). There is no inconsistency here. In Philippians 1, the problem was personal antipathy to Paul, while in Acts 16, it was essentially hostility to Christ.

Paul realized that the girl was possessed by an evil spirit and he turned to her and said, **'In the name of Jesus Christ I command you to come out of her!'** The spirit promptly departed and the girl was healed. We have every reason to believe she was also saved. Paul's response, you will note, was not one of angry repudiation, but of compassion and a desire to do her some real good. We are to pray for those who despitefully use us and we are to love our enemies. If, by God's grace, they then become our friends, we have even greater reason for rejoicing.

*Paul and Silas jailed* (16:19-24)

Paul had not only healed the girl; he had hit her masters where it really hurt them — in their pockets! Their business was ruined and they knew it. Satan, too, had lost his mouthpiece, so, to use Calvin's words, 'The same devil that was recently trying to catch Paul with its flattering and enticing words through the mouth of the girl, now whips up her masters into a fury, to drag him off to death.'[3] It now served their interests to *denounce* what Paul was preaching and this they did with a false accusation of disorderly conduct and sedition — the time-honoured method of suppressing the truth of the Christian message, now as then. The result was the usual arrest, beating and imprisonment of the missionaries. Heathens and Jews could rest easy — the Christian genie was safely in the bottle! Or so they thought.

**Crisis: what must I do to be saved?** (16:25-34)

Secured in the stocks in the inner cell, Paul and Silas were praying and praising God about midnight **'and the other prisoners were listening to them'** (16:25). The gospel may be locked *up*, but it cannot be locked *out*. To the outward view, their situation was grim — flogged and imprisoned, they perhaps faced even death on the morrow. But God was in all their thoughts and as they poured out their deepest petitions before the Lord, their sense of being in his everlasting arms evoked lively singing of his praises. They had been beaten up, but they were not beaten down!

*Convicted of need* (16:26-30)

While the praise of God resounded through the prison, **'a violent earthquake'** shook the place and **'All the prison doors flew open, and everybody's chains came loose'** (16:26). All at once, the situation was transformed. Roles were instantly reversed, for while the apostles were freed, the jailer became the prisoner of his own fears. Seeing the open doors, he assumed his charges had escaped, and suddenly gripped with terror over anticipated punishment for losing them, he **'drew his sword'** in order **'to kill himself'** (16:27). The sad irrationalism underlying suicidal impulses comes into sharp focus. To a man floundering in a flood of fear, death seems to be the only way of escape! And so it would be, were there no eternity, no God and no judgement to come. The jailer, you see, was more afraid of the effects of an earthly disaster than he was of coming before the living God! He was more afraid of those who can kill the body but cannot kill the soul, than of the Lord who can destroy both body and soul in hell (Matt. 10:28). 'To escape from the misery of the present hour, he was about to rush, unprepared and unsummoned, into the presence of his judge.'[4] He was a man without hope, because he was without God. And so he hovered over hell, unconverted and in the most desperate need of a Saviour!

God, however, had other plans for him and arrested him by a timely cry from Paul: **'Don't harm yourself! We are all here!'** (16:28). In contrast to the earlier occasion in Jerusalem, when the Lord miraculously delivered Peter from jail, the apostolic prisoners stayed put when they might have escaped. This, says John Calvin, was so that God might disclose 'the power of his hand, to set a seal upon the faith of Paul and Silas, and to make the name of Christ truly illustrious among the others'.[5]

The jailer must have known something of Paul's missionary work. He may well have heard of the new Christians. Certainly, he would be aware of the healing of the slave girl. Now, with his own ears, he had heard Paul and Silas praising God! And, wonder of wonders, they had voluntarily remained his prisoners and saved him from taking his own life! 'What kind of men are these?' he must have asked himself. 'What kind of faith is this that they proclaim? Who is this God that has followers like these?' It dawned on him that he had been spared from death. But why, he could not fathom. He was clearly awakened to his lost state, because he **'fell trembling'** before Paul and Silas and asked the most vital question any lost person can ask in this world: **'Sirs, what must I do to be saved?'** (16:29-30), i.e., 'How can I have eternal life?' He was still lost, of course. He didn't know what to do. Indeed, his question indicates that he may have thought that he could *do* something — in the sense of doing some good work — to save himself, to commend him to God. 'He had strong remorse,' observes Buchanan, 'but remorse is not repentance; he had a deep sense of fear; but fear is not faith,' and like everyone who is still to be brought to saving faith in Jesus Christ, 'he looks to some efforts or doings of his own as the means of his deliverance.'[6] He was certainly desperate. He was willing to change his ways. He would do better in future. He would clean up his life. He would listen to Paul's God. He just wanted to be told what to do.

*Called to saving faith* (16:31-32)

How amazing Paul's reply must have seemed to him! **'Believe in the Lord Jesus, and you will be saved — you and your household'** (16:31). Paul told him not to *do* any deed, but to *believe* in a person — Jesus Christ! It is important to grasp the dramatic contrast between the question and the answer. He asked for *works* to *do*: Paul told him to come in *faith* to the *Saviour Jesus*. He reached out for some attainable works-righteousness: Paul pointed him to the grace of God in Christ, received through faith. Faith, you see, is not a 'work' — it is the opposite of any self-generated good act. Why? Because saving faith is always 'the gift of God' (Eph. 2:8). Paul was saying, in the clearest possible language, that the way of salvation was not to be found through any programme of good deeds. It was rather to be found through faith in Jesus Christ and his finished work! What Paul did was simply to *proclaim Jesus Christ!* He declared the Word about Jesus, beginning with something of an echo of Jesus' own words to another enquirer, Nicodemus: 'Whoever believes in him [the Son] shall not perish but have eternal life' (John 3:16).

Paul did not stop there: he and Silas **'spoke the word of the Lord to him and to all the others in his house'** (16:32). There was nothing of the modern evangelistic sales-pitch technique, with its well-rehearsed sequence of questions, answers and proof-texts leading to a 'sinner's prayer', on uttering which the enquirers are assured they are 'receiving Jesus' and 'will go to heaven' if they die that night. It should be clear enough that such techniques in fact do exactly what Paul was so careful to avoid: that is, they give the enquirers something to 'do' (come while the organ is playing, give the right answers, pray to accept Jesus), as opposed to exercising, from the heart, repentance towards God and faith in the Lord Jesus Christ, as the Holy Spirit applies the Word and effectually draws them to the Lord.[7]

Paul proclaimed the gospel of Christ and waited for the Holy Spirit to do his secret work in the hearts of his hearers. In so doing, he emphasized two essential points. The first is that the very heart of the message is the risen Jesus Christ. He is the 'Lord Jesus' — the author of salvation, able to save all who believe because, through his death on the cross, he accomplished salvation for all who would trust in him.

*Converted to Christ* (16:33-34)

The second essential point is that true conversion is much more than words. As with Lydia, the evidences of true conversion to Christ were a transparent joy, a desire for baptism and an open-hearted love for, and hospitality towards, the Lord's servants. Too many professions of faith are accepted on the basis of no more than a bare assent to a form of words. A 'decision for Christ' is often accorded an unchallengeable validity, long after the so-called 'convert' has given little or no practical evidence of living the Christian life. If we are really saved, we are justified by faith alone — but not that faith that is alone. A saving change immediately evidences itself, not in instant doctrinal knowledge or a comprehensively perfect transformation of behaviour, but in the practical following of Jesus with a child-like devotion that shines with the Saviour's love. The conversions recorded in Scripture sometimes mention the content of the converts' words — Peter, Thomas and the woman of Samaria are good examples — but they invariably focus on the practical fruits of faith. The test of living faith is faithful living. Speaking of hospitality, Matthew Henry asks, 'What have we houses and tables for but as we have opportunity to serve God and his people with them?' On Christian joy, he adds, 'One cheerful Christian should make many.'[8] Amen!

**Aftermath: progress for the gospel** (16:35-40)

The earthquake no doubt impressed the magistrates as being somehow related to their treatment of Paul and Silas, for no sooner had daylight come than they quietly ordered the prisoners' release. Paul, however, refused to leave and insisted that the magistrates escort them from the jail personally, reminding them, by the way, that he was a Roman citizen and they, by jailing him without a trial, had broken the very law they were appointed to uphold!

Why did Paul stand on his rights in this way? And why now — rather than before landing in jail? The best answer to the latter question is probably that he just did not get a word in edgeways in all the tumult of the crowd. The magistrates certainly did not accord him his right of a defence. But why now? Would it not be best — some might even say, more gracious — just to slip away without any fuss? The answer would appear to be that Paul thought it extremely important to hold the magistrates accountable for their actions. Their public abuse of their power required some public acknowledgement and redress. The wounds inflicted by the lictor's rods still racked the frames of Paul and Silas. For the sake of future Christian witness and the order of society, it was necessary to call the civil power to responsible and righteous behaviour. They too were answerable to God. Implicit in Paul's action, then, is the doctrine he later enunciates, in which civil magistracy is defined as the God-appointed institution responsible for civil order, as 'God's servant, an agent of wrath to bring punishment on the wrongdoer.' (Rom. 13:1-5).

On a more personal level, Paul perhaps wanted these men to experience some of the fear that had been so instrumental in the conversion of the Philippian jailer. And, indeed, when they heard he was a Roman citizen, they did become alarmed. Their response, however, was quite different from that of the jailer. Far from asking how they could be saved, they rather urgently requested that Paul leave the city and get out of their lives! We are reminded that the gospel is greeted differently by people who are equally lost at the time of hearing. 'To the one,' Paul later says, 'we are the smell of death; to the other, the fragrance of life' (2 Cor. 2:16). Some never ask the vital question: 'What must I do to be saved?' They put away disquieting thoughts of death and eternity, or simply remain unconcerned — they have no fear of God before their eyes.

The gospel marches on notwithstanding the apathy and resistance of the careless and gainsaying. The Philippian jailer and his family were added to Lydia and her household and with others formed the nucleus of the church to which Paul would later write, 'I thank my God every time I remember you. In all my prayers for all of you, I always pray with joy because of your partnership in the gospel from the first day until now, being confident of this, that he who began a good work in you will carry it on to completion until the day of Christ Jesus' (Phil. 1:3-6). The 'first day' had seen the first harvest in Europe for the gospel. Nearly two thousand years later, while we still await the coming of the 'day of Christ Jesus', the gospel calls people everywhere to ask the vital question, 'What must I do to be saved?' and offers the same answer: 'Believe in the Lord Jesus, and you will be saved.'

# 22.
# The world turned upside down

**Please read Acts 17:1-15 and 1 and 2 Thessalonians**
*'These that have turned the world upside down are come hither also'* (17:6, AV).

When the British Army surrendered at Yorktown, effectively ending the American War of Independence, it marched away to a tune entitled 'The world turned upside down'. It was the end of one era and the beginning of another for both Britain and the United States. The idea of 'upsetting' the world did not, however, originate in the eighteenth century. In an infinitely more profound way, the world was turned upside down in the first century A.D. as the gospel of Jesus Christ changed the hearts of men and women, transformed their lives and upset the very social fabric of the times. The advent of Jesus, his death and resurrection and the inauguration of the New Testament church in the outpouring of the Holy Spirit, heralded an irreversible change for the world and for human destiny. The impact of the gospel has meant that the world could never be the same again!

The assertion that the apostolic church had turned the world upside down came, of course, not from the friends of the church, but from her enemies. This was a complaint, not a commendation! To them, it was a bad thing, something to be resisted and if possible suppressed. But their analysis was correct. Hate it they might, but it remained a glorious truth. And so, just as it was unbelievers who gave to history the name by which the followers of Jesus have ever since been known — 'Christians' (11:26) — so also did detractors of the gospel accurately describe and predict the impact of the then fledgling Christian faith upon the course of human history: they 'turned the world upside down' (17:6, AV). How this happened is beautifully illustrated by the effects of Paul's ministry in Thessalonica and Berea. From this we may draw the lessons for the effective ongoing mission of the church in our own day. First, we are told *how* the Lord will turn the world upside down (17:1-3) and, second, we are shown *what* happens when the Lord turns people's lives upside down (17:4-15).

## The gospel: how God is turning the world upside down (17:1-3)

The gospel would never have been preached anywhere, if the followers of Jesus had worried about the consequences. To preach Christ was to invite a lot more than a sideways glance or a chuckle in the crowd. Paul was beaten from pillar to post on his missionary journeys. His wounds were still smarting on his back when he had to face potentially hostile hearers all over again. Paul certainly asked himself why he put himself through the mill like this again and again: 'And as for us, why do we endanger ourselves every hour? I die every day — I mean that, brothers.' He also had an answer. He was discussing the resurrection of the body with the Corinthians, some of whom evidently denied this doctrine. 'If I fought wild beasts in Ephesus for merely human reasons, what have I gained? If the dead are not raised, "Let us eat and drink, for tomorrow we die"' (1 Cor. 15:30-32). There is a glory that remains to be revealed in us, Paul says, and he considered that his present suffering was 'not worth comparing' with that heavenly reward (Rom. 8:18). 'For to me', he wrote, 'to live is Christ and to die is gain' (Phil. 1:21). Proclaiming Christ to a sin-sick world cannot but engender some opposition. The 'present sufferings', therefore, just come with the territory. God's servants look beyond the horizon of these difficulties and see both the glory of God in the salvation of sinners here and now and the glory yet to be revealed hereafter.

*Holy boldness* (17:1; 1 Thess. 2:2)

In his earliest inspired epistles, Paul wrote to the church in Thessalonica which had grown from his ministry on the second missionary journey. He recalled their beginnings: 'You know, brothers, that our visit to you was not a failure. We had previously suffered and been insulted in Philippi, as you know, but with the help of our God we dared to tell you his gospel in spite of strong opposition' (1 Thess. 2:1-2). Ejected from Philippi, Paul made a beeline — of 100 miles! — for the next major city and, once there, went straight to the Jewish synagogue (17:1). What this tells us is that before any of us speaks a single word for Jesus Christ, we will need to be *courageous* in our innermost being, as was the apostle Paul. This is not the same as the absence of fear in the anticipation of the kind of troubles the apostles faced. But it does mean going ahead anyway! Calvin speaks of Paul as having that 'unconquerable mental courage and indefatigable endurance of the cross' which showed that 'he was equipped with the heavenly power of the Spirit'.[1]

Now, of course, not everyone is called to be an evangelist and Paul was gifted by God according to the requirements of his calling. Nevertheless, all Christians need the enabling power of the Holy Spirit for whatever challenges they may face in their own Christian life and witness. Boldness is part of the warp and woof of all Christian witness (Ps. 27:14; 31:24; Prov. 28:1; Acts 13:46; 2 Cor. 10:1-2). Thomas Manton defines Christian courage in terms of a willingness to suffer great things out of 'faith and submission to God's will'. This requires, he says, four things: '(1) A heart weaned from the world (Matt. 6:24)... (2) A heart entirely devoted to God (Luke 14: 26). (3) A heart purged from sin, or else our zeal is not uniform, besides that our lusts will weaken our courage... (4) A heart that lieth under a deep sense of eternity, and things to come (1 John 5:4), "This is the victory we have over the world, even our faith."' And what his means in practice, says Manton, is this: 'Not any looking backward, but forward.'[2] Paul kept his eyes on the goal — and so must we, wherever the Lord has placed us.

*Reasoning from the Scriptures* (17:2)

As usual Paul went to the synagogue. There he **'reasoned with them from the Scriptures'** on three successive Sabbaths. His *method*, in other words, was to appeal to the authority of Scripture from the start. 'In the teaching of the faith,' says Calvin, 'the authority of God alone ought to be sovereign, and we ought to be dependent upon it.'[3] Paul always went to the heart of the matter. These Jews knew the Scriptures and were looking for the Messiah. Paul therefore went straight to the Word of God. In Athens, even with the heathen philosophers, the apostle continued to 'stick to his text', for although he later discussed with them some quotations from their own writers, he began by 'preaching the good news about Jesus and the resurrection' (17:18). The preaching of Paul always went straight to the doctrinal heart of the gospel, without apology to those who had no prior knowledge of the biblical data. Today, we face a society that is increasingly biblically illiterate. The temptation is to soft-pedal the biblical content of the message, on the ground that people will be put off, or at least confused, by material with which they are unfamiliar. The apostle's methodology is, however, conclusive for our own approach. It is *the Word of God* that is sharper than any two-edged sword in opening up the hearts of the lost and ignorant — it is the Word which 'is able to save your souls' (James 1:21, AV). No such promise is attached to story-telling, moralizing or reasoning, which is in abstraction from the explicit content of the Word of God. Our reasoning must be from the Scriptures!

*Proclaiming Jesus Christ* (17:3)

Paul's discourse would have been similar to his sermon in Pisidian Antioch, of which Luke gives a full outline in Acts 13:17-41. Here Luke only mentions the most basic points.

First, he proves from Scripture (the Old Testament) the doctrine that **'The Christ** [i.e., the promised Messiah, at this point unidentified] **had to suffer and rise from the dead.'** Luke does not list the passages Paul cited and expounded, but they would probably have included such texts as Genesis 3:15; Psalms 2; 16:9-11; 22; Isaiah 52:14-15; 53:9-12; Daniel 7:13-14; 9:24-26; and an exposition of the meaning of the Old Testament ceremonies along the lines of Hebrews 9:11-28 and 11:17-19. 'Methinks,' writes Charles Simeon, 'he would dwell with delight on these unanswerable topics, and strive with all his might to fix conviction on their minds.'[4]

Secondly, he identified 'the Christ' of the Old Testament with Jesus: **'This Jesus I am proclaiming to you is the Christ.'** He would have shown how all the prophecies and fore-shadowings of Messiah in Scripture were perfectly fulfilled in Jesus of Nazareth, of whose resurrection he was himself a witness. He would have testified to his own conversion to Christ and spoken of the great events of Pentecost and the work of the Holy Spirit through the ministry of the apostles and the church. Everything he said would have proclaimed Jesus as the Saviour of sinners. The gospel *is* Jesus and his death, burial and resurrection. Preaching the gospel is proclaiming Jesus as 'the Christ'. It is not substituting story-telling for biblical exposition, or using some (otherwise unexplained) Scripture text as a peg on which to hang a string of illustrations. Still less is it moralizing on social questions or speculating about 'prophecy' from television news of events in the Middle East. These are not the means God has appointed by which his ministers will come to 'know nothing ... except Jesus Christ and him crucified' among their people (1 Cor. 2:2). If lost people are to be converted, and the converted made holy, they will need to hear constantly of Christ and his claims upon every area of their lives. This remains the task of his church today.

## **Changed lives: what happens when the gospel is preached** (17:4-13)

The gospel came to the Thessalonians 'not simply with words, but also with power, with the Holy Spirit and with deep conviction' (1 Thess. 1:5). The result was that people were decisively affected by the message. To some it was a 'fragrance of life', to others the 'smell of death' (2 Cor. 2:16). You cannot get away from it — people always react to the gospel message, one way or the other! And so it was in Thessalonica and Berea.

### *Opposition in Thessalonica* (17:4-9)

In only three weeks, people were converted to Christ in considerable numbers: **'some of the Jews ... a large number of God-fearing Greeks and not a few prominent women'** (17:4). Although we know that Paul also preached to the pagan Greeks and many of them 'turned from idols to serve the living and true God' (1 Thess. 1:9), the initial success of the gospel was achieved in the context of the synagogue, in which God was worshipped and the Scriptures were read and explained, as they had been since the days of Nehemiah (Neh. 8:8). The gospel had, as it were, 'a toe in the door' in the synagogue, because that was the one place where the light of God's

Word shone, not only in the reading of the Scriptures but in the hearts of true Old Testament believers. Indeed, these were the covenant people of God and the very people who could be expected to rejoice in the good news of Jesus Messiah.

But here was the rub. When Jesus was proclaimed as the promised Messiah (Christ), only **'some'** of the Jews believed. On the other hand, **'a large number'** of Gentiles, including prominent women, embraced the gospel. There was widespread opposition among the Jews, and they were further disturbed by Paul's 'stealing' so many of their Greek proselyte 'sheep'! But instead of reflecting on the possibility that God was telling them something they really needed to hear, they closed ranks in opposition to the word, work and servants of God and fomented a riot against them. With an unscrupulous disregard for their own vaunted principles, they hauled **'Jason and some other brothers before the city officials'** (they could not find Paul) on trumped-up charges of political subversion. The politarchs, to their credit, quieted the situation by releasing the Christians on bail (17:6).

The charge of political subversion was false, as it always is when the gospel is faithfully proclaimed. The gospel is very relevant to the conduct of politics and the formulation of policy, of course, because the spiritual lordship of Jesus Christ has very practical, down-to-earth ethical and moral implications for civil government and social relations. The gospel is, nevertheless, not a political credo *as such*, Jesus is not a candidate for political office and the church is not a political party. Nowhere did the apostles say, 'Vote for Jesus: don't vote for Caesar!' The Lord himself made this quite clear on the occasion when the 'Pharisees and the Herodians' attempted to trap him into a political entanglement: 'Give to Caesar what is Cæsar's and to God what is God's' (Mark 12:17). Church and state are distinct. The church is not a political entity, but her message is as prophetic for the behaviour of the body politic as it is for that of families and individuals. We have already noted that the Jewish establishment correctly discerned where the gospel was going: the followers of Jesus were turning the world **'upside down'**! (17:6, AV). These Jews knew that this was an essentially spiritual movement. They felt it, rightly, as a profound threat to their status quo Judaism. They also realized that the apostle's kind of commitment to the comprehensive lordship of Christ was bound to transform the whole Roman world if enough people could be persuaded of its truth. Their instincts were accurate in that way which only those who see living faith in Christ as the antithesis of all they hold so dear correctly perceive the radical claims of the gospel.

The challenge for modern Christians, then, is to grasp the apostolic vision for transforming the world and not to be put off by the opposition. The world is downside up! It will stay that way, until the power of the gospel of Christ turns it upside down (i.e. right-side up)! Yet many Christians think of their faith as a private, special-interest activity, one option among many in a pluralist spectrum of varied religions, beliefs and opinions. They want to be left alone and aim to trouble no one. They are embarrassed by the clear clash of Christian principles with public policy on issues like abortion, labour re-lations and capital punishment. They prefer not to think about what the Bible says on a vast range of practical principles as these apply to their own daily lives, far less the order of society and the integrity of civil government. Nevertheless, it is clear that the gospel is *meant* to transform the world. Christ is *declared* the Lord not only of individuals and the church, of inward piety and the corporate worship of God's people. He is Lord of the nations themselves! And they must 'kiss the Son,' or they will perish in his wrath! (Ps. 2:12).

### *Blessing in Berea* (17:10-13)

Jesus had told his disciples, 'When you are persecuted in one place, flee to another' (Matt. 10:23). The Thessalonian believers took this advice and sent **'Paul and Silas away to Berea'**, sixty miles towards the south. Their reception in that place still shines brightly in the annals of the gospel. **'Many'**, not just 'some', of the Jews believed and we have the impression that the synagogue became the church almost overnight. If that was indeed the case, it is the only instance in the New Testament of a fellowship of Old Testament believers doing what their Lord and their doctrine required them to do all along, namely, to receive Jesus as the promised Messiah and become New Testament believers.

The reason for the unique success for the gospel in Berea was that the people there were **'of more noble character than the Thessalonians'** (17:11). They were *real* Old Testament believers. They believed the substance, not just the outward form. Because of this, they reacted to Paul's preaching in two ways. They first **'received the message with great eagerness'**. Their heart-response to Scripture was one of accepting and believing it. They were prepared to be led wherever the Word of God led them. They were excited about hearing from the Lord, about learning more of his will and putting it into practice in their lives. 'There is a readiness in holy souls,' says Thomas Manton, 'to believe sooner and easier than others.'[5] As a result, they **'examined the Scriptures every day to see if what Paul said was true'**. They regarded the Scriptures as the authoritative test of truth (1 Thess. 5:21; 2 Tim. 3:16). Man's words were to be measured by God's words (Isa. 8:20). It is a mark of the work of the Holy Spirit when people search the Scriptures to be persuaded of the truth.

When God is at work, the powers of darkness are never far away. On hearing of Paul's preaching in Berea, the Thessalonian Jews came down and repeated their earlier performance, **'agitating the crowds and stirring them up'** (17:13). Some commentators, noting that no further mention is made of any Berean church in the New Testament, speculate that the work fizzled out. 'A strong church grew in Thessalonica in adversity, whereas none was born in Berea,' says one, suggesting that there was too much 'ease and lack of conflict' for it to be a great work of the Spirit.[6] It must be said, however, that this interpretation flies in the face of the positive evidence of a work of God's grace among the Bereans. In any case, trouble soon arose to banish any 'ease and lack of conflict' and the work evidently went forward, supervised by Silas and Timothy. The absence of any later references to the church in Berea is not an argument for anything, except perhaps that this was one place, no doubt among many, where the church thrived quietly, unheralded and unsung.

It ought to be said, for the comfort of God's people, that while it is true that it is not a good sign when all men speak well of us, neither is persecution a necessary mark of godliness. The Bible tells us to pray for a 'quiet life' (1 Thess. 4:11; 1 Tim. 2:2). And if we actually enjoy such a life — call it 'ease and lack of conflict' if you like — ought we not to regard it as an answer to our prayers? In any case, there is enough conflict and anguish in the normal 'quiet life' of Christians everywhere to be the occasion of the refining work of the Holy Spirit, without adding the riotings and intimidations of the Thessalonian mob! If you love the Lord, serve him devotedly and your life can still be called 'quiet', then praise the Lord for it and do not think yourself deficient because you have not been ridiculed or beaten in the streets!

*Doors open as others close* (17:14-15)

The apostle Paul moved on to Athens. Even in this fact lies a vital truth: persecution has promoted more than it has prevented the spread of the gospel. The door closed in Berea to open in Athens; it would close in Athens to open in Corinth; and so on until, one day, no door will be left unopened and the whole work of salvation will be completed. It is true, of course, that the gospel spreads by less distressing means: by migration and by missions. It remains a fact that the extension of God's kingdom, as witnessed by the history of churches around the world, was not the result of human planning, but the amazing providences of God as he opened and closed doors and sent his people out in the power of the risen Christ.

> Oh, fill us with thy Spirit,
> Like morning dew shed down,
> And with our praises loyal
> King Jesus we shall crown.

(Clement of Alexandria, *c.* A. D. 170-220).

# 23.
# Proclaiming the unknown God

**Please read Acts 17:16-34**

*'Now what you worship as something unknown I am going to proclaim to you'* (17:23).

The campus of the University of Pittsburgh, Pennsylvania, is dominated by a vast multi-storey pile that looks strangely reminiscent of a neo-Gothic cathedral. This building, known as 'The Cathedral of Learning', is not a church, but a gigantic monument to human learning, incorporating facilities necessary to a great university. But it is indeed a parody of a church building: a grove of humanist Academe impudently pointing to heaven and posing as a vehicle of the divine revelation it has effectively supplanted. And only a few yards away, a real church building, Heinz Chapel, crouches tiny and impotent, in mute confirmation of the triumph of secularism in the modern university. Jerusalem cowers in the shadow of Athens. Revealed truth yields to the wisdom of the world. The God of the Bible lies prostrate at the feet of autonomous man.

Ancient Athens was the world centre of art, science and philosophy. Here, says J. C. Ryle, lived 'the most learned, civilized, philosophical, highly educated, artistic, intellectual population on the face of the globe'. Here was the very best of the wisdom of the world. The impact of the gospel on this place cannot but be instructive for modern Christians as they face the neo-paganism increasingly prominent in Western intellectual life today. The coming to Athens of Jerusalem — in the person of the apostle Paul — was bound to result in a tremendous clash between the accumulated wisdom of godless civilization and the gospel of Jesus Christ, the living Word of the living God.

**The problem: a city full of idols** (17:16-21)

Luke's account highlights three characteristics of the great heathen metropolis.

First and most visible was its *idolatry*. The city was **'full of idols'** (17:16). Temples abounded. The Acropolis was dominated by a forty-foot-high statue of Minerva. 'The Athenians', said Pausanius, 'surpassed all states in the attention which they paid to the worship of the gods.'[1] They tried to cover all the angles. And perhaps the most astounding example of this was their monument to hopeful agnosticism inscribed, **'To an unknown God'**! (17:23).

A second characteristic was its *learning*. Paul was questioned by **'a group of Epicurean and Stoic philosophers'** who, Luke records, mostly **'spent their time doing nothing but talking about and listening to the latest ideas'** (17:18-21). Anyone with experience of academics and ecclesiastics today will recognize this scene! There is a kind of learning which is both idle and an idol: a plaything of the mind, yet also its master. Ideas, treated like hallucinogenic drugs, can provide thrilling trips to deadly destinations. The Athenians were always learning, but never coming to a knowledge of the truth. Paul Johnson's memorable epitaph for modern intellectualism applies equally well to ancient Athens: 'The worst of all despotisms is the heartless tyranny of ideas.'[2] They were prisoners of their own spiritual blindness.

The third characteristic was their confident *contempt for the gospel message* which Paul proclaimed. They called Paul a **'babbler'** — literally 'a seed-picker' (17:18). Just as a bird will pick up a seed here and drop it there, without knowing what it is doing, so Paul the 'seed-picker' was being characterized as a man who picks up ideas here and there and talks about them to all and sundry, without really understanding what he is talking about! Later, having heard an exposition of the gospel, many **'sneered'**, although, to be fair, some expressed a willingness to hear him again (17:32). For the former, the courtesies extended to purveyors of speculative philosophies were supplanted by abuse for the messenger of God's truth! No one is as intolerant as a 'liberal' when he is confronted by the Word of God. 'Although they claimed to be wise, they became fools and exchanged the glory of the immortal God for images made to look like mortal man and birds and animals and reptiles' (Rom. 1:22-23).

Small wonder, then, that Paul was **'greatly distressed'** by Athens. Here was the best of human wisdom and accomplishment, and it all added up to the desperate truth that 'the world through its wisdom' did not know God (1 Cor. 1:21). Athens was a glittering morgue, in which the cadavers of worldly wisdom vied with one another in the beauty contest of the spiritually dead. This moved Paul with compassion. Clever lost people are arguably the last to see their folly and the least willing to heed the gospel. Like the rich, they have learned to despise so many people as their inferiors that they are all but impervious to the voice that tells them of their own helplessness and need of a Saviour. But this is exactly what the world of thought needs to hear — and embrace — most urgently. Athens demonstrates that intellectualism without Christ is really an anti-intellectualism, because its entire tendency is to deny God's reality and the absolutes of his Word. Our world is as full of its own idols as was ancient Athens, and the remedy is still Jesus Christ and him only.

### **The solution: a call for repentance** (17:22-31)

In the face of the finest pagan minds of his time, Paul was determined to declare the Word of God. He was taken before the court of the Areopagus (literally, 'Mars Hill' after the place where it met), an ancient Athenian institution responsible for settling religious and philosophical matters in the city. He then **'stood up in the meeting'** and delivered an address which stands for ever as a model for the evangelism of the unbelieving academics of the world.

It is worth pointing out that this was on *their* home ground, in *their* meeting and in *their* mode of discussion. New Testament evangelism followed people into their world with an unpretentious naturalness and an unhurried urgency. It did not depend, as is too often the case today, on drawing the unconverted into Christian 'mission services', to be bombarded by emotional singing and appeals for commitment to Christ. We certainly should invite our friends to church. Evangelism happens whenever and wherever the gospel is preached. But if all our evangelism is locked up in church services, we certainly cannot be said to be going into all the world to teach and disciple the nations, as Christ commanded and the apostles exemplified![3] Paul, then, evangelized the philosophers where he found them. Like his Lord, he went among lost people, not only in the synagogues, but in the streets and market-places of his world. And so should we.

The apostle's address unfolded in five distinct steps: he perceived their need, picked a starting-point, pointed them to their problem, pricked their consciences and proclaimed the gospel of Jesus Christ. And in the process, he has given us a most elegant example of apostolic evangelistic methodology, for us to digest and to apply in our own witness for Jesus Christ.

*Perceiving the need* (17:22-23)

Paul first identified the Athenians' spiritual situation. He made a careful assessment and, once clear in his own mind as to where they stood, he put his finger on their particular need as he discerned it. In the process, he picked up something peculiar to the Athenians which gave him an entrance into the wider issues of their false religion.

He opened by noting how **'religious'** they were (17:22). This term was as vague then as it is today.[4] It simply meant that there was evidence they had 'religion' of a kind. They had plenty of it, for there were **'objects of worship'** all over the place. Paul saw that the shortest way of getting the gospel to these folks was to begin with *their* religion. Here is a principle of universal application: find people's 'religion' and go for it! Today, the 'objects of worship' are more secular, but they are 'religious' all the same. Many people today worship secular idols—their sport, their hobby, their pleasures, their possessions. Others are into New Age pantheism and all sorts of cultism, spiritualism and just plain superstition. All of these are suitable targets for Christian personal evangelism. Whatever people love most is their 'religion'. It is this we must identify. It is this which our strategy for personal witness must address. Only then will we be able to present the gospel to them with intelligence, sensitivity and, with the blessing of God, effectiveness.

One of their objects of worship caught Paul's eye: an altar inscribed **'to an unknown God'** (17:23). There appear to have been a number of similar altars in Athens, some to unknown *gods*.[5] It appears that the Athenians sought to cover their ignorance of gods not known to exist, on the assumption that if they did turn out to exist, they could claim to have made an effort to reverence them. Paul saw this attitude as both the bench-mark of their need and his opportunity to proclaim the gospel. **'What you worship as something unknown,'** he declared, **'I am going to proclaim to you.'** It was not that Paul thought they *really* worshipped the God of whom they had no knowledge. He simply meant to say that whatever they thought they were doing, he would point them to the real thing — to the real worship of the real God! Paul looked for the most empty spots in the lives of lost people: that is, the places where *they* revealed, whether they knew it or not, their own uneasiness and vulnerability. People's needs do show. They cannot hide them. But if we do not look for them, we shall miss the mark. If we merely trot out our canned gospel message or moral outrage, without identifying the sinner's specific need, we shall only be talking to ourselves. Paul never preached the gospel in the abstract. He scratched where people itched.

*Picking a starting-point* (17:24-25)

Integral to the process is picking the right starting-point. The Athenians were concerned about gods, 'known' or 'unknown'. So Paul seized the moment! He spoke of the **'God who made the world and everything in it'** and unabashedly told them, in utter contradiction of their heathen notions, who this (to them) unknown God was, what he was really like and how he was to be worshipped! No 'beating about the bush' with this apostle! He knew how to get to the point, speak to the point and keep to the point! He began with God!

Why did he start here? Why did he not get straight into the gospel of Jesus Christ? The answer is, surely, that he had to lay the correct basis for understanding the gospel. So, with the Jews in Antioch, he spoke of God's dealings with their 'fathers' (13:16-23) and led them to Jesus as the culmination of the history of redemption — a redemption of which they were well aware from their knowledge of the Scriptures. The Athenians, by contrast, had minds full of polytheistic clutter and not the slightest conception of their lostness before the one true God. They first needed to know to whom they were really accountable. And so, Paul leads them — very gently, you will notice — to a right view of God. He is the Creator, who made all things; he is the **'Lord of heaven and earth'**, who is self-existent and self-sufficient and neither lives in man-made temples nor needs what people can do for him. He is not a superman in the sky. He *is* 'spirit' and those who worship him must worship him 'in spirit and in truth' (John 4:24). Hence George Gillespie's characterization of God in a prayer, later incorporated into the *Shorter Catechism*: 'God is a Spirit, infinite, eternal and unchangeable, in his being, wisdom, power, holiness, justice, goodness, and truth' (Question 4). Without such a view of God, the Athenians could only have seen Jesus as just another candidate for their already teeming pantheon. They needed to know the one and only God and Jesus Christ, his Son.

Choosing the starting-point in our witness for Christ is a matter of discerning the need of the particular people to whom we are speaking. This involves at least four steps:

1. Paul first *found out* where his target audience stood on basic issues. He kept his eyes and ears open. He first observed and listened.
2. His second step was to choose *the core issue*. He weighed up their positions in relation to biblical doctrinal priorities.
3. He then went on to *tackle them* at that most basic point.
4. Finally, he rapidly linked this to the gospel of *Jesus Christ*.

His approach throughout was dynamic and flexible. He was never bound to a set of memorized questions or a form of words. Paul's method was to suit the message to the person and the need. We are bond-servants to *Christ*, not the slaves of one particular *form of words* presenting Christ. Parrot evangelism is not *personal* evangelism! In proclaiming Christ, we need to feel and convey a personal interest in the one to whom we hold forth the Word of Life. True personal evangelism is 'custom-made' for its hearers.

*Pointing to the problem* (17:26-28)

From the character of God, Paul turns to the origin and purpose of man. The problem is, of course, the Athenians' ignorance of God and their lack of a reconciled fellowship with him. They dreamed that they had arisen from the soil of Attica and fancied they could worship even an unknown God! Well, said Paul, the real God brought all the nations into existence from the **'one man'** — humanity is God's creation and we are all the descendants of Adam. Furthermore, he **'determined the times set for them and the exact**

**places where they should live'** (17:26) — human history is God's providence. If people are to know the Lord, they must be gripped by an awareness of who they are and where they stand in relation to him.

Indeed, this is the very reason for our existence. God's purpose in human history is first **'that men would seek him'**. The implication is that human beings have lost the true knowledge of their Creator. In parallel with Romans 1:18-20, Paul emphasizes that there is a witness to the reality of God both in the world he made and within our own constitution as men and women made in the image of God. The Athenian concern for their 'unknown god' was evidence of that innate awareness of the existence of God (what later theologians would call the *sensus deitatis*) which is an indelible part of our creaturehood. Hence God's right to expect that people would **'indeed** [not 'haply' (AV), 'perhaps' (NIV, NASB) or, still less, 'in the hope' (RSV)] **reach out for him and find him'** (17:27).[6] The point is that no one has the slightest excuse for not seeking the Lord (Rom. 1:20).

And if we do not 'find him', it is not because he is too far away — for **'He is not far from each one of us'** (17:27). To drive this home, Paul reminded them of what their own poets had written. Epimenides the Cretan had said that **'In him** [the supreme being] **we live and move and have our being,'** while Aratus had asserted that **'We are his offspring.'**[7] Paul was not suggesting that these pagans and their Athenian kinsmen were worshipping the true God all along, but he was saying that they knew enough of the natural revelation of God to know that he is *there,* that he *made us* and is to be *sought* by us. Man knows in his innermost being that he is answerable to God. But such is his spiritual darkness — and this is a wilful, culpable and sinful disposition — that he looks everywhere but in the right direction for the solution to the problem. They actually tend to 'suppress the truth' and give themselves to the worship of 'created things rather than the Creator' (Rom. 1:18,25).

### *Pricking the conscience* (17:29)

Even if his hearers accepted intellectually the force of Paul's assertion of the reality of an unseen Creator-God, this would not in itself constitute the acceptance of God himself. I know that Moscow exists, but, never having been there, I do not know Moscow. And I never will know Moscow until I make it a matter of conscience that I actually go there. The Athenians would never know God, until and unless they became conscience-bound to come to him! Paul therefore makes a beeline for their consciences, so that they would be convicted of the sin of not only not knowing God (ignorance) but of denying him in favour of false gods (idolatry): **'Therefore since we are God's offspring, we should not think that the divine being is like gold or silver or stone — an image made by man's design and skill.'** Conviction of sin is essential to becoming a Christian. Conversion to Christ presupposes the conviction of being lost and estranged from him by reason of personal sin and rebellion against God.

*Proclaiming the gospel* (17:30-31)

Last, but never least, Paul comes to the proclamation of the gospel of Jesus Christ itself.

He first prefaces this with a striking statement about the patience and *forbearance* of God: **'In the past, God overlooked such ignorance'** (17:30). God was, and is, long-suffering. He is 'slow to anger'. For centuries, he let the Gentile nations go on their way in idolatry and sin. He did not wipe them out in his righteous wrath. This is not, of course, the same as approving of that sin. God is always of purer eyes than to behold iniquity. Sinners still died and went to hell. God nevertheless preserved the nations for that day when Christ would be revealed. He so loved the world that he gave his only begotten Son to be born of a woman, under the law, in the fulness of his chosen time. With the advent of Jesus Christ and his proclamation as Saviour of the lost, the times of 'ignorance' were over for the Athenians.

The same principle applies today, to the extent that God still holds back from mass judgement of the world's lost. He has a purpose of grace to save a people for himself from among them. On the other hand, there is implicit in Paul's words a more pointed guilt for those who hear and reject the gospel of Jesus Christ. The very brightness of the light all the more condemns the darkness. This also implies, for those who love the Lord and the lost, and desire to see people come to Christ, that a deeper urgency must attend their witness to the world. The fields are, in every generation, 'ripe for harvest' (John 4:35). We must reap, or that harvest will rot where it stands.

The appropriate response to this is *repentance*: **'Now he commands all people everywhere to repent'** (17:30). **'Now'** means 'in this present age' — from now on! This is the era of the universal preaching of the gospel of grace in Jesus Christ. The whole world is called to repent. Paul's emphasis upon repentance, without any parallel reference to faith, has led some commentators to regard this as a deficient presentation of gospel truth. This criticism, however, overlooks the richness of the New Testament doctrine of repentance. The Greek *metanoia* means an inner change of heart that is decisive for the whole personality. It means turning away from sin and unbelief, with their guilt and pollution, and turning to Christ, in faith and for his righteousness. Repentance is a distinct grace from faith, but is inseparable from it in its exercise. One cannot truly repent and not believe. One cannot truly believe and not repent.

Peter showed the intertwining of repentance and faith in his charge to the crowd at the temple gate: 'Repent ye therefore, and be converted, that your sins may be blotted out ...'(Acts 3:19, AV) and Paul records its reality in the lives of the Thessalonian believers, who 'turned to God from idols to serve the living and true God' (1 Thess. 1:9).

The preaching of repentance is essential to proclaiming Christ. Repentance itself, from the heart, is essential to a saving knowledge of Christ. The gospel is about who will be Lord in your life. Christ does not save sinners so they can go on living as they did in practice, while feeling 'saved' in their hearts because they think warm and trusting thoughts about Jesus. Faith without works is dead — that is, it is not real faith at all. Real faith gets to work. Repentance is the core of that drive to new obedience which flows from the experience of true conversion to Jesus Christ. The Athenians were not told to 'ask Jesus into their hearts', or called upon to pray a so-called 'sinner's prayer' and on that basis given a so-called 'assurance' that they were thereby right with God and saved from a lost eternity. No! Paul told them to change their ways — body and soul, heart and hand — and commit themselves in repentance to the Lord. A naked assent to truths about Jesus, or even a sincere feeling that Jesus is your Saviour, without repentance and a commitment to doing the will of the Lord, is half a conversion and may well be no conversion at all! The cost of discipleship is unconditional surrender. The modern church needs to relearn the truth that saying you are a Christian is not equivalent to being one. Faith and repentance are sides of a single coin. As we have already seen, we are certainly justified by faith alone, but not that faith which is alone.[8]

Thirdly, the *certainty of final judgement* makes this a matter of supreme urgency (17:31). To reject Jesus as Saviour and Lord is to invite a meeting with him as Judge. Jesus is **'the man he** [God] **has appointed'**, by whom the world will be judged in the last great day. There is a reckoning for every human being.

Finally, the *resurrection* of Jesus is **'proof of this to all men'** (17:31). Paul thus came full circle, for it had been his 'preaching the good news about Jesus and the resurrection' that had won him the invitation to address the Areopagus (17:18-19). The point is that the fact that *Jesus has risen* is proof that he has the authority to be both Redeemer and Judge. Had Jesus remained in the grave, there would be no reason to believe the gospel or fear his wrath. The gospel and all the claims of God would have rested in his grave for ever! 'If Christ has not been raised,' Paul would later say with utter honesty, '[our] faith is futile; [we] are still in [our] sins,' and 'If only for this life we have hope in Christ, we are to be pitied more than all men' (1 Cor. 15:17-18). Luke's record focuses on those elements of Paul's address which dramatize his assault on the Athenians' idolatry, but there can be no doubt that Paul proclaimed Christ as the crucified and risen Saviour in the fullest sense of preaching the gospel.

### **The result: a challenge to faith and action** (17:32-34)

The proclamation of the 'resurrection of the dead' — that is to say, the fact that Jesus Christ has risen and all that this implied for the response of the philosophers — brought Paul's presentation to a climax and elicited an immediate reaction. As on every occasion before or since when Christ has been preached, there were those who said, 'No' — **'some of them sneered'** — those who said, 'Maybe' — **'We want to hear you again ...'** — and those who said, 'I believe' — **'A few ... believed ... among them ... Dionysius, ... a woman named Damaris, and a number of others.'** Far from being a discouragement, this ought to energize God's people to spread the gospel as far and wide as they possibly can. Paul was serious about reaching lost people with the Christian message and it is this intense seriousness that needs to grip Christians today.

Do you really believe the world is full of idolaters of one kind or another, who are going to hell very shortly, if they do not repent and believe in the Lord Jesus Christ? Paul did, and he put his life on the line to do something about it! Lost people are all around you. They have many different idols, but these all amount to ignorance and unbelief. Some lost people go to churches and think they are right with God, but they too have never repented of sin and committed themselves to Jesus. And what of you? Have you come to Christ? Have you repented of sin? For if you have not, Paul asks you, 'Do you think that you will escape God's judgement? Or do you show contempt for the riches of his kindness, tolerance and patience, not realizing that God's kindness leads you towards repentance?' (Rom. 2:3-4).

There is nothing 'nice' about the gospel message. It is hard, it is urgently insistent and it is addressed to people who are dying while they live. But it is the only message of real love for sinners the world will ever hear. There is nothing trivial or incidental about it. The gospel is not an optional extra that makes life go better for people who like that sort of thing. It is a matter of life and death — eternal living or everlasting dying. Paul's message on Mars Hill calls us to repentance and new life and challenges us to proclaim our Saviour to others, that they too might enter into life in him.

## 24.
# Discouragement and encouragement

**Please read Acts 18:1-17**

*'Do not be afraid ... for I am with you ...'* (18:9-10).

The apostles did not have an easy time. There is no triumphalism in the New Testament, none of the glory-stories that so permeate Christian biographies and fund-raising letters today. The apostles certainly experienced triumphs, but the trials of God's people, and some of their failures, are also reported very honestly in Scripture. Their normal experience was that of hard work and hardship in the ministry of the gospel. We tend to associate the 'hardships' of the apostles with those occasions when they were beaten and imprisoned, or run out of town. Dramatic as such instances are, they did not happen everywhere and all the time. Their regular hardships were the ordinary things: the long dusty miles trudging the highways of the Roman world, the sore legs, the tiredness, the sickness, the discomforts, the indifference of happy pagans, the suspicion of proud Jews, the sheer effort of going on and being faithful followers of Jesus Christ.

After Athens and, to say the least, rather modest success, they moved on to Corinth, the great commercial centre that sat astride the isthmus of the same name. Even as he drew nearer to the city, Paul was determined to 'know nothing' while he was with the Corinthians, 'except Jesus Christ and him crucified' (1 Cor. 2:2). Coming on the heels of his brush with the Athenian intellectuals, this sounds like a reaffirmation of his resolve to keep to the plain gospel and resist the temptation to use 'wise and persuasive words' to woo the world to Christ (1 Cor. 2:4). It is as if Paul is debating with himself and is persuading himself to stick to his task against the niggling of some of his discouragements. If this is indeed the case, his ministry in Corinth provides a picture for us of the tension between the discouragement and encouragement that all of God's people feel in the normal course of their lives. Paul's Corinthian experience therefore speaks pointedly to us, even though we live in a very different world from his.

**Discouragement** (18:1-6)

The Corinth of A.D. 51 was enough to discourage anyone who had the slightest sense of decency. It was a vast, teeming, thoroughly immoral place. If Athens represented the sins of the mind and intellect, Corinth exemplified the corruptions of the flesh. Situated there was the Temple of Venus with its thousands of prostitutes. Corinth had a deservedly proverbial reputation for sexual sin.

Small wonder, then, that the apostle felt somewhat daunted by the task of evangelizing the place. Yet in his discouragement — and, not least, his triumph over it — he touches our hearts, for we feel our own weaknesses just as keenly and very easily identify with Paul's sense of the difficulty of bearing a Christian witness in an unsympathetic world. Three points in particular seem to have troubled the apostle.

*Feelings of personal inadequacy* (1 Cor. 2:1-5)

Paul was not a 'super-hero' who breezed through his life in a corona of unclouded confidence. He was indeed a man of great gifts, but these by no means immunized him from the normal human susceptibilities to tiredness, fear, doubt and discouragement. 'I came to you,' he later reminded the Corinthian Christians, 'in weakness and fear, and with much trembling' (1 Cor. 2:3). So disheartened was he on one later occasion — probably during his time in Ephesus (19:23-41) — that he 'despaired even of life' (2 Cor. 1:8). Yes! The apostle to the nations almost gave up hope! By God's grace, he persevered. But by honestly revealing that his feet, too, were made of clay, he surely helps us with our felt weaknesses. He strengthens us because he proves conclusively that his adequacy for his calling rested not on his own gifts and abilities, his native intelligence or his tough-mindedness, but on the free grace of God in Christ sustaining him day by day.

*Lack of success in the ministry* (18:1-4)

Paul had, for the most part, faced indifference in Athens. Only 'a few' believed (17:34). Corinth proved to be as difficult a proposition. The only encouragement was meeting **'Aquila ... who had recently come from Italy with his wife Priscilla'**. They were very probably believers in Christ[1] and since they were tent-makers, the apostle was able to work with them at their trade and lodge in their home. On the Sabbaths, Paul **'reasoned in the synagogue, trying to persuade Jews and Greeks,'** apparently without much success.

Nothing is more discouraging in the ministry than seeing little fruit in terms of people converted to Christ or Christians maturing in their faith. The modern epidemic of so-called 'pastoral burn-out', especially common among younger pastors in the U.S.A., is no doubt in large measure attributable to the intense disappointments of ministry among gospel-hardened people, both inside and outside the churches. Trained in theological seminaries that are short on sound doctrine and long on a triumphalist 'practical' theology, touting methods that can be expected to 'work' if correctly implemented, many young men are simply not prepared for the rigour and the pain of coping with real people and their problems. Paul did not give up preaching because a lot of people would not listen, but he knew the feeling as well as any preacher today.

*Experiences of personal rejection* (18:5-6)

It hurts to be rejected. When **'Silas and Timothy came from Macedonia'**, presumably with some financial resources, Paul **'devoted himself exclusively to preaching'**. The Jews, however, **'opposed Paul and became abusive,'** to such an extent that Paul was moved to cease ministering to the Jews and instead turn to the Gentiles. This decision was marked by the dramatic gesture of shaking the dust from his clothes, signifying separation from even the dust of their synagogue (cf. Acts 13:51; Matt. 10:14). With echoes of the prophet Ezekiel, Paul also declared himself **'clear of** [his] **responsibility'** for their relationship to God and the judgement: **'Your blood be on your own heads'** (cf. Ezek. 18:30; 33:5).

For all his boldness, Paul was touched deeply by rejection. That was why he so sympathized with Timothy, who was more easily discouraged than Paul, and reminded him that God had not given Christians 'a spirit of timidity, but a spirit of power, of love and self-discipline' (1 Tim. 4:12; 2 Tim. 1:7). Paul knew very well that the tendency of all discouragement in the Christian life is to tempt us to say, with Jeremiah, 'I will not mention [the Lord] or speak any more in his name' (Jer. 20:9). Moses, for example, felt at one point that his efforts had brought more trouble on the Israelites than anything else (Exod. 5:22-23). Even Joshua was ready to give up on one occasion (Josh. 7:7). Paul himself really believed that he was not 'equal to such a task' as spreading the gospel. Even though he could see that the Lord was making him an able minister of the new covenant, he was profoundly aware of his need of God's enabling strength every step of the way (2 Cor. 2:16; 3:6; 12:9). Those who experience the strengthening and enabling grace of God are more, not less, sensitive to their own frailties and more, not less, humbled in their daily dependence upon the Lord. 'When I am weak,' says Paul, 'then I am strong' (2 Cor. 12:10).

And when we grasp, with submissive understanding, that the Lord's promise of ultimate victory is not a guarantee of exemption from hard times, we discover God's work of grace in our hearts to be a powerful and precious stimulus to be always giving ourselves 'fully to the work of the Lord' in the assurance that 'we will reap a harvest if we do not give up' (1 Cor. 15:58; Gal. 6:9). 'If we have fightings without and fears within,' counselled Charles Simeon, 'we must go the more earnestly to God for help, and rely the more firmly on his promised aid. Instead of sinking under discouragements of any kind, we must say to every enemy that obstructs our way, "Who art thou, O great mountain? Before Zerubbabel thou shalt become a plain."'[2]

## **Encouragements** (18:7-17)

Even relatively small discouragements make us prone to think that all is gloom and doom and that there are no encouragements at all. Paul might well have been tempted to be so cast down that he could see no evidence of God's goodness to him, God's presence with him, or God's blessing through him. Our passage says otherwise about God's goodness to his people.

*God always has some encouragements for us* (18:7-8)

However difficult our experiences, if we would but open the eyes of faith, we would see the hand of God at work for our blessing in many ways.

Paul was not without *fellowship with Christian friends*. He had strong support from Aquila and Priscilla and later Silas and Timothy. Such blessing is too often taken for granted. Christian friends are too easily treated as hearers of our complaints rather than as causes of encouragement and, more, as resources provided by the Lord to counsel and strengthen us in our Christian life.

The apostle was also not without *usefulness in his ministry*. Even if the synagogue as a whole rejected the gospel, **'Titius Justus ... Crispus, the synagogue ruler, and his entire household ... and many of the Corinthians who heard him'** believed in the Lord and were baptized. Are we without fruit? Entirely? Have we *no* usefulness to Christ? Surely not! The Lord has done things through us and the fruit is in new lives! Sometimes we only hear of this years later. And only heaven will reveal fully the blessing we have been to others. The Lord never sends out his Word so that it returns empty of blessing, even if we do not see that immediately. There is an old song that goes: 'Look for the silver lining, whenever clouds appear in the sky.' God has his silver linings in all the clouds of the Christian life. The eye of faith will see his work in our lives.

*God has given us precious promises* (18:9-11)

One night, after the apostle had launched out into Gentile ministry, the Lord **'spoke to [him] in a vision'** (18:9). The Lord's words strongly suggest that Paul was less than buoyant about the way things were going. Notice five things the Lord says.

1. **'Do not be afraid'** (18:9). Fear is the fruit of forgetting who is really in control of your life and circumstances. This was the Lord saying, 'Remember your God! He is your loving heavenly Father! Remember his Son! He is your Saviour and sits at the Father's right hand, the Mediator-King over all things, on behalf of his church' (Eph. 1:22). His 'perfect love' is the antidote to our fear (1 John 4:18). Dwell on Christ's love. When fear comes, flee to Jesus. 'Do not be afraid, little flock,' says Jesus, 'for your Father has been pleased to give you the kingdom' (Luke 12:32).

2. **'Keep on speaking, do not be silent'** (18:9). Be faithful to your calling! 'Be prepared in season and out of season'(2 Tim. 4:2). Your feelings are to be irrelevant to the discharge of your calling before God. Act according to principle and truth. And if you are caught unprepared, 'Do not worry beforehand about what to say. Just say whatever is given you at the time, for it is not you speaking, but the Holy Spirit' (Mark 13:9-11).

3. **'For I am with you...'** (18:10). Fix your eyes on Christ. He has said, 'And surely I am with you always, to the very end of the age' (Matt. 28:20). The Lord is with his people, at all times — again, whether they feel it or not. His favour surrounds us 'as with a shield' (Ps. 5:12).

4. **'No one is going to attack and harm you...'** (18:10). The Lord assured Paul that on this occasion he would be kept in complete safety. This is not to be taken as a universal promise for every situation Paul or any other Christian might face. Martyrs have been suffering and dying in every generation of the present New Testament era. Paul himself was not spared martyrdom. We are reminded, however, that even the forfeiture of our lives cannot negate the ultimate reality of God's promise to keep his own from harm. 'No one', says Jesus, 'can snatch them out of my Father's hand' (John 10:29). Like the eye of a hurricane, which is an island of calm surrounded by 100 m.p.h. wind, the Christian heart that grasps experientially the promises of God knows a peace that passes all understanding, even in the maelstrom of a troubled life.

5. **'Because I have many people in this city'** (18:10). The Lord had a future for the church in Corinth. As yet unsaved people were marked out for conversion to Christ. That is to say, his power would penetrate that city in such a way as to transform the prospects that the apostle now anticipated with some dread. In any case, the Lord is the true ruler of Corinth, whatever the clamour of the masses against the gospel. Even the lost are under his sovereignty: 'The king's heart is in the hand of the Lord; he directs it like a watercourse wherever he pleases' (Prov. 21:1); 'And God placed all things under his feet and appointed him to be head over everything for the church, which is his body, the fulness of him who fills everything in every way' (Eph. 1:22).

God has spoken to us! The very fact that he has given us his Word opens the way to innumerable encouragements to faith. All the doctrines of the Word must be, and can only be, music in a believer's ear. Rehearse in your mind the teachings of Scripture. Go through the divisions of systematic theology — the doctrines of Scripture, of God, of man and sin, of Christ and salvation, of the church and sacraments, of the last things and the coming of Christ. Some will say that 'doctrine' is not practical! Shame on them! These are the meat of Christian growth, the engine of discipleship, the warp and woof of a lively faith. Recall often how God has dealt with you in the course of your life — the events, the passages of Scriptures, the breath of the Holy Spirit in prayer times, the happy influence of Christian friends, the love of Jesus Christ your Saviour — and reaffirm the truth that the Lord is near to all who call upon his name.

*God is at work in the world* (18:12-17)

The last point in the vision, namely that God is in control of people and events, is powerfully illustrated in the incident involving Gallio, who was the Roman governor of the province of Achaia in A. D. 52-53.[3] Gallio came from a famous family. His younger brother was Seneca, the Stoic philosopher and teacher of the Emperor Nero, on whose order both would one day commit suicide. Paul had probably been in Corinth for about nine months when Gallio assumed his office. The Jews evidently saw the coming of a new governor as an opportunity to get rid of Paul and nip the growing church in Corinth in the bud. They **'made a united attack on Paul'** and dragged him to court, where they charged him with **'persuading the people to worship God in ways contrary to the law'** (18:13).

The synagogue leaders undoubtedly meant to convey to Gallio that Paul was teaching *against* the law of Moses.[4] The background to this is that under Roman law there were legal and illegal religions. The old religions of conquered territories were recognized as legal for the same pragmatic political reasons that in the days of the British Empire, Catholicism in Lower Canada (Quebec) and Islam and Hinduism in India were protected by law — to keep the populace relatively happy under a foreign yoke. New religions, however, had no legal sanction, also for political reasons — they threatened the status quo! Thus, if Gallio could be convinced that Paul was preaching a *new* religion, then the apostle could be convicted of illegal activity and banned from Corinth (see also 16:20; 17:6).

Gallio saw through this stratagem immediately and, before Paul could offer a defence, he threw the plaintiffs and their case — the former quite literally — out of his court (18:14-16). He refused to sit in judgement on what was, to him, an exclusively Jewish theological problem. And so Paul came to no harm, just as the Lord had told him (18:9-10). Ironically, the Jewish leader Sosthenes received some of the 'medicine' he had earmarked for Paul, for he was set upon and beaten outside the court, probably by an anti-Jewish crowd. Gallio '**showed no concern whatever**' — not the last time the persecution of a minority was winked at for political advantage.

Whatever Gallio's personal attitude, his action as an interpreter of the Roman law was very important for the church. It granted legitimacy before the law of the empire, and was the first legal step on the road to the establishment of Christianity as the religion of Rome under the Emperor Constantine. 'The Church of Christ', wrote Alexander McLeod, 'is a kingdom not of this world, but the kingdoms of the world are bound to recognize its existence... Jehovah has raised Jesus from the grave to a throne in heaven (Eph. 1:20,21). He raised him from the dead, and set him at his own right hand in the heavenly places, far above all principality, and power, and might and dominion. The Mediator, thus exalted over the highest grades of creature authority, demands of all his subjects to bow the knee before him. He requires of the powers that are named in this world, that in their official stations they would remove *impediments* to the progress of religion, and *afford protections* to his church.'[5]

When Paul stepped out of Gallio's court, he must have been a different man from the one who had plodded his discouraged way from Athens less than a year before. His trials were not over. The world would never offer a primrose path for the gospel of Jesus Christ. But the arm that is not shortened so that it cannot save had been laid bare. The world had seen it. The lost had been found. Christ had been lifted up. His glory was in the earth! He had kept his promise, first given in his Great Commission and republished in the night vision in Corinth: 'And surely I am with you always, to the very end of the age' (Matt. 28:20; Acts 18:10). To such evidences of God's goodness, the Christian responds with the words of the psalmist:

'Yet I am always with you;
you hold me by my right hand.
You guide me with your counsel,
and afterwards you will take me into glory'
(Ps. 73:23-24).

# Part VI

# The third missionary journey

Acts 18:18 - 20:38

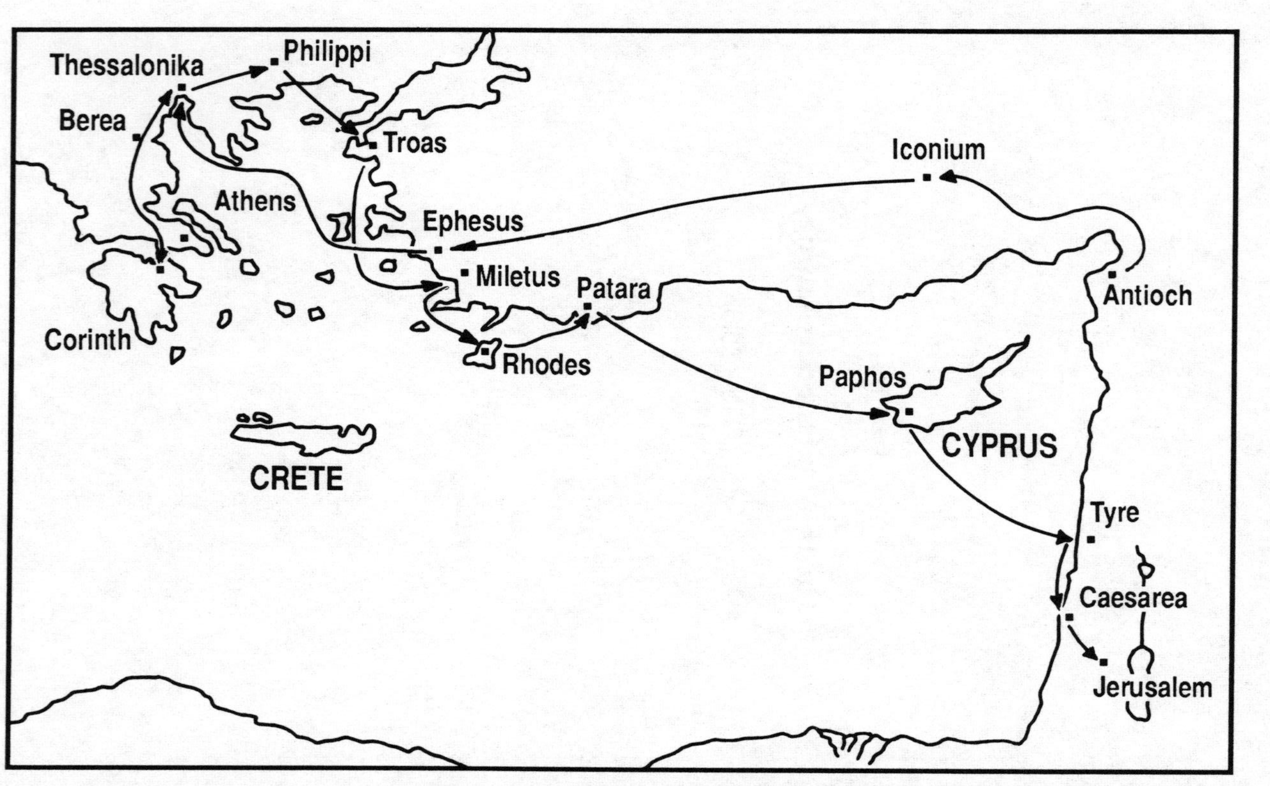
Thessalonika
Philippi
Berea
Troas
Iconium
Athens
Ephesus
Miletus
Patara
Antioch
Corinth
Rhodes
Paphos
CYPRUS
CRETE
Tyre
Caesarea
Jerusalem

# 25.
# More than a name

**Please read Acts 18:18 - 19:20**

*'Jesus I know, and I know about Paul, but who are you?'* (19:15).

Abraham Lincoln is said to have asked someone, 'If you call the tail of a dog a leg, how many legs does a dog have?' 'Five, of course,' came the answer. 'No,' chuckled Lincoln, 'it still has four legs. Calling the tail of a dog a leg doesn't make it one!' Calling an unbeliever a Christian doesn't make him one, either. One of the most searching descriptions of hypocrisy in Scripture is that given by the Lord in his letter to the church in Sardis: 'You have a name that you are alive, but you are dead' (Rev. 3:1, NKJV). To take a name is to make a claim! But that still begs the question: does it actually square with the facts? In Sardis, sadly, it did not!

If you call yourself a Christian, you are saying that you are a follower of Christ. You are saying that you want people to know that you are a Christian. You are saying that you want them to be Christians too! And so the Bible is full of challenges to Christians to live up to the *name* of the Lord, whom they profess to believe and trust. We are not to forget the name of our God (Ps. 44:20). We are to glory in his holy name (Ps. 105:3). His name is to be on the foreheads of his people (Rev. 22:4). The point is that 'the name' represents all that Christ is: the mere name is not enough, there must be the reality of knowing the person, Jesus Christ. It is not enough to be called a Christian; you must actually *be* a Christian. There is no such thing as a non-practising Christian. You need more than a name. The 'name' is just not enough! In his account of how the gospel came to Ephesus, Luke describes a number of people whose experience illumines this single theme. These are Priscilla, Aquila and Apollos (18:18-28), the disciples of John the Baptizer (19:1-7) and the sons of Sceva (19:8-20).

**Priscilla, Aquila and Apollos** (18:18-28)

Some time in A. D. 52, Paul left Corinth to return to Antioch in Syria.[1] On the way, he stopped briefly in Ephesus, promising the Christians there that he would return, the Lord willing. With his arrival in Antioch, the second missionary journey was formally concluded (18:18-21).

*'Accompanied by Priscilla and Aquila'* (18:18-23)

Paul was **'accompanied by Priscilla and Aquila'** as far as Ephesus, in which place that remarkable couple were to provide hospitality for Apollos, much as they had for Paul in Corinth. Their labours of love offer a beautiful picture of how devoted and talented Christians can quietly and indispensably support, facilitate and foster the effectiveness of the ministry of other, more publicly visible, servants of the Lord. They may well have kept Paul from despair in Corinth. They certainly provided him with a stable home base and workplace, as well as congenial fellowship. Without such 'salt of the earth' families, the finest preachers in the world would have been little better than vagrants, and lonely ones at that! Now transplanted to Ephesus, this godly pair were about to have a ministry to a future preacher of the gospel, who would, by an appropriate providence, be sent to Corinth to take up where Paul had left off.

*'An eloquent man and mighty in the Scriptures'* (18:24-26)

Apollos was **'a Jew ... a native of Alexandria'**, the great Egyptian metropolis, and a man of fine character and obvious gifts (18:24-26). He was a 'natural' for public ministry. Luke details no fewer than six leading qualities of this remarkably gifted man.

He was **'eloquent'** (18:24, AV).[2] That is to say, he had definite gifts as a communicator. He could use words well to make his points. This means far more than a good voice and a turn of phrase. Apollos had a mastery of communicative skills. This is little thought of today, but there is still no substitute for it in the gospel ministry. True, a loving pastor will do his people much good, even if he is deficient as a speaker. But the blessing will be in spite of the preaching, when it ought to be greatly facilitated by it. Preaching is to be a mighty vehicle of the Spirit's work in the church.

Secondly, he demonstrated a **'thorough knowledge of the Scriptures'** (18:24). He knew his Bible. Even before he came to a full knowledge of Christ, he was no novice in biblical knowledge. Afterwards, that grasp of Scripture furnished him almost overnight with a mature theology.

Furthermore, he had been instructed in **'the way of the Lord'** (18:25) — an expression used with reference to John the Baptizer's ministry of preparing 'the way of the Lord'. He knew that Jesus was the Christ. He believed him to be the Saviour, but did so according to the incomplete understanding of the disciples of John. We have no reason to believe that he did not love Jesus with his whole heart. But it is clear that his grasp of the fulness of New Testament revelation about Jesus was deficient. He was at this point in the twilight zone between the Old and New Testaments — something that must have been common in the apostolic period, as the Holy Spirit filled up the canon of Scripture revelation.

Fourthly, he spoke with **'great fervour'** (18:25). He did not give 'quiet talks'. He was enthusiastic and animated in his speaking. He broke some sweat in the pulpit, precisely because he was fervent in his commitment to the message he proclaimed! It is one of the scandals of the modern church, and a symptom of its powerlessness, that a *passion* for Christ and the gospel is so conspicuously absent from so many of its pulpits. Fervent preaching is never comfortable to those who sit under it, but those who treasure God's truth and value their own souls will love to be disturbed by such ministry and will bless the Lord for the privilege!

Fifthly, he was a gifted teacher — he **'taught about Jesus accurately'** (18:25). This counterbalances Luke's comment about his 'fervour'. Apollos was not a fanatic. His fervour was informed and intelligent. His passion grew from his grasp of truth and his concern was to teach that truth as clearly as he could. Luke qualifies this, however, by pointing out that he **'knew only the baptism of John'**. That is to say, he did not yet know the fulness of apostolic doctrine about Jesus. He knew Jesus from the Old Testament (i.e., prophetic) perspective, but had still to hear the retrospective revelation of God about the full implications of the death and resurrection of Jesus and the coming of the Holy Spirit to the church. He had 'the root of the matter', but stood in need of its fruit.

Finally, he was bold — he **'began to speak boldly in the synagogue'** (24:26). He spoke out for Christ. He witnessed to the

Jews about their Messiah. He was not ashamed of his message. He wanted others to embrace it for themselves.

All of this speaks of a man who was being prepared by God for effective ministry. The application ought to be clear enough. Are we looking for such abilities and accomplishments in our men today? Are we encouraging and calling such men to the ministry? Are we praying that such men would be raised up? Or are we letting men call themselves to a ministry for which they are not manifestly equipped by the Lord, because we are afraid to contradict what seems to be their inward conviction of a call to the ministry. Apollos obviously had an inward call and that is vital for anyone who wants to preach the gospel. But it is not enough and it is not conclusive on its own. Apollos' case shows us that manifest gifts — gifts obvious to all and scriptural in character — are absolutely essential to the proper outward call by the church of men to the ministry. This is what desperately needs to be recovered in our day, if we are to see a powerful ministry in our land.

*'They... explained the way of God more adequately'* (18:26)

Part of this recovery has to include the involvement of people like Priscilla and Aquila in the lives of those who would be God's messengers. Apollos had a measure of faith, learning and enthusiasm, but something was missing. Priscilla and Aquila discerned that he 'needed to know the way of God more adequately'. Lloyd Ogilvie is near the mark when he says that 'Apollos needed what all religious people desperately need — an experience of the substitutionary sacrifice of Calvary as the only basis of righteousness with the Lord, and an infusion of His Spirit as the only source of power to live life as it was meant to be lived.'[3] Whatever the state of his heart — remember, he was not an unconverted heathen but an Old Testament believer who was fully persuaded that Jesus was the Messiah — Apollos needed a full-blown, clear understanding of New Testament salvation by grace alone. It is quite likely that he was confused on the role of the law of Moses in relation to salvation and it was this that Priscilla and Aquila saw needed to be corrected. A clue as to what was missing may lie in the mention in 18:27 that, when he did go on to minister in Corinth, he was said to be a great help to those who 'by grace had believed'. True believers can easily remain enmeshed in a legalist view of righteousness and treat the gospel like a new law or see good works as instrumental in their salvation, as opposed to being the necessary fruit of that salvation.

What is particularly impressive is that Priscilla and Aquila did not hold back and wait for Paul to return. They took the responsibility and **'explained'** to Apollo what in their estimation he needed to know. They could have done what some church members today feel quite justified in doing — complain about the minister's deficiencies behind his back or raise opposition to him in a public congregational meeting. Making any effort to help the man with loving and thoughtful counsel seldom seems to enter the heads of such critics. Here is another symptom of our contemporary need of spiritual revival. We need an involved and informed membership in the churches, which will take responsibility for building God's kingdom and foster the establishment of a godly ministry.

*'He was a great help...'* (18:27-28)

The fruit was not long in following. Apollos was able to go on to Corinth with the blessing of the emerging church in Ephesus. Here, too, we see some basic practical aspects of genuine gospel ministry, particularly from the perspective of the church itself. There are three points we may note.

The first is the *recognition of enthusiasm* in Apollos to preach the gospel. He **'wanted'** to go to Achaia. Remembering Paul's experience there, this amounts to a courageous readiness to march, so to speak, towards the sound of the guns. Apollos was not looking for a sinecure, or even a 'career'. He was committed to reach lost people for Christ. That commitment was obvious to other Christians. It was manifestly unselfish. It was proof of his love for Christ. And the principle as it applies to the church's assessment of potential ministers is just this: evidence of genuine enthusiasm for the gospel ministry is absolutely essential before any man receives the approval of the church.

The second aspect is the necessity of *unqualified support* from the church for those whom she may call and send out to minister for Christ. The emerging church in Ephesus both **'encouraged'** Apollos and wrote a letter of recommendation to the disciples in Corinth, so that they would welcome him. Apollos was not a self-appointed 'lone ranger'. He was certified by the church. He had credentials to take with him.

Finally, the *faithfulness* of Apollos' ministry was soon evident to both the church and the world. He worked hard in building up the people of God — he was **'a great help to those who by grace had believed'**. He also engaged in public debate with the Jews, **'proving from the Scriptures that Jesus was the Christ'**. The church was aware of the power and goodness of God in and through Apollos' ministry. The hand of God was on his work.

### **John's disciples** (19:1-7)

While Apollos was in Ephesus and then Corinth, Paul had begun his third missionary journey (see Map 3, p.228). He travelled overland through Galatia and Phrygia, 'strengthening the disciples' wherever he found them (18:23). Eventually he arrived in Ephesus and, while there, he came across some other **'disciples'**, twelve in number, who turned out to be followers of John the Baptizer (19:1,3,7). Like Apollos they were only acquainted with John's baptism, which, though a baptism of repentance, was less than Christian baptism. It is not clear if they were, also like him, sincere believers in Jesus as the promised Messiah. John Stott, following Michael Green, is persuaded they were not Christians at all, even though they claimed to be his 'disciples'.[4] Most commentators, however, regard them as pre-Pentecost believers in Christ — people who were truly trusting in Christ as their Saviour, but were as yet ignorant of the outpouring of the Holy Spirit.[5] The latter appears to be the more natural reading of the situation. What is clear is that their knowledge of the gospel was deficient in certain respects and owed more to Old Testament Messianism than to the full New Testament revelation of Jesus Christ.

This comes out in Paul's conversation with them. He asked them, **'Did you receive the Holy Spirit when you believed?'** (19:2). Calvin sees this as an enquiry as to their having received the special apostolic gifts of the Holy Spirit, as opposed to a simple enquiry into the validity of their professed faith in Christ.[6] Coming to Christ in faith certainly involves the workings of the Holy Spirit in the human heart. But it does not include an experience of the Holy Spirit *distinct from* the experience of believing in Jesus. True, believing in Christ only happens in and through the Holy Spirit. Faith is, experientially, in *Christ* and in him *alone* as our Saviour, and is not dependent on our precise doctrinal awareness of the Holy Spirit's operations. These disciples believed in Jesus, but were totally uninformed about the Holy Spirit's actual work in their own conversion. They did not know anything about the Holy Spirit — not even that he existed! (19:2). They therefore knew nothing of Pentecost, or of the extraordinary gifts associated with that definitive outpouring of the Spirit.

Paul immediately took up the question of their baptism: **'Then what baptism did you receive?'** To this they replied, **'John's baptism'** (19:3). Now why did Paul turn to baptism, when he discovered they had not even heard of the Holy Spirit? He did so because this indicated that they were probably John's disciples and were largely untaught about the fulfilment aspects of Jesus' ministry. Paul explained to them that John's baptism was about repentance and the promise of Christ — about believing in **'the one coming after him, that is, in Jesus'** (19:4). It was therefore less than Christian baptism, which is baptism **'into the name of the Lord Jesus'** — the baptism which, upon being instructed by the apostle, they then received (19:5).

Paul would also have told them of the Holy Spirit and the gifts of the Spirit. He then gave them, as it were, their own mini-Pentecost, in which **'The Holy Spirit came on them, and they spoke in tongues and prophesied'** (19:6). This was a republication of Pentecost marking the induction of the disciples of John into the church. It had the effect of commissioning these twelve disciples to tell all the scattered followers of John to embrace the fulfilment of the promises about Jesus of which John had preached to an earlier generation. This, then, is not to be seen as a separate 'second blessing', in which, in addition to conversion to Christ, they now came to experience the Holy Spirit. As believers in Christ, they had already been regenerated and indwelt by the Spirit, in spite of their doctrinal ignorance of his person and work. To know Christ is to have the Spirit. What happened to them on this occasion was a specific endowment of the apostolic charismata in connection with a public manifestation and re-statement of the original Pentecost. In this way, God definitively demonstrated the giving of the Holy Spirit to the church as a whole (2:1-13,38-39), the Samaritans (8:14-17), the Gentiles (10:44-48) and finally the disciples of John. Each was an 'exceptional procedure' in the unfolding of redemptive history expounding the fact of the Holy Spirit's ministry in and through the church from Pentecost to the Second Coming of Christ.[7]

We are confronted once again, in practice, with the theme that threads through our passage: having a name that we belong to Christ is not enough. We must evidence his saving power. We must know the presence of his Spirit. We must live as informed disciples, who have been led by his Spirit into the truth of the revealed Word. We must live the name that is above every name and follow Christ in all the fulness of gospel grace.

## **The sons of Sceva** (19:8-20)

Paul preached in the synagogue for some three months, and, upon his ejection from that place, continued to minister **'daily'** in **'the lecture hall of Tyrannus'**. We are reminded somewhat of the output of John Calvin, who preached every day in Geneva and filled the world with the published fruit of these labours, and of George Whitefield, who preached forty times a week at the height of the Great Awakening in colonial America, and is said to have generated 18,000 sermons in his thirty years of ministry. Paul's output as a missionary pastor-teacher condemns most modern one-sermon-a-week ministers as miserably unproductive, if not indeed plain lazy! He kept it going for two years with the happy result that **'All the Jews and Greeks who lived in the province of Asia heard the word of the Lord'** (19:8-10).

### *Extraordinary miracles* (19:11-12)

During this time, **'God did extraordinary miracles through Paul.'** So extraordinary were these — Luke uses the adjective *tychousas* to emphasize that these were not the regular kinds of apostolic miracles[8] — that people were healed of illness and of demon-possession even through contact with **'handkerchiefs and aprons'** which had touched Paul. Sceptics and charlatans alike love this passage, though for different reasons. The former can dismiss it as incredulous fantasy and with it the claims of the whole Bible, while the latter employ it to justify swindling people out of money for so-called 'prayer cloths' which will allegedly heal what ails them upon contact. We must remember that the miracles of apostolic times were attestations of the validity of the apostolic ministry, pending the completion of the canon of Scripture, and not normative components for ministry today.

*The error of the sons of Sceva* (19:13-16)

If this is not always properly understood today, it was also not grasped clearly by everyone at the time. They saw the miracles and, instead of seeing that they specifically attested Paul and his message, jumped to the wrong conclusion that they were acts which resulted from the mere invocation of the name of Jesus. Such were the seven sons of a Jewish priest named Sceva. They assumed that if Paul could say the magic words, they could also! They thought that the mere utterance of a form of words was the cause of the miracles.

The Lord promptly disabused them of this notion. When they attempted to cast out demons in Jesus' name, their powerlessness was dramatically exposed. The **'evil spirit answered them, "Jesus I know, and I know about Paul, but who are you?"'** (19:15). The demon-possessed man then proceeded to give them a thorough hiding! And what was the point? Just what we have seen throughout this study: claiming the name of Jesus is not enough! God's blessings are attached to faith. Saving grace issues in changed lives, from the inside out. The sons of Sceva missed the point and the Lord took occasion from their blunder to make it clear for all time that whatsoever is not of faith is sin. He also made it clear that the miracles were connected with Jesus and Paul — that is, were unique divinely given attestations of Christ's authorization of Paul as the apostle to the nations. This is the message that modern charismatics so sadly ignore in our day, to the disservice of those they promise to heal!

*Living the name of Jesus* (19:17-20)

Many of the people in Ephesus did get the message! They **'believed'** and **'came'** to Paul and **'openly confessed their evil deeds'.** And they acted on their convictions, for those who had been involved in **'sorcery'** destroyed the scrolls, valuable though they were, in evidence of true repentance for their former ways.

## Summing up

No one in our passage denied that it was *necessary* to call upon the name of the Lord Jesus Christ in order to be one of his. Even the sons of Sceva in their deluded way acknowledged this truth. What ought to be clear to us by now is that merely claiming the name of Jesus is not enough. Paul makes plain to us that a living profession of Jesus Christ exists in a particular context — one in which there is, firstly, a sound and growing grasp of the whole doctrine of God's Word about Jesus, the fulness of gospel teaching; secondly, a profound inward faith and personal trust and dependence on Christ as one's own Saviour and Lord, and, thirdly, an inward walk with the Holy Spirit who is, as it were, Christ in us, the hope of glory.

Apollos and the disciples of John show us how possible it is to be very sincere, even truly believing and rather orthodox in doctrine, and yet not know the fulness of Christ in the power of his resurrection. There is, in other words, tremendous room for spiritual growth in every Christian's life. What a privilege to know that our limitations can be opened to the filling of the Holy Spirit himself!

The sons of Sceva teach a darker lesson. They show how possible it is to seem to be very sincere, but in fact to be unconverted and utterly opposed to Christ! The heart is deceitful above all things and desperately wicked. Who indeed can know it? Jeremiah's warning still stands and the answer is always to come to the test of God's Word. Where true faith lives, the name of Christ will be exalted in the practical lives of those who are his. There will be open confession of sin and a turning in practical repentance from the old wicked ways. The power of the Lord will be *seen* in its transforming effects! (19:18-20). 'Rise then, to this, my brethren,' cried Charles Simeon, 'and beg of God so to assist you by his Holy Spirit, that you may come short of it in nothing, but "be lights" to all around you, and "salt" that shall keep you and all, who come in contact with you, from corruption. If ye profess to believe in Christ, and have a "hope in him", see that ye follow him in all things, and "purify yourselves, even as He is pure."'[9]

# 26.
# The best-laid schemes...

**Please read Acts 19:21 - 20:1**
*'Paul decided to go to Jerusalem...'* (19:21).

While ploughing his field in November 1785, the poet Robert Burns inadvertently unearthed the winter quarters of a mouse. Moved by the panic of the 'wee sleekit cowrin' timrous beastie', Burns penned the poem, 'To a Mouse,' in which he mused on the uncertainties of life and gave to the English language one of its most famous and pensive expressions.

But Mousie, thou art no thy lane [alone],
In proving foresight may be vain:
The best-laid schemes o' mice an' men
  Gang aft agley,
And lea'e us nought but grief an' pain,
  For promised joy.

And so it often seems! The ploughshare of the unanticipated can destroy our 'best-laid schemes' at a stroke! This is a fact of everyday life — the stark exposure of man's inability to exercise comprehensive foresight, far less sovereignty, over his own future. 'Do not boast about tomorrow,' said Solomon, 'for you do not know what a day may bring forth' (Prov. 27:1). We need to plan, we cannot live our lives at random, but the control of our tomorrows always eludes our grasp.

Our passage quietly demonstrates this reality in the life of Paul and the church in Ephesus and offers us some insight into the way we frame our personal plans and respond to the events which overtake them. In 19:21-22 we see Paul setting some goals for himself, while in 19:23 - 20:1 we have a record of things that happened to affect the apostle and the church in a significant way.

## **Man proposes — Paul makes his plans** (19:21-22)

Paul had first visited Ephesus early in A.D. 52 with Priscilla and Aquila. For once, the Jews actually requested him to *stay*, but the apostle declined, although he did promise to return, should it be the Lord's will (18:18-21). In the meantime, Priscilla and Aquila remained as a seed-family for the emerging church in Ephesus. They had opportunity to minister to the newly arrived Apollos, who soon moved to Corinth to take up the work Paul had left some months earlier (18:24-28).

Paul meanwhile returned to Ephesus after a journey of some 1,500 miles[1] and settled into a two-year ministry (18:22-23; 19:1,10). Great spiritual blessing attended his preaching. A definitive outpouring of the Holy Spirit was given to certain disciples of John the Baptizer (19:1-7). 'Extraordinary' miracles attested the apostle's ministry and, as a direct result of the humbling of the sons of Sceva by a demoniac, many believed and left their former lives as magicians. 'In this way,' Luke records, 'the word of the Lord spread widely and grew in power' (19:8-20). Lest we think that this was all plain sailing, we should note that Paul told the Corinthians that it was in Ephesus that he 'fought with wild beasts' and suffered such 'hardships' that he 'despaired even of life' (1 Cor. 15:32; 2 Cor. 1:8-9).

It was at this point, his ministry in its third year and clearly bearing tremendous fruit, that Paul made some plans for his future work. He **'decided'** to go to Jerusalem *via* Macedonia and Achaia and eventually on to Rome (19:21). The literal reading of the text is, 'purposed Paul in his spirit...' (Gk, *etheto ho Paulos en to pneumati).* It is not clear whether this should be rendered 'in *his* spirit' or 'in *the Spirit*' There is an unresolved ambiguity here, which is very probably deliberately designed to emphasize that this was not a decision made by the direct revelation of God to Paul — compare Acts 20:22, where he is later *compelled* by the Spirit to go to Jerusalem — but one resulting from the normal interplay of the faculty of thought and the grace of spiritual discernment. Paul was indeed led by the Holy Spirit, but it was in the application of a godly mind to his calling and circumstances.

This is the ordinary experience of Christians then and now. On the one hand, the Holy Spirit leads the Christian in his reflection, and not least his prayers, on the principles of God's Word as they bear on his real circumstances and prospects. On the other hand, we recognize that we are not given to see the future, even though the Holy Spirit leads and guides us. His work is to produce wise, discerning Christians, not seers and clairvoyants. The secret things still belong to the Most High (Deut. 29:29). The Holy Spirit's powerful influences in our lives do not eliminate the need to depend on the Lord day by day. Indeed, it is his design to deepen that dependence, so that we walk by faith and not by sight (2 Cor. 5:7). Genuine confidence in God's leading in our lives is not the same thing as a monolithic certainty that things will happen according to our personal plans and goals. It is rather a trust in the promise that the Lord will, on a dynamic ongoing basis, lead us in the way of his blessing, in spite of and even because of whatever does *not* go 'according to [our] plan'![2]

As it happens, Paul did not set off immediately for Macedonia, Achaia and Jerusalem. Instead, he despatched Timothy and Erastus, probably in connection with the collection for the famine victims in Judaea (cf. Acts 24:17; 1 Cor. 16:1; 2 Cor. 8). His plan, then, was modified as soon as it was conceived. Why? Because, as he told the Corinthians, 'a great door for effective work has opened to me, and there are many who oppose me' (1 Cor. 16:9). What is most striking is that Paul regarded opposition, just as much as success, as a valid reason for staying in Ephesus. He knew that where Satan fights hardest, the gospel must be having a greater effect, even than that which is obvious.

## **God disposes — circumstances affect the plans** (19:23 - 20:1)

Things were bound to come to a head some day. And so they did, for just as Paul was delaying his trip to Macedonia, **'There arose a great disturbance about the Way'** (19:23).[3] This is Luke's third use of the term 'the Way' in describing the church (9:2; 19:9, 23). There is some-thing quietly yet radically uncompromising about this name. It says that this Christian faith is a new way of salvation and a way of life. It also carries an implied claim to exclusivity — it is *the* way, which everyone must follow at their peril. Anyone who thought about things could see that this 'Way' spelled radical changes for society and culture, if enough people were persuaded to follow its teaching.

Pagans, ancient and modern, are not blind to the implications of the gospel for their cherished way of life. When they hear the real biblical gospel, they see clearly that it strikes at the norms and vested interests of their non-Christian, or post-Christian cultures. And eventually they rise up in defence of their unbelief. This is why, for example, the British establishment is so afraid of Christian cable television channels. Ostensibly the government aims to protect the poor undiscerning British masses from the venality of American-style 'tele-evangelists'. In fact, they are afraid of a genuine market-place of ideas in which real biblical truth will challenge both the religious and secular charlatans of the time. Establishment religion in England is 'safe' because it merely talks to itself. It challenges no one. It is dead and irrelevant — a dumb dog that has no bark (Isa. 56:10). Truly apostolic preaching, however, makes people shake in their shoes, because it suspends men and their societies over the edge of hell, shows them where they are going and calls them to repentance, faith and reformation in Jesus Christ, who is the only way to redemption!

*Demetrius' speech* (19:23-28)

Needless to say, perhaps, it was the business community of Ephesus that first discerned the threat posed by 'the Way'. **'Demetrius'** was evidently a leading member of the silversmiths' guild in Ephesus. He correctly saw that if enough people became Christians, the worship of Artemis (Diana) would suffer and the market in **'silver shrines'**, which was their bread and butter, would be adversely affected. His appeal was first directed to their economic self-interest. They made **'a good income from this business'** (19:25). This 'Way' was some day going to hit them in their pockets! But he also offered a more pious reason for outrage against the gospel. It would discredit the temple of Artemis, one of the seven wonders of the ancient world, and **'The great goddess herself ... will be robbed of her divine majesty'** (19:27). In the circumstances of the time, this was no doubt a frantic exaggeration, for the Christians were still only a small number in what was a very large city. Nevertheless, Demetrius correctly discerned that the growth of the Christian faith would be the 'writing on the wall' for the cult of Diana. As such it stands as proof, if ever it were needed, that the Christian faith is not merely a matter for the individual and his personal life, but it reforms the whole life of individuals, communities, nations and cultures. Demetrius saw it. Modern secular humanists see it. They see there is no middle ground. Christian faith produces Christian culture and Christian culture destroys the religious infrastructure of unbelieving societies and begins to reconstruct it on a biblical basis.

*Paul's companions seized by the mob* (19:29-34)

The crowd, incited by Demetrius' prophecy of doom, swept up **'Gaius and Aristarchus, Paul's travelling companions from Macedonia'**, and converged on the theatre, a 25,000-seat arena which still stands to this day. Paul wanted to go to the aid of his friends, but was dissuaded both by his disciples and some of the provincial officials. Things were getting out of hand and Paul's presence would only fuel the frenzy of the mob. Confusion was the order of the day. Most people **'did not even know why they were there'**. Even the Jews got into the act. Wanting to make sure everybody knew they did not approve of Paul, they **'pushed Alexander to the front ... to make a defence before the people'**, and, no doubt to their monotheistic mortification, succeeded only in setting off two solid hours of shouted pagan praise for **'Artemis of the Ephesians'**!

*The city clerk defuses the situation* (19:35-41)

If the Jews showed whose side they were really on, it fell to the Roman officials to retrieve the situation for a sense of justice and, not least, for the health and welfare of Paul's companions. The faithful disciples of Jesus Christ have often received more consideration from high-minded pagans than from apostate churches.[4] The **'city clerk'** was the soul of rationality and good sense, exemplifying how a pagan civil government can be a ruler, as described in Romans 13, who holds 'no terror for those who do right'. That courageous official could have been willing, like the Jews, to sacrifice the Christians to placate the angry mob and save his own skin. But, like Gallio in Corinth (18:10,14-16), he stood for law and order against them all ... and prevailed. Behind this stands, of course, the sovereign rule of Christ, the King of kings. The Lord acted through this man to deliver his people from harm.

*Paul leaves for Macedonia* (20:1)

The riot had the effect of setting Paul back on track with his former plan. The 'great door for effective work' in Ephesus had closed for him. It was time to move on, and so, like any minister who has been called to a new sphere of labour, he encouraged the people, said goodbye and set off. There is a real breath of normality here, notwithstanding the dramatic circumstances which precipitated Paul's move. Life goes on. God opens and closes doors. But he will never leave us or forsake us, wherever his paths may lead.

**God and your plans**

We may draw a number of practical conclusions from these events in the life of Paul and the Ephesian church.

First of all, *it is proper for Christians to make plans and set goals*. This is not inconsistent with a genuine trust in the sovereign will of God. Indeed, it is essential to seek the leading of God the Holy Spirit. The Word of God, prayer, circumstances, the counsel of pastors, elders and Christian brothers and sisters, and the application of a Christian mind to the realities of our life-situations constitute together the means by which the Lord is pleased to guide us. The essential thread which binds them into one blessed unity of purpose and action is the work of the Holy Spirit in the inner person of the Christian. Given the reality of God's provision for our guidance, it would be folly indeed to 'drift from one challenge to another without a clear destination'.[5] Paul had *short-term* goals — Macedonia (Thessalonika and Philippi), Achaia (Corinth) and back to Jerusalem. He also had *long-term* goals — Rome and Spain (Rom. 15:24,28). Above all, he had an *ultimate* goal — heaven itself. These constituted his sense of direction in his life and ministry.

Secondly, *we must lay our personal goals before the Lord* and reassess them in the light of his Word and his dealings with us. However persuaded we may be in our own minds as to what we want to happen, we have to acknowledge humbly that in fact we just do not know what a day will bring forth (Prov. 27:1). Furthermore, however committed we may be to our goals we must say with James, 'If it is the Lord's will, we will live and do this or that' (James 4:15). Our goal ought never to be turned into 'fixed ideas' in abstraction from the Word of God. Personal holiness requires a dynamic trust in the Lord and a healthy reticence about our own infallibility!

Thirdly, *our personal goals are not a substitute for looking to Christ.* The Lord has promised not to leave us, but to be with us always, even to the end of the age (Matt. 28:20). This is an ongoing relationship, in which we progressively change our ways to conform with his ways. We see this in the different ways in which Jesus and Paul handled their plans and goals. Jesus knew exactly where he was going at every point. He knew and executed the eternal purpose of the Father for his mediatorial work with unvarying precision. Paul, on the other hand, listened to the Holy Spirit, followed in faith and found that his plans were modified by all sorts of unforeseen (by him) circumstances.

Finally, *our goals are to be set in the context of hope and the promises of God.* Paul was able to encourage the Ephesians as he left them, because he himself was in a state of spiritual encouragement. He saw the hand of God in the worst calamities. Contrast the mournful self-pitying outlook of Robert Burns in the same poem with which we began this study. The mouse was homeless thanks to Burns' ploughshare, but the poet felt worse off than the rodent.

Still thou art blest, compared wi' me!
The present only toucheth thee:
But och! I backward cast my e'e
  On prospects drear
An' forward, tho' I cannot see
  I guess and fear!

And, do you know something? Rabbie Burns was right about himself for once! The fact is that an unconverted sinner *is* worse off than a homeless mouse! He is without God and hope in the world. Outside of living faith in Christ, he has 'no advantage over the animal' (Eccles. 3:19).

There is an answer. It is the gospel. It is in coming to Christ and being saved. Paul could say, with vibrant confidence, 'I know whom I have believed, and am convinced that he is able to guard what I have entrusted to him for that day' (2 Tim. 1:12). Our plan must be to be in Christ's redemptive plan every day and for ever, by grace through faith.

# 27.
# A living fellowship

**Please read Acts 20:1-16**

*'Don't be alarmed,' he said. 'He's alive!'* (20:10).

Autumn in the north-eastern United States is one of the greatest sights on earth. When the first frost kisses the trees, the green leaves of summer begin a gentle transformation into a riot of brilliant reds and oranges and yellows and browns. To walk in the woods is to enter a vast cathedral of colour. Of course, you have to take your time and look up if you are to enjoy it to the full. Go too fast and you will miss something of the wonder, or stub your foot upon a rock!

It is every bit as possible to walk through a passage of Scripture and miss the beauties of its teaching. Some parts of the Acts narrative are rather vulnerable to neglect just because they are sandwiched between accounts of particularly dramatic and significant events. Lest we miss the jewels that lie in quiet reaches of the Scripture, we must train ourselves, by God's grace, to pause, look up and take in the riches of all of his Word. Acts 20:1-16 is just such a passage, for the reason that it unspectacularly recounts Paul's movements around the Ægean Sea between the close of his three-year ministry in Ephesus and his powerful farewell to the Ephesian elders at Miletus while on his way back to Jerusalem.

Yet here we have cameos of church life, which together present a picture of a vibrant church. Together, they tell us what every church ought to be, if she is worth her Master's salt. Four leading characteristics emerge, all of them vital elements in the profile of a living gospel church. These are *heartfelt love* (20:1-3), *supportive fellowship* (20:4-6), *lively worship* (20:7), and the message and experience of *new life in Jesus Christ* (20:8-16).

**Heartfelt love** (20:1)

After the riot, Paul evidently concluded that departure was the better part of ministerial valour, so after **'encouraging'** the Ephesian Christians, he **'said goodbye and set out for Macedonia'**. Many a congregation has had cause to mourn the removal of a faithful pastor to another sphere of service and none more so than the fledgling fellowship in Ephesus. Who would fill Paul's shoes? What would become of them? Many thoughts and some fears coursed through their minds. But most poignant would be the simple fact of separation, possibly never to meet again on this side of eternity. 'Loving friends know not how well they love one another till they come to part, and then it appears how near they lay to one another's hearts.'[1] If this were the case — can we doubt it? — then it must have been a solemn moment, even a watershed, in the experience of everyone present.

Yet there is no hint that they were unwilling to let him go. They did not cling to him as their exclusive possession. As a matter of fact, Paul had spent more time in Ephesus than in any other place, Corinth included. They knew that Paul was the apostle, not just to the province of Asia, but to the nations of the world. It is certain he parted from them with their blessing, for the very atmosphere in the Ephesian church was fragrant with the love of Christ received and shared. What a contrast with the disharmony which too often has stained the life and progress of churches. It was, after all, professed Christians who looked down on Timothy because he was young (1 Tim. 4:12) and Christian ministers who were inclined to lord it over the people of God (1 Peter 5:3). But the Lord's way is always the way of heartfelt love for our brothers and sisters in Christ: 'Love is patient, love is kind. It does not envy, it does not boast, it is not proud. It is not rude, it is not self-seeking, it is not easily angered, it keeps no record of wrongs. Love does not delight in evil but rejoices with the truth. It always protects, always trusts, always hopes, always perseveres' (1 Cor. 13:4-7).

**Supportive fellowship** (20:2-6)

Paul ministered in Macedonia, **'speaking many words of encouragement to the people'**, but soon moved on to **'Greece, where he**

**stayed three months'**, until forced to move on by the threat of persecution (20:2-3). Thus was completed an especially productive period for his writing, for after his arrival in Macedonia, he wrote 2 Corinthians (see 2 Cor. 8:1; 9:2-4) and once in Greece — in Corinth — he penned his letter to the Romans.[2] It was also fruitful for evangelism, as witness Romans 15:19, where Paul was able to record that he had 'fully proclaimed the gospel of Christ' from 'Jerusalem all the way around to Illyricum' — that is, from modern Israel to Croatia, on the Adriatic — an achievement unparalleled in all the annals of Christian missions!

The apostle did not do this on his own. Titus was with him in Macedonia, and for part of the way back to Syria he was accompanied by a team of no fewer than seven men, who were responsible for carrying the collection of funds for the relief of the Judean churches (see 1 Cor. 16:1-4; 2 Cor. 8 - 9; Rom. 15:25-27). They left Paul in Philippi, sailed over to Troas (Troy) and waited there for him to catch up a little later. They made an interesting group. **'Sopater'** is probaby the 'Sosipater' of Romans 16:21 and one of those Bereans whom Luke records as being of 'more noble character' (17:11). **'Aristarchus'** was the one seized in the Ephesian riot, later Paul's fellow-prisoner (19:29; Col. 4:10). Of **'Secundus'** we know nothing. From Galatia came **'Gaius'** of Derbe and **'Timothy'** of Lystra, later the recipient of two New Testament letters which bear his name. From the province of Asia came **'Tychicus'**, the 'dear brother ... faithful minister and fellow-servant in the Lord' of Colossians 4:7 and Ephesians 6:21, and **'Trophimus'**, the disciple later noted as being 'sick in Miletus' (21:29; 2 Tim. 4:20).

For these men, Paul's company on the long miles to Jerusalem was truly a 'school of the prophets', in which they received 'on-the-job training' for their future ministries for Christ. That journey made the wait in Troas well worthwhile. We 'should not think it hard to wait a while for good company in a journey,' is Matthew Henry's word for us today.[3] Real gospel fellowship is much more than mere camaraderie or even a strong fellow-feeling. It is learning, growing, sharing, waiting and fighting the good fight of faith *together*, as God's people! It is membership of one another in one body (Eph. 4:25; 1 Cor. 12:12-26).

Notice also that the basic ingredients of healthy ministry and church life are here: strong leadership, good team-work and the supportive fellowship of the church, all undergirded by the manifest leading of the Holy Spirit (20:22). A 'church' of spectators is not really a church at all, for the biblical model envisages the active involvement of the whole membership and the progressive integration into the body of those who are converted to Christ through the preaching of the gospel.

## **Living worship** (20:7)

Upon Paul's arrival from Philippi, the reunited apostolic band spent a week in Troas, resting in preparation for the journey to come. Of this time, Luke records only the major events of the Lord's Day prior to their departure and so has left us not only a record of the miraculous revivification of Eutychus, but a description of public worship in New Testament times. Four principal features can be identified and, although the passage is descriptive rather than prescriptive,[4] these can properly be regarded as normative for Christian worship today.[5]

### *Meeting together*

The first principle is that Christians are to *meet together for worship* (1 Cor. 11:17,20; 14:23-26). This is not an optional extra — an added blessing, say, on top of individual devotions. It is the essential, invariable core of the spiritual life and health of the child of God. The secret place and the family altar are no less important arenas of worship, but are co-ordinate with the assemblies of the church, not alternatives to them. People who have to 'think' about 'maybe' going to church betray a seriously defective grasp of the nature of biblical worship. Those to whom the Lord is 'sun and shield' yearn for 'the courts of the Lord' with hearts that 'cry out for the living God' (Ps. 84:2,11). Where there is genuine love for the Lord and worship 'in Spirit and in truth', there cannot but be heartfelt rejoicing with those who say, 'Let us go to the house of the Lord' (Ps. 122:1). Individualism and familyism — stay-at-home religion — deny this covenantal and corporate experience which is of the very essence of biblical worship. Even private worship derives much of its meaning and power from the broader covenant context and is inseparable from the life of the people of God as a whole. We worship God in the plural. In solitary confinement, the persecuted saints of God cry out as those unnaturally deprived of the fellowship of the people of God. They may be *isolated*, but *isolationist*, never! The first impulse of new Christians is, therefore, to join the public worship of Christ's church. 'Let us not give up meeting together, as some are in the habit of doing, but let us encourage one another — and all the more as you see the Day approaching' (Heb. 10:25).

*On the first day of the week*

The Troas church met on **'the first day of the week'** — the Greek *mia sabbaton* means literally 'the first (with reference to) the (Jewish) Sabbath'. This expression is used in six other places in the New Testament in reference to what we call Sunday (Matt. 28:1; Mark 16:2; Luke 24:1; John 20:1,19; 1 Cor. 16:2). In Revelation 1:10, this is called the 'Lord's Day'. This is the Christian sabbath, the New Testament publication of the one-in-seven day of rest established at creation, inscribed in the fourth commandment of the moral law and promised in the eternal glory yet to be revealed (Gen. 2:2; Exod. 20:8-11; Heb. 4:9). The day is moved from the seventh to the first day of the week on account of the resurrection of Christ, but the sabbath principle was preserved.[6] The Lord's Day is, observes Matthew Henry, 'a sign between Christ and them, for by this it is known that they are his disciples; and it is to be observed in solemn assemblies, which are, as it were, the courts held in the name of our Lord Jesus and to his honour'.[7] Public worship is accordingly forever the centre-piece of the Christian keeping of the Lord's Day.[8]

*To celebrate the Lord's Supper*

The Troas believers assembled, Luke says, **'to break bread'**. He is referring to the celebration of the Lord's Supper. This probably included a fellowship meal, or 'love feast', which was so abused in Corinth (1 Cor. 11:20-22). Even allowing for Paul's clear disapproval of 'love feasts', this strongly suggests that the Lord's Supper was meant to be observed weekly, alongside the ministry of the Word. If this is so, the quarterly and even half-yearly observances of many churches can only be regarded as an unwarranted withholding of one of the means of grace from the Lord's people. The notion that frequent communion is somehow equivalent to the devaluation of the sacrament finds no support in apostolic teaching or practice.

*Attend to the ministry of the Word*

Paul **'spoke to the people'**. That is, he preached a sermon. And, because he was to leave the next day, he preached until midnight — 'longer than usual', says Calvin, on account of 'the eagerness and attention of his audience'.[9] As Stott points out, this conjunction of the proclamation of the Word and the administration of the sacrament has rightly been maintained in the church ever since.[10] This ought to be a corrective to the tendency of our day to replace sermons with drama, puppets, magic and so-called 'special music'. However legitimate such things may be in other Christian social contexts, they have no biblical warrant for incorporation into the worship of God, far less as substitutes for the preaching of the Word by the Lord's appointed ministers. There was no such flummery in the service in Troas and there should be none in ours today! The biblical and apostolic primacy of preaching and the sacraments in the worship of God's people is precisely what marks out true gospel churches from those of the ear-ticklers and the false prophets of our time.

What we see in the Troas worship service is that pure, precious presence of the Holy Spirit at work in true worshippers as they give themselves to the Lord in the way he has commanded that he be worshipped. It is too serious to be turned into a variety show, too joyous to be abandoned to frivolity, and too much a celebration of Christ to be made a vehicle for the expression of human 'gifts', however God-given they might be.[11] Worship 'in spirit and in truth' is nothing if it is not worship God's way. Worshippers imbued with the life in the Spirit delight to hear the Word preached because the Scriptures are 'the living oracles of God'. If we would share the apostolic experience of living worship, we must give ourselves to the means of grace which the Lord has provided for our growth and blessing.

**New life in Christ** (20:8-12)

The combination of Paul preaching 'until midnight', a crowded **'upstairs room'** — on the **'third storey'**, Luke tells us — and an atmosphere heavy with the fumes of **'many lamps'** was too much for a young lad[12] named Eutychus. Perched at a window, no doubt to get some fresh air, he sank into a **'deep sleep'**, fell out of the window and **'was picked up dead'** from the ground. The whole scene is an emblem of human frailty. Even the boy's name — Eutychus means 'good fortune' — breathes something of the vulnerability of human hopes. And so an occasion of great blessing was shattered by a dreadful tragedy.

Why did it happen? We are tempted, of course, tacitly to presume that a good God should not permit a young boy to fall out of a window while an apostle is preaching! When promising young Christians die, whether by an accident or an incurable disease, we respond in similar fashion: 'Why should God bring him this far, only to let his potential be obliterated by an untimely death?' The tendency is to push the blame onto God, as if he owed us all a trouble-free existence. It might be more to the point, for example, to ask where Eutychus' parents were at the time, or for what biblical reason Christians should imagine themselves to be exempt from the common vicissitudes of life in a fallen world. What *is* different for Christians is the promise of the grace of God as that which is sufficient for our needs (2 Cor. 12:9). And even though the Lord promises a measure of temporal prosperity and well-being, this is not the same thing as guaranteed immunity from the inherent frailties of life in a fallen, finite world. Indeed, the very power of the witness of Christians lies not so much in their *exemption from* the problems of life, as in their *persevering through* their difficulties, looking to Christ as their Saviour and Friend in both sorrows and joys. The truth remains that God *has* provided for his people's need, remembering that their calling is to live in a dying world. This world is not heaven and believers are not yet made perfect in terms of the glory which is yet to be revealed.

An even more unprofitable approach is to assume that specific calamities are to be tied to particular sins. This would see Eutychus' fall as a judgement for falling asleep during the sermon. Calvin rightly dismisses such a suggestion with indignation: 'I see no reason why certain commentators condemn the young man's sleepiness so strongly and sharply, by saying that he was punished for his lethargy with death. For what is strange about his struggling with sleep at the dead of night and finally succumbing?'[13] The simplest explanation is the best: the lad was so tired, he lost the fight to stay awake! We fall ill because we are simply susceptible to illness — sometimes, it is true, because our behaviour lays us open to it, as for instance with sexually transmitted diseases, or smoking and lung cancer. It is the way of the world. To ask endlessly, 'Why? Why? Why?' as if there has to be some answer beyond these basic realities, is not only pointless, because it is unanswerable in these terms, but unhelpful, because it tends to self-pity and delays getting to grips with the problem itself.

The proper response is to turn to the Lord *in faith* — not in self-pitying disbelief ('Why me?') or self-righteous judgementalism ('He must have done something bad'). The significance of Eutychus' death and restoration to life is, as Calvin perceptively observes, that 'The Lord wished to awaken the faith of his own people not only by the sleep, but also by the death of this young man, so that they might receive Paul's teaching more eagerly, and keep it thoroughly imprinted on their minds.'[14] God took occasion from the tragedy to demonstrate his power to give new life. The raising of Eutychus, so reminiscent of Elisha's raising of the Shunammite's son (2 Kings 4:34), attested the validity of the gospel message as proclaimed by the apostle Paul and so was a parable of that even greater life — the eternal life of which saving faith in Jesus Christ is the entrance and experience. Eutychus was raised to die another day, perhaps in old age. Sinners who are converted to Christ will never perish. The miracle of raising the lad from death speaks of the greater — yes, *greater* — work of the Holy Spirit in taking dead souls and making them new creations in Christ!

We so often turn this on its head and imagine that conversion to Christ is less a supernatural act of God than the physical miracles we read of in the Bible — as if conversion were merely a species of education, like learning the alphabet or thinking through a mathematical problem. But this is not the case! The visible miracles are emblematic of the invisible transformations effected by the Holy Spirit when men and women are saved by grace through faith in Jesus Christ!

The revived Eutychus was a sermon proclaiming God's love for his people and his determination to save sinners. No wonder, then, that the people continued to fellowship with Paul **'until daybreak'** and later went home **'greatly comforted'** (20:12). Paul, likewise, could leave for Jerusalem next morning in the assurance that the Lord was with his people in Troas and doing a great work among them (20:13-16). Christ had shown them all that 'In him was life, and that life was the light of men' (John 1:4).

The liveliness of the church in Troas rebukes the emptiness of so much church life today and, indeed, the spiritual torpor of many so-called Christians. Today, 'life' in a church is too often equated with a varied programme, contemporary music and drama and an attention to comfortable facilities. From this viewpoint, Troas was a disaster. Meeting in a house, cramped together in a poorly lit and smoky atmosphere, with a sermon lasting several hours and a fellowship meeting through the small hours — it is all wrong for today's model of a successful church in Britain or North America. The enthusiasm of the Troas believers burns brightly in the young churches of places like Korea and Singapore, but is almost extinct in the cradles of the Reformation. Here then is the challenge — to stir up a new fervour for the things of God, a renewed interest in the gospel of Jesus Christ! 'Let us', said Charles Simeon to his people in Cambridge two centuries ago, 'rather come together as that assembly [in Troas] did: I to preach and you to hear, as though we were never to meet again in this world. The subjects of the Apostle's discourse are as important to us as they were to the [early] Christians: let us beg of God to impress them more deeply on our minds, that they may be to us "a savour of life unto life", and not, as they are to too many, "a savour of death unto death".'[15] Love your brothers and sisters in Christ, give yourself enthusiastically to the supportive fellowship of God's people, join together wholeheartedly in the worship of God and walk every day in newness of life, looking to Jesus as the Author and Finisher of your faith.

# 28.
# A word to the leadership

**Please read Acts 20:17-38**

*'I commit you to God and to the word of his grace'* (20:32).

Faithful ministers of the gospel desire passionately to see their hearers commit themselves to Jesus Christ and go on to maturity in the 'faith once for all entrusted to the saints' (Jude 3). Too often many have had cause to agonize over the slow progress of their church members in personal godliness and discipleship. As a result, some have despaired of their own effectiveness as preachers, or questioned the sincerity and teachableness of the people. Sometimes they have even entertained doubts about the power of God to transform people's lives. Joy over sinners coming to faith is not infrequently clouded by sorrow, occasioned by subsequent evidence of lack of spiritual growth.

The apostle Paul no doubt knew something of these emotions. He had been 'through the mill' many times in his ministry. He knew plenty of both joy and sorrow in the Christian ministry. Nowhere do these two intertwined strands of Christian experience shine out more poignantly than on that day in A. D. 55 when Paul made his farewells to the elders of the Ephesian church. He was leaving a work which was newly established and parting from believers whom he had faithfully nurtured. He did so in the knowledge that he would probably not see them again on this side of eternity and in the anticipation that false teachers would soon arise from their own ranks. He knew that they would soon be severely tested in their Christian lives. His parting counsel accordingly expresses this great fact of true Christian experience: that it is normal for joy and sorrow to exist side by side in the emotional life of each and every believer. In sorrow we discover afresh the joy of belonging to the Lord. In joy we find the sorrow of being in a world still blighted with human sin and misery. This is a great and deep mystery. We can see the tears in Paul's eyes as he speaks to his friends for the last time. Such partings are indeed 'sweet sorrow'.

The address is very personal and speaks to the past, present and future experience of the Ephesian church. It is also unique, in that it is the only example of a sermon given to an audience entirely composed of ordained elders. It is first and foremost a word for the leadership of the church, although its message is thoroughly relevant to everyone who has ears to hear. Paul speaks to them of their past blessings (20:17-21), future trials (20:22-31) and present prospects (20:32-38) in the gospel ministry.

## Past blessings (20:17-21)

When Paul arrived in Miletus, he **'sent to Ephesus for the elders of the church'** (20:17). Since it is about thirty miles from Ephesus to the port of Miletus, it would have taken a few days for the elders to come up for the meeting. It is noteworthy that there were a good number of elders in the Ephesian church, for it establishes one of the basic principles of New Testament church government, namely, that the spiritual leadership of the church resides, according to God's appointing, in a *plurality* of elders. The church in Ephesus may have been subdivided into particular congregations, or may have been one united congregation. We do not know. What is clear is that it was regarded as organically united — a church in the singular. These elders — here called 'presbyters' and later described as 'bishops' (NIV, 'overseers'), who are to 'pastor' (NIV, 'shepherd') the flock (20:28-29) — were neither 'one-man band' ministers nor diocesan bishops. They were a college of ordained officers working together in the leadership of the congregation (or congregations, as the case may be) of the Ephesian church. In 1 Timothy 5:17, Paul later distinguishes between those elders 'whose work is preaching and teaching' (the pastors, ministers or teaching elders), and those who, with them, 'direct the affairs of the church' (the ruling elders, usually simply called 'elders').[1] The men who came to Miletus were these ordained elders, whether ministers or ruling elders, who had been set apart to lead the church in Ephesus.

Paul began by reminding them of their past experience of the ministry of the gospel. It was, of course, their experience of his ministry among them. He focuses on two points: how he lived and what he preached.

*How Paul lived* (20:18-19)

His manner of life was well known to them. They witnessed how he **'served the Lord with great humility and with tears'**. They saw how he handled being **'severely tested by the plots of the Jews'**. These answer the two main questions in anyone's life: 'What does he live for?' and 'How does he react when the pressure is on?' Paul was selflessly committed to the Lord and he proved his commitment when he stood fast against his persecutors. It was no accident that Paul mentions this first. Why? Because how we live will make or break the usefulness of what we say. Hypocritical preachers are the most despised in the world — and it must be said that they deserve to be! We are letters 'read and known by everybody' (2 Cor. 3:2). Paul lived a life of gospel holiness with humility and consistency. And that lent powerful wings to his message about Christ. His life testified to the power of the gospel. He practised first what he went on to preach! We must do no less, if we would have any integrity and credibility with people.

*What Paul preached* (20:20-21)

His work was also an open book. Paul details three basic aspects of honest, God-honouring ministry.

First, *his motive had always been to do them good.* He had not held back **'anything that would be helpful to [them]'** (20:20). The idea is that of not shrinking back from telling the truth they needed to hear for their salvation and their life of faith, even though it involved taking risks and facing certain difficulties he could otherwise do without. Preachers are often tempted to shrink back from pressing home the whole gospel to people's consciences. Plenty of so-called Christians want easy, comfortable messages, not words that challenge and shake them and require the transformation of their lives. Paul wanted to be approved of. He never relished the pain of dealing with angry hearers who objected to his plain words about the issues of life and death. Yet he knew that the whole gospel message, the tough parts and all, was necessary to their blessing, even salvation itself.

Second, *he was diligent in his work.* He taught them **'publicly and from house to house'** (20:20). One gets a sense of tremendous *output* from this. In 'the pulpit', so to speak, and in their homes, Paul worked, worked, worked with the people. He was not lazy. He produced! You see this kind of energy in the Reformers and the Puritans and the Jonathan Edwards and George Whitefields of the world. Richard Baxter of Kidderminster, an exceptional case to be sure, visited 800 families a year and exercised a ministry that amounts to nearly 40,000 pages of print! Contrast the modern preacher who told a young man that in five years of ministry to the one congregation, 'You've said all you've got to say,' and should move on! How we need a revival of apostolic ministerial diligence! Furthermore, it can still be said, with J. A. Alexander of Princeton, that 'The church has yet invented nothing to supply the place or rival the effect of church and household preaching.'[2]

Third, *he had proclaimed the whole counsel of God.* He **'declared to both Jews and Greeks that they must turn to God in repentance and have faith in our Lord Jesus'** (20:21; cf. 20:27). To summarize the scope of the apostolic preaching in terms of the twin focus on repentance and faith does not indicate a minimalist 'Christian basics' approach to the content of revealed truth. It is obvious from the biblical record of Paul's ministry that it comprehended a wide range of doctrinal subjects. The point is that, in the last analysis, the purpose of all of God's truth is to bring us to repentance and faith — that is, to new life in Christ. Every truth has an evangelistic, transforming impact, when rightly understood and properly applied.[3]

To sum up, Paul's past ministry in Ephesus was selfless, earnest, faithful and manifestly blessed by the Lord. People were converted to Christ. Lives were transformed. The gospel was really 'good news' to many people.

### **Future challenges** (20:22-31)

From the past, Paul turned to the future. One thing was clear: the future of the Ephesian church was going to be without the apostle to lead and guide them. Paul first emphasized that his going to Jerusalem was due to the leading of the Holy Spirit and that he was under no illusions as to the hardships that lay ahead for him. He was able to face all this, however, because the very meaning and purpose of his life was to **'finish the race and complete the task'** given to him by the Lord Jesus — **'the task of testifying to the gospel of God's grace'** (20:24). Here we have a wonderful echo of his earlier words to the Corinthians: 'I resolved to know nothing while I was with you except Jesus Christ and him crucified' (1 Cor. 2:2).

Now, why does Paul lay this out with such realism? He pulls no punches. He does not try to cover up the costs of being a faithful minister of Jesus Christ. Why? Surely and simply to provide an example for the Ephesian elders to follow. Paul leads from the front. He knows that the soul of true leadership is to ask nothing of one's followers that one is not prepared to do first. He leads them, like Shakespeare's Henry V, 'unto the breach' as he assaults the citadels of unbelief with the gospel of Christ. Their task — and ours — is essentially the same.

Paul, then, knew that none of his Ephesian friends would **'ever see [him] again'** (20:25). He was 'about to take his leave of them and of his country'.[4] To encourage them for the future, he then gave them parting counsel — a challenge to faithfulness that is as fresh in its application to us today as ever it was to the elders of the young church in Ephesus. The apostle offers three points with respect to their future task.

*'You have the truth!'* (20:26-27).

Once more, Paul reminds them that he has declared to them **'the whole will of God'**. The form is that of calling them to witness that he has discharged his duty as 'a watchman for the house of Israel' (Ezek. 3:17-21; 33:1-9) and is **'innocent of the blood of all men'**. His point was not merely to vindicate himself, but to impress on the elders that they, having heard the truth from the apostle, were now the bearers of the gospel flame. They had the whole counsel of God and they also bore the responsibility for teaching it faithfully, so that they too could declare their innocence of the blood of those to whom they ministered in the Lord's name. They were amply provided with the tools with which to fulfil their calling as elders!

*'You are to shepherd the flock of God!'* (20:28-30)

Elders have a challenging task. It is to pastor — that is what the Greek word for 'shepherd' *(poimeno)* means — the church, which Jesus **'bought with his own blood'**. The imagery is that of the sheep, the shepherd and their enemies, the wolves. The measure and content of pastoring is, of course, the whole counsel of God. The goal is the spiritual and eternal welfare of the Lord's people. The work is as daunting as it is necessary, for God's people are the primary target of errorists who are out to destroy their faith and subvert the work of the gospel.

First, elders must always remember that it was **'the Holy Spirit'** who made them **'overseers'** (20:28). True, they were elected, (see 14:23, where the NIV 'appointed' obscures the full import of the Greek *cheirotoneo* and 2 Corinthians 8:19 where NIV renders the same word '*chosen* by the churches'). The church is not, however, a democracy and an elder is not the elected representative of a constituency. The people are to choose those whom the Holy Spirit is raising up to serve him. The ministry of the elders flows from him. There is a *divine* mandate to serve. If this is forgotten, the eldership soon degenerates into sterile committeeism, more concerned to make the church run smoothly and keep people happy than to do the real work of the gospel. The eyes of the elders must be upon the Lord.

Second, *problems* are certain to arise. **'Savage wolves will come in among'** the Lord's people. Bad attitudes, false teaching, contentiousness, personal animosities will arise. Whatever form it takes, this is the work of the devil, who seeks to 'deceive even the elect — if that were possible' (Matt. 24:24).

Third, and most sinister, is the prediction that **'from [their] own number men will arise'** and distort the truth in order to gather a following for themselves. These are called 'men' rather than 'wolves', not because they are any less predatory, but because they begin as part of the flock. They are 'wolves in sheep's clothing'. They are Satan's fifth columnists! Churches rarely divide over straightforward doctrinal disagreements. A thirst for power and influence is more commonly the genesis of disruption (James 4:1). Distorted teaching often merely provides an excuse for divisions already in existence. The point is that elders worth their salt will have to take care to preserve the doctrinal purity of the church.

*'You must follow in my footsteps!'* (20:31)

How will this be done in practice? 'Well,' says Paul, 'do as I have done! Follow my example! See how I was constantly on guard and

**"for three years I never stopped warning each of you night and day with tears".**' There is warmth, earnestness and fervent commitment here. Paul's ministry was no 'cold and heartless exhibition of the truth'.[5] He poured himself into his work. And that is what it would take for the Ephesians to prevail in the battles that lay before them. 'Remember your leaders, who spoke the word of God to you. Consider the outcome of their way of life and imitate their faith' (Heb. 13:7).

## Present prospects (20:32-38)

Having led their thoughts back to the blessings of the past and forward to the challenges of the future, Paul then brings all these threads together in a focus upon their present prospects and brings his address to a powerfully encouraging crescendo. The truth is that they have every reason for expecting to see continued progress for the gospel. The reasons for this are writ large upon the apostle's parting benediction.

### *The God of grace* (20:32)

Paul committed the Ephesians **'to God'**. This was no mere form of pious words. The temptation is to trust men, especially great men. So the apostle pointed them away from any reliance they might wish to lay upon him and directs them to the one and only *source* of all that they need in order 'to contend for the faith that was once for all entrusted to the saints' (Jude 3). He, 'the only God our Saviour,' the same writer adds, 'who is able to keep you from falling and to present you before his glorious presence ... with great joy' (Jude 24).

Furthermore, he has provided a *means* by which he communicates his enabling grace to his people — **'the word of his grace'**. This is the word that reveals and conveys grace: the word by which we may know the Lord. The primary reference is to the inscripturated word, the Scriptures, what Peter calls 'the pure spiritual milk' (1 Peter 2:2). Jesus expressed the same thought when he said, 'Man does not live on bread alone, but on every word that comes from the mouth of God' (Matt. 4:4; Deut. 8:3). Jesus is the living Word revealed in the Scriptures. He loved the church, gave himself for her, to make her holy, 'cleansing her by the washing with water through the word, and to present her to himself as a radiant church...' (Eph. 5:25-27). 'The Holy Scriptures are justly called "the word of God's grace",' said Charles Simeon, 'because they contain a wonderful revelation of grace, suited to, and sufficient for, our every want... By that the whole work of grace may be carried on and perfected within us. It is by that that we are at first begotten to God: and by that shall we be nourished unto life eternal.'[6]

*Established faith* (20:32)

Speaking of Christians, John Calvin writes, 'We are like an unfinished building. Indeed all the godly must be founded on Christ, but their faith is a very long way from being perfect and complete. On the contrary, although the foundation remains firm, certain parts of the building sometimes totter and fall. Accordingly, there is need, both of constant building, and, from time to time, of fresh supports.'[7] This, says Paul, is what the 'word of his grace' is able to do in you.

First of all, it **'can build you up'**. The Greek word is itself a picture of the process — *oikodomeo* comes from *oikos* (house). Thus Paul says that Christians are 'members of God's household [literally, the buildings (*oikeioi*) of God], built on the foundation of the apostles and prophets, with Christ Jesus himself as the chief cornerstone' (Eph. 2:19-22; cf. 1 Cor. 3:9). We are by spiritual growth to become 'the whole measure of the fulness of Christ' (Eph. 4:12,16,29; Col. 2:6-7). This is the doctrine of *progressive sanctification* — of growth to maturity through being built up in faith and life.

Secondly, this 'word of his grace' can **'give you an inheritance among all those who are sanctified'**. This is eternal life — beginning now. It is 'possession by a filial right, the portion of sons'.[8] Here is where we experience the reality of what the psalmist speaks of when he says, 'The Lord will accomplish what concerns me' (Ps. 138:8, AV) and what Paul means when he says, 'He who began a good work in you will carry it on to completion until the day of Christ Jesus' (Phil. 1:6). Our eyes are to be on the prize of our 'heavenward' calling in Christ Jesus (Phil. 3:14). The prize is not only heaven, but our present calling 'heavenward' — not only the ultimate destination, but the journey itself. We are marching through Emmanuel's land... right now!

*Practical godliness* (20:33-35)

Paul concludes by once again holding up the transparent godliness of his own example. Unlike the bejewelled prelates of the Middle Ages or the evangelical voluptuaries of the electronic church today, he sought nothing for himself. He showed them by his **'hard work'** that we **'must help the weak'**. This he seals with a quotation, recorded nowhere else in Scripture, from Jesus: **'It is more blessed to give than to receive'** (20:35).

This text is often used to stimulate people to give to the church — a legitimate application, no doubt, but not the main idea at all. This is rather a universal principle of Christian life and experience, flowing from the cross itself, where Jesus gave himself as the ransom for the many (Matt. 20:28). Christ is more blessed by dying to save his people from their sins than even they are in receiving by faith the redemption he purchased. It is the mercy of God; the desire to do lost people everlasting good; the love that lays down its life for the spiritually blind and dead, that they might live for ever in reconciled fellowship with God. It is the attitude which took Jesus to the cross.

As they knelt in prayer and grieved to see Paul sail away for ever, the Ephesian elders knew for certain that Christ must be their 'all' (Col. 3:11). This was the message they must live and proclaim. It is the message we must hear today! 'What we may meet with in life,' Charles Simeon told his Cambridge congregation, 'or whether we shall ever behold each other's face again in this world, God alone knows. But let us live for God, and for eternity; let us live as we shall wish we had lived, when we shall stand before the judgement-seat of Christ to receive our eternal doom. Let us go forward in the path of duty, assured that the rest which awaits us will richly repay our labours, and the crown of righteousness our conflicts.'[9]

# Part VII

## The road to Rome

Acts 21-28

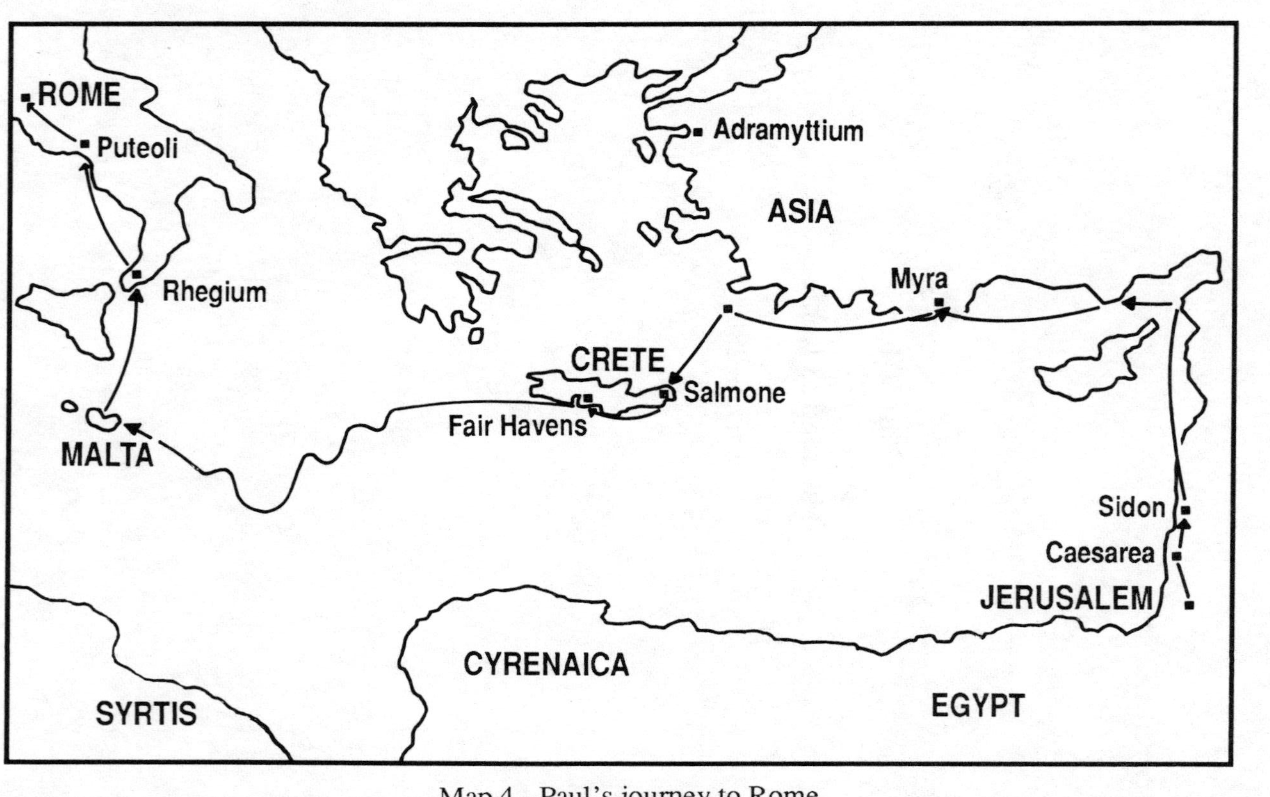


Map 4 - Paul's journey to Rome

## 29.
## The courage of convictions

**Please read Acts 21:1 - 22:21**

*'I am ready... to die in Jerusalem for the name of the Lord Jesus'* (21:13).

In Matthew Arnold's epic poem, *Sohrab and Rustum*, 'The pale Persians held their breath from fear,' as they watched the approach of the Tartar horde and anticipated defeat in the coming battle. There are occasions in every life when we may well feel like Arnold's 'pale Persians'. The inevitable has to be faced. We know, or think we know, the outcome of some unavoidable situation or decision, but we just have to do what we have to do. And we are afraid of the pain, the effort and the uncertainty that this carries in its train.

Paul found himself in just such a position at the close of his third missionary journey. While saying farewell to the Ephesian elders at Miletus, he disclosed that he was 'compelled by the Spirit' to go to Jerusalem, notwithstanding the fact that 'in every city' the Spirit had warned him of the 'prison and hardships' he would face in the Jewish capital (20:22-24). What is striking about this is that the Holy Spirit revealed both the mission and the *cost* of engaging in the mission. There is no promise of painless and unhindered triumph. God did not offer Paul a rose-garden. He could anticipate, in fact, sharing in the fellowship of Christ's sufferings. Jesus tells us plainly that 'A student is not above his teacher' and later adds, 'If the world hates you, keep in mind that it hated me first' (Luke 6:40; John 15:18). The world is hostile to Christ and therefore to those who proclaim and live the gospel. But God's purpose is to save a people out of that hostile world, inch by inch, soul by soul, generation after generation, until the whole number of the elect are gathered in. It is a testimony to the total honesty of Scripture that it pulls no punches about the true nature of discipleship to Christ. 'If anyone would come after me,' said Jesus, 'he must deny himself and take up his cross and follow me. For whoever wants to save his life will lose it, but whoever loses his life for me and for the gospel will save it' (Mark 8:34-35). The Christian's life and calling *is* one of victory, but it involves warfare and requires a courage that is born and sustained by the power of God!

Luke's account of Paul's sojourn in Jerusalem demonstrates three aspects of the courage of Christian convictions as exemplified by the apostle. These are, respectively, the courage to face suffering (21:1-16), to be gracious (21:17-26), and to speak out for Jesus (21:27 - 22:21).

## **The courage to face suffering** (21:1-16)

The apostle sailed from Miletus (see Map 4, p.266) to Cos, Rhodes, Patara, round Cyprus and on to Tyre, where he stayed for a week. It was there that the Tyrian believers **'through the Spirit ... urged Paul not to go on to Jerusalem'** (21:4; cf. 20:23). Nevertheless, Paul sailed for Ptolemais, stopped there overnight, and then walked to Cæsarea, where he stayed in the house of Philip the evangelist and his four unmarried daughters who prophesied (21:7-9). It was while he was in Cæsarea that Paul experienced the strange culmination of these revelations of the Holy Spirit warning him of troubles to come in Jerusalem.

The prophet Agabus, whom we last met in Antioch (11:28), symbolically[1] acted out what was going to happen to Paul if he went to Jerusalem — **'the Jews of Jerusalem'** would **'bind'** him and **'hand him over to the Gentiles'**. This set the people off weeping and they pleaded with Paul not to go up to Jerusalem (21:10-12). The apostle, however, was not to be deflected from his course. In his handling of the matter, he has left us a model for settling our own challenges to difficult discipleship.

### *Starting point — 'ready... to die'* (21:13)

We are taken straight to the heart of the matter. Paul asked why his friends were weeping and breaking his heart. He was **'ready not only to be bound, but also to die in Jerusalem'**. Self-preservation was not the main goal of his life. He had already enunciated the principle in his address to the elders at Miletus: 'I consider my life worth nothing to me, if only I may finish the race and complete the task the Lord Jesus has given me — the task of testifying to the gospel of God's grace' (20:24). It was not that Paul did not value the gift of *life*, that he did not cherish it and did not love his own body. But it is true, as John Calvin says, that he was not 'so gripped by a blind love of living' that he lost sight of the 'reasons for living'. Life is not an end in itself, it is 'arranged for us like a racecourse' and so we must 'always ... make haste to the winning post and ... overcome obstacles ... so that nothing may... delay us on the course'.[2] Paul does in fact put the proper biblical Christian value on life. He desires to live only to satisfy the will of the Lord, expend it in his service and fulfil his heavenward calling in Jesus Christ.

The apostle did not mean this to apply only to those who preach the Word. When he told the Corinthians, 'We who are alive are always being given over to death for Jesus' sake, so that his life may be revealed in our mortal body,' he was reflecting on his own ministry and that of preachers in general (2 Cor. 4:7-12). But elsewhere his application is to every Christian. We are to offer our bodies 'as living sacrifices' (Rom. 12:1). 'If we live, we live to the Lord; and if we die, we die to the Lord. So, whether we live or die, we belong to the Lord' (Rom. 14:8-9; cf. 2 Cor. 5:14-15). Paul's confession must become the living confession of every follower of Jesus: 'For to me, to live is Christ and to die is gain. If I am to go on living in the body, this will mean fruitful labour for me. Yet what shall I choose? I do not know! I am torn between the two: I desire to depart and be with Christ, which is better by far; but it is more necessary for you that I remain...' (Phil. 1:21-24). Calvin summarizes the central point correctly when he says, 'It is only those who will freely lay down their ... lives as a testimony for the truth, that will ever be properly disposed to live for the Lord.'[3] Is your life, truly and from the depth of your heart, *forfeit* to Christ? This is what it means to be his disciples.

*Stimulus — 'the name of the Lord Jesus'* (21:13)

The motive for such devotion to Christ is simply that he is *worthy* of it! Paul is willing to die **'for the name of the Lord Jesus'**. The 'name' stands for Jesus himself.

He is worthy of our self-sacrificial discipleship because of *who he is*. He is the eternal Son of God, our Creator, 'the radiance of

God's glory and the exact representation of his being, sustaining all things by his powerful word' (Heb. 1:3).

Jesus is also worthy of our devotion because of *what he has done.* He died for 'sinners' like us, when we know that only rarely is anyone willing to die even for a 'good man' (Rom. 5:6-8). He was obedient to death, 'even death on a cross' (Phil. 2:8). He bore the penalty of sin as the substitute for lost sinners and won salvation for all who would come to him, believing. He 'paid the penalty of the law (Isa. 53:8; Rom. 4:25; Gal. 3:13; 1 Peter 2:24), and merited eternal life for the sinner (Rom. 8:4; 10:4; 2 Cor. 5:21; Gal. 4:4-7.'[4]

And, finally, Jesus is worthy of our service, because of what he *is doing now* and what he *will do* in the future. He is active on our behalf. He intercedes for us with his Father. Unprofitable servants as we are, he blesses us with everlasting mercies. By the Word and the Holy Spirit, he sanctifies his own and converts enemies to be his own. And he is coming again in glory at the end of the age. Why should not Christ's love compel us, who, in him, are 'new creations'? Why should we not desire to be, and work at becoming, 'the righteousness of God' in him? (2 Cor. 5:14,17,21).

### *Steadfast trust — 'the Lord's will be done'* (21:14-17)

Paul's Christian friends gave up when they saw he was not going to change his mind and said, **'The Lord's will be done'** (21:14). This should not be interpreted as a kind of grim resignation. The right acceptance of the Lord's will is a *believing* acquiescence. They were agreeing with Paul that God really did want him in Jerusalem and meant him to be bound by the Jews and handed over to the Gentiles for some as yet undisclosed fate. Trusting the Lord means trusting when we can see and when we cannot — when fearing the known consequences of obedience and dreading the unknown potential for suffering and loss. Paul and his companions had no illusions, but were steadfast in the trust that God would be with him, whatever might happen. And so, in due course, they went up to Jerusalem and lodged in the home of Mnason, a Christian originally from Cyprus.

## **The courage to be gracious** (21:17-26)

As it turned out, Paul's first trial in Jerusalem arose not from the Jews, but from within the church. This was of a different character altogether from the hostility of those opposed to the gospel, but it was enough to be potentially damaging to his ministry and the church's unity. In facing up to it, Paul shows that just as it took God's grace for him to be steadfast while suffering persecution, it was also going to require grace to be conciliatory towards Christian brothers who had become critical of his teaching and practice as a missionary.

*Praise* (21:17-20)

Upon his arrival in Jerusalem, Paul was warmly received by the **'brothers'**, i.e., the members of the church. He was also well received by the Lord's brother, **'James'** and **'all the elders'**, who were assembled as they had been in the famous meeting recorded in Acts 15.[5] Paul reported in detail **'what God had done'** through his ministry to the Gentiles and this was greeted with spontaneous praise to God (21:20). Whatever problems had to be dealt with, the basic substratum of the church's fellowship was one of rejoicing in the blessing of God among them.

*Criticism* (21:20-21)

Jewish believers had heard it alleged that Paul was telling Jews **'to turn away from Moses ... not to circumcise their children or live according to our customs'**. They rejoiced in the conversion of Gentiles. They were not saying that circumcision was necessary for salvation (see 15:1-35). It troubled them, however, to think that what had been the practice of godly people for centuries should now be set aside altogether, as if it were a sinful thing to do.

It is important to remember that, at this point in time, Paul had already written his Galatian, Corinthian and Roman epistles.[6] He had taught freedom from the law as the ground of justification (Gal. 3:13; 5:1-4). He had thoroughly expounded justification by faith alone (Rom. 4:2-8). And to the Corinthians, while asserting the essential freedom of the Christian from the observances of the law, he had indicated his personal accommodation to its provisions in certain contexts. So, 'to the Jews' he 'became like a Jew ... for the sake of the gospel' (1 Cor. 9:19-23). Far from telling Jews to 'turn away from Moses', he had in fact taken special care to avoid misunderstanding and offence by observing without compromise the ceremonial and dietary practices of the Mosaic law. His critics simply had no case!

*Conciliation* (21:22-26)

Even though this was true, the Jerusalem elders felt it necessary for Paul to make a decisive gesture which would show the people that he really did respect the law of Moses. It so happened that four young Christian men had taken a vow and were seeking to be released from it according to the provisions of the Mosaic law. That this was a Nazirite vow is indicated by the necessity for their heads to be shaved. This was a commitment to a limited period, usually thirty days, of intense focus on the things of God and was signalled by ceremonial cleanness (no contact with dead bodies) and abstinence from grape products including wine, and the cutting of the hair. Grapes and wine symbolized the temptations of the flesh, while untrimmed hair — remember Samson? — represented unimpaired strength devoted to the Lord. James suggested Paul **'join in their purification rites and pay their expenses'** (21:24; cf. Num. 6).[7]

Paul had taken such a vow himself in the past (Acts 18:18) and readily consented. He only did so, you will note, after being assured by James that this was consistent with the decision of the earlier (Acts 15) Jerusalem 'council', that is, that this would not imply that Gentile Christians should be expected to take Nazirite vows (21:25-26).

The question is, of course, ought Paul to have accommodated in this way to the mistaken zeal for the law of Moses on the part of the Jewish Christians? After all, the same Paul had roundly condemned Peter to his face for Judaizing tendencies (Gal. 2:11-14). The answer is that Paul drew a very clear line between what was to be required of non-Jewish converts to Christ as necessary for salvation, and what was permissible devotional observance for Jewish Christians raised under the Mosaic law. Peter was wrong to 'force Gentiles to follow Jewish customs'. The Judaizers were wrong to require circumcision as a condition of salvation (Acts 15:1-11). But it did not suddenly become wrong to continue to observe the dietary laws or take a Nazirite vow. On these points there was freedom of conscience. Paul explains: 'Though I am free and belong to no man, *I make myself* a slave to everyone, to win as many as possible. To the Jews I became like a Jew, to win the Jews. To those under the law I became like one under the law (though I myself am not under the law), so as to win those under the law. To those not having the law

I became like one not having the law (though I am not free from God's law but am under Christ's law), so as to win those not having the law. To the weak I became weak, to win the weak. I have become all things to all men so that by all possible means I might save some' (1 Cor. 9:19-22). Note that Paul is not advocating insincerity or a disregard for the revealed will of God. What he recognized is that there was a large area of his own behaviour in which he could accommodate to the likes and dislikes of others, without compromising the gospel. Paul wanted to cross barriers, not put them up.

The apostolic period was unique in that it was a transition period in which the Old Testament ceremonial law was passing away in favour of the establishment of the New Testament fulfilment in Christ. Between Pentecost and the destruction of the temple in A. D. 70 a whole generation of Jewish believers had to grapple very practically with the claims of Old Testament piety and not least with its rabbinic accretions which had added so much to Mosaic law and taught human traditions as the commands of God. Paul was dealing with a one-off problem — the lingering claims of obsolete Old Testament rituals.

The challenge to be 'all things to all men' in order to win people to Christ remains, however, for Christians today. It means, for a start, that there is no room for a 'holier-than-thou' attitude to the unconverted. And this does not need to be in words. It can be the body-language that reacts to a hair-style, a swear-word or the way the person dresses. Then there is the frosty stare that says, 'I don't really want to be around types like you.' When we do speak, are we ready to overlook the peripherals and keep our focus on the heart of the matter? It hardly advances the cause of the gospel merely to sound off to some young fellow that he drinks too much or is a layabout. We have great noses for single, black-and-white moral issues, when what we need is to get into that lost person's heart with the issues of life and death and of the gospel of Christ. Pontificating about the symptoms has always been easier than tackling the disease. Paul's holy elasticity was born of the deepest desire for the welfare of those to whom he brought the message of eternal life.

This is equally true in dealing with believers. Paul accommodated the believing Jews in Jerusalem for the same reason that he adapted his approach to unbelieving Gentiles on his missionary journeys. He submerged his comfort and his preferences so as to avoid putting unnecessary religious and cultural obstacles in the way of his hearers. This took great wisdom and sensitivity to people. Most of all, it took a profound love for souls.

Some Christians not only find this difficult (which it is!); it seems to be beyond them, to never have entered their heads! Such is their view of their own purity and of the righteousness of their own conviction that they are prepared to break fellowship and even divide churches on what are, in truth, very slight points indeed. I once met a zealous and gracious young man who would not attend a service at an annual church meeting he was visiting, because there would be women present with their heads uncovered and it offended his convictions so much. There are some who attend *no* church fellowship because there is none that meets their standards. Such folk are invariably very sincere, but they are never 'all things', but always 'their own thing' to 'all men'! These are extremes, of course, but they illustrate the tendency to look inward to the point that all sight is lost of the kind of generosity of spirit which Paul exemplified.

This also suggests the observation that Christians can get to the place of only talking to themselves. I do not mean that they *literally* never talk to other people. I mean that their thinking, their language, their concerns and therefore their witness for the Lord become an exercise in maintaining and bolstering their own confidence, instead of what it needs to be — an outward-looking communication of the truth of God to the world, that actually speaks with understanding and understandably to lost people. A good example of this is the 'outrage' genre of Christian communication, such as the telegrams a certain Scottish church used to send to Buckingham Palace any time a member of the royal family did something frivolous on the Lord's Day. Paul could have gone around shouting protests at the sins of the powers that be and have quickly won a reputation as a self-righteous crank, good for a laugh if he ever came to your town! But he made a powerful and lasting impact on people. And he did so principally because he was able to get close to them. He spoke their language. He understood them. He loved them enough to accommodate them, without compromising his principles. He was never self-righteous, even when speaking of God's wrath. He was willing to get close to unbelievers and get his hands dirty, so to speak. His example calls us from just talking to ourselves, from being concerned merely to be 'right', and impels us to give of ourselves sacrificially, uncomfortably, humbly and lovingly, that we might win lost people for Christ — to have, like Paul, the courage to be gracious.

## **The courage to speak out for Christ** (21:27 - 22:21)

Paul's sponsorship of the four Christian Nazirites no doubt allayed the fears of those Christians who suspected him of a poor attitude to the law of Moses, but it was of no avail with certain elements of the Jewish populace at large. Towards the end of the seven-day purification period, some Jews from Asia raised a hue and cry against Paul while he was inside the temple, with the now standard accusation that he was teaching **'all men everywhere'** against **'our people and our law and this place'**. The trigger for this was the conviction that Paul had brought **'Greeks into the temple area'**, so defiling that **'holy place'**. Luke notes that they had earlier seen Paul with Trophimus, a Greek Christian known to them from home, *outside* the temple. When they later spotted the apostle *inside* in the Court of Israel, they jumped to the conclusion that Trophimus was also there, although in fact he was not (21:27-29).

The result was a riot in which Paul was only saved from a lynching by the prompt intervention of the Roman garrison. Paul was arrested and taken to the barracks adjacent to the temple, all the while closely pressed by the mob. It was at this point — on the steps of the Antonia fortress — that Paul spoke to the Roman commander and sought opportunity to speak to the crowd.

### *Paul's approach* (21:37 - 22:2)

Before any speaker can get an audience for his message, two things need to happen. First, he needs to speak in a language his hearers understand and, second, he needs to identify himself with them in some tangible way. He has to command a hearing even before one word of substance is said. Paul achieved these goals on the steps of the temple as the soldiers took him away in chains. And in doing so, he provided a model for preachers of the gospel and, indeed, for all witnessing Christians.

Paul spoke *in the language of the people*. He first spoke to the Roman commander in Greek. This surprised the soldier, because he had apparently thought Paul was an Egyptian terrorist. But it had two helpful effects. It immediately disposed the Roman to listen to what Paul had to say for himself by disarming his prior prejudicial assumptions, and, secondly, led him to give permission for the apostle to speak to the crowd, once he had discovered something about who he really was (21:37-40). This afforded Paul his hearing. So he duly applied the same principle in his address to the people. He spoke to them in their language, Aramaic, and when they heard this, **'They became very quiet'** (22:1-2).

A large part of that quiet readiness to hear Paul was the realization among the crowd that he was one of them — **'a Jew, born in Tarsus of Cilicia, but brought up in this city'** (22:3). Paul *identified* with his hearers. He touched the common ground they shared as Jews. In other words, his starting-point in communicating the gospel to them was the point at which they had *most in common* and on which there was *no point of offence* between them. Paul's principal aim was to show that a Jew can be a Christian, even that a true Jew *must* be a Christian and that it was not inconsistent of him, as a Jew, to preach Jesus of Nazareth as the Messiah promised in the Scriptures. Paul accordingly started with them where they were — and where he himself had started — their common Jewishness! Notice, also, how respectful Paul was towards them. He addressed as **'brothers and fathers'** men who would have killed him a moment before — and he meant it! He carefully avoided offering the slightest insult. Paul had very impressive Jewish credentials, but there was no affectation of superiority, no holier-than-thou attitude. He was warm, personal and the very soul of tact and grace. This is surely the essential requirement for all Christian evangelism. In this he took his cue from Jesus, who said of his own mission, 'God did not send his Son into the world to condemn the world, but to save the world through him.' After all, the world was, as Jesus added, 'condemned already' (John 3:17-18). Anybody can read the Riot Act. Evangelism means reaching out in love.

*Paul's testimony* (22:3-21)

The apostle's address is in three parts, each of which builds on the preceding one to present a coherent defence of his actions and personal testimony to his faith.

First, he builds upon his identification with them by stressing their *common Jewish heritage* (22:3-5). He was **'a Jew'**, bone of their bone and flesh of their flesh. He was **'thoroughly trained in the law'** under Gamaliel, 'the most eminent teacher of that time'.[8] He was **'as zealous for God'** as any of them and had **'persecuted the followers of this Way to their death'**, even, on one occasion, going to Damascus under a commission from the Sanhedrin to arrest the Christians and take them to Jerusalem **'to be punished'**. Paul was grabbing their attention by showing them that he knew exactly what they were concerned about. He had their ears. Now he would go for their hearts.

Paul then told them about *how he was converted to Jesus Christ* on his Christian-chasing expedition to Damascus (22:6-16). He testified to the encounter with the risen Jesus that changed his life for ever (see Luke's account in Acts 9:3-7). At high noon on the Damascus road he discovered that he was in fact opposing the God of his fathers and persecuting his Son and the promised Messiah, Jesus of Nazareth! Blinded by the light of God and humbled by the revelation of his spiritual blindness, Paul was brought to the place of submission to Jesus: **'"What shall I do, Lord?"'** (22:10). Once in Damascus, a man named **'Ananias ... a devout observer of the law'** (a phrase intended to catch the attention of his hearers) came to him with a revelation of God's will: **'The God of our fathers has chosen you to know his will and to see the Righteous One and to hear words from his mouth. You will be his witness to all men of what you have seen and heard'** (22:14-15). Here was the core of Paul's testimony: what had happened to him was not because he was some crazy heretic who had thought up some new ideas, but rather was the result of God, in Jesus the Messiah, revealing his perfect will. By the sovereign grace of God, Paul had been converted from being an enemy of God — something he did not believe himself to be at the time — to becoming a servant and apostle of Jesus Christ, his Son. This was the doing of *their* God and his!

Finally, Paul explained his subsequent calling to minister to the *Gentiles* (22:17-21). This, too, was the revealed will of God — revealed, be it noted — by **'the Lord** [Jesus]**'**, while Paul was **'praying at the temple'**! Jesus had told him to leave Jerusalem because **'They will not accept your testimony about me.'** Paul had objected to this, on the ground that he, as a converted former persecutor of the church and of Stephen, could expect to be given a good hearing, but the Lord had insisted and earmarked him for ministry to the Gentiles.

That was as far as he got. The crowd was merely enraged and there were calls for the apostle's death (22:22).

*Christian witness today*

Perhaps the first lesson of Paul's defence for us today is that our testimonies for Christ must always be *personal, yet Christ-centred.* The genius of true Christian testimony is that while we explain 'how the Lord changed my life', we really are pointing to our Saviour, Jesus. Even when Paul speaks of himself, there is no self-centredness. He recedes before the work of God and the light of Christ. He speaks clearly of the risen Christ. He does so in scriptural language, thus pointing his hearers to the Word of God, as opposed to his own experience or opinion. He also maintains a sense of the awesomeness of Christ. He never speaks casually of Jesus, as if he were a schoolboy chum instead of the divine Mediator he really is. He reverently, firmly and faithfully told the truth about Jesus, the Son of God.

Secondly, it is worth emphasizing again the *sensitivity and tact* with which Paul bore witness to Jesus. Too many Christians seem to think you can shout people into the kingdom of God. They stand up, blast away about sin for a while, 'present Jesus' as the only Saviour and invite a 'decision' on the spot. It is as if merely hectoring people with biblical truths is a means of grace! Paul could, after all, just as well have rebuked the mob loudly for trying to kill him. He could have told them what he later told the Philippian believers, that he counted his Pharisaic advantages in life as 'loss' and 'rubbish' compared to 'knowing Christ Jesus' (Phil. 3:8). But he knew that before they could understand these points, they needed to understand that his devotion to Jesus was not inconsistent with his Jewish heritage — indeed, that this was the real point of God's dealings with them as a people. That is why Paul did not throw the gospel in their faces, but sought to woo them by showing that their God had sent Jesus to them.

Thirdly, Paul testified to the people of Jerusalem, even though he knew by a direct revelation of Jesus Christ that they would not listen to him. He *persevered* in spite of meagre prospects of success. Why?

Because, in the last analysis, the testimony of God will stand, whether or not people come to faith, besides which, it is every Christian's calling to be ready at any time to give a reason for the hope that is in him or her. Our witness is not to be silenced because *we* feel it will do little good. The majority of that crowd no doubt remained unpersuaded by Paul's defence. But his faithful stand has echoed around the world and surely encouraged the Christians in Jerusalem at that time. Our calling is to plant the gospel seed. God provides the harvest.

Finally, it is obvious that the key to bearing testimony for Christ is *having a testimony to bear*! Paul believed in Jesus. Paul loved Jesus with every fibre of his being. Paul's testimony was of Jesus' work of grace in saving him from his sins and making him his disciple. Paul rejoiced in Jesus. He lived for Jesus. He could not but testify to the Jesus who had died on the cross as his substitute and rose from the dead for his justification. That is why he could stand before a raging mob and speak for Jesus. That is why he never hid his witness from the world. That is why he wore his heart for Jesus upon his sleeve. Should this not challenge us to ask ourselves, 'What testimony do I bear for Christ? What testimony do I have in my heart of his saving grace? How do I witness for him?'

James Alexander offers an appropriate challenge to new faithfulness, when he writes, 'There is a low cowardly disposition in certain Christians, to seek the world's approval, and almost ask the world's pardon for their faith. Are they asked to some questionable activity? They stammer out their apology for being Christians. Are they laughed at for not loving this world enough? They plead religious habit or church rules, or their friends' opinions, instead of simply glorying in their birthright in the world to come. That which they should wear as a crown and should hold forth as an irresistible attraction for unbelievers to come over to their side, they sometimes hide in a corner, and blush when people think they have it.'[9]

Paul's example calls Christians afresh to have the courage of gospel convictions. It is evident from his testimony that day, as he faced that murderous crowd, that Stephen's martyrdom had come to mean to him something quite different from what it did that day on which 'he gave approval to his death' (8:1). Then he had felt hatred; now he knew the love of Christ. Then he had despised Stephen; now he understood him. Now, like Stephen, he rejoiced to witness to his Saviour. This is the calling of every believer.

# 30.
# The Lord was near

**Please read Acts 22:22 - 23:11**

*'The Lord stood near Paul and said...'* (23:11).

'No prophet is accepted in his home town,' said Jesus to the people of Nazareth when they rejected him (Luke 4:24). Paul's experience was no different. Although he came originally from Tarsus, in modern Turkey, he was brought up in Jerusalem. There he spent his student days. There he began a promising career as a zealous Pharisee and a persecutor of Christians. Jerusalem was really his home town. But after he became a Christian, he ceased to be the 'blue-eyed boy' of the establishment and soon discovered that he was no longer really welcome in Jerusalem (cf. 22:18).

The Holy Spirit had predicted the dangers of going to Jerusalem (21:4,10-11). Paul could expect trouble, because the Lord had forewarned him. And as things turned out, even the Christians were suspicious of him, on account of (false) rumours that he taught the Jews of the Dispersion to 'turn away from Moses' (21:20-26). The unconverted Jews, however, were more than suspicious. They were furious and even wanted him dead (22:22).

We would surely forgive Paul for feeling discouraged by all of this and for regretting coming to Jerusalem. Yet nowhere do we have the slightest suggestion that he felt that way. All we know is that he went to Jerusalem both realistically anticipating the opposition and powerfully motivated by a desire to serve the Lord (20:22-24). He went there with his eyes open and he rejoiced in doing the will of the Lord, risks and all. It was his calling and his joy to testify 'to the gospel of God's grace'. He was moved, impelled and energized by a profound grasp of the gospel of Jesus Christ, the promises of God and his commission to preach the Word, in season and out of season — when the going was easy and when it was tough.

Now, with the shouts of the mob ringing in his ears, **'Rid the earth of him! He's not fit to live!'** (22:22), and the prospect of a Roman flogging soon cutting furrows in his back (22:24), Paul demonstrated once again what it meant to be faithful for Christ in a hostile world. In his ordeal with Claudius Lysias, the Roman commander, and the Jewish council, the Sanhedrin, we have a profile of Christian courage in the face of adversity, in his case unjust and murderous persecution. Luke's account reveals five aspects of Paul's carriage and state of mind as he faced what might have been the last hours of his life on earth. He had a clear head (22:22-30); a good conscience (23:1); holy boldness (23:2-5); a resurrection hope (23:6-10) and, most important of all, he knew *t*he nearness of the Lord (23:11).

## A clear head (22:22-30)

When the Romans **'stretched [Paul] out to flog him'**, it was in order to extract the truth from him. On other occasions the apostle came under the 'rod' three times and five times received 'forty lashes' (2 Cor. 11:24-25). This time he faced the *flagellum*, a whip consisting of thongs with sharp metal and bone inserts. Few endured this cruel instrument of punishment without permanent injury. Many died. Paul was in a tight spot, to say the least. From the 'frying pan' of the mob, he had fallen into the 'fire' of the *flagellum*! He took two steps, however, that served to extricate him from his predicament: he kept a clear head and he spoke up! Simple enough, you might think, but not so easy when under extreme pressure.

Paul *kept a clear head.* He thought fast, he applied his mind and he remembered that Roman citizens were exempt from the kind of punishment he was about to receive.

So he *spoke up* for his civil rights under the laws of Rome. He grasped at his every legal advantage. This contrasts with the way Jesus responded to his persecutors, for he hardly defended himself at all (Isa. 53:7; Acts 8:32). Why the difference? The answer is that, whereas Jesus' purpose was to *die* in order to *be* the gospel in his atonement for sin, Paul's goal was to *live* to *preach* the gospel of Jesus' perfect sacrifice. The effect on the Romans was electric, for they had unwittingly placed themselves under the censure of their own law. 'Police brutality' was allowed for subject peoples but not for the citizens of Rome! This was accentuated by the further revelation that whereas the commander had had to purchase his citizenship, Paul was able to say he was **'born a citizen'**! (22:28).

The encouragement for all of us is to ask the Lord to give us a clear head and a bold tongue. Pray for quiet composure under pressure. And study to be wise. Know the Word of God and understand your world. Seize every opportunity for Jesus Christ. In particular, take advantage of the law of the land to advance the gospel. Some Christians regard this as somehow 'unspiritual'. Well, it did not bother the apostle Paul — and for the simple reason that he believed that the authorities are *supposed* to be God's servants to do good! (Rom. 13:4). Paul's privileges as a Roman citizen were used by God to get him to the heart of the empire and to extend his ministry into the household of the wicked Nero! Let us not be so (falsely) heavenly-minded, that we are no earthly good! *Carpe diem* — seize the day — for Jesus Christ!

### A good conscience (23:1)

Since the Roman commander really had no idea what Paul was charged with, he called for the Jewish Sanhedrin to examine the apostle and render some judgement in the matter. Paul was duly brought before this body. We can assume that he was well enough known to many of the councillors. We can also assume that it was generally understood that Paul was being charged with heresy with respect to the Mosaic law and sacrilege in regard to the temple (see 21:28). At this point, however, no formal determination had been made, for this was merely the first stage in the investigation of the problem.

Paul knew, however, that he was on trial for his life and, accordingly, he opened his defence with an appeal to God and to a good conscience, with respect to all that he had done in the course of his ministry. There is a majestic, and yet humbly fragrant, simplicity to his words. He **'looked straight at the Sanhedrin and said, "My brothers, I have fulfilled my duty to God in all good conscience to this day."'** He thereby turned a plea of 'Not guilty' into a personal testimony for his Lord! We tend to think of legal procedures as a kind of 'game' in which technicalities are juggled this way and that, either to secure a conviction or 'get' the accused 'off'.

The apostle's appeal to a 'good conscience' emphasizes that the central concern in his life, never mind court cases, ought to be honesty before the Lord and a willingness to be accountable to him for every aspect of his behaviour. The word for 'conscience', the Greek *suneidesis,* means literally 'awareness together with' — that is, self-knowledge as measured against a particular standard of conduct. Lloyd Ogilvie puts it very well when he observes that Paul 'energetically lived *in* the truth he had', and that 'his conscience was *the servant* of a congealed thought and action'.[1] Conscience is the mind functioning in the context of a known standard. Scripture speaks of conscience as a faculty of the human mind — the mind of human beings made in the image of God. It is part of what it means to be human (2 Cor. 4:2). Paul speaks of the 'consciences' of 'Gentiles, who do not have the law', nevertheless 'bearing witness' to the reality that 'the requirements of the law' were 'written on their hearts', so that they did 'by nature the things required by the law'. The conscience, he says, operates through our thoughts, 'now accusing, now even defending' our actions in terms of that moral standard (Rom. 2:14-15).

Of course, it is possible to be wicked and have a clear conscience. People can have very different standards of right and wrong. Conscience is only the so-called 'voice of God' in so far as it is informed by God's revealed will, the Bible. Hence the need for Christ to cleanse our consciences from dead works, so that we can serve the living God (Heb. 9:14). The effect of unbelief is that 'Minds and consciences are corrupted' (Titus 1:15). The unrenewed mind is 'hostile to God' (Rom. 8:7) and that is always reflected in the conscience of the unconverted. Hence the goal of the preaching of God's Word is 'love, which comes from a pure heart and a good conscience and a sincere faith' (1 Tim. 1:5). Consequently, the common proverb, 'Let your conscience be your guide', is fundamentally misleading. It is *God* who must be our guide, *through* a sanctified conscience. Why? Because 'conscience' is not some sinless abstraction — like some mental computer chip implanted in the brain and programmed to produce perfection, a supposed surrogate of God deep in the mind. No! Our consciences are simply the sensitivity or hostility, as the case may be, of our minds to the things of God. The harder the heart, the easier the conscience about doing bad things. Hitler and Stalin no doubt let their consciences be their guides in the murderous annihilation of their millions of victims. Paul warns us of the apostate false teachers 'whose consciences have been seared as with a hot iron' (1 Tim. 4:1-3). To be born again to a living faith in Christ, in contrast, means 'having our hearts sprinkled to cleanse us from a guilty conscience' (Heb. 10:22).

One further point: Paul's 'good conscience' was not 'good' because he was sinlessly perfect, for no one is (James 3:2). It was not 'good' because it never accused him of sin (1 John 3:20). It was not 'good' because, in modern parlance, he 'felt good about himself'. Paul had a good conscience because he really knew God's will and could testify to a sincere consistency between that truth and his actions. That is not a claim of sinless perfection, but it is to say that in terms of both his inward mental awareness of God and his practical faithfulness and integrity before God and the world, his ministry was not characterized by the promotion of known error, the practice of habitual sin or the neglect of positive righteousness as defined by God. A *good* conscience is a *godly* conscience. Anything less is a lie — a lie to ourselves, a lie to others and a lie to God.

### **Holy boldness** (23:2-5)

The high priest Ananias evidently took great offence at Paul's opening statement and ordered those standing near him **'to strike him on the mouth'** (23:2). This arrogant and illegal assault on a man who had not yet even been charged, far less tried and convicted, understandably provoked the apostle and he responded with a very sharp rebuke: **'God will strike you, you whitewashed wall! You sit there to judge me according to the law, yet you yourself violate the law by commanding that I be struck!'** (23:3). This robust statement has occasioned some division among the commentators.

Some tend to censure the apostle for these stern words and treat them as evidence of his 'humanity' — a euphemism for personal sin.[2] They readily allow that he was sorely provoked and that what he said was true in itself, but point out that the apostle appears to apologize later for criticizing the chief priest. This, then, is seen as something of a lapse and is held to be inconsistent with Jesus' example of meekness before his persecutors. As such, it fits in with the squeamishness that is rife in evangelical circles today about being 'judgemental' — a jargon word for speaking the truth in a plain and forthright way. It is just not 'nice' to confront anybody in the vigorous way exemplified by Paul on this occasion. 'Niceness', however, is too often used to cover a retreat from being honest about the real issues of life and earnest for the salvation of lost people.

The general and, we may say, historical understanding of Paul's statement regards it as a righteous, and indeed prophetic, rebuke of the apostate chief priest, Ananias. Paul says three things, all of which were true and one of which was a prophecy that was fulfilled just a few years later.

First, he told the priest, **'God will strike you.'** J. A. Alexander notes that the language denotes 'simple futurity' and that 'The only sense consistent with this form is that of a prediction or prophetical denunciation, not of the general fact that condign punishment awaits such sinners (compare Gen. 9:6; Matt. 26:52), but of the specific fact that this man was himself to be smitten of God.'[3] And indeed, Josephus records his assassination by Jewish zealots during the Jewish War which culminated in the destruction of the temple and the final obliteration of the trappings of the Old Testament order. The fact is that this man died under that great judgement of God predicted by Jesus, when he lamented over the Jerusalem he longed to gather together, 'but [they] were not willing' (Matt. 23:37-39).

Secondly, Paul identified the man as a **'whitewashed wall'**, echoing Jesus' trenchant denunciation of the Jewish establishment, a generation earlier. Jesus used the even stronger expression, 'whitewashed tombs' (Matt. 23:27). This priest was a hypocrite — like a crumbling mud-brick wall whitewashed to make it seem better than it really was. This was true and, while vividly stated, was unexceptionable, not simply in view of the picturesque language of the time, but in the context of the truth as it was and as it had already been revealed by the mouth of the Son of God. F. F. Bruce, who is 'not disposed to join in the chorus of disapproval voiced by many commentators' over Paul's statement, points out that 'Had [Paul] known the man intimately, he could not have spoken more aptly.'[4] This was not answering reviling with reviling (1 Peter 2:23). It was facing a fool with his folly and his eternal danger. And that can never be a passionless pursuit. It was also something of an epitaph for the whole Sanhedrin.

Thirdly, Paul stated a reason for this characterization: **'You sit there to judge me according to the law, yet you yourself violate**

**the law by commanding that I be struck.'** This was not even a trial. No charges had been heard and no defence offered. It was sheer demagoguery. Paul's protest was thoroughly deserved and, for reasons already mentioned, is not to be censured on the grounds that Jesus was relatively silent before his judges. Calvin points out that if we give way to impatience, or merely moan, we are to be blamed to a degree. But 'If a clear and serious accusation comes from a composed mind, then it does not go beyond the limits laid down by Christ,' citing our Lord's words in Matthew 5:22. Paul spoke, not for the sake of personal revenge, he adds, but 'because he was a minister of the Word of God, he did not want to pass over in silence an outrageous act, that deserved a grave and earnest rebuke, especially since it would be a beneficial thing to drag out the gross hypocrisy of Ananias from its hiding place into the light of day'.[5] He was, after all, addressing one of those of whom Jesus had said, 'You belong to your father, the devil' (John 8:44). Jesus and Paul cared enough to tell sinners the truth and with a costly earnestness that left them in no doubt as to the seriousness of the problem.

If this was all that had been said, the matter would have been settled beyond all dispute. But Paul said more, and what he said has been hotly debated ever since. Some bystanders objected that the apostle had insulted **'God's high priest'** and Paul responded by saying, **'I did not realize that he was the high priest; for it is written: "Do not speak evil about the ruler of your people"'** (23:4-5; Exod. 22:28). At first glance this looks like a retraction of some kind, and many have taken it as an admission of fault, even if it clearly falls short of being an apology. The standard line is to compare Paul unfavourably with Jesus' response to being struck in John 18:22-23. But this, as already pointed out, takes no adequate account either of the particular contexts in each case, i.e., Jesus was aiming to die on a cross, whereas Paul aimed to live and go to Rome. Neither does it take note of Jesus' very robust forthrightness on other occasions. Furthermore, we have every reason to believe that when Paul defended himself, he did so in terms of the experience of Jesus' promise to his disciples that the Spirit of God would give the words to speak on just such occasions (Matt. 10:19-20; Mark 13:11).

In this light, Paul's statement is more properly understood as an elaboration of his rebuke of Ananias, rather than an admission of sin. John Calvin, following Augustine, had 'no doubt that [Paul's] excuse was ironical'.[6] James A. Alexander, the eminent Princeton theologian, whose exposition of this passage is without equal, shows Paul was actually calling into question the very validity of Ananias' authority as being that of which the Mosaic law spoke in Exodus 22:28. The 'most satisfactory solution', says Alexander, 'is, that Paul means to deny that Ananias was in any such sense High Priest, as to make him a violator of the law in Exodus'.[7] There were, by this time in Jewish history, a number of titular 'high priests', so that any resemblance with the Mosaic pattern had all but vanished. Paul could not but have known who Ananias *the man* was, but to recognize him as a *high priest* according to the law was out of the question. Yes, Scripture enjoined against rebuking those whom God had placed over his people! But this ecclesiastical poseur — 'whitewashed wall' — was entitled to no such exemption from the true messengers of the living God! Let the church today speak with holy boldness and call sinners, in high places or low, to account before the bar of God's revealed Word! How will people repent and turn to the Lord, if God's messengers are too timid to speak plainly about the need of their souls and the only Saviour who can save them?

## A resurrection hope (23:6-10)

The foregoing interpretation is confirmed by what Paul now did. In one brilliant stroke, he exposed just how ludicrous it was to imagine that Ananias and his gang were the legitimate inheritors of the mantle of Moses. He drove home the point of the utter incongruity between the current ecclesiastical leadership and the doctrine of the Word of God, of which they were supposed to be the defenders. He knew the Sanhedrin consisted of Sadducees and Pharisees and that these were bitterly opposed to one another. The Sadducees were the 'liberals' who, like many of today's 'Protestant' clerics, were anti-supernaturalists and sceptics in their doctrine. The Pharisees, like the mainstream of the church of Rome, were the 'legalists', who were supernaturalist in their doctrine, but devoted to a scheme of salvation by works and ethno-religious heritage. Paul aimed straight for this fault-line by declaring his doctrinal commitment to his **'hope in the resurrection of the dead'** (23:6). This served two purposes.

It first emphasized that the heart of Paul's message was the *resurrection* of Jesus of Nazareth. He does not mention Jesus by name, but does in fact focus on the doctrinal root of the matter. This is the logic of 1 Corinthians 15:13, where he says, 'If there is no resurrection of the dead, then not even Christ has been raised.' He appeals to the orthodoxy of the Pharisaic party, as far as it went. In this, he seized the initiative and moved the controversy away from the legalistic grounds upon which the crowd rioted and he was later charged and placed the focus on a basic doctrine of the gospel, which it so happened the Pharisees shared.

Simultaneously, this turned over the stone under which the Sadducees were hiding, namely their fundamental rejection of the supernaturalism of the law of Moses. Hence the **'great uproar'** which immediately ensued and reduced the Sanhedrin to what it really was, an apostate shadow of what God had intended the leadership of his church to be under the Old Testament order! So great was the violence that the Roman commander ordered in the troops to retrieve the apostle and carry him to safety! The pretended upholders of Moses' law, not for the first time, demonstrated that they had turned the house of God into a den of thieves! Paul's prophetic condemnation of Ananias and the council received a double confirmation!

What this ought to say to us today is that we, like Paul, ought to live as the children of our risen Saviour, keeping the focus of our testimony upon the heart of the gospel — the resurrection of the crucified Jesus — and confront the world with our Lord's claims whenever we can. It is to be feared that we too often let the world set the agenda by choosing the subjects upon which to debate and justify their rejection of Christ. When they ask, 'What does your church believe?' we launch into the impossible intricacies of denominational peculiarities. When they challenge us on 'predestination', we end up discussing infra- and supra-lapsarianism. When they rail against corrupt tele-evangelists, we explain how pure we are. Paul kept his eyes on the heart of the matter — and *he* is the risen Christ! 'Ah!' we say, 'that was Paul and we are not apostles or theologians.' To which we answer: here, once again, we see Paul 'given what to say', just as Jesus had promised (Matt. 10:19), and here, for us as well, is a promise of the power of the Holy Spirit as he works within our hearts. He leads all his people into all truth. He never leaves faithful people to their own devices. Christ has promised, by his Spirit. to be with us, even to the end of the world!

## The nearness of the Lord (23:11)

After two terrible days, Jesus **'stood near Paul and said, "Take courage! As you have testified about me in Jerusalem, so you must also testify in Rome."'** This was a unique event, in that it was a visible manifestation of Jesus and it was a specific confirmation of his apostolic commission to testify in Rome. Jesus said (critics of Paul's address to Ananias please note!) that Paul had faithfully and successfully testified in Jerusalem. Now he was to know that he would also accomplish God's mission for him in pagan Rome! As the apostle to the Gentiles, he would not be silenced, nor would the will of God be thwarted. The gospel would win through to victory!

It nevertheless touches the lives of all of God's people in that it assures us that the encouragement afforded to Paul that night is promised to every believer in the exercise of his calling as a follower of Jesus. He is as surely with us now as he was with Paul that night. Paul saw him with his eyes. We see him with the opened eyes of Spirit-filled understanding. The promises of our Lord never to leave us and never to let anyone pluck us out of his hand are as fresh and real today as they were to Paul.

The Lord is always near his witnessing people. His encouragements are breathed across their hearts by the Holy Spirit. His purpose of grace remains their calling and will not be overthrown. 'Do not be afraid, little flock,' Jesus tells us, 'for your Father has been pleased to give you the kingdom' (Luke 12:32).

# 31.
# 'That's enough for now!'

**Please read Acts 24**

*'When I find it convenient, I will send for you'* (24:25).

Everyone knows from personal experience that 'Procrastination is the thief of time' and that wisdom teaches that we ought 'never put off till tomorrow what [we] can do today'. Some people take this advice very seriously and plan their lives with the utmost care and foresight. When it comes, however, to the things of God — to Christ, the gospel, salvation, personal holiness, worship, discipleship, heaven and hell — there is plenty of evidence that large numbers of people are not in any hurry to listen to the most important advice in the world. Procrastination *in spiritual things* can be the thief not only of time, but also of eternity!

Think of the rich young man. He listened to what Jesus had to say about selling all he had to give to the poor, but 'He went away sad, because he had great wealth' (Mark 10:22). Remember the farmer who was too busy building bigger barns for his accumulating wealth to give attention to the real issues of life and death. 'But God said to him, "You fool! This very night your life will be demanded from you. Then who will get what you have prepared for yourself?"' (Luke 12:20). And there were the girls in Jesus' parable who had put off preparing for the wedding reception, only to find themselves left out in the cold — a parable, of course, of the plight of those who die in their sins, having falsely persuaded themselves that they are right with God (Matt. 25:1-13).

A similar case is that of the Roman procurator Felix, before whom Paul was to be tried in Cæsarea. He is a prime example of the mind-set of those who are willing to dabble with eternal questions but who soon lose interest and leave any conclusions for 'a more convenient time', which, like the proverbial tomorrow, 'never comes'. In the record of Paul's trial, Felix for the most part lurks quietly in the background. It is Paul who is in the foreground, as he defends himself against the false accusations of the Jews. And yet Felix is the true focus of Luke's account — it is the story of a man who was touched by the gospel, for a moment, but recoiled from it, and remained committed to his unbelief.

The narrative is full of reversals: the *judge*, the 'most excellent' Felix, is just another lost sinner (24:1-4); the *trial*, ostensibly of Paul, becomes God's arraignment of Sadducean Judaism (24:5-21); while the *verdict* reverses the role of judge and accused, so that while Paul is shown to be truly free, Felix is seen to be the slave of his own unbelief (24:22-27).

## The judge — 'most excellent Felix' (24:1-4)

Less than a week after his arrival in Cæsarea, Paul was put on trial before Felix. The presence of Ananias, the high priest, and his special prosecutor Tertullus, is a testimony to the political and religious significance of the event and the impact of Paul's ministry. For those Jews who were determined to reject Jesus as their true Messiah — that is, the religious establishment — the suppression of the Christian faith was a major priority. They correctly realized that the claims of the church, as represented by the preaching of Paul, implied the disappearance of the ceremonial and legal superstructure of the Old Testament and the rabbinical teachings and traditions. They should have welcomed this as something entirely consonant with the teaching of the Scriptures. But they had turned the true faith of the Old Testament era into the cult we know as Judaism by teaching for doctrines the commandments of men (Matt. 15:9, AV), and set their faces against their own God and his Anointed — a position from which their descendants have, as yet, only rarely departed in the millennia since.[1]

The proceedings began with an address by Tertullus, the prosecutor for the Jewish establishment. With traditional oriental effusiveness, he extolled the virtues of the Roman procurator, Marcus Antonius Felix, whom he addressed as **'most excellent Felix'** (24:4). This man had risen from humble beginnings to considerable prominence in the Roman administration.[2] He had been greatly aided by his brother's influence with the Emperor Nero and by a series of political marriages — his latest wife, Drusilla, was the daughter of Herod Agrippa I. Felix had served as procurator, or governor, of Judea since A. D. 52 — it was now A. D. 59 — and before that had been prefect in Samaria.[3]

From the New Testament and other contemporary sources, we have a picture of a man who was intelligent and resourceful. He had made the most of his opportunities and abilities. He was an astute politician, who used people on his way to the top and never looked back. Tacitus recorded that he 'exercised the prerogatives of a king with the spirit of a slave' (cf. Eccles. 10:16-17). He was an independent thinker, who was not inclined to be swayed by honeyed words (like those of Tertullus), but who was intrigued by courageous and strong-minded men (like Paul). He was known for his avarice (cf. 24:26), and was later relieved of his office on account of corruption. The world might call him 'excellent', but Felix was a wicked man. Although he knew something about the Christian movement and its message (24:22), he was ignorant of the gospel. He did not know Christ as his Saviour. He was dead in his trespasses and sins.

There is an inescapable irony in this scene. Here was the man before whom the apostle Paul was to be tried. Yet, in ultimate terms, their roles were actually the reverse! Under the searchlight of the apostle's witness to the good news of Jesus Christ, the judge became the judged. Thus Paul arraigned Felix at the bar of heaven! It is in this sense that the saints already judge the world (cf. 1 Cor. 6:2). Their testimony for Christ confronts lost people with the issue to end all issues: the question as to where they will spend eternity.

### **The trial — Paul for the defence** (24:5-21)

Felix settled down to hear the meat of the case. Tertullus continued for the prosecution. In due course, Paul would have his day in court.

#### *The case for the prosecution* (24:5-9)

Tertullus' argument was in three parts. The first was a distinctly *political* charge (24:5). Paul was a **'troublemaker, stirring up riots among the Jews all over the world'** (cf.17:6). The impression conveyed is that Paul was a subversive, who instigated these riots for political reasons, when in fact it was those Jews who objected to his teaching about Jesus and the gospel who actually initiated the disturbances. These men knew that to get a favourable decision from the Roman administration, they had to make a political charge stick. A narrowly 'religious' question would not guarantee Roman intervention in the interest of their religious agenda — the suppression of the Christian church.

The same tactic is employed today. Whenever Christ and his truth are proclaimed clearly and courageously applied to all of life, you will often hear the charge that this represents 'narrow sectarian interests', or it is 'bringing religion into politics' and is then 'interference of the church in the state'. It is true, of course, that public morality is addressed by the gospel — the issue of abortion is a case in point. It is true that the doctrine of the lordship of Christ commands change in people's lives, and that includes how they behave in their political lives. Nevertheless, the 'troublemaker' charge reaches far beyond the interface between gospel preaching and the hearts and lives of those who rule in the body politic. The apostles never preached sedition against 'the powers that be', although they did not shrink from outlining the duty of the state to be 'God's servant, an agent of wrath to bring punishment to the wrongdoer' (cf. Rom. 13:1-7; 1 Peter 2:13-15). Needless to say, unbelievers can easily calculate what will happen in both church and state if more and more people are converted to Jesus Christ. They know this can only presage the rise of new constraints upon them to be more morally responsible and less corrupt. Those who reject Jesus, then and now, correctly discern the significance of a Christ-proclaiming, gospel-living church for their comfortable set-up and try to persuade the authorities that it is in their interests to suppress it, if at all possible.

The second charge was *religious*. Paul was alleged to be a **'ringleader of the Nazarene sect'** (24:5). This was the somewhat prejudicial way in which the Jewish establishment labelled a leader of the Christian church. F. F. Bruce notes that in Arabic and Hebrew today the word for Christian is 'Nazarene'.[4] For the Jews of Paul's day, the Christians were a sub-Jewish sect, lumped with other groups, like the Zealots, who had radical political goals, and so the term had a contemptuous edge to it. If, however, such 'guilt by association' was implied, it was not supported by the evidence, as we have already seen.

The final charge was not only religious in nature, but was *criminal* in character (24:6-9). Paul, they said, had **'tried to desecrate the temple'**. This referred to the original reason for his arrest, which was a rumour, escalated into mob hysteria, that he had *actually* brought 'Greeks into the temple area and defiled [that] holy place' (21:28-29). This was a tilt against Claudius Lysias, the Roman tribune in Jerusalem,[5] who had dismissed their complaint and had only sent Paul to Cæsarea because he did not want to handle the Jews' plot against Paul, a Roman citizen, on his own. He 'passed the buck' to his superior, Felix. Tertullus, you will notice, presented a modified charge — he only accused Paul of *attempting* to defile the temple, implying that only his prompt seizure by the Jews had forestalled doing the deed. This charge could not easily be proved or disproved. It was surely a case of throwing mud and hoping some of it would stick! Perhaps he hoped that Felix would see it was a Jewish police matter, overturn Lysias' action and restore Paul to their tender mercies.

The modern parallels are only too clear. Proclaim openly, intelligibly and practically the claims of Jesus Christ as revealed in the teaching of Scripture; apply the Word to issues like abortion, the death penalty, homosexual behaviour, heterosexual sin, corruption in government, oppression in the workplace, exploitation of the poor, integrity in the judiciary etc.— all matters upon which God has a well-known position — and it will be attacked as 'meddling in politics' or 'legislating morality', two things 'the church' is not supposed to do! Against this it must be asserted that the Word of God teaches *both* church and state how to obey Jesus Christ and declares him the Lord of men and nations!

*Paul speaks in his own defence* (24:10-21)

First of all, he respectfully *acknowledged the legitimate civil authority*, in the person of the Roman procurator Felix, and made particular mention of the procurator's personal experience of Jewish affairs (24:10). We are to 'honour the king' (1 Peter 2:17; Eccles. 8:2). Even if we disagree with the policy of the government or the behaviour of individuals in high places, it is vital to the effectiveness of any Christian witness we may bear to them that we always carry ourselves with quiet respectfulness. We must, indeed, obey God rather than men, but civil government has been appointed by God and it is God who tells us to 'submit to the authorities, not only because of possible punishment, but also because of conscience' (Rom. 13:5).

Secondly, the apostle *pleaded not guilty* to the charges and confidently asserted that the facts of the case were easily verifiable (24:11-13). He had gone **'to Jerusalem to worship'** twelve days before, but no one found him **'arguing with anyone'** or **'stirring up a crowd'**. There was no evidence to prove the charges levelled by his accusers.

Last but not least, Paul *gave his personal testimony* as to what he had done and why he had done it (24:14-21). He gave a reason for the hope that was in him and he did so, says Charles Simeon, with 'firmness of mind ... tenderness of spirit' and 'purity of heart'.[6]

First, he testifies as to his *doctrine*: **'I admit,'** he said, **'that I worship the God of our fathers'** (24:14-16). This is a statement of personal faith. He believed in the God who revealed himself to the fathers of Israel — the God revealed in what we call the Old Testament. This was a matter of fact, but it was not the whole story. Paul therefore was completely open about his belief in the gospel as the fulfilment of Old Testament teaching. Four points, all of which are essential to every Christian's faith and witness, receive particular attention.

1. Paul says he worshipped the God of the Old Testament **'as a follower of the Way, which they call a sect'** (24:14). There are three things to note here. The first is that he confesses his faith as a *New Testament believer* — 'a follower of the Way' — and in so doing confesses Jesus Christ. Secondly, he clearly affirms that 'the Way' is the *true* way to follow the God of their fathers. It was not a 'sect', as his accusers alleged, but the fruition of all that God had promised in the old covenant. Paul believed in the God of his completed Word, Old and New Testaments. Thirdly, he thereby declares that he is *not ashamed* to be counted with those who believed in the Lord Jesus Christ.

2. He goes on to declare his belief in the revealed Word of God: **'everything that agrees with the Law and that is written in the Prophets'** (24:14). Our authority for following Jesus as the Messiah is in the Scriptures and not in any merely subjective impressions or

speculative teachings. Notice that Paul does not appeal to his own apostolic inspiration, but 'to the law and to the testimony' (Isa. 8:20).

3. He declares his hope of the **'resurrection of both the righteous and the wicked'** (24:15). His Sadducean accusers did not believe this truth, but the more orthodox Pharisaic party did. So when the apostle said he had the same hope as **'these men'**, he was identifying with the Pharisees and effectively driving a wedge between them and the Sadducees! The former believed in the future advent of the Messiah and in the general resurrection associated with his triumph. If anyone was 'sectarian', it was those who rejected this dual hope — that is to say, as Lenski comments, 'in regard to this point, these Sadducees alone constitute the sect. And ... Felix, who knew the Jews, could not but see the point.'[7]

4. Last of all, the apostle declares his **'conscience clear before God and man'** (24:16). As we have already seen, the word 'conscience' (Gk. *suneidesis*) means 'knowing together with [something else]'. That 'something else' is the absolute standard of truth — the revealed Word of God. By our very constitution as men and women made in the image of God, we have a conscience — a 'voice' in our inner being attuned to a greater or lesser degree to the moral law of God. That is why people, whether or not they are Christians, have some sense of right and wrong (Rom. 2:14-15). Sinners can and do suppress and sear their consciences (1 Tim. 4:1-3) and frequently come to what they feel is a 'clear conscience', even though they live in utter disregard of God's revealed will. But those who come to faith in Christ experience the progressive cleansing and enlivening of their consciences as they devote themselves to discipleship to their Saviour (Heb. 9:14; cf. 10:22; 2 Cor. 4:2; 1 Tim. 1:5; 2 Tim. 1:3). A 'clear conscience' must be measured against God's moral standard. The apostle was not sinlessly perfect, but his conscience testified to a consistency between his actions and the Lord's will. When Paul claimed this before Felix and his accusers, he challenged *their* consciences, they knew it, and, had it been revealed to public view, many of them also knew that they had *bad* consciences before God and even each other. The challenge to all of us is to purge our consciences from dead works to serve the living God! (Heb.9:14, AV).

After stating his doctrine, Paul offers a two-part defence of his *actions*, giving an account of what he was doing in Jerusalem at the time he was arrested and offering a challenge to the very morality of the trial itself (24:17-21).

1. He had gone there, in the first instance, for unimpeachable purposes — to take **'gifts for the poor'** and **'to present offerings'** at the temple (24:17). Indeed, when apprehended at the temple, he was **'ceremonially clean'**, had gathered no crowd and caused no disturbance (24:18-19).

2. He further pointed out the essential injustice of his arraignment before Felix. Where were the Asian Jews who created the original disturbance? (21:27-29). Of what crime had the Sanhedrin found him guilty? (23:1-10). Was it not true that it was Paul's affirmation of **'the resurrection of the dead'** that occasioned the trial — the very doctrine which the orthodox Jews believed, against the Sadducean establishment liberals? (24:20-21).

With this, Paul rested his case. It was not so much a legal defence as a confession of faith and a testimony for truth. He kept the focus on the real point, which was the will of God and the gospel of the risen Jesus Christ. Whatever the politics of his predicament, the real problem was a theological one. And this remains the case for us. There is hardly a public question today which is not fundamentally a theological problem, the resolution of which depends on the proper application of God's law. Christians need to awaken to the reality that there is no 'secular' sphere of life where our faith cannot go. Paul grasped this fact and wasted no time getting to the spiritual heart of every matter he confronted. Christ is Lord of *all* of life. Sound theology ought to be our philosophy of life.

### **The verdict — the judge condemns himself** (24:22-27)

By any standard, Paul's defence was masterly. Felix was impressed and intrigued by the apostle. Furthermore, he **'was well acquainted with the Way'** — which is to say that he knew full well the Jews, whatever their theological disagreements, had no civil case against Paul. So he **'adjourned the proceedings'**, indicating that he would decide the matter later — **'when Lysias the commander'** came to Cæsarea (24:22; cf. 23:26-30). At the same time, Felix was a politician. He used the coming of Lysias, who was never called to give evidence anyway, as an excuse for fobbing off the Jews.

However, he did not release Paul. He gave him considerable freedom and allowed him the comforts of home, but kept him under guard. And so, at least for a while, he placated the Jews, avoided riding too roughshod over Paul's rights as a Roman citizen and, as we shall see, gave himself some time to develop his own interest in the apostle.

Then, a few days after the trial, Felix and his wife Drusilla called for Paul and **'listened to him as he spoke about faith in Christ Jesus'** (24:24). To some modern Christians today, speaking about 'faith in Christ' is limited to basic facts about Jesus and an appeal for the barest mental commitment to him as Saviour. 'Leading people to Christ' has become, for some, the work of an evening's conversation, sealed by a 'prayer to receive Christ'. Scriptural examples of personal evangelism present an entirely different picture. From Jesus' encounters with Nicodemus, the woman at the well and the rich young man, through the witnessing of Peter and Philip, to the personal ministry and preaching of the apostle Paul, we see time taken, doctrine explained, sin confronted, consciences searched, the costs of discipleship counted and well-considered commitments made. Jesus and the apostles do not appear to have worried, as modern Christians do, about 'turning people off' by telling them too much about sin and salvation, repentance and faith and the cost of discipleship. When Paul spoke 'about faith in Christ', he not only spoke about Jesus, the cross and the way of salvation, but also **'discoursed on righteousness, self-control and the judgement to come'** (24:25). There was both gospel and law. And he did not, as many so-called 'soul-winners' do today, confine himself to the *act* of believing — a gospel sales-pitch on saving faith — but expounded the *content* of the life of faith. This is vital in all gospel presentation, for we cannot understand the true meaning and implications of faith — both the doctrine of justification by faith and the act of believing, savingly, upon the Lord Jesus Christ — until and unless we face up to the truth about our spiritual state and condition before God. 'We must see our desert and danger as transgressors of the law, before we can ever fully appreciate the Gospel,' observed Charles Simeon.[8] Paul covered the whole field. He spoke of Jesus, of his death for sinners, of the resurrection, of justification by grace through faith, of the claims of Christ upon our lives, of judgement and eternity.

As he spoke, however, it was not conviction of sin, repentance and faith, and a turning to Jesus that were kindled in Felix's mind. It was, rather, the fear and trembling of someone who wanted to stay the way he was and not be upset by dark thoughts of accountability to God and future judgement. **'Felix was afraid'** — the Greek, *emphobos*, indicates the *condition* of fear — and with good reason. His conscience ought to have troubled him. He had never let God's law get in the way of what he wanted to do with his life. The apostle's challenge was only too clear. 'The law', notes Lenski, 'strikes with great power like a hammer; it pierces the sinner's armour like a sword that reaches the vitals... When a man is struck in an unprotected spot, he inevitably winces even when he does not yield.'[9]

Felix did not yield. He sidestepped the issue. **'That's enough for now! You may leave. When I find it convenient I will send for you'** (24:25). Felix did find it convenient to talk with Paul on many later occasions, but it is clear that he did so mainly in the hope that Paul would **'offer him a bribe'** (24:26). As to the gospel, his mind was made up. He loved his sins more than he feared their consequences. Whatever his qualms, that appears to have been that.

Paul remained a pawn in Felix' endless quest for favour and preferment, for when he was replaced as procurator by Porcius Festus, **'to grant a favour to the Jews, he left Paul in prison'** (24:27).

## The valley of decision

God keeps mercy for thousands. He is slow to anger and plenteous in mercy. But he has told us plainly that he will by no means clear the unrepentantly guilty. He does not keep calling sinners to repentance and faith for ever. There comes a point when he no longer contends with people who are determined to oppose him. Such a moment precipitated the destruction of the human race at the Flood (Gen. 6:3). But such moments come in individual lives and not necessarily at their death. Felix heard the gospel and trembled. His conscience stirred. He saw the issues. But he then took the fatal turn and fobbed God off. We have every reason to believe that this was the moment he chose hell for ever. It is often assumed that everyone has the whole of life in which to turn to Christ and be saved. This is not the case. Scripture makes it clear that 'If we deliberately keep on sinning after we have received a knowledge of the truth, no sacrifice for sins is left, but only a fearful expectation of judgement and of raging fire that will consume the enemies of God' (Heb. 10:27). It is, as the same writer sums up, 'a dreadful thing to fall into the hands of the living God' (Heb. 10:31).

The fact is that with respect to the gospel of Jesus Christ, we live in a valley of decision. To hear the gospel, to know what Scripture says about sin and salvation, imposes the urgent necessity of response. Such experiences are overtures of God's grace and episodes of the Holy Spirit's reaching to our hearts and minds. The Lord is patient and longsuffering. He often besieges unbelieving hearts over many years, sometimes even to the edge of the grave, but at no point can anyone assume or presume that his current encounter with the gospel is not his last. At every point, *now* may be the final opportunity. Urgency is always at the forefront of the gospel call to repentance and faith. Delay is consistently represented as potentially fatal. The message is: '*Today,* if you hear his voice, do not harden your hearts...' (Heb. 3:15 ; cf. Ps. 95:7). Felix's example is a vivid caution to everyone who ever hears the gospel to 'seek, without delay, that godly sorrow which worketh repentance unto salvation' (2 Cor. 7:10).[10] He heard the truth, he trembled, but he turned away.

As for you, heed the advice of William Jay, the great preacher of Bath: 'Bless God if you tremble at his word; but remember, conviction is not conversion. Depend not on excitement in religion, without principle. Pray that you may tremble to purpose. Let your fear induce you to flee for refuge, to lay hold of the hope set before you. Beware of losing your burden on the wrong side of the hill. Lay it down nowhere but at the feet of him who cries: "Come unto me, all ye that labour and are heavy laden, and I will give you rest. Take my yoke upon you, and learn of me; for I am meek and lowly in heart: and ye shall find rest unto your souls. For my yoke is easy and my burden is light."'[11]

## 32. Almost persuaded?

**Please read Acts 25:1 - 26:32**

*'Almost thou persuadest me to be a Christian'* (26:28, AV).

If Felix is an example of someone who showed some interest in the gospel and then quickly backed off when he counted the cost of discipleship, Herod Agrippa II has long been thought of as one who seemed to get very close to becoming a Christian, only to fall at the very last hurdle. He is often portrayed as the one that got away — the 'almost Christian' of a host of gospel sermons![1] This appealing and dramatic perspective does not, however, hold up under closer scrutiny. It owes more to the English of 1611 and the Authorized Version than to the Greek of the New Testament. On a careful reading of the latter, Agrippa turns out to be not quite as much of an 'almost' Christian after all. What he actually said to Paul indicates a man who was quite decided as to his personal attitude to the Christian message.

Furthermore, Agrippa is not primarily significant for his personal unwillingness to trust in Jesus Christ. Many individuals in the New Testament record exemplify the unbelieving response to the gospel. What marks out Agrippa is not so much *what* he did, as *who* he was. He was one of the leading figures in the Jewish community. There is, accordingly, a corporate dimension to his unbelief. Indeed, his response to Paul's evangelistic witness stands as a kind of ratification of the rejection of the gospel by the Jewish establishment of the time. Agrippa's turning away from Christ is emblematic of the hardening opposition to the gospel of the mainstream of Judaism. Because of this, the gospel was thereafter sent to the Gentiles as the primary focus of the evangelization of the world.

The state of Agrippa's individual religious experience, then, must be viewed in the context of this broader reality. He was the reigning Jewish monarch at the time of the destruction of the temple in A. D. 70 and as such he presided over the last days of the Old Testament order. Together with the high priests, he represented the blindness of the Jewish establishment to their own Messianic hope, as that was fulfilled in Jesus of Nazareth. Agrippa was, so to speak, a nail — one of many, certainly — in the coffin of the apostate church of the Old Testament age. In his encounter with Paul he drove his nail home. Within a decade the Old Testament church disappeared for ever. What is left in modern Judaism is a cultic memory of the Pharisaic tradition of New Testament times.

### **Paul's appeal to Cæsar** (25:1-12)

Before we can examine the encounter between King Agrippa and the apostle Paul, we must understand how it came about in the first place. After his initial skirmish with the Jerusalem establishment, Paul had been sent to Cæsarea to have his case heard before the Roman procurator Marcus Antonius Felix (24:1-23). There he remained, under house arrest, for some two years, until the appointment of a new procurator, Festus, led to the reopening of his case.

Just three days after his arrival in Cæsarea, Festus went up to Jerusalem to meet the Jewish leadership. The latter, always having an eye to the main chance, quietly requested that the new procurator reopen their case against Paul. They suggested that Paul be transferred to Jerusalem for trial, secretly intending that he be killed in an ambush along the way (25:1-3). Festus agreed to reopen the case, but was careful to reserve his procuratorial prerogatives by insisting that the Jews come to Cæsarea to press their charges in the proper court and before the proper judge (25:4-5).

Paul's trial was duly convened over a week later. The Jews made **'many serious charges'**, which, adds Luke, **'they could not prove'**. It was '*déjà vu* all over again'.[2] They presented the same three points they had made before Felix and, as before, the apostle denied them all. He had, he said, **'done nothing wrong against the law of the Jews or against the temple or against Cæsar'** (25:6-8). The onus was squarely upon the accusers to prove their case. This they were, of course, incapable of doing.

Festus soon saw that there was no case on which he, as a Roman judge, could find Paul guilty. But the politician in him did not want to offend the Jews in the first fortnight of his period of office. So he made what effort he could to curry their favour. Like Pilate before him, he wished to wash his hands of his inconvenient prisoner. He offered Paul the option of being tried in Jerusalem, adding, no doubt as an inducement, that this would take place before him (25:9). What this meant was that Festus, in effect, wanted to pass the matter back to the lower court, the Jewish Sanhedrin, and have them try once more to resolve the case.[3] The earlier proceeding had ended in total disarray, when Paul had triggered a doctrinal division between the Sadducees and the Pharisees (23:1-11). The Sadducean party had no illusions about the difficulties of conducting a successful prosecution, even in the Sanhedrin. All they wanted was an opportunity to murder Paul, something a journey to Jerusalem would afford. Festus was probably ignorant of the plotting and just hoped somehow to be rid of the embarrassment. He would no doubt gladly have acquiesced to any verdict pronounced in the Jewish court.

But Paul did not let Festus off the hook! He saw clearly that the tendency of the Roman's pragmatism was going to deny him justice. He would be prepared **'to die'** if guilty of a capital crime, but as an innocent man he was certainly not prepared to be handed over to the dubious mercies of his false accusers! He therefore invoked his privilege of last resort as a Roman citizen — **'I appeal to Cæsar!'** — and in a single stroke removed himself from the clutches of both his accusers and his temporizing judge, for, under imperial law, Festus was obliged to send him to Rome (25:11-12). What is significant for modern Christians in this appeal is that Paul was prepared to use every civil right afforded to him by the laws of Rome. He was ready to exhaust every legal avenue. He was challenging the civil authorities to be 'God's servant to do [him] good' (Rom. 13:4), by upholding such righteousness as was enshrined in their laws. We need likewise to hold our 'powers that be' accountable — to judge righteously and do their people good, according to the enduring principles of the Word of God for social order. True justice is biblically defined and is the task of civil government, however secular and unbelieving the times may be.

## **Paul's testimony before Agrippa** (25:13 - 26:27)

**'A few days later King Agrippa and Bernice arrived at Cæsarea to pay their respects to Festus'** (25:13). This Agrippa was the son of the Herod Agrippa who died so dramatically at Cæsarea (Acts

12:23). He was king of a Roman satellite state in northern Palestine and, as we have already noted, a prominent figure in the Jewish establishment. Bernice, his sister, was the widow of her own uncle and a woman of easy virtue, suspected of what Calvin decorously calls 'being excessively familiar' with her brother.[4]

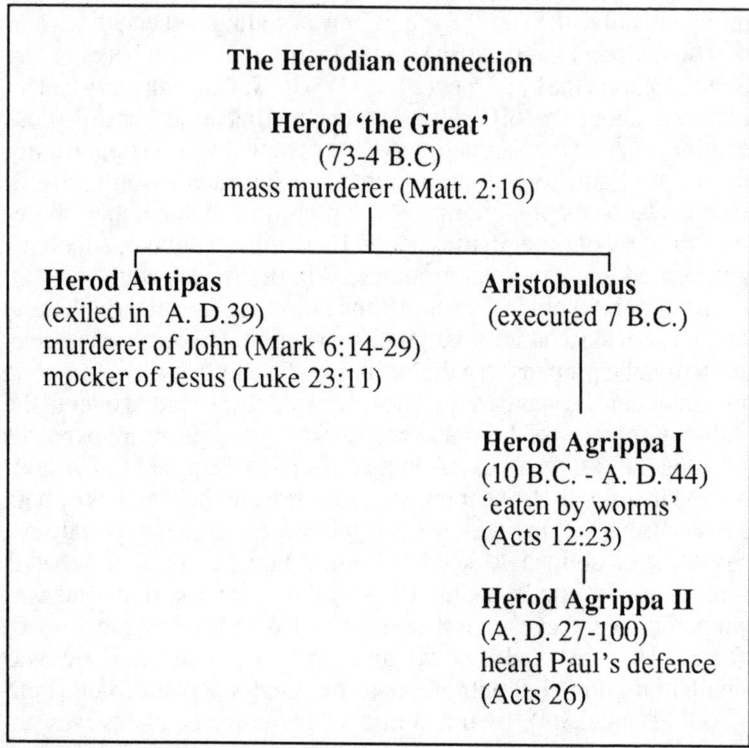


Festus told Agrippa about Paul's case and this so intrigued the king that he asked for an opportunity to hear what Paul had to say for himself, thereby unwittingly setting the stage for one of the greatest defences of the Christian faith the world has ever heard. To Festus the whole thing was a mystery. It was, he thought, a Jewish religious controversy about **'a dead man named Jesus who Paul claimed was alive'** (25:19). He obviously could not care less about Paul's theology, but he wanted some idea of what was going on, so that he would have **'something to write'** to the emperor in Rome.

The next day Paul was brought before the assembled dignitaries and invited to **'speak for [him]self'**. With a motion of his hand, the apostle began his **'defence'** (26:1). Note that this is the third account in Acts of Paul's conversion, so please refer to our expositions of 9:1-19; 22:5-16 for details.[5] The chief significance of this account is that it affords us a model for the way Christians bear personal testimony for Christ. There are six parts.

*1. A humble appeal for a hearing* (26:2-3)

Paul always made his hearers aware that he considered it a privilege to have opportunity to speak to them about his Saviour and faith. He considered himself **'fortunate'** and praised Agrippa's knowledge of **'Jewish customs and controversies'**. In contrast to the fellow whose opening evangelistic question to a college student, in a somewhat reproachful tone, was 'Are you epistemologically self-conscious?' Paul was always respectful in tone, even with those who did not deserve it (e.g. 22:1), and thoroughly down-to-earth and to the point. People naturally react against what they perceive to be a threatening approach and it is probably fair to say that several decades of exposure to door-to-door visitation and raucous street preachers have, if anything, hardened the general populace against gospel witnessing. The need for gentle-spirited evangelists was never greater than it is today in our cynical, burnt-out, gospel-hardened communities. We cannot merely *expect* a hearing because we have a great message; we must *win* a hearing with humility and a discernibly caring attitude to people.

*2. An identification with the hearers* (26:4-8)

Paul always sought to reach people through some point of common and immediately relevant interest. He had his own agenda, of course, but he began with *them*. Agrippa was a Jew and his accusers were Jews. So Paul took full advantage of his Jewishness and of the doctrinal background which he knew that Jews knew from the Scriptures. He spoke directly to the needs and concerns of his hearers. Jesus did this all the time. With Nicodemus he talked theology; with the woman of Samaria he focused on morals; with the rich young man it was money. Had he talked theology with the woman, or morals with the young man, he would have failed to make any impact on them. In point of fact, the woman wanted to talk theology and the young man wanted to talk morals, but they did so in order to get away from Jesus' very pointed claims!

*3. An honest admission of past attitudes to Jesus and his followers* (26:9-11)

Paul could have given Agrippa a sermon on the evils of the Roman political system or on the moral standards of Jewish ecclesiastics. This would have, as the Americans say, 'gone over like a lead balloon', but he could always have said he had told them the truth. Some Christians 'witness' like that and merely manage to come off sounding self-righteous. No one is persuaded by being shouted at, even with home truths. Being 'right' is not enough. There has to be a touching of souls, an element of personal warmth, of vulnerability, of humility, of sincerely seeking the other's good, without any pretension to being above them, without 'talking down' and affecting an air of having, as they say, 'arrived'.

Paul freely admitted that he had once felt as they did about opposing **'the name of Jesus of Nazareth'**. Paul wanted Agrippa to know that he had been where they were. He had not been a Christian all his life. He had really hated Jesus' followers and proved it by his actions, when he **'went to foreign cities to persecute them'**. Calvin notes that 'He did not spare his own character, but freely makes known his own disgrace, so long as the mercy of God may be revealed more clearly out of it.'[6] If we would see people saved, we must both *be* saved ourselves, deeply *feel* the force of that salvation and humbly *testify* to others about that reality in our lives. Jesus does not make nice people nicer; he makes 'alive' those who were 'dead in transgressions' (Eph. 2:5). Lost people need to know that. They are not impressed by blow-dried Pollyannas. Paul showed Agrippa his heart.

*4. An account of conversion to Christ* (26:12-18)

Surely it is obvious that, if we want people to believe in Christ and give their lives to him, we must tell them why and how we came to be Christians ourselves. At the heart of our personal witness for our Saviour is giving the reason for the hope that we have (1 Peter 3:15). Paul, therefore, naturally spoke of his personal experience of *conversion* — his coming to faith in Christ.

This is basically the same as the two earlier accounts of his conversion (9:1-19; 22:5-16), but does offer some new information. Here we are told that Jesus spoke **'in Aramaic'** and quoted a common saying of the time, **'It is hard for you to kick against the goads'** (26:14). This proverb was roughly equivalent to the modern 'You can't buck the system!' It is difficult to face a reality you have been doing your best to deny for years. Paul's proud spirit was humbled and he was convicted of his sin by the real objective appearance of the Jesus he had regarded as totally dead and gone! He wanted Agrippa to know that he had been changed by the sovereign grace of the Lord Jesus Christ at a point when he was full of hostility to him and deserved rather to be crushed by his righteous anger.

Furthermore, he wanted Agrippa to know that the Lord had *commissioned* him to be **'a servant'** and **'a witness of what [he had] seen'** of Jesus, so that the nations **'may receive forgiveness of sins and a place among those who are sanctified by faith in [Jesus]'** (26:16,18). Conversion 'includes a radical transfer of allegiance and so of environment. It is both a liberation from the darkness of satanic rule and a liberation into the sphere of God's marvellous power and light.'[7] Everyone who is saved by grace through faith in Jesus as Saviour and Lord experiences such a transformation and knows that it is his calling to live every day for the Lord.

Paul's calling as apostle to the nations was unique, as was his eyewitness testimony to the risen Jesus. But there is nothing unique about the calling of every Christian to shine as a light in a dark place or to be a city on a hill, which cannot be hidden. And this is in the nature of true Christian testimony. The idea that people can be Christians because they 'go to church', or 'try to be good', or in some way coldly accept there is a God and think Jesus came to do some good, is completely exploded by everything the Bible reveals about the nature of Christ, the gospel and the way of salvation. Real Christians *love* Jesus from the heart. They *know* that they do. And whether they were converted dramatically, as Paul was, or quietly, as many growing up in Christian homes have been, they confess him as the Saviour they have come to know in their *experience*. More than that, they seek daily to *live* for him as their Lord. They offer their whole life to him, and though they are the first to confess their failure to measure up to their Redeemer, they confess with hand on heart that he is who he is and that they are his.

*5. A testimony to continuing commitment to Christ* (26:19-23)

Paul also stressed that he had consistently given himself to this calling ever since his conversion. He couches what he says in terms of an implicit appeal to Agrippa to agree that this was the right thing to do. It was, after all, a **'vision from heaven'** which changed him (26:19). Would the king expect him to do otherwise? And what did he do except preach everywhere that people should **'repent and turn to God and prove their repentance by their deeds'**? (26:20). Again, Paul brought Agrippa up hard against his conscience. Was not faith, repentance and doing what God commanded exactly the point of God's Word? Why then, when he was in the act of keeping God's law in the **'temple courts'** (see 21:26-27), were the Jews so angry that they tried to kill him? Was he not simply doing *God's* will? Furthermore, the truth was that he was **'saying nothing beyond what the prophets and Moses said would happen — that the Christ** [i.e., the Anointed One, the Messiah, *ho christos*] **would suffer, and as the first to rise from the dead, would proclaim light to his own people and to the Gentiles'** (26:21-23). This was a masterly defence. Every syllable forced Agrippa to face the teaching of his own Scriptures and ask himself whether or not what Paul was saying was true.

The message for us, two millennia on, is to steep ourselves in God's Word and live holy lives, so that we, too, may say with open faces and clear consciences that what we say and do is the consistent expression of obedience to God's plainly revealed will. It is to take what the Bible says about the human condition and ask lost people to face what they know to be true from the television news and their own lives, namely, that the wages of sin is death. It is applying the good news of salvation to a world that is rotting before their eyes. If we have courage and speak plainly and biblically, we cannot avoid touching the consciences of unconverted, Christless, lost people. Paul shows us the way.

*6. A challenge to the hearers to come to Christ* (26:24-27)

Festus simply thought Paul was crazy: **'"You are out of your mind, Paul!" he shouted. "Your great learning is driving you insane!"'** (26:24). He just was not interested and, like so many since, shrugged it off as so much nonsense.

Paul, however, was not to be deflected from driving home his message to Agrippa's conscience. Asserting the soundness of both his mind and his argument, and reminding the king of his knowledge of these matters, he looked Agrippa in the eye and said, **'King Agrippa, do you believe the prophets? I know you do'** (26:27). We shall examine the king's response in a moment. The point to be noted here is that Paul moved from a first person singular explanation of his faith to a second person singular challenge to Agrippa's faith. This has to happen in all preaching and in all personal witness, if men and women are to be called to repentance and faith at all. There must come the point where we say: 'What about *you?* Where do *you* stand? What will *you* do with Jesus?'

Everything Paul said had led to this point. He stalked Agrippa's conscience and then he pounced to face him with a decision. Paul was no longer defending himself from legal guilt; he was evangelizing his royal auditor and calling him to the bar of heaven! The roles were reversed in that moment and the judge became the man in the dock! This is the aim of all evangelism — to arraign lost and guilty sinners before God's justice and call them, helpless, to the Saviour whose blood cleanses from all sin. Paul's challenge left Agrippa naked before heaven and the claims of God. Did he believe the prophets? Yes, he did, to a certain degree. Then he must believe in Jesus as the Christ, for he is the one of whom the prophets had spoken! He was at the crossroads of his life and his eternal destiny! The issue was clear. This he knew. He had been invited to believe the gospel.

## Was Agrippa 'almost persuaded'? (26:28-32)

Agrippa was clearly affected by Paul's direct challenge. We have already noted that Agrippa became known to generations of English-speaking Bible readers as the classic 'almost Christian', because of the Authorized Version of 1611: '*Almost thou persuadest* me to be a Christian' (26:28, AV). He is the man who seemed seriously open to the gospel, but held back at the very last moment. One writer went as far as to say that the king was 'convinced that Jesus was the Christ'.[8] But how convinced was Agrippa? Was he really 'almost' a Christian? The answer hinges on two points relative to the translation of the verse.

The first is that the Greek *(en oligo)* appears to refer to *time* rather than to a measure of either Agrippa's *persuasion* (AV, 1611) or Paul's *persuasiveness* (RV, 1881).[9] The best rendering of the text is: 'In a *short time* you will persuade me to become a Christian' (NASB).[10] *En oligo* means literally 'in a little' and is the same expression used in Paul's reply, where he clearly takes up Agrippa's intended meaning: **'Short time or long...'** (26:29).

The second point is that when Agrippa refers to being persuaded, it is not at all obvious that he means to be taken at face value. The tenor of the whole passage strongly suggests that Agrippa, while a thinking person with a sincere enough interest in hearing what Paul had to say, remained detached throughout. When the apostle challenged him directly, the king reacted with a rather rueful, defensive, and even ironic put-down, as if to say: 'I have to hand it to you, Paul! In no time at all you'll be talking me into becoming a Christian!' He fobbed Paul off. He felt the power of his message, but held back decisively. He was actually quite a distance from being, in the words of the well-known chorus, 'almost persuaded'. He was, if anything, persuaded to be unpersuaded! He was undoubtedly impressed by Paul's masterly arguments. His conscience was pricked. He saw that the real issue was coming to Jesus as the risen Christ in repentance and faith, and with a commitment to follow him. But Agrippa did not want Jesus to be his Saviour and Lord. And he was unable to refute Paul — in this he reminds us of the rich young man who 'went away sad' from Jesus (Mark 10:22). So he shrugged him off and turned away.

John Calvin hit the nail on the head: 'The apostle accomplished at least this, that he wrested an involuntary confession out of King Agrippa; just as those who cannot resist the truth any longer are in the habit of nodding, or at any rate giving some kind of assent. Agrippa indeed means that he will not be a Christian willingly, and what is more has no intention of becoming one, yet that he is unable to resist, but is somehow being drawn in in spite of himself. That goes to show how great the stubbornness of human nature is, until it is reduced to obedience by the Spirit of God.'[11]

The sad fact is that Agrippa chose unbelief. He had to admit Paul was innocent of anything deserving death or imprisonment and no doubt regretted, with Festus, that he now had to be sent to Rome (26:30-31). But as to the heart of the matter, the gospel of Jesus Christ, he still loved darkness more than light (John 3:19). He knew the right thing to do and did not do it (James 4:17). He had heard the truth and, having gone his way, had no excuse for his sin (John 15:22).

What does this mean for us? First of all, it reminds us that a mere knowledge of the facts of biblical truth does not make anyone a real Christian. Agrippa knew what Scripture taught. He understood Paul and only too clearly grasped the implications of his message. Yet no amount of argument was going to take him to the foot of the cross, to trust in Jesus. He is often thought of as one who was 'not far from the kingdom of God' and in a sense this is true. Yet, it is more accurate to say that it was the kingdom of God that was not far from him! New life in Christ was offered to him on a platter, but he would not repent and believe. In terms of attitude, intentions and response, he might have been a million miles away. In fact, he resisted the gospel to the last.

Finally, it tells us that we must not, like Agrippa, flirt with the gospel and remain committed to being uncommitted. There is a parallel of a kind here with the way the rich young man responded to Jesus' charge to sell all he had and give to the poor (Mark 10:21). That young man accepted God's law, but only in such a way as to resist the spiritual claims of both the law and the gospel. He went on his way because he would not leave everything to follow Jesus. Agrippa went on his way, albeit with an interest in Pauline theology and some religiosity of his own, and all because he would not give himself to Christ.

Paul's prayer calls us to Christ: **'Short time or long — I pray God that not only you but all who are listening to me today may become what I am except for these chains'**(26:29). With nothing but the utmost humility and overflowing gratitude to the Lord, he could say that it was the greatest thing in the world to be a Christian, to know the love of Christ, to be washed in the blood of the Lamb, to be filled with the Holy Spirit and to enjoy the liberty of the children of God. And this he wished most earnestly for all who heard him that day. Agrippa chose the path that leads to destruction. Christ still calls you to choose the path of life.

# 33. Kept by the power of God

**Please read Acts 27:1 - 28:16**

*'Who are kept by the power of God...'* (1 Peter 1:5, AV).

Luke's account of the 'acts of the apostles' is fast drawing to a close. Most of the 'meat' of his story is behind him and he now concludes his narrative with the record of Paul's journey to Rome and his reception in that great city. The physician's readers might perhaps be forgiven for passing more lightly over these closing chapters, for there is no doctrinal teaching in them which has not been covered more thoroughly elsewhere in his account. To do so, however, would be to neglect the record of some significant events in God's unfolding work of redemption in the Roman world.

Paul's journey to Rome was one of the most remarkable ever recorded in the annals of missionary endeavour. After a long and stormy voyage, the apostle was shipwrecked and his life and that of his companions spared in fulfilment of direct revelation from God. He was left destitute on a beach in Malta and shown hospitality by complete strangers. He was bitten by a viper, but not injured. He was accused of being a murderer and then hailed as a 'god'! Luke shows us that the hand of God was upon Paul through this whole business, preserving him for the work he still had for him to do in Rome and beyond. He was 'kept by the power of God through faith unto salvation ready to be revealed in the last time' (1 Peter 1:5, AV).

The passage unfolds a four-act drama, in which we see Paul sailing into trouble (27:1-12), in a storm at sea (27:13-38), saved by the power of God (27:39 - 28:10) and arriving in Rome (28:11-16).

**Sailing into trouble** (27:1-12)

Luke's journal records the course of the voyage in some considerable detail and gives us a distinctly authentic 'feel' for maritime travel in the ancient world. The prisoners were first embarked, probably at Cæsarea (see Map 4), on a ship from Adramyttium in Greece. They sailed up the coast to Sidon, to the east and north of Cyprus — **'the lee'** being the opposite side of the island from that of the prevailing wind, which is from the west in the eastern Mediterranean. After some two weeks of what must have been very skilful ship-handling, they docked at Myra on what is now the south coast of Turkey.[1] There they changed ships for one that was heading for Italy, out of Alexandria in Egypt, and made **'slow headway'** over to Crete, finally dropping anchor at a place called Fair Havens. It was now early October (**'after the Fast'**, i.e. Yom Kippur, 27:9) and the weather was closing in on them. Nevertheless, the decision was made to press on a further forty miles to the Cretan port of Phœnix (perhaps the modern Phineka) and spend the winter there.

Two points in this narrative call for some comment. The first is almost incidental, but highlights a truth that has been of great encouragement to many Christians over the years. When Paul's ship landed at Sidon, the centurion **'in kindness ... allowed him to go to his friends so they might provide for his needs'** (27:3). As far as we know, Paul had never been in Sidon. Perhaps he had made these friends while in nearby Tyre, or on his travels. It may even be just a reference to the fellowship that exists between Christians who are meeting for the first time, as a result, certainly, of contacts and intermediaries through the networking of people of like mind. Whoever they were, they were friends to Paul, because they provided for his needs. It was to be the last time before his arrival in Rome that he would rejoice in the fellowship and family worship of a Christian home and a wider company of believers. It was in a sense his valedictory service as he left on his great mission to Nero's capital. Strengthened and encouraged by the warmth of Christian friends, Paul was fortified against the sea of trouble that lay before him.

The second point concerns the apostle's warning against sailing on late in the year and in the face of worsening weather (27:10). The pilot and the ship-owner regarded it as advisable to seek a better port in which to winter. Clearly, they were between a rock and a hard place: they could stay put and risk losing the ship in port, or sail and risk losing both ship and crew at sea, should conditions deteriorate further. In this context Paul's warning is more prediction than prescription. He foresaw disaster and said so. It was not that Paul did not believe that God was sovereign over wind and wave and would not get him to Rome, come what might. He simply emphasized the path of prudence and responsibility. Better to be safe than sorry, and arrive in Italy in one piece in the spring, than hazard the dangerous billows of a wintry sea. The absolute sovereignty of God is the context, not the contradiction, of the proper exercise of human responsibility. He who foreordains whatever comes to pass also foreordains the means by which it should happen — and the intelligent application of the human brain is often a part of those means! Taking the longer view, we may say that Paul's advice set the scene for those later incidents on the voyage in which God again confirmed his apostolic discernment and calling by mighty and miraculous deliverances, even if it had no immediate effect on those responsible for the decision to put to sea. The old cliché is as true as ever: man proposes, God disposes.

## Storm at sea (27:13-38)

The sailors were not foolhardy. They waited till the weather improved before they **'weighed anchor and sailed along the coast of Crete'** (27:13). Their optimism was soon shattered, however, by a **'wind of hurricane force, called the "north-easter"'**, which drove them inexorably towards the African coast and the dreaded **'sandbars of Syrtis'** (27:14,17). Day after day they ran before the wind until, bereft of cargo, tackle and even hope, they waited helplessly for the ship to take them to a watery grave.

When hurricane 'Hugo' slammed into Charleston, South Carolina, on 21 September 1989, killing twenty people and causing three billion dollars worth of damage, one woman interviewed on national television commented that many in Charleston had no time for the Lord and that the hurricane was a message from God calling people to turn to him. It was a word in season. Such calamities do give pause for serious reflections on the issues of life and death. They also reveal people's deeper commitments — or the lack of them. Paul was no exception — and he soon showed the other 275 people on board something of the stuff of which God had made him by his grace. Three times in these harrowing days Paul intervened to encourage their flagging spirits.

*1. A call for faith* (27:21-26)

By this time, everybody on board must have been only too well aware that the decision to sail on, against Paul's advice, had proved a costly error of judgement. Why, then, did Paul remind them of his earlier warning? (cf. 27:10). Certainly not just to say a smug 'I told you so!' And surely not to cast the blame in rueful recrimination. In fact, God had given him more to say and this reminder of his earlier wisdom grabbed their attention and commanded a hearing. They must **'keep up [their] courage'**, for, even though they would **'run aground on some island'** and the ship would be destroyed, **'not one of [them]'** would be lost! But why should they believe him? Because God had sent **'an angel'** to assure Paul that he would arrive in Rome to **'stand trial before Cæsar'** and that he had been given **'the lives of all who sail[ed] with [him]'**. He had **'faith in God'** that it would happen just as he had been promised. They should take courage!

We should note, first of all, that this incident illustrates the basic fact that the whole human race is in the same boat in this life. All men, whether believers or unbelievers, share a common life and are subject to the same kinds of ups and downs. Yet running through this shared tapestry is a thread of blessing peculiarly attached to the Lord's people. For ten righteous men the Lord would have spared Sodom (Gen. 18:32), and he blessed Potiphar's house for Joseph's sake (Gen. 39:5). For many thousands he presently spares a London and a New York. Godless sailors lived because of godly Paul. The unconverted do not realize how great are the blessings that have flowed to them from the presence of God's people among them. 'It is', as Calvin observes, 'a remarkable pledge of God's love toward us that he makes some drops of his kindness flow from us to others.'[2]

We must also grasp, in the second place, a more solemn truth, namely that 'All the blessings that God lavishes on the ungodly finally make for their destruction, just as, on the other hand, the punishments which the faithful suffer in common with the reprobate are to their advantage.'[3] The pagan sailors might escape Davy Jones' locker this time, but hell still yawned open for the unconverted. Whatever their temporal blessings, the lost stay lost if they do not embrace Christ by faith. On the other hand, for Paul to live was Christ and to die, gain (Phil. 1:21). Whatever their trials, believers discover that they work in them a great weight of glory in Jesus their Saviour (2 Cor. 4:17). The real issue is not how easy or difficult this life may be; it is rather what we do with Jesus Christ!

Finally, we can see that Paul's exhortation to the men to take courage was more fundamentally a call to faith. The message was muted, but it was there. No doubt he had earlier told them why he was going to Rome and about this Jesus whom he served. Paul's day-to-day life was one exercise in holistic evangelism. He did not need to give a formal gospel presentation for them to get his message. He simply testified to the promises of the one **'whose I am and whom I serve'**, and affirmed his personal faith in his God. They could not escape the claims of his testimony. It was an invitation to believe as he did. When modern Christians begin to live their faith with such a natural, open-faced witness for the Lord, we shall see among us the power of God to save.

*2. A call for unity* (27:27-32)

The crisis came at midnight on the fourteenth day out of Crete. They were in fact about to make landfall on Malta, after being driven across the central Mediterranean (the name **'Adriatic'** then covered more than the area north of the Straits of Otranto). The terror of that night defies even Luke's description. In the end they could only **'pray for daylight'**. Some sailors, however, thought to escape the sinking ship by stealing off with the lifeboat. Paul insisted that all hands were needed if any were to be saved, and the centurion duly prevented them from abandoning the ship. Keeping together, striving together and, not least, believing together are necessary to human progress.

The selfishness of the sailors recalls an incident in 1991 in the Indian Ocean, when a cruise ship foundered in a storm. The captain and many of the crew abandoned the ship and left the passengers to their fate. Tragedy was averted — amazingly without any loss — by the heroic efforts of South African rescue helicopters and ships, in stark contrast to the conduct of the crew.

In Paul's case, of course, the focus was on a unified response to God's promise that they would be spared. Disunity was simply unbelief in the promise and therefore a counsel of despair and a self-fulfilling prophecy of impending doom.

*3. A call for effort* (27:33-38)

The promise of God always includes the means of fulfilling the promise. 'God certainly does not commend his power to the faithful,' writes Calvin, 'in order that they may give themselves up to laziness and inactivity, with contempt for intervening means, or rashly rush into danger, when there is a definite reason for taking care.'[4] Responsibility is the context for receiving what God has promised. God's sure decree never implies a fatalistic response — it is rather an encouragement to optimistic, expectant effort. Before dawn Paul intervened for a third time and urged them to **'take some food'**. He also reminded them of God's promise. Then he took some food and **'gave thanks to God in front of them all'** and **'broke it and began to eat'** (27:35). In this way, too, he evangelized the men. He testified without any affectation or shame that his God was the Lord and the Giver of every good and perfect gift. He did not hide his faith or his devotion from the unconverted. What they saw was what they got — a real Christian, living for Jesus Christ.

John Stott says it best when he comments that here we see 'aspects of Paul's character which endear him to us as an integrated Christian who combined spirituality with sanity, and faith with works... He was a man of God and of action, a man of the Spirit and of common sense.'[5] Because he was truly 'heavenly-minded', he was a great deal of 'earthly use'! Christians, you ought to be the most practical people in the world, because the Lord has given you the real truth about the real world and its real needs!

## **Saved by the power of God** (27:39 - 28:10)

Daylight brought land, which turned out to be the island of Malta, and with it the delivery upon the shore of the whole company, safe and sound, if exhausted and bedraggled (27:39-44). In the process, the truth of Paul's earlier revelation that God had given their lives to him was powerfully confirmed in the centurion's forbearing to kill the prisoners because he wanted to preserve Paul alive (27:24,43).

Luke tells us little of Paul's three-month stay on Malta, but he does record two significant events which powerfully attested his apostolic commission and message.

*The viper on the beach* (28:1-6)

The local Maltese people were of largely Phœnician origin. They were not 'barbarous people', as the AV wrongly translates the Greek *barbaroi* — a word which simply refers to foreigners, neither Greeks nor Jews, who spoke their own languages.[6] And they proved just how civilized and compassionate they really were by mounting a relief effort which was to extend to caring for all 276 for the entire winter! Marooned the travellers were, but not on a desert island populated by 'barbarians'!

They immediately built a fire on the beach for the shivering castaways. Paul gathered some brushwood for this fire and so unwittingly triggered the incident which led many to think he was a god. When he put the wood on the fire, **'A viper, driven out by the heat, fastened itself on his hand'** (28:3).

The first reaction of the islanders was to jump to the conclusion that he was **'a murderer'**, who, having escaped from the sea, was now being caught by **'Justice'** — which, for these pagan folk, was 'the goddess *Dike*, the personification of justice and revenge' (28:4).[7] This reaction is not to be brushed off as so much superstition. There is, indeed, a certain sense in which the events we observe express God's judgements in the earth (Rom. 1:18). Any and every calamity ought to cause us to reflect on our relationship with the God who is holy and just and who is righteously angry with human wickedness every day. It is also true that certain evils have predictable, clearly identifiable, consequences — sexually transmitted diseases being a case in point.

Where we make the mistake — and this was what the Maltese did with Paul's viper — is when we assume that there is *always* a one-to-one correlation between public disasters and personal sins and jump to the conclusion that everyone who suffers anything must be receiving punishment for some specific sin. This was what Job's celebrated 'comforters' thought about Job's personal tragedies —

and they were wrong. Sufferings, like the rain that falls on the just and the unjust, are experienced by all sorts of people and for no specifically attributable reason of gross sin (Eccles. 9:1-3). What we can say is that when these things happen to godly people, they have the ultimate purpose of refining their faith and showing through them, in them and to the watching world, the glory of God (John 9:2-3; 2 Cor. 4:17; Heb. 12:6). We therefore cannot make judgements about people and their relationship to the Lord on the basis of their sufferings. Jesus made this absolutely and for ever plain. Somebody raised the question of the Galileans who had died at the hands of Pilate's police in a fracas at the temple. The implication apparently was that they had to have been special sinners to perish in this way. Jesus' answer was an emphatic, 'I tell you, no!' and a solemn exhortation, 'But unless you repent, you too will all perish.' To make it even clearer, he asked if the eighteen men who died in an accident — the collapse of a tower in Siloam — were greater sinners than the rest of the people in Jerusalem. 'Of course not!' was the answer he assumed they would (correctly) give. Then, he repeated, 'Unless you repent, you too will all perish' (Luke 13:1-5). All calamities, rightly understood, call all men everywhere to repent towards God and believe in the Lord Jesus Christ.

Paul, however, was miraculously preserved from the viper's poison. He **'suffered no ill effects'** (28:5). This, not surprisingly, effected a complete reversal in the Maltese attitude to Paul. They promoted him from being a murderer to being **'a god'**! (28:6). This, of course, is the other side of the error we have just discussed — the crude correlation of beneficial circumstances with personal goodness. It is the error of the so-called 'prosperity gospel' that promises health and wealth in this life as the necessary and invariable reward and proof of a living faith. This does not square with Jesus' teaching about having troubles in this world and taking up 'the cross' and following him. Whatever temporal blessings God may give us, the true and abiding reward of the believer is the life everlasting (Rom. 2:5-10).

In any event, the glory is God's and Paul was no doubt as horrified to hear the Maltese attribute divinity to him as he had been in Lystra years before (14:11-18). If, therefore, we have plenty and have the blessing of a quiet life, this should impel us to gratitude to God and redoubled personal commitment to a holy life. If we merely conclude that prosperity proves that we are right with God, we not only misread the Bible and history, we set ourselves up for a terrible fall. God resists the proud, but gives grace to the humble.

*The healing of the sick (28:7-10)*

Paul was not the only one to be preserved from a life-threatening situation. Publius, the leading local official, entertained Paul's company — i.e. the centurion and his chief charges — for three days. Paul healed his father and soon, **'The rest of the sick on the island came and were cured.'** Again, we have an instance of the attestation of both the apostolic message and the apostolic messenger — tying in the message of salvation by grace in Christ with the tangible compassion of healing miracles. We are not told of any conversions at this time, but the fact that Paul was **'honoured ... in many ways'** gives reason to hope that many Maltese may have become believers.

**God's promise kept — arrival in Rome** (28:11-16)

In due course, Paul set sail again for Italy. He landed at Puteoli, in the Gulf of Naples, and stayed there a week with **'some brothers'**. Then he went on to Rome and a meeting with more Christians, who had come as much as forty miles from the city to meet him. No wonder **'Paul thanked God and was encouraged'** when he saw these men! The Lord had kept him by his power to fulfil his promise that he would come to Rome to stand trial before Cæsar! (27:24).

Paul had again experienced what he had long known to be true, both from the doctrine of God's Word and from his experience of God's dealings with him: namely, that whatever happens to us in life, falls within the purpose of God. No storm, no shipwreck, no viper, no Sanhedrin, no riots, no murderous threats — nothing could separate him from the love of God or thwart God's purpose for him. This, too, is a truth for every Christian today. We are 'kept by the power of God' says the apostle Peter (1 Peter 1:5). 'Our faith', comments Robert Leighton, 'lays hold upon this power, and this power strengthens faith, and so we are preserved; it puts us within those walls, sets the soul within the guard of the power of God, which, by self-confidence and vain presuming in its own strength, is exposed to all kinds of danger. Faith is an humble, self-denying grace; it makes the Christian nothing in himself and all in God... It is the property of a good Christian to magnify the power of God, and to have high thoughts of it, and therefore it is his privilege to find safety in that power.'[8] And so we can sing with joy and thanksgiving:

I love you, Lord! You are my strength,
The Lord, my rock, my fort, my power,
My God, my hiding place, my shield,
My horn of safety, and my tower.[9]

# 34.
# The unfinished task

**Please read Acts 28:17-31**

*'Salvation has been sent to the Gentiles, and they will listen'* (28:28).

Paul arrived quietly in Rome and settled into a ministry which was to continue for some two years. During this time he seems to have been spared any dramatic confrontations with the authorities. If the Emperor Nero knew that Paul had appealed to him, there is no evidence that he paid any attention to the case. Luke only records an exchange between Paul and the local Jewish community. Then it just seems to tail off. There is no neat, final and happy ending. The book of Acts ends, not with a full stop, but with a dotted line. This is reminiscent of the book of the prophet Jonah, which also ends rather abruptly, leaving unanswered questions about the state of Jonah's faith and the implications of God's grace towards Nineveh for the Gentile world. In the same way, Luke leaves us hanging ... wondering what came next. This open-endedness, in both Acts and Jonah, is clearly quite deliberate. God did not want either historian to conclude his account with a fully-rounded finale or a sentimental 'happy ending'. He intended rather to leave us with what are essentially unfinished stories. And they are unfinished because the work of God remains unfinished and because the preaching of the gospel is to go on until the Lord returns at the end of the age. The Lord is still saving lost people and calling them to love and serve him with all their hearts and minds and strength throughout all their days. The unfinished task of the church is to proclaim the gospel of saving grace in Jesus Christ to the ends of the earth while the world lasts.

The book of Acts, then, is about the continuing work of God in and through his church. For that very reason, it is also about the unfinished work of faithfulness: faithfulness in reaching out (28:17-22); faithfulness in persevering when people will not listen (28:23-

29) and faithfulness in proclaiming Jesus Christ, the only Saviour (28:30-31).

**Faithfulness ... in reaching out** (28:17-22)

Paul's arrival in Rome was the fulfilment of the Lord's words to him in a Jerusalem prison: 'Take courage! As you have testified about me in Jerusalem, so you must also testify in Rome' (23:11). The apostle wasted no time. As soon as he had settled into house arrest, he began to reach out to the Jews of Rome. **'Three days later he called together the leaders of the Jews'** (28:17). Considering all that had transpired between the apostle and the Jewish church over the years, it is remarkable that the Jewish leaders in Rome would accept an invitation to meet with him. It is also striking that he should approach them as he did. Paul had a heart for his own people, that they might be saved (Rom. 10:1). This illustrates one of the hallmarks of the evangelistic impulse: it is the spirit that not only takes, but *makes,* opportunities to spread the good news of Jesus Christ. There was nothing passive about apostolic evangelism. Paul did not wait for things to happen. He targeted synagogues and market-places and hostile crowds. He made the most of his arrests, trials, shipwrecks and imprisonment. He was always working on ways of reaching out with the gospel. He never exhibits that all-too-common unwillingness of modern Christians to give a reason for the hope that is in them — until and unless it is virtually *forced* out of them by circumstances or insistent enquirers! Paul was not shackled by worries about embarrassing or offending people, or invading their privacy, or 'forcing his opinions down people's throats'.

His world was a market-place of ideas. He forced nothing upon anybody. But he refused to let anyone, far less his own fears and inhibitions, prevent him from proclaiming Jesus Christ as the only Saviour of sinners! This liberty did not, however, issue in the almost obnoxious approach of those who, with near-robotic detachment, shout the gospel at passers-by in shopping centres or collar some young girl on the street with insistent words about hell and sin. There is nothing unlovely or insensitive about Paul's approach. He never tried to shout people into the kingdom of God. He told people the truth, but did so with honesty, sensitivity and a spiritual focus that breathed a personal concern for their souls.

*An honest approach* (28:17-18)

Paul was completely honest about the circumstances which brought him to Rome. He did not want the Jews of Rome to hear second-hand about his arrest and his appeal to Cæsar. If he had been furtive about these matters, it would only have led to suspicious speculation and must have seriously harmed the reputation of the fledgling Christian witness in the metropolis. Paul told them that in spite of all this judicial activity, he had done nothing against their — or his — people and ancestral customs.

*A sensitive approach* (28:19-20)

Notice also that Paul did not indulge in any complaining or accusation over his past treatment by the Jews. His appeal to Cæsar was to secure his release, in accord with the decision of the lower court that he had done nothing worthy of death. He had no hidden agenda. He had no charge to bring against his own people. And it was to explain this that he had asked to meet with them. If Christians want to win people for Christ, they will have to avoid introducing harmful, irrelevant and unnecessary distractions into their efforts to communicate the gospel. We think of a Roman Catholic we once knew, whose first approach from a local evangelical church's evangelistic outreach was to receive through the door a tract on how the church of Rome is the biblical Babylon, the Mother of Harlots! Some Christians need to learn that winning points is not the same as winning people! Loving the lost means sensitivity to their susceptibilities as well as their need.

*A spiritual approach* (28:20)

Paul's motive for appealing to Cæsar, then, was not for revenge against the Sanhedrin. But neither was it merely for his legal vindication and personal freedom. It was, he said, on account of **'the hope of Israel'** that he was in chains. The 'hope of Israel' is, of course, the promise of a Messiah in the Old Testament, now fulfilled in the person and work of Jesus Christ. The glory of the Saviour is to be the consuming motive and goal of all Christian witness. Paul, of course, was really saying that he was a true Jew — a believer in the Messiah — and was assuring the Jews in Rome that, far from representing some weird new heresy, he was actually serving God according to the soundest scriptural orthodoxy! He was wooing his hearers towards considering the claims of Jesus Christ.

*A successful approach* (28:21-22)

The goal of Paul's first approach was really quite limited. He wanted to gain a hearing. He did not want to be turned away even before he could say a word. In this he succeeded, for the Jews were prepared to listen, and, although they had heard nothing of his particular case, they had heard plenty of talk **'against this sect'**. Here is a lesson Christians need to learn and apply today: pre-evangelism is almost as important as evangelism itself. Like the golf ball hit towards the pin — 'If you're never up, you're never in' — we must win a hearing *for* the gospel, if the gospel *itself* is to be heard at all.

**Faithful ... when people will not listen** (28:23-29)

Getting a hearing does not guarantee acceptance of the message. The Roman Jews listened to Paul, but their initial interest turned to a decisive rejection of the gospel message. This is startling for several reasons. First of all, this is the last specific incident recorded in the book of Acts. We are left with a starkly candid picture of the difficulty of preaching Christ in an unsympathetic world and the necessity of trusting the Lord to do his work in people's lives. Secondly, this is the last instance of a Jewish rejection of Paul's ministry and is the moment when he turns exclusively to the Gentiles. Henceforth, the hitherto prevailing Jewish character of the church would give way to the multi-ethnicity that has characterized her to this day. Thirdly, Paul confirms Jesus' principle that rejection in one place is a mandate to take the message of salvation elsewhere (Matt. 10:14). The gospel moves on, seeking the lost wherever they may be found.

*When some won't listen...* (28:23-27)

If the Roman Jews rejected the gospel, it was not for lack of hearing the message. Paul preached Christ from the Old Testament Scriptures **'from morning till evening'** (28:23). The large crowd was evidently very attentive, but as the day advanced, decisions were made in many minds: **'Some were convinced'** and **'Others would not believe'** (28:24). It is clear from what follows that the latter were in the majority.

Winding up his address, and no doubt keenly aware of the hardening attitudes among his hearers, Paul quoted Isaiah 6:9-10 to them. The original passage, as J. A. Alexander has pointed out, presents three distinct elements, each of which contributes to the judgement on the people's unbelief. These are, 'the ministerial agency of the Prophet, the judicial agency of God, and the suicidal agency of the people themselves'.[1] The role of the prophet is emphasized in Isaiah 6 itself. In John's quotation in John 12:39-40 the apostle emphasizes the sovereign judgement of God as that which shut the eyes and ears of those who witnessed Jesus' miracles and still did not believe. The third element — the self-destructive attitude of the people themselves — is emphasized by Jesus in his use of Isaiah's words in Matthew 13:14-15 and by Paul in Acts 28.

'What you are doing,' Paul was saying to the Roman Jews, 'is to put yourselves in the same category as your unbelieving ancestors, who repeatedly rejected the prophets and were themselves finally rejected by God for their hardness of heart.' It was an earnest appeal for them to turn back and *not be* **'ever hearing but never understanding ... ever seeing but never perceiving'**. It was a call for them not wilfully and deliberately to harden their hearts, close their eyes and shut their ears, because they were afraid that the Lord might **'heal them'** if they did **'see ... hear ... understand ... and turn'** (28:27). Nothing could have been made more clear to that audience than that *they* were acting, on their own responsibility, to reject the overtures of God's grace and, at the same time, point them to the Christ as the only name given under heaven among men whereby they had to be saved! They did not listen, but it was not for lack of hearing the gospel.

*Go to others who will listen* (28:28-29)[2]

It is important to realize that the Roman Jews' rejection of the gospel is not just another incident among a myriad of such events. This particular moment was, in fact, the end of an era for unbelieving Judaism. Hitherto, the gospel had been taken 'to the Jew *first*, and also to the Greek' (Rom. 1:16, AV). Henceforth, the gospel would go to the nations of the world: **'God's salvation has been sent to the Gentiles, and they will listen.'** Judaism would meanwhile have its own rendezvous with destiny in A. D. 70, with the destruction of Jerusalem and the temple — less than a decade after Paul, under the inspiration of the Holy Spirit, spoke this solemn word from God.

Given its reference to this unique event in redemptive history, what, if anything, can we say about its application to succeeding generations of Christians? We may certainly say that Paul did not mean to say either that no Jews would ever listen to the gospel thereafter, or that no Gentiles would ever reject the gospel. When Paul said that the Gentiles 'will listen', he simply meant that the church of the future would be preponderantly made up of Gentile converts. And so we may take it that Isaiah's words apply as much to the twentieth century and most pointedly (but not exclusively) address the rejection of the truth *within* the visible church. Remember that Paul was speaking to the Old Testament *church,* when he spoke to the Jews. The central application of this passage today is to the New Testament church — to the covenant-breakers and apostates within the church, or what calls itself the church — to the end that we really listen to the word of the Lord. 'Well', said Charles Simeon, 'be it known to you, that if you, who call yourselves Christians, will not value the gospel as you ought, it shall be taken away from you, and will be given to others who will bring forth the fruits thereof with gladness.'[3]

## **Faithful ... to proclaim the Lord Jesus Christ** (28:30-31)

There is, however, also a somewhat less threatening application for us here and an appropriately encouraging one on which to close the Acts of the Apostles. **'For two whole years'** Paul was able to preach the gospel in Rome, and all this time he was under house arrest! Notice the three main characteristics of his ministry during that two-year period.

1. He **'welcomed all who came to see him'**. His door was open to all enquirers. If he could not go to them, he would not turn away any who came to him. He maximized his opportunities to speak of Christ and minister to men and women.
2. He consistently **'preached the kingdom of God and taught**

**about the Lord Jesus Christ'**. The gospel of saving grace in Jesus Christ was his consuming passion. Christ entirely dominated his horizon. When Paul said 'for me to live is Christ', he was revealing his innermost priority. He loved the Lord and constantly lifted him up before people.

3. He did this **'boldly and without hindrance'**. Although displaced in the NIV rendering, these words are in fact the very last in the Greek text of Acts. This emphasizes, as John Stott points out, that 'Though his hand was still bound, his [Paul's] mouth was open for Jesus Christ. Though he was chained, the Word of God was not.'[4] This sums up the entire theme of Acts. Christ cannot be contained! The gospel cannot be silenced! The salvation of sinners cannot be stopped!

The message of Acts is that the work goes on. Jesus told his disciples that they would be his witnesses 'in Jerusalem, and in all Judea and Samaria, and to the ends of the earth' (1:8). The fulfilment of this commission continues today as the modern followers of Jesus proclaim him the only name given under heaven among men, by whom we must be saved. This is the unfinished task: 'You will be my witnesses ... to the ends of the earth.'

# Appendix — Miracles and healing[1]

There has always been too much loose talk about miracles. Getting a job you didn't expect is not a miracle. Babies are not miracles. A prodigal son becoming a fine young Christian is not a miracle. The so-called 'miracle of Dunkirk', in which the British Army escaped from France in 1940, was not a miracle. Neither are healings from psychosomatic illnesses, nor even the not infrequent unexplained healings of otherwise incurable diseases, whether in hospitals or through the fervent intercessory prayers of Christian people. All of these are undoubtedly wonderful and amazing events. Many things happen which defy explanation, boggle the mind and appear clearly to be the work of God. They are all evidences of God's hand — providence — acting in time and space. But that is not to say they are miracles in any biblical sense. Biblical miracles are not to be equated with any event that happens to defy a so-called 'natural' or 'rational' explanation. 'Miracle' is not to be regarded as a catch-all category for anything we cannot explain 'on our own'. This is true whether we are talking of the healing of some disease, the birth of a baby or the conversion of a sinner to Jesus Christ. The power of God is essential to them all, but that is not what makes an event a miracle.

### What is a miracle?

The point is that the essence of biblical miracles is not their defiance of explanation *per se*, but their revelatory and redemptive significance. The best definition of a miracle (i.e., what are called in the Bible 'signs, wonders and mighty acts') I know is this: 'A miracle is an extraordinary, visible, redemptive event ordained by God to reveal his redemptive purposes to men and to arouse their awe and wonder.'[2] We can see all these elements in the healing of the lame beggar at the Beautiful Gate (Acts 3).

1. It was *extraordinary* in that the witnesses and the physicians were unable to explain it within the terms and limitations of their normal experience. The science of our own day would not be able to provide a naturalistic explanation of this healing.

2. It was *visible* — obviously — in that it was seen and understood to be a sign, even by the bystanders. It goes without saying that an 'invisible miracle' would be a contradiction in terms — an unseen 'sign', as every advertiser knows, is no sign at all!

3. It was *redemptive* in that it accomplished and revealed something in the unfolding of the history of redemption. As such, it was an act of God in history attesting the validity of the revelation of God in Christ and affirming the efficacy of the message of the gospel. For believers this means that it both reveals and edifies (builds them up in their faith).

4. It was *awesome and wondrous* in that it attracted widespread attention, even to the extent of eliciting worship towards God. Miracles are not marginal events of the 'stranger than fiction' variety. They grab and convince because they are mighty acts of God.

5. It was an *attestation from God* confirming the one who performed the miracle and set the divine seal upon his message.

The miracles in the Scriptures generally exhibit these characteristics. They occur at specific points in history for the purpose of establishing divine truth and securing its impact upon that era. This is why miracles and miracle-workers are most obviously associated with certain periods in redemptive history. Four such periods stand out: the Exodus from Egypt; the struggle with Baalism in the time of Elijah and Elisha; the time of the Exile, with Daniel particularly prominent; and the coming of Christ and the apostles in the first century of the Christian era. Outside of these periods, miracles are relatively rare events in Scripture history. One as yet future period in history — the return of Christ — will be accompanied by signs and wonders attesting the final and consummated revelation of his glory. Until that time, however, the Bible gives us no reason to expect 'signs, wonders and mighty acts' after the pattern of the prophets, the Lord and the apostles. Why is this so? Because in three particulars, God has given a completeness and sufficiency for the New Testament era between the two advents of Christ.

1. A complete and sufficient *revelation* of himself in Christ in the now closed canon of the Old and New Testament Scriptures. The inspired, infallible and inerrant Word of God has been definitively set down and will see neither addition nor deletion while the world lasts.

2. A complete and sufficient *sign* which ends all 'signs' beside or apart from the Word itself, namely 'the sign of Jonah,' i.e., the resurrection of Jesus Christ (Matt. 12:39-41). This is the true and final 'sign' until the Lord comes again.

3. A complete and sufficient *power* to sustain, bless and heal the people of God in every aspect of their lives as the disciples of Jesus. He sent the Holy Spirit to be our Counsellor in his absence and gave us the watchword for the life of New Testament believers as they work and witness in preparation for the coming of the Lord: 'My grace is sufficient for you.' The New Testament is the era of *sufficiency* with respect to the Lord's revelation and provision for the salvation of his people. We are positively commanded *not* to seek a sign. We have no warrant to expect *new* revelations from the Lord. And we are given no encouragement to believe that God will send miracles and miracle-workers to perform healings and the like in our midst. This said, we must also address the question whether God in any way does works of healing above and beyond the current limitations of known medical and surgical accomplishment.

## The sufficiency of Scripture

Let us first deal with the question of miracle-workers. If the above definition of 'miracles' is correct — and I believe this is the Scripture's own definition — then it becomes clear that the closure of the canon of Scripture implies that such miracles have ceased and will only appear again in the events surrounding the Second Coming, when they will attest the final outpouring of divine revelation upon the fallen and about to be renovated world. No new revelation means no new revealers to attest and no miracles to attest them! In this respect the New Testament era is unique — it alone has a complete and sufficient Scripture. This economy of divine redemptive activity simply does not require 'miracles' to attest either the Word of God or the messengers of God!

As you can see, this biblical understanding of miracles encapsulates a much tighter definition than our modern usage of the word, both within and without the Christian community. It implies that whatever the 'healings' we see today — and please note that I am not arguing that genuine healings never take place — they cannot be miracles of the type recorded in the Bible. And they cannot attest the revelatory agency of apostles or prophets, for there simply are no such activity to attest and no such messengers to be gifted with such attestatory powers. An immediate practical implication is that in the era of a sufficient Scripture, an indwelling Holy Spirit and a risen Christ who says his grace is sufficient for our every need, believers are not to be looking for so-called miracle-workers, miracle services, 'power evangelists' and the like, to heal their diseases. Rather, they may rest in the assurance that God will provide for them by the means he has appointed, namely, the all-sufficient grace of Jesus Christ ministered in terms of the biblically appointed means of grace — the ministry of the Word, the sacraments and prayer.

### A wonderful world

Although we have no warrant in the New Testament to expect that miracles of the biblical pattern will occur between the end of the apostolic period and the return of Christ, this in no way limits the *power* of God to do as he wills in the earth. The same power which healed the crippled beggar and raised Lazarus from the dead operates now in the world, with this difference: that it is covert rather than overt and is not connected with the office of a class of God's servants, to whom a particular gift has been given for the purpose of heightening the public perception of both the Word and the compassion of Christ.

This has powerful implications for those who claim a specific 'gift of healing' today. It suggests that some of these practitioners may be sincere believers who have a deficient understanding of the scriptural teaching on miracles and healing and who lack a truly discerning knowledge of themselves and their actual gifts and calling. But looming darkly behind them are two other possibilities about which the Bible is not silent. One is that there is an extensive class of cynical charlatans who exploit a peculiarly vulnerable sector of the population — the troubled and the sick. Another possibility raises the spectre of satanic 'counterfeit miracles, signs and wonders' (2 Thess. 2:9; Matt. 7:22; 24:24). None of this, however, implies that healings which defy medical explanation do not take place.

To put this matter in proper perspective, we need to understand the natural order of things in the world. As John Murray said in one of his lectures on the doctrine of God, 'We must avoid the thought that what we call the order of nature is a system that operates according to laws and forces within it, quite apart from the will of God.'[3] Many Christians have not heeded Murray's advice and have come to think of the natural world, and natural causation, in a deistic way — as if God merely made the world with a built-in set of natural laws and then left it to operate on its own, pausing only now and again in the course of history to 'intervene' with miracles and *in that way* sustain the working out of his purposes. There is a double error in this. On the one hand, there is an unbiblical view of *nature*, which takes for granted that all causes and effects can be explained exhaustively without recognizing the will and power of God in operation. On the other hand, in order to restore the balance and bring God back into the natural order, an unbiblical *divine interventionism* has to be posited, complete with overt 'signs and wonders' and miracle-workers to go with them.

Scripture, however, reveals a *unified doctrine of nature*. All things consist in God, says Paul. 'In him we live and move and have our being' (Acts 17:28). While it is proper to talk about the 'order of nature' because it is a biblical concept (James 3:11-12), we must remember that God's creation is more than *things* — it is also the way the things fit together and work. The 'naturalness' of things, in itself, is marvellous and awe-inspiring when seen by the eye of faith. The natural world bears the stamp of a personal Creator and his amazing providence. The natural world is God's world in the most intimate sense. He holds it in being moment by moment. The Hebrew word *pele'*, meaning 'wonder', is used both of God's mighty acts in creation and the parting of the Red Sea and of the ordinary providences in which the Lord supplies the basic daily needs of his people (Ps. 136:4; 145:4-6,9,12; Job 37:5-6; Prov. 30:18-19). This is, at one and the same time, the presupposition of, and the stimulus to, Christian scientific endeavour. It is God's wonderful world that opens up before our eyes, its every fact undergirded by the power of God and redolent of his creative handiwork. You can see that this is the opposite of the approach that assumes the neutrality of the facts and the inadmissibility of understanding them in the context of creation and providence as revealed in the Scriptures.

**God heals**

On a more mundane level, perhaps, but one which has touched all our lives at one time or another, is the matter of sickness. Why pray to be healed if all you need is a particular medicine? Is healing merely a matter of causality anyway? Are the causes of sickness and therefore of healing exhaustively knowable? If they are, we are a long way from exhausting them and solving the problems definitively! What we do know is that things are not very simple. Medical science, for all its amazing accomplishments, is like all science in that it is not so much *explanation* as it is sophisticated *description* of the causes and effects it investigates. It is a complex of 'working hypotheses' which are subject to modifications based on further observation of phenomena.

Even though it is by means of this process that God blesses us with the healing mediated by reliable medication and skilful surgery, there is always an element of mystery in the healing process itself. Cause and effect drift from sight in the *unknown territory* of God's invisible and inscrutable providence.

Integral to this experience in the believer's life is the exercise of faithful prayer, in which he looks to the Lord that he might exercise his power, personally and lovingly, to the end of healing. The definitive Scripture passage on the means of dealing with sickness is not the accounts of the miracles of Christ and the apostles, but that oft-neglected section at the close of James' epistle: 'Is any one of you sick? He should call the elders of the church to pray over him and anoint him with oil in the name the Lord' (James 5:14). The anointing with oil probably refers to contemporary medical practice, although it may be symbolic of the work of the Holy

Spirit (or both of these). What is beyond debate is that *prayer* and, at that, the prayer of the *elders* — not the ministrations of those who fancy themselves to have a 'gift of healing' — is the normative context in which sickness is to be faced and the means appointed by God by which the promise of healing will be claimed. Surely it is precisely in this context that we can and must conceive of medically inexplicable healing taking place today — and this without either the public acclaim or the redemptive-historical signification of the healings of the Scriptures. When we grasp the wonder of God's ordering and sustaining of the created ('natural') order, we shall neither be surprised by the frequency with which his dealings with us defy rational(istic) description, nor shall we cease to be amazed by the wonders he does through the medium of human discovery and ingenuity.

**The glory of God in Jesus Christ**

God had glorified **'his servant Jesus'** in his resurrection from the dead! That glory was made manifest at Pentecost in the coming of the Holy Spirit. That glory was further declared in act (healing the lame man, 3:1-10) and word (Peter's preaching in explanation of the miracle, 3:12-26). The lame man knew the meaning of what had happened, for he walked and jumped and *praised God*! He saw that the essence of it was not his restored ability to walk! He saw, by faith, that it was the grace of God in the person and work of Jesus Christ! Commenting on this, John Calvin offers us this counsel: 'Let us therefore learn reverently to consider the works of God, that our wonder at them may serve as an entrance for doctrine. When doctrine is cold and unprofitable to us, God is thereby justly punishing us for our ingratitude in despising the glory of his works. Again, because we do not possess insight enough to discern as much as we ought in the works of God by themselves, let us learn, if we would attain to the mark, to join with it the help provided by doctrine. In brief, the one is not to be separated from the other. Experience is rich in evidence for this. For it is this fault which has caused the world to abuse miracles so shamefully.'[4] Calvin's point is that God's work (the healing) led the lame man to glorify God himself. That is to say, he grasped the truth (doctrine) about God in terms of personal faith in God's Son, the Lord Jesus Christ (3:16). The miraculous works of God recorded in Scripture are striking proof of the reality and certainty of God's revealed purpose of redemption in Christ. That these miracles have ceased ought not to dismay us, because, firstly we see that they had a purpose in a specific context and, secondly, we also see that God's Word teaches us that he still works in the world and in our lives with all the power and grace that is necessary to supply *all* our needs. The love that reached out a healing hand to the man at the Beautiful Gate still reaches out to us today, however different the manner in which that healing is accomplished.

But the day came when that healed cripple died. His healing blessed his life but did not make it endless. The once-risen Lazarus also died. The best of earth-bound gifts are fleeting. But these men both had an everlasting gift — they possessed an inheritance that could not fade away. Christ was their Saviour once for all and for ever. They rejoice in glory with their Saviour this very day and on the Great Day will, with all the saints, be clothed with the incorruptibility of a resurrection body for which there will be no lameness, no sickness and no death. They praise the Lord and say, 'Thanks be to God! He gives us the victory through our Lord Jesus Christ' (1 Cor. 15:57). This is the healing men and women really need.

# References

**Chapter 1 — Prelude to Pentecost**

1. John Calvin, *The Acts of the Apostles, (Calvin's New Testament Commentaries)*, Eerdmans, 1965, vol. I, p.23. The two volumes on *Acts* are volumes 6 and 7 in the series of modern translations of Calvin's New Testament Commentaries, originally published in Britain under the editorship of Thomas F. Torrance and David W. Torrance. *Acts*, vol. I, was translated by W. J. G. McDonald and vol. II by J. W. Fraser.

2. See T. V. Moore, *The Last Days of Jesus*, Banner of Truth, 1981, for a full treatment of this forty-day period.

3. F. F. Bruce, *The Book of Acts*, Eerdmans (NICNT), 1971, p.35.

4. Calvin, *Acts*, vol. I, p.24.

5. G. Smeaton, *The Doctrine of the Holy Spirit*, Banner of Truth, 1961 (first published 1882), p.48.

6. As above, p.49.

7. Matthew Henry, *A Commentary on the Whole Bible*, World Bible Publishers, vol. 6, p.7, quotes an ancient Jewish scholar as saying, '*Rumpatur spiritus eorum qui supputant tempora*' ('Perish the men who calculate the time')! A hard judgement perhaps, but one which many Christians today would do well to heed.

8. Calvin, *Acts*, vol. I, p.31.

9. The company consisted of the Eleven, who are named for the record, 'the women', whom Calvin (*Acts*, vol. I, p.40) believes to have been their wives, and 'Mary the mother of Jesus and his brothers'. The Roman Catholic doctrine of the perpetual virginity of Mary founders on the plain meaning of the latter part of this text.

10. Henry, *Commentary*, vol. 6, p.10.

11. The New Testament proto-church numbered at least these 120 men (plus women and children) in Jerusalem and the 'more than five hundred of the brothers' who witnessed his resurrection (also plus women and children) in Galilee (1 Cor. 15:6). There must have been many more scattered around the country.

12. Joseph Smith, the founder of Mormonism, is on record as saying in one of his 'revelations' that the disciples kicked Judas until his intestines gushed out, so that in the shedding of *his own* blood, he could atone for his sin of betraying Jesus (C. W. Penrose, *Blood Atonement*, Salt Lake City, 1884, p.13). This gave rise to the Mormon doctrine of human self-atonement by the shedding of the sinner's own blood (for certain sins not covered by the blood of Christ)! It is no coincidence that to this day execution by firing squad is an option in Utah for any convicted of capital crimes!

13. For an explanation of the connections between these passages and particularly

the fact that Matthew ascribes to Jeremiah what is specifically said by Zechariah, see T. Laetsch, *The Minor Prophets,* Concordia, 1970, pp.470f.
14. Henry, *Commentary,* vol. 6, p.12.
15. Bruce, *Book of Acts,* p.50 (see also Rev. 21:12,14).
16. Consider the case of the Catholic Apostolic Church (the Irvingites), a strange mixture of sacerdotal, charismatic and evangelical teaching. They had twelve 'apostles' and an eschatology that held that Christ would return before these men had all died. The death of the last 'apostle' in 1901 left the denomination stranded above the high-water mark of their own false prophecies — 'a devotional guild with an impossible eschatological agenda,' observed J. R. Fleming.
17. The choice of Matthias has come under fire from some biblical scholars. E. M. Blaiklock (*Acts,* IVP, 1977, p.73) suggests that this was an act of immaturity and haste and that Paul was destined for Judas' place as the twelfth apostle. But we have no reason from the text to suspect divine disapproval or apostolic incompetence. Paul was called separately to be an apostle to the Gentiles. Nowhere is there a hint that Matthias is a pseudo-apostle. Neither is there any warrant to accuse Peter of an improper understanding of those texts he quoted from the Psalms to show that Judas should be replaced.

**Chapter 2 — The coming of the Holy Spirit**
1. Smeaton, *Doctrine of the Holy Spirit,* p.48.
2. Henry, *Commentary,* vol. 6, p.14.
3. E. J. Young, *A Commentary on Daniel,* Banner of Truth, 1978 (first published 1949), p.201; cf. Henry, *Commentary,* vol. 6, p.17.
4. Henry, *Commentary,* vol. 6, p.14.
5. F. H. Chase, quoted by F. F. Bruce (*Book of Acts,* p.55). Bruce seems to approve of Chase's thoroughly anti-supernaturalist view when he suggests it may be 'relevant'.
6. Henry, *Commentary,* vol. 6, p.15.
7. Smeaton, *Doctrine of the Holy Spirit,* p.50.
8. Henry, *Commentary,* vol. 6, p.16.
9. Smeaton, *Doctrine of the Holy Spirit,* p.52.
10. R. B. Gaffin, Jr, *Perspectives on Pentecost,* Presbyterian & Reformed, 1979, pp. 38-9.
11. Calvin, *Acts,* vol. I, p.54.

**Chapter 3 — Christ is preached**
1. Bruce, *Book of Acts,* p.69.
2. As above, p.67.
3. R. C. H. Lenski, *The Interpretation of the Acts of the Apostles,* Augsburg Press, 1961, p.73.
4. Calvin (*Acts,* vol. I, p.59) points out that Peter is not saying that Joel's prophecy is to be fulfilled in terms of every believer uttering prophecies (new word-revelation) from God, but that all may have 'spiritual wisdom to the extent of excelling in prophetical gifts'. In applying it to us today, Calvin says with reference to the extraordinary apostolic gifts of word-revelation (prophecy and tongues), 'For, although the visible gifts of the Spirit have ceased, God has not yet withdrawn his Spirit from his church.'
5. Lenski, *Interpretation of Acts,* p.77.

6. D. Chilton (*Paradise Restored,* Dominion Press, 1987, p.101), insists that a 'day of the Lord' in A. D. 70 is the finishing-point of the fulfilment of Joel 2. Lenski (*Interpretation of Acts,* p.79), Bruce (*Book of Acts,* p.69) and Laetsch (*Minor Prophets,* pp. 128-9) see this as the last Day of Judgement. J. A. Alexander (*Acts,* Banner of Truth, 1980 (first published 1857), vol. I, pp. 65-6), Calvin (*Acts,* vol. I, p.89), Henry (*Commentary,* vol. 6, p.21) and C. F. Keil & F. Delitzsch (*Commentary on the Old Testament,* 1970, p.218), all subscribe to a rolling fulfilment throughout the New Testament age.
7. Lenski, *Interpretation of Acts,* p.79
8. Alexander, *Acts,* vol. I, p.67.
9. Psalm 132:11.
10. *The Book of Psalms for Singing,* Reformed Presbyterian Church of North America, 1973, selection 110.
11. Lenski, *Interpretation of Acts,* p.103.
12. Henry, *Commentary,* vol. 6, p.26.
13. As above.
14. For a survey of New Testament usage see *The New International Dictionary of New Testament Theology,* (*NIDNTT*), ed. Colin Brown vol. 1, pp.357f., article on *'metanoia'*.
15. *Shorter Catechism,* 87: 'Repentance unto life is a saving grace, whereby a sinner out of a true sense of sin, and apprehension of the mercy of God in Christ, doth, with grief and hatred of his sin, turn from it unto God, with full purpose of and endeavour after, new obedience.'
16. James Fisher, (ed.), *The Westminster Assembly's Shorter Catechism Explained* (Philadelpia, 1818 — 3rd Glasgow edition, 1765 — p.120) defines unrepentant sorrow: '[This] legal sorrow, or horror of conscience, which the men of the world may have, from a dread of God as a vindictive judge, ready to pour out the vials of his wrath and vengeance upon them, without any uptaking of his mercy through Christ, is nothing else but the beginning of eternal death, and inconceivable misery, as was the case with Cain, Judas and others.'
17. Bruce, *Book of Acts,* p.77.
18. As above.
19. The question as to whether or not the children of believers are included in the covenant community in the New Testament church, as they were in the Old Testament church — and with it the question of the baptism of the infant children of believers — is often discussed in connection with Acts 2:39. No one disputes that this text is only intelligible in the context of the place of children in the Old Testament covenant. The element of continuing promise in the line of the generations implies that God has a purpose of grace for the children of New Testament believers, just as surely as he had a purpose of grace for children in the Old Testament — the fruition of which promise consists in coming to faith in Christ. This promise to the children cannot be spiritualized to refer to 'spiritual' children as oppposed to literal children. Christian parents have a promise to claim for their own children. How this is to be understood and applied is, of course, at the heart of the paedobaptist/anti-paedobaptist debate. Paedobaptists, including the present writer, take this to indicate the inclusion of the children of believers in the New Testament covenant community and argue that such 'covenant children' ought therefore to receive the sign of inclusion in that community — hence the practice of baptizing the infant children of believers. Anti-paedobaptists (i.e.

Baptists), while not denying that believers' children are privileged in terms of the gospel, do not accord them a place in the covenant community, which they see as including only those who may be presumed, by reason of a credible profession of faith, to be of the elect. They emphasize the connection in Acts 2:37 between repentance and baptism, set baptism exclusively in the context of profession of faith and reject the application of baptism to children. The problem cannot be discussed further in this context. Acts 2:37 and 39 pose their own problems for paedobaptists and anti-paedobaptists alike and the subject deserves the most careful study. For a short but helpful treatment, see the articles by G. Beasley-Murray (for the Baptists) and R. T. Beckwith (for paedobaptists) in *NIDNTT*, vol. 1, pp. 143-62 ('Baptism/Infant Baptism'). For a vigorous head-to-head discussion of the wider issues see David Kingdom, *Children of Abraham*, (Carey Publications, 1973) and the reply by Herman Hanko, *We and our Children: the Reformed Doctrine of Infant Baptism*, (Reformed Free Publishing Association, 1981).
20. F. F. Bruce, *The Acts of the Apostles — the Greek text*, Eerdmans, 1970, p.98, notes: 'The promise of the "covenant of grace" is not only to the present generation but also to those yet to come: cf. the promises to Noah (Gen. 9:9) to Abraham (Gen. 13:15; 17:7ff.; Gal. 3:16), and to David (Ps. 18:50; 89:34ff.; 132:11f.).'
21. Henry, *Commentary*, vol. 6, p.28.

**Chapter 4 — The growing church**
1. J. I. Packer, 'Nothing Fails like Success,' *Christianity Today*, 12 August 1988, p.15.
2. The figure of '144,000' in Revelation 7 is symbolic of the whole number of the elect, also defined in the same chapter as 'a great multitude that no one could count'. In the execution of God's plan of salvation, we are to be concerned with the *quality* (faithful ministry), while he says he will handle the *quantity* (giving the increase — see 1 Cor. 3:5-9).
3. *NIDNTT*, vol. 1, p.643.
4. Henry, *Commentary*, vol. 6, p.28 (his emphasis).
5. Alexander, *Acts*, vol. I, p.90.

**Chapter 5 — When God heals**
1. For a fuller treatment of the significance of miracles and their relevance for us today, see Appendix, 'Miracles and healing'.
2. Simeon, *Expository Outlines*, vol. 14, pp. 270-71.

**Chapter 6 — The true healer**
1. L. J. Ogilvie, *The Communicator's Commentary*, vol. 5, *Acts*, Word, 1983, p.85.
2. Calvin, *Acts*, vol. I, p.97.
3. As above, p.98.
4. Simeon, *Expository Outlines*, vol. 14, p.272.
5. As above, pp. 272-3.
6. *NIDNTT*, p.648 (article on 'Name' by F. F. Bruce). For a remarkable and stimulating discussion on the significance of names in human societies and in Scripture see 'What's in a Name?', in Arthur C. Custance, *The Doorway Papers*, vol. IX, *The Flood: Local or Global?'*, Zondervan, Academie Books, 1979, pp. 167-92.
7. *NIDNTT*, p. 654.

8. Ogilvie, *Acts*, p.84.
9. Henry, *Comm entary*, vol. 6, p.36.
10. As above, p.38.
11. Calvin, *Acts*, vol. I, p.106.
12. Lenski, *Interpretation of Acts*, p.148.
13. As above, p.149.
14. Alexander, *Acts*, vol. I, p.122.
15. Lenski, *Interpretation of Acts*, p.151.
16. Simeon, *Expository Outlines*, vol. 14, p.286.

**Chapter 7 — Holy boldness**

1. Calvin, *Acts*, vol. I, p.111.
2. John Owen, *The Works of John Owen*, Banner of Truth, 1968, vol. 4, p.512.
3. Bruce, *Acts — the Greek text*, p.120.
4. Gaffin, *Perspectives on Pentecost*, p.34.
5. Ogilvie, *Acts*, p.98.
6. J. Howie, *The Scots Worthies*, p.452.
7. The plural, '*They* raised *their voices* together in prayer,' no more indicates that the prayer was uttered in unison than the earlier observation that 'Peter and John' reported what had happened meant that they both spoke in unison. Someone led the prayer of the assembly, but, as with all the public prayer of the church, it is represented as the prayer of *all*. See Lenski, *Interpretation of Acts*, p.177, for a good explanation of this.
8. Calvin, *Acts*, vol. I, p.123.

**Chapter 8 — All things in common**

1. Thomas Manton, *The Complete Works*, Maranatha, vol. 21, p.89.
2. Simeon, *Expository Outlines*, vol. 14, p.308.
3. Lenski, *Interpretation of Acts*, p.186.
4, The NKJV's 'all things in common' is to be preferred to the NIV's inept paraphrase, 'They shared everything they had.' The NIV rendering describes actions ('they shared'), whereas the noun '*koina*' ('in common') at this point denotes a commitment or attitude. The actions resulting from this attitude of *koina* are recorded in verses 34-37.
5. The fact that Luke appears to suggest this as a translation of the name Barnabas has occasioned no end of debate among interpreters. The Hebrew name, Bar-nebua, denotes a 'son of prophecy'. Luke's Greek interpretation is *huios parakleseos* — son of encouragement, or consolation. The connection in Luke's mind would appear to be the Holy Spirit, the Paraclete *(parakletos)* of John 14:26. The Holy Spirit, who is the source of all prophecy, is also the source of Barnabas' faith in Christ and generosity of spirit. The 'son of prophecy' is truly the 'son of [Spirit-given] encouragement'! Luke is not merely translating a Hebrew name: he is interpreting the man himself — a man who has been powerfullly changed by the work of the Holy Spirit. (See Alexander, *Acts*, p.183 and Ogilvie, *Acts*, pp.115-17 for further explanation.)
6. Ogilvie, *Acts*, p.118.
7. Calvin, *Acts*, vol. I, p.133.
8. Ogilvie, *Acts*, p.119.
9. Lenski, *Interpretation of Acts*, p.196.

10. Calvin, *Acts*, vol. I, p.133.
11. Not-so-secret benefaction can backfire in an amusing, but suitably humbling way. For instance, the magnificent Eastminster Presbyterian Church in Pittsburgh (U.S.A.) was built with money from the Melllon family just as the Depression began to blow away the false prosperity of the twenties. This great building has ever since been known locally as 'the Mellons' fire-escape'!
12. The same Greek verb (*nosphizo* — 'to appropriate') and preposition '*apo* — 'from') are used in Acts 5:2,3 and the Septuagint text of Joshua 7:1.
13. F. Schaeffer, *Joshua and the Flow of Biblical History*, IVP (USA), 1975, p.116.
14. Ogilvie, *Acts*, p.120.

**Chapter 9 — Reactions to the gospel**

1. The modern church-growth movement generally favours the primacy of small groups (six to ten people meeting two to four times a month) in its models of the church and her ministry. Large gatherings are seen as of secondary importance. They claim Acts 2:46 as the basis for this position. The text itself, however, not to mention the entire experience of the apostolic church, confirms the contrary view that public worship and private (small-group) fellowship, in that order and in balance with one another, constitute a healthy community-building structure for the church (cf. 5:42). Hebrews 10:25 is just not satisfied by faithful mid-week attendance at a small group.
2. See Appendix 1, 'Miracles and healing', for a discussion of the place of miraculous healing today.
3. Calvin, *Acts*, vol. I, p.138.
4. Owen, *Works*, vol. 8, p.83 ('Sermon on the Beauty and Nature of Gospel Worship').
5. John Calvin, *Acts*, Calvin Translation Society ed., vol. I, p.205. Christopher Fetherstone's 1585 translation is much livelier on this point than W. J. G. McDonald's 1965 translation.
6. The text does not say Peter's shadow *was* efficacious or give sanction to any superstitious views some of the people might have entertained. This is merely an indication of the impact the apostles had on the populace in Jersualem, many of whom would be quite inclined to a superstitious view of healing miracles.
7. J. G. Machen, *Christianity and Liberalism*, 1968 (first published 1923), p.2.
8. Merrill C. Tenney, *New Testament Times*, IVP, 1965, p.95.
9. J. G. Machen, *The New Testament: An introduction to its Literature and History*, Banner of Truth, 1976, p.87.
10. Simeon, *Expository Outlines*, vol. 14. p.319.
11. Ogilvie, *Acts*, pp. 130-31.
12. Lenski, *Interpretation of Acts*, p.235.
13. Calvin, *Acts*, vol. I, pp. 152-3.
14. Lenski, *Interpretation of Acts*, p. 238.

**Chapter 10 — A man full of faith**

1. Owen, *Works*, vol. 16, p. 143 (chapter 9 of his treatise, *The True Nature of a Gospel Church*).
2. As above, p.144.
3. The biblical office of deacon is neither a grade of the clergy (as in Episcopalianism or Roman Catholicism) nor a ruling/administrative office (as in

some Baptist churches). The permanent offices of the New Testament church are those of elder (teaching and ruling) and deacon (mercy).
4. Bruce, *Book of Acts*, pp. 129-30.
5. Calvin, *Acts*, vol. I, p.165.
6. R. B. Rackham, *The Acts of the Apostles*, Baker, 1964 (first published 1901), p.87.
7. The NIV identifies 'synagogue' in verse 9 with a building, the 'Synagogue of the Freedmen'. It is probable, however, that no building *title* is in view here, but rather the 'assembly' or congregation which was made up of freedmen (Roman Jews formerly in captivity of some sort), Cyrenians and Alexandrians (from Africa) and Cilicians and Asians (from what is now Turkey).
8. Calvin, *Acts*, vol. I, p.167.
9. Heard from a speaker in a church-growth seminar, 2 February 1990.
10. Lenski, *Interpretation of Acts*, p. 257.

**Chapter 11 — The first martyr**

1. T. M. Lindsay, *Luther and the German Reformation*, T. & T. Clark, 1900, p.131.
2. Calvin, *Acts*, vol. I, p.171.
3. Rackham, *Acts of the Apostles*, pp.99-102, gives a lucid account of those instances in which Stephen refers to events recorded in Scripture and includes points of detail not obviously provided in the Old Testament texts themselves. We cannot discuss the solutions to these apparent discrepancies in this short volume. Suffice it to say that, firstly, Stephen spoke under inspiration of the Holy Spirit; secondly, careful exegesis of the Old Testament texts demonstrates the accuracy of both the text and Stephen's information; and thirdly, there is corroborating material from contemporary extra-biblical sources in a number of cases. See also Lenski, *Interpretation of Acts*, pp. 251ff., for a thorough treatment of these points.
4. Calvin, *Acts*, vol. I, p.216.
5. Rackham, *Acts of the Apostles*, p.106.
6. Lenski, *Interpretation of Acts*, p. 305.
7. J. H. Merle d'Aubigné, *The Reformation in England*, Banner of Truth, 1972, vol. 2, p.76.
8. Bruce, *Book of Acts*, p.172.
9. Henry, *Commentary*, vol. 6, p.95.

**Chapter 12 — Reaching out**

1. Tertullian, *Apology*, I, 11-13, in J. Stevenson, (ed.), *A New Eusebius*, SPCK, 1970, pp.167-8.
2. See Richard Ganz and William Edgar, *Sold Out!*, Onward Press, 1990, for a thought-provoking treatment of this theme.
3. Lenski, *Interpretation of Acts*, p.318.
4. Calvin, *Acts*, vol. I, p.234.
5. For an example of the notion that 'Baptism is essential for salvation,' among Protestants, see Edward C. Horton, *The Church of Christ*, Howard Book House, 1970, pp.41ff.
6. John Dick, *Lectures on the Acts*, p. 129. John Dick also wrote the excellent *Lectures on Theology* (see chapter 13, note 2, below).
7. G. W. Marston, *Tongues Then and Now*, Cherry Hill, 1974, pp.17ff.
8. Lenski, *Interpretation of Acts*, p.324.

9. A. A. Hodge, *Outlines of Theology*, Eerdmans, 1949, p.471.
10. It was common until recent times for civil service and household duties under the monarchies of the Middle East to be largely delegated to a class of *castrati* deliberately groomed for these purposes.
11. Calvin, *Acts*, vol. I, p.252.
12. As above, I, p.255.
13. *Book of Psalms for Singing*, selection 72A.

**Chapter 13 — A chosen instrument**

1. James R. Willson, 'The conversion of Saul of Tarsus,' *Evangelical Witness*, vol. IV, pp.296-7 (June 1826). Willson edited this, the first periodical of the Reformed Presbyterian Church of North America, in Coldenham, New York (1822-26).
2. John Dick, *Lectures on Theology*, Applegate, Cincinnatti, 1864, p.356. Dick (1764-1833) was a minister in Glasgow and Professor of the United Secession Church. He uses the expression 'invincible grace' in referring to the effectual power of God in regeneration and conversion. The conventional description of the classic fourth point of Calvinism is 'irresistible grace'. Dick correctly points out that sinners do *resist* repeatedly the overtures of the gospel and in fact are resisting God's grace, right up to the moment when God chooses to apply that grace, with *invincible* force, to bring that lost person from darkness into light.
3. Ogilvie, *Acts*, p.167.
4. Buchanan, *The Office and Work of the Holy Spirit*, Banner of Truth, 1968, p.159.
5. The Greek *ekloge* — from which we get the English words, 'elect', 'election' and 'eclectic'.
6. See the AV renderings of 2 Corinthians 4:7 and 1 Peter 3:7. The NIV destroys the beauty and power of the biblical language in these texts with flatly paraphrastic substitutes. In the former verse, 'earthen vessels' become 'jars of clay' and in the latter the 'weaker vessel' becomes 'weaker partner'.
7. Calvin, *Acts*, vol. I, pp.265-6.
8. Bruce, *Acts — the Greek text*, p.205.
9. As above, p.208.
10. Henry, *Commentary*, vol. 6, pp.119-20.

**Chapter 14 — A new direction**

1. The NASB accurately renders the Greek and is to be preferred to the NIV, which manages to disrupt the flow of Luke's thought by shifting the phrase 'the fear of the Lord' from second to last place. The NIV translators appear to have wished to connect 'strengthened' (NASB, 'being built up') with 'encouraged by the Holy Spirit' (NASB, 'the comfort of the Holy Spirit') and so identify it as a co-ordinate work of the Spirit. If this is a case of the supposed benefits of the NIV's 'dynamic equivalence', it is, alas, the equivalence of confusion and obfuscation. It shows how easily even an uncomplicated Greek text can be muddled, when the translators miss the precise intent of the inspired writer's train of thought.
2. Jesus said, *'Talitha qumi'* ('Little girl, arise!'), while Peter said, *'Tabitha, qumi!'* ('Tabitha, arise!').
3. Calvin, *Acts*, vol. I, p.278.
4. Ogilvie, *Acts*, p.177.
5. Henry, *Commentary*, vol. 6, p.123.
6. Ogilvie, *Acts*, p.179.

7. Bruce, *Book of Acts,* p.218.
8. Calvin, *Acts,* vol. I, p.299.
9. As above, p.316.
10. This 'Gentile Pentecost', with the events of Acts 8 and 19, is to be seen as an element in 'the initial foundational spread of the gospel' which correlates with 'the events of Acts 2' as part of 'a unique, non-repeatable (i.e. non-typical, non-modular) complex of events' (Gaffin, *Perspectives on Pentecost,* p.24). There is no basis here for the position of charismatics who identify the baptism of the Holy Spirit as a 'second blessing' after conversion to Christ, and tie to it a normative gift of 'speaking in tongues' for all Christians who have received Spirit-baptism.

**Chapter 15 — First called 'Christians'**
1. Ralph Buchsbaum, *Animals without Backbones,* Penguin Books, 1961, vol.2, p.114.
2. Theological formulations of the marks of the church define up to three which are deemed essential for a church to be regarded as a true church: the faithful preaching of the Word of God, the right administration of the sacraments and the faithful exercise of discipline. Calvin held the first *two* only to be essential. The *Westminster Confession* only insists on the first (the preaching of the Word) as being of the essence of a true church, and views the others as indicating the relative purity of churches (chapter XXV, 2, 4, 5).
3. In a recent seminar under the aegis of the Charles E. Fuller Institute for Church Growth (California, U.S.A.) I heard a prominent speaker tell how 'older' couples who came to his growing church (average member — twenty-three years old and unmarried) were referred to other churches, as they fell outside the target group and ministry goals for their church, which were (although he did not state it so baldly), all-white, suburban and 'yuppie'!
4. Lenski, *Interpretation of Acts,* p.454.
5. There has always been a strong strand of biblical expository preaching in British evangelicalism, exemplified by men like Martyn Lloyd-Jones and William Still and their spiritual children in the gospel ministry. The Word is, of course, its own best interpreter and the recovery of exegetical-experiential exposition is but the inevitable expression of the power of the Spirit who divinely inspired the Word in the first place.
6. Probably the trip mentioned in Galatians 2:2.
7. Ogilvie, *Acts,* p.195.

**Chapter 16 — Persecution and progress**
1. Dick, *Lectures on the Acts,* p.176.
2. Lenski, *Interpretation of Acts,* p.480. It is not clear what they believed about the guardianship of angels over God's people. Suffice it to say that Scripture does teach that angels watch over us and minister to us in various ways. There is no warrant for the common notion that there is *one* 'guardian angel' assigned to each person. Scripture speaks of varying numbers, according to the demands of the situation (cf. Exod. 14:10; 2 Kings 6:17; Dan. 10:5,12; Ps. 34:7; 91:11; Matt. 18:10; Heb. 1:14).
3. This word, *demos,* occurs only four times in the New Testament (Acts 12:22; 17:5; 19:30,33), in every case referring to the formal political assembly of the

people, convened for business by their rulers. The hundreds of other occurrences of words for 'people' are comprised of the Greek *ethnos* (nation), *laos* (people at large) and *ochlos* (unorganized mob).
4. There are only five words in the Greek *(Theou phone kai ouk anthropou)* and these are easily translated in just five Engish words, thereby preserving the raw force of the original. Most English versions, however, add several words to make the spontaneous exclamation into a proper sentence. This has the effect of making the people's acclaim somehow sound more like a civilized overstatement than the pagan blasphemy it was.

**Chapter 17 — Free indeed!**
1. Bruce, *Book of Acts,* pp.260-61, suggests that Simeon may be 'Simon of Cyrene', who carried the cross for Jesus (Luke 23:26). Of Manaen, who was of aristocratic origin, having been brought up as a companion to Herod Antipas (uncle of Herod Agrippa), he says, 'What a commentary on the mystery and sovereignty of divine grace that, of these two foster-brothers, one should attain honour as a Christian leader, while the other should be best known for his shameful behaviour in the killing of John the Baptist and in the trial of Jesus!'
2. Ogilvie, *Acts,* p.208.
3. Calvin, *Acts,* vol. I, p.356.
4. Simeon, *Expository Outlines,* vol. 14, p.410.
5. Calvin, *Acts,* (CTS edition), vol. I, p.504.
6. Brownlow North, *The Rich Man and Lazarus — An exposition of Luke 16:19-31,* Banner of Truth, 1979, p.106.

**Chapter 18 — Coping with rejection**
1. Ogilvie, *Acts,* p.221.
2. Henry, *Commentary,* vol. 6, p.176.
3. This is a key definition of the role of miracles in the New Testament. See Appendix I.
4. This claim has been made in connection with efforts to find Noah's ark on Mt Ararat.
5. Henry, *Commentary,* vol. 6, p.179.
6. One thinks, for example, of the origins of Chalmers' Church, West Port, Edinburgh (the church, now defunct, into which I was born). In his last years, Thomas Chalmers, the leader of the Free Church in the 1843 Disruption of the Church of Scotland, gave himself to planting a church among the slums below Edinburgh Castle. This involved a team of twenty, one to each section, visiting every home repeatedly over a period of years. Chalmers himself was turned away from one door *twenty-three times* before gaining a hearing for the gospel! The work was blessed with success and grew through conversions to over 500 members within a few years.
7. Simeon, *Expository Outlines,* vol. 14, p.433.
8. Ogilvie, *Acts,* p.220.
9. On this occasion, the 'door of faith' refers to 'coming to Christ'. Elsewhere Paul uses the word 'door' with reference to opportunities to preach the gospel (1 Cor. 16:9; 2 Cor. 2:12; Col. 4:3).

**Chapter 19 — By grace alone**

1. D. D. Bannerman, *The Scripture Doctrine of the Church,* Baker, 1976 (first published 1887), pp.405-11. It is exegetically impossible to interpret these terms as representing grades of clergy, as do prelatist and episcopalian churches.
2. A modern parallel would be the doctrine of 'baptismal regeneration', both in its Roman Catholic and Protestant (Disciples of Christ, Christian Church) forms, in which baptism is deemed necessary for salvation.
3. W. Hendriksen, *A Commentary on Galatians,* Banner of Truth, 1969, pp.14-15. Galatians 2:1 evidently refers to the same journey recorded in Acts 15:1-4.
4. Only to be revived, with modified eclecticism, by medieval Roman Catholicism, with its elaborate ritualism and sacerdotalism.
5. Owen, *Works,* vol. XVI ('The True Nature of a Gospel Church'), p.47. See also Thomas Witherow, *The Apostolic Church,* Free Presbyterian Publications, 1983, pp.48-54.
6. Owen, *Works,* vol. XVI, p.207.
7. R. J. Rushdoony, *The Institutes of Biblical Law,* Craig Press, 1973, pp. 87, 297.
8. Owen, *Works,* vol. XVI, pp. 207-8.

**Chapter 20 — 'Come over and help us!'**

1. Simeon, *Expository Outlines,* vol. 14, p.443.
2. Calvin, *Acts,* vol. II, p.61.
3. As above, p.64.
4. As above, pp. 68-9.
5. For a marvellous exposition of this truth, see 'The Exercise of Mercy Optional with God,' in W. G. T. Shedd, *Sermons to the Natural Man,* Banner of Truth (originally published 1873), pp.358-78.
6. Simeon, *Expository Outlines,* vol. 14, p.448.
7. It is likely that the Jews were expelled from Philippi, a Roman colony, at the time that Claudius expelled the Jews from Rome (Lenski, *Interpretation of Acts,* p.655).
8. Buchanan, *Office and Work of the Holy Spirit,* pp. 188-9.
9. Simeon, *Expository Outlines,* vol. 14, p.449.
10. Buchanan, *Office and Work of the Holy Spirit,* p.190.
11. This is true for both paedobaptists and anti-paedobaptists. In the former case, the children of believers are baptized because they are regarded as 'covenant children', who belong to the Lord according to promise, although they are not yet able to make a profession of faith. They are baptized because they are regarded as *already* being members of the church, not *because* baptism makes them members of the church. What anti-paedobaptists object to in this is not the significance of baptism as a sign of the covenant, or its relationship to church membership (sound Baptists no more believe that baptism 'makes' anyone a member of Christ than do sound Presbyterians!); their objection is the extension of the covenant administration to include the children of believers. The real heart of the baptist/paedobaptist controversy is not the doctrine of baptism *itself* (i.e., as a sign and seal of God's covenant), but the theology of the *place of believers' children* with respect to the covenant of grace.
12. Simeon, *Expository Outlines,* vol. 14, p.452.

**Chapter 21 — 'What must I do to be saved?'**
1. Simeon, *Expository Outlines*, vol. 14, p.456.
2. Calvin, *Acts*, vol. II, p.76.
3. As above, p.79.
4. Buchanan, *Office and Work of the Holy Spirit*, p.133.
5. Calvin, *Acts*, vol. II, p.84.
6. Buchanan, *Office and Work of the Holy Spirit*, p.135.
7. For an incisive exposition of this subtle form of works-righteousness and its inroads into modern evangelicalism, see Tom Wells, *Christian: Take heart!*, Banner of Truth, 1987, pp.130-31.
6. Henry, *Commentary*, vol. 6, p.215.

**Chapter 22 — The world turned upside down**
1. Calvin, *Acts*, vol. II, p.91.
2. Manton, *Works*, vol. 8 (Sermons on Psalm 119), pp.126-7.
3. Calvin, *Acts*, vol. II, p.92.
4. Simeon, *Expository Outlines*, vol. 14, p.462.
5. Manton, *Works*, vol. 17, p.149.
6. Ogilvie, *Acts*, p.254.

**Chapter 23 — Proclaiming the 'unknown God'**
1. Lenski, *Interpretation of Acts*, p.708.
2. Paul Johnson, *Intellectuals*, Harper & Row, 1988, p.342. This incisive analysis of modern intellectualism ought to be read by every thinking Christian.
3. For a searching discussion of this theme, see Kenneth F. W. Prior, *The Gospel in a Pagan Society*, IVP (USA), 1975, pp.29-39.
4. Bruce, *Book of Acts*, p. 355. The Greek is the adjective *deisidaimonesterous*, from *deido* ('I fear') and *daimonia* (elsewhere in the New Testament this is rendered 'demons', but to the Athenians it simply meant 'divinities' — see Lenski, *Interpretation of Acts*, pp.721-2 for a discussion of this point).
5. Bruce, *Book of Acts*, p.356.
6. Lenski, *Interpretation of Acts*, p.731.
7. Bruce, *Book of Acts*, pp. 359-60.
8. Much of modern fundamentalism/evangelicalism has effectively adopted the eighteenth-century Sandemanian view of faith, as no more than an assent to the truth about Jesus without a commitment to follow him. Especially in the U.S.A., this manifests itself in the (false) teaching that a person can accept Jesus as Saviour, but not as Lord, and be what is often called a 'carnal Christian' — someone who has supposedly been saved but lives like an ordinary unbeliever. On Sandemanianism, see D. Martyn Lloyd-Jones, 'Sandemanianism,' in *Profitable for Doctrine and Reproof*, Puritan Conference Report 1967, pp. 54-71. For an analysis of the tragic impact of this error on American religion see John MacArthur, *The Gospel According to Jesus*, Zondervan, 1988.

**Chapter 24 — Discouragement and encouragement**
1. John Stott, *The Spirit, the Church and the World*, IVP (USA), 1990, p.296.
2. Simeon, *Expository Outlines*, vol. 9, p.166.

3. Lenski, *Interpretation of Acts,* pp. 754ff. This is known from an inscription found at Delphi in 1909.
4. Calvin, *Acts,* vol. II, p.137, notes that they 'took pains to cover bad grounds with a decent excuse' (i.e., they hid a false accusation about Paul's use of the Mosaic law behind an apparent concern for observing Roman law).
5. Alexander McLeod, *Messiah, Governor of the Nations of the Earth,* Reformed Presbyterian Press, 1992 (first published 1803), p.31. Alexander McLeod (1774-1833) was a native of the Isle of Mull in Scotland, who emigrated to the United States and became the first minister of the Reformed Presbyterian Church (the church of the emigrant Scottish Covenanters) in New York City.

**Chapter 25 — More than a name**
1. Paul may have taken a Nazirite vow at Cenchrea (18:18). If this is so, it involved him in not only cutting his hair, but abstaining from all use of grapes and wine and avoiding contact with dead bodies. The purpose of this was deeper devotion and thankfulness to God. It may be that he was recognizing the mercies of God in his second missionary journey.
2. The AV 'eloquent' is probably to be preferred to the NIV's 'learned'. The Greek, *logios,* has reference to being 'gifted and well-trained dialectically' (Lenski, *Interpretation of Acts,* p.769).
3. Ogilvie, *Acts,* p.271.
4. Stott, *The Spirit, the Church and the World,* p.304.
5. Alexander, *Acts,* vol. II, p.186; Bruce, *Book of Acts,* p.385; Calvin, *Acts,* vol. II, p.149.
6. Calvin, *Acts,* vol. II, pp.148-9.
7. Bruce, *Book of Acts,* p.387.
8. Stott, *The Spirit, the Church and the World,* p.306.
9. Simeon, *Expository Outlines,* vol. 14, p.495.

**Chapter 26 — The best-laid schemes...**
1. Bruce, *Book of Acts,* p.379.
2. This was Paul's second visit to Corinth and is to be distinguished from his third visit, mentioned in 2 Corinthians 12:14; 13:1, but nowhere referred to by Luke.
3. With deplorable lack of accuracy and style, the NIV replaces the Greek double negative, '*no litttle* trouble' *(tarachos ouk oligos),* with the blandly positive, '*a great* distubance'. Curiously, the NIV retains the double negative in 19:25 — 'no little business' *(oukoliganergasian).* One is thankful for the accuracy in this verse, but wonders if it owed more to accident than design!
4. The fiercest persecutions in the British Isles were perpetrated not by Roman Catholicism, as many assume, but by a supposedly 'Protestant' Episcopalian establishment determined to subjugate the Presbyterians and Puritans of the seventeenth century. The Marian persecutions of the sixteenth century were horrendous, but were to be surpassed by the almost genocidal fury that was visited on Scotland in the 'Killing Time' of the 1680s.
5. Ogilvie, *Acts,* p.282.

**Chapter 27 — A living fellowship**
1. Henry, *Commentary,* vol. 6, p.257.

2. The approximate dates and locations for those of Paul's epistles which were written during the second and third missionary journeys are as follows:

| | | |
|---|---|---|
| 1 and 2 Thessalonians | from Corinth | *c*.A.D. 50-51 |
| 1 Corinthians | from Ephesus | *c*.A.D.54 |
| 2 Corinthians | from Macedonia | *c*.A.D.55 |
| Romans | from Corinth | *c*.A.D.55 |

3. Henry, *Commentary*, vol. 6, p.257.
4. Stott, *The Spirit, the Church and the World*, p.320.
5. See also the exposition of Acts 2:42-47 in chapter 4 ('The growing church').
6. Francis Nigel Lee, *The Covenantal Sabbath*, Lord's Day Observance Society, 1972, pp.202ff.
7. Henry, *Commentary*, vol. 6, p.258.
8. It should be noted that the proper designation for the New Testament sabbath is 'the Lord's Day'. The word 'sabbath' invariably refers to the Old Testament sabbath, which was the seventh day of the week. Consequently, Christians should use John's name for the day (Rev. 2:10), even though the Lord's Day is truly 'the sabbath' for the Christian era, to be remembered according to the principle of the Fourth Commandment.
9. Calvin, *Acts*, vol. II, p.169.
10. Stott, *The Spirit, the Church and the World*, p.321.
11. A common line of argument for the inclusion of song, dance and drama in public worship is to claim that God wants us to glorify him with our gifts and since we have such abilities among us, who are we to stifle them in the house of God? The simple answer is, as the *Westminster Confession* (XXI, I) so succinctly puts it, that 'The acceptable way of worshipping the true God is instituted by himself, and so limited by his own revealed will, that he may not be worshipped according to the imaginations and devices of men, or the suggestions of Satan, under any visible representation, or any other way not prescribed in the Holy Scripture.' This is the general 'regulative principle' of Scripture as applied specifically to worship.
12. In 20:12 Eutychus is called a *pais* — a term for lads aged eight to fourteen.
13. Calvin, *Acts*, vol. II, p.170.
14. As above.
15. Simeon, *Expository Outlines*, vol. 14, p.505.

**Chapter 28 — A word to the leadership**

1. In some Baptist churches, the 'deacons' do the work of elders as defined in 1 Timothy 5:17, and the eldership has been wrongly locked up in the professional pastor/minister. At the other end of the spectrum, Episcopalianism has erected a whole hierarchy of ecclesiastical aristocrats on the basis of an unwarranted division between the equivalent and interchangeable words 'bishop' and 'presbyter', making separate offices of each, and the supposed authority of Timothy and Titus over groups of churches. Presbyterian, Congregational and many Baptist churches have maintained, albeit with some minor variations, the simplicity of the biblical pattern, where each particular (local) church consists of a body of believers led by a plurality of elders (one or more of whom may be set apart for preaching/teaching), assisted in mercy ministry by a body of deacons.
2. Alexander, *Acts*, II, p.243.
3. This implies that preaching which abstracts any given biblical teaching from its

practical import for the Christian's life is not worthy of the name. This is especially true of subjects relating to church order, or to speculative theological themes. There is a difference between a lecture on a controversial subject and the preaching of the Word, which is too often confused and/or ignored.
4. Alexander, *Acts,* vol II, p.248.
5. As above, p.253.
6. Simeon, *Expository Outlines,* vol. 14, p.524.
7. Calvin, *Acts,* vol. II, p.188.
8. Alexander, *Acts,* vol II, p.254.
9. Simeon, *Expository Outlines,* vol. 14, pp.525-6.

**Chapter 29 — The courage of convictions**
1. For other examples of this procedure see Isaiah 20:2; Jeremiah 27:2; 32:7; Ezekiel 4:2,7.
2. Calvin, *Acts,* vol. II, p.179.
3. As above, p.197.
4. L. Berkhof, *Summary of Christian Doctrine,* Eerdmans, 1988, p.114.
5. To call the Acts 15 and 21 meetings 'councils' obscures the simple fact that these were assemblies of the elders (Gk *presbuteroi,* presbyters) from the congregations of the church. This was the aggregate of the presbyters (21:18; cf. 1 Tim. 4:14) and no prelatic council of high-grade clerics. When we stick to the Bible's own language, the impression of some basis for diocesan episcopalianism entirely evaporates and we see that the biblical pattern for church government rests upon an eldership drawn from the people. The preachers, excepting, of course, the apostles, were just those elders who were set aside to labour in the Word and doctrine. There is not much comfort here for radical independency either. The fact that the Acts 15 and 21 meetings took place indicates that particular churches under the New Testament are not granted absolute autonomy. They have a real but circumscribed independence, under the pastoral guidance of the wider presbyterate in its role as an appellant, deliberative and delegated body to which the theological and disciplinary problems of particular churches may be submitted for resolution as seems good to the Holy Spirit and the whole church (15:28).
6. R. H. Gundry, *A Survey of the New Testament,* Zondervan, 1970, pp.384-5.
7. For an exposition of the Nazirite vow, see G. J. Keddie, *According to Promise — the message of Numbers,* Evangelical Press, 1992, pp.44-8.
8. Stott, *The Spirit, the Church and the World,* p.347.
9. J. W. Alexander, *Consolation,* Charles Scribner, 1853, p.93.

**Chapter 30 — The Lord was near**
1. Ogilvie, *Acts,* p.315, emphasis mine.
2. See, for example, Stott, *The Spirit, the Church and the World,* p.352 and Ogilvie, *Acts,* p.316.
3. Alexander, *Acts,* vol. II, p.321.
4. Bruce, *Book of Acts,* pp. 450-51.
5. Calvin, *Acts,* vol. 2, p.228.
6. As above, p.229.
7. Alexander, *Acts,* vol II, p.326. See pp. 324-7 for his masterly exposition of Acts 23:5. For various shades of the 'Paul-at-fault' school, see Lenski (*Interpretation of Acts,* p.931), who thinks Paul 'inadvertently sinned against an office ' (i.e., that

of the high priest); Stott (*The Spirit, the Church and the World*, p.352), who thinks Paul was 'rude'; and Ogilvie (*Acts*, p.316), who believes Paul 'failed'.

**Chapter 31 — 'That's enough for now!'**

1. Many Christians seem to think that modern Judaism is fairly sound Old Testament religion, marred only by the refusal to accept the New Testament teaching about Jesus. This overlooks the fact that orthodox Judaism is essentially a Pharisaic cultic remnant of the old covenant faith. The authority of the rabbinic teaching entirely controls the interpretation and application of Scripture, in a manner very similar to the influence of the *Testimonies* of Ellen G. White on the Seventh Day Adventist use of Scripture and, more decisively still, the paramount authority of the *Book of Mormon* and *Doctrine and Covenants* over Mormon interpretation of the Bible. The Judaism of today is not the faith of Abraham, Moses and David, minus Jesus. It is a living fossil — the last remnant of the legalist heresy of the Pharisees — as much, if not more, in need of reformation as Rome, the cults and liberal Protestantism. The destruction of the temple in A.D. 70 marks the end, for ever, of the old covenant religion as the received orthodoxy.
2. See entry 'Felix, Marcus Antonius', in *The New Bible Dictionary*, IVP, 1975, p.421.
3. Rackham, *Acts of the Apostles*, p.445.
4. Bruce, *Book of Acts*, p.465 (footnote 8).
5. The *Textus Receptus* includes a verse (24:7 in the AV) which explicitly criticizes the role played by Claudius Lysias: 'But the chief captain Lysias came upon us, and with great violence took him away out of our hands...'
6. Simeon, *Expository Outlines*, vol. 14, pp. 550-51.
7. Lenski, *Interpretation of Acts*, p.971.
8. Simeon, *Expository Outlines*, vol. 14, p.567.
9. Lenski, *Interpretation of Acts*, p.983.
10. Simeon, *Expository Outlines*, vol. 14, p.568.
11. W. Jay, *Morning and Evening*, Harper, 1858, 'Evening', p.71.

**Chapter 32 — Almost persuaded?**

1. Matthew Mead, *The Almost Christian Discovered*, Presbyterian Board of Publication (first published 1661) is a discourse of 211 pages on Acts 26:28.
2. This immortal redundancy was perpetrated by the irascible American baseball player and manager, 'Yogi' Berra, a man famed for verbal atrocities that somehow vividly captured the feeling of the moment.
3. Lenski, *Interpretation of Acts*, p.996.
4. Calvin, *Acts*, vol. II, pp.264-5.
5. The three accounts differ only in minor details. Stott, *The Spirit, the Church and the World*, pp. 379-82, has a helpful note on these passages and very effectively disposes of the alleged discrepancies between them.
6. Calvin, *Acts*, vol. II, p.274.
7. Stott, *The Spirit, the Church and the World*, p.374.
8. Simeon, *Expository Outlines*, vol. 14, p.
9. The Revised Version has, 'With but little persuasion...,' thereby making Agrippa comment on how near Paul thought he was to succeeding. This suggests that Agrippa, with tongue in cheek, was teasing Paul — as if to say, 'Keep trying, Paul! A bit more of this stuff and you might win me over!'

10. The NASB renders the Greek with strict accuracy, but could have recognized it for the less than positive expostulation it was, by including either an exclamation mark or a question mark. The NIV correctly renders this sense and translates *en oligo* as '*in* such *a short time*' but then spoils it by inserting the words, 'Do you think that ... such' (which are not in the Greek text) just so that we know that Agrippa is actually taking a dig at what Paul was trying to do. English always needs more words than Greek to say the same thing, but here is a case where the NIV added five words just to convey the *tone* of the original!
11. Calvin, *Acts,* vol. II, p.283.

**Chapter 33 — Kept by the power of God**
1. Alexander, *Acts,* vol.II, pp. 438-9, shows how the AV rendering ('under' Cyprus) has misled many into thinking Paul sailed to the south rather than the north of Cyprus (see also Stott, *The Spirit, the Church and the World,* p.387, who notes that the Western text records that it took two weeks to reach Myra).
2. Calvin, *Acts,* vol. II, p.292.
3. As above.
4. As above, p.293.
5. Stott, *The Spirit, the Church and the World,* p.392.
6. Lenski, *Interpretation of Acts,* pp.1098-9. The NIV's rendering ('islanders') is less offensive but no more accurate. 'Natives' would be the closest approximation, not excluding its patronizing connotations.
7. Stott, *The Spirit, the Church and the World,* p.394.
8. Robert Leighton, *Commentary on First Peter,* Kregel, 1972, pp.39-40.
9. *Book of Psalms for Singing,* Selection 18A.

**Chapter 34 — The unfinished task**
1. Alexander, *Acts,* II, p.493.
2. Acts 28:29 is not found in many manuscripts and appears only as a footnote in the NIV. It repeats in substance the content of 28:25.
3. Simeon, *Expository Outlines,* vol. 14, p.603.
4. Stott, *The Spirit, the Church and the World,* p.400.

**Appendix — Miracles and healing**
1. This chapter originally appeared in article form in *The Covenanter Witness,* XCII, 5 of 3 March 1976, and is used by permission from the Reformed Presbyterian Board of Education and Publication, Pittsburgh, Pa. It has been revised and retitled for this volume.
2. This definition is from Professor John Frame's lectures on 'The Doctrine of God', during my time in Westminster Theological Seminary, Philadelphia. It struck me then as very helpful, and still does, after twenty years. It ought to be noted that the Protestant/Reformed understanding of miracle radically departs from medieval Scholasticism which saw miracle as any contravention of so-called 'natural law'. Miracles are never presented in Scripture as violations of the natural order, but rather as responses to God's will as he projects it in and through the structure of the cosmos as he has made it.
3. John Murray, unpublished class notes (Westminster Theological Seminary).
4. J. Calvin, *The Acts of the Apostles,* Beveridge edition, vol. I, p.141.